This book is a gift

to

Cecilia van Zyl

From

Cecile de Jager

Date

22 September 2002

My message to you for the new year

"I will never leave you nor forsake you." Joshua 1:5

SOLLY OZROVECH

You are my my fortress, my God in whom I trust

My Father God

Lux Verbi.BM

PO Box 5, Wellington 7654
Tel. (021) 873-3851

Designed and set in 12,5 on 14,5 pt Weidemann Book
by Lux Verbi.BM

Printed and bound by
NBD, Drukkery Street,
Goodwood, Western Cape

First edition, first print 2001

ISBN 0 7963 0002 X

*This book is gratefully dedicated
to the childminders in our orphanages who,
with so much love and tenderness,
heal the wounds and scars of children.*

*May the great Friend of children give
you the necessary wisdom
and strength each day
for your almost humanly
impossible labour of love.*

A grateful testimony by the author

As a little boy in the orphanage at Ugie in the Eastern Cape, there were many days of intense and almost uncontrollable longing for my parents, whom I had lost through a car accident at a very early stage of my life; so early, that I did not even know what they had looked like. I had no photograph or keepsake of them, and can clearly remember how I often sat for a long while on my iron bed with the coir mattress, wondering in painful longing: What did they look like? What kind of people were they? If only I had a photograph of them! And then, all of a sudden, another Father spoke to me from his Word, loud and clear. His words are written down in Psalm 27:10: *Though my father and mother forsake me, the LORD will receive me.* It hit me like a knockout blow right between my eyes: I do have a Father. I do have a photograph of him – the Bible.

My Father talks to me. He leads me in love and grace. He reprimands me. He comforts and encourages me. Everything a father and a mother could do for me and infinitely more, He has done for me through all the years. It would be less than honest of me to claim that my longing for my father and mother was totally dispelled, but my Father God talks to me to fill this gap in my life with his love.

From that hour onwards, this was the adage with which I faced the world: I have a Father, more wonderful and loving than any earthly father could ever be. And He talks to me through his Word and his Spirit. He cares for me. My future is assured, now and until eternity. Jehovah Jireh! The Lord will provide! With these words I held on to his Word during days of stinging loneliness and longing, of suffering and groping like a drowning person: My heavenly Father will take me in his care. God is my Father. I am his child. Hallelujah! Praise the Lord!

This book is a thankful testimony to the Father God who talks to his children. May you, dear reader, hear his voice clearly day by day, and may it help you to be his obedient child. Through Christ Jesus you and I have become his children. *Give thanks to the Lord, for he is good. His love endures for ever* (Ps 136:1).

Soli Deo Gloria!

Solly Ozrovech

January

Prayer for January

1. God is the great "I am"
2. A glimpse of heavenly holiness
3. All in heaven worship God
4. All of creation speak of God
5. God is the ultimate victor
6. God's loving plan for redemption
7. Do not reject God
8. To honour God
9. Focus on things divine
10. God knows our hearts
11. Exalt his righteousness and faithfulness
12. God saves us to attain his goals
13. God – the source of our joy
14. God is a merciful judge
15. Find goodness and wisdom with God alone
16. God steps in to save us
17. The wisdom of God
18. God, the source of true wisdom
19. God demands a holy life
20. God is patient and compassionate
21. God is truth
22. God gives comfort in times of hardship
23. Do you know God's power to save?
24. God cares for his scattered flock
25. Paul speaks of the true God
26. With God on our side …
27. God helps his children
28. God expects us to do the right thing
29. The creation testifies
30. Nothing can separate us from the love of God
31. Do not reject the kingdom of God

Prayer for January

Holy God and our heavenly Father through Jesus Christ,
we thank you for revealing your Person and your will to us
through your Word.
Help us to get to know you better and to learn to love you more
through our interaction with your Word.
With John we confess,
*In the beginning was the Word, and the Word was with God,
and the Word was God* (Jn 1:1).
Lord Jesus, we worship you as the incarnation of the Word
that came from God to redeem us.
You came to reflect God in the Word
so that we might know and love him.
Holy Spirit of God, we praise you as the One
who inspired people to write the Word,
and to make it available to us.
Thank you that you interpret and explain the Word
and that you open the Word so that we can discover
God's intention in it.
Triune God, we worship you as the God of the Word.
With joy and thankfulness we confess,
"O Word of God incarnate, O Wisdom from on high,
O Truth unchanged, unchanging, O Light of our dark sky,
We praise Thee for the radiance that from the hallowed page,
A lantern to our footsteps, shine on from age to age"
(Hymn 303:1 – Methodist hymnbook).

Amen

January 1

GOD IS THE GREAT "I AM"

God said to Moses, "I am who I am. This is what you are to say to the Israelites: 'I am' has sent me to you" (Ex 3:14).

God is the Alpha and the Omega; the Beginning and the End; the First and the Last. This means that he wants to be our everything at all times and in all circumstances. Many people are Alpha people: they get stuck at the beginning of faith. Here, where you confess that you believe in God, it is very safe, but you make no progress. You do not grow spiritually.

"I am" tells you to move forward. Withstand the storms of trials, and achieve victories in his name. God is the Finisher, the Omega. Lift your eyes at the starting block and focus on what lies ahead and on what awaits you at the finishing line. Get to know God intimately; devour his Word; take your communion with him seriously. God is your essence, your energy. He guides you through struggles and strife right to the finishing post, which is not the end, not the point where you collapse from exhaustion. No, it is where God freely lives though you.

FOOD FROM THE WORD OF GOD
Exodus 3:14; Psalm 41:13; 90:1-4; 102:25-27; Isaiah 43:13; 44:6; 48:12-13; Revelation 1:1-20.

God's Omega means new developments, new discoveries, new challenges, new victories, and new instructions for you to follow. The most effective of God's servants are those who live with complete faith – Omega people. There is no need to fear the mighty "I am". When John fell at God's feet in worship, he touched John lovingly and told him what to do (Rev 1:17-20). What is your personal instruction from "I am" for today?

Eternal and holy God, grant that I might, through your grace, be an Alpha person, but moreover that I might be an Omega person who will serve you sincerely and obediently right to the end.

Faithlessness leads to a hopeless end; faith in God leads to endless hope.
GILBERT BRENCKEN

January 2

A GLIMPSE OF HEAVENLY HOLINESS

Each of the four living creatures had six wings and was covered with eyes all around, even under his wings. Day and night they never stop saying: "Holy, holy, holy is the Lord God Almighty, who was, and is, and is to come" (Rev 4:8).

The apostle John was guided into the presence of the Mystery behind the universe. However, John knew of no way to describe God. He could only describe his reaction to the holy presence of God. To John, God remained an inexplicable mystery, even when he appeared before God. The same applies to us. God is the Mystery who was, and is, and will ever be: the Mystery behind creation; behind our redemption; the Mystery worthy of receiving the praise, thanksgiving, and worship of our hearts.

FOOD FROM THE WORD OF GOD
Revelation 4:1-6; 6:2; Isaiah 6:1-8; Ezekiel 1:3-6, 22, 26-28.

The risen Saviour called John into the holy presence of God, so that he may know – and we, too, through him: the almighty God is the force behind the universe. He did not create us in order to be left forgotten on planet Earth. We do not roam aimlessly through space. We are the children of a great God of great miracles, who sits in omnipotence on his throne, and achieves his goals for his creation and for the creatures within it.

Read, therefore, every detail that John uses to describe the holiness of God. Purposefully and prayerfully, picture yourself within the scenes, the sounds, and the magnitude of God's omnipotence and holiness. Praise the Lord, and strive to live a holy life so that you can draw closer to his holiness, even though it is in trembling worship.

You are worthy, our Lord and God, to receive glory and honor and power, for you created all things, and by your will they were created and have their being (Rev 4:11).

There is only one true faith: faith that is certain of God's love.
OSWALD CHAMBERS

January 3

ALL IN HEAVEN WORSHIP GOD

After this, I heard what sounded like the roar of a great multitude in heaven shouting: "Hallelujah! Salvation and glory and power belong to our God" (Rev 19:1).

There is great joy in heaven because those who wanted to destroy the children of God have been defeated. A new spirituality, pledged by God, has begun. Those who are reconciled with the Lamb cannot but exclaim: Hallelujah! Those who were once persecuted know no limits to their joy and worship.

Many of the most authoritative biblical scholars agree that the name Babylon in Revelations (18:10) refers always to the prevalent society in which Christians must live here on earth. When Babylon falls – for, as all Babylons, it surely will – what will your reaction be? As the merchants (Rev 18:3) who grew rich from her limitless wealth, and as the kings of the earth who behaved immorally with her? Or will you join the angels in singing hymns of praise to God?

FOOD FROM THE WORD OF GOD
Revelation 19:1-16; Exodus 15:11-13, 17-18; Psalm 104:31-35; 148:1-6; 150:1-6.

Do you dedicate your time and energy to acquiring the possessions that will fall with Babylon? Or do you entrust your life to the kingdom of God so that, even if earth and heaven were to perish, that which really matters to you will remain eternally? Only then will you be able to eventually sing in that eternal choir, together with all those who stored their treasures in heaven (Mt 6:19-21).

Can you imagine anything more glorious than praising God in heaven all day? Have you yet accepted the invitation to the Lamb's eternal banquet?

I praise and glorify your Name, my Lord and my God, because the victory and the glory and the power are yours!

There are three things that only God knows: the beginning, the course, and the end of things.
FRANCIS BACON

January 4

ALL OF CREATION SPEAK OF GOD

The heavens declare the glory of God; the skies proclaim the work of his hands (Ps 19:1).

Time and again, God's creation reaffirms my faith in him. Creation belongs to my heavenly Father, and around me I hear music, which reaffirms my faith: in the wind that blows through the leaves; in the babbling of streams; in the rainbow after a thunderstorm; in the moonlight gleaming on the ocean; in the snow on mountain peaks; in the mighty mountains and rocks; in the skies and in the clouds. Knowing that my God created all of this by his power and love strengthens my soul.

FOOD FROM THE WORD OF GOD
Psalm 19:1-4; 50:1-6; 97:1-6; 119:89-91; Romans 1:1-27.

Time and again, God's creation reaffirms my faith in him. The songs of birds on the wind; the red morning skies to which the dark night yields; the purity of the lily that grows from God's good earth – everything proclaims our Creator's glory and honour. I see his reflection in all that is breathtakingly beautiful. I hear his footsteps on the rustling of the wind. Everywhere and all the time, he is talking to me; and I listen to him.

Time and again, God's creation reaffirms my faith in him. Therefore, I know that, even when it seems as if creation is being wrenched from his control, God is in control. The world belongs to him. Moreover, even though the battle against evil is not yet over, my crucified Saviour will triumph, and heaven and earth will become one. Thus, I, along with all creation, shall proclaim the glory and honour of the Creator God, from now until eternity.

O God, the nations have invaded your inheritance; they have defiled your holy temple, they have reduced Jerusalem to rubble. Pour out your wrath on the nations that do not acknowledge you, on the kingdoms that do not call on your name (Ps 79:1, 6).

God is known through quietness and reveals himself through mysteries.
ROBERT H BENSON

January 5

GOD IS THE ULTIMATE VICTOR

... for true and just are his judgments. He has condemned the great prostitute who corrupted the earth by her adulteries. He has avenged on her the blood of his servants (Rev 19:2).

For thousands of years, Satan has deceived people into thinking that they can build a peaceful, loving world without Jesus Christ. He tricks people into believing that their problems can be solved by upbringing, education, and wealth. But, the foul work of the evil one will pass. For a time it will appear as if he is triumphant and many believers who live with King Jesus as the loving and merciful Ruler will revolt against even God.

FOOD FROM THE WORD OF GOD
Revelation 19:17-20:5; Isaiah 24:21-22; 29:6-8; Ezekiel 39:1-4; Daniel 2:40, 44.

When, at the end of this time, Satan is released for a short while, he will gather his old cronies: Gog and Magog, the nations that hated Israel. Once more they will descend upon Jerusalem. But this battle will not last for long because fire will rain down from heaven and devour them (Rev 20:9). Satan will have his final place of unrest: *And the devil, who deceived them, was thrown into the lake of burning sulphur ... They will be tormented day and night for ever and ever* (Rev 20:10). On that day, God in Jesus Christ will be the ultimate Victor. And all who have been washed by the blood of the Lamb will reign with him eternally.

Astounding times are predicted for us in this passage. However, a frightening future awaits those who are not faithful to God. Therefore, whatever the future might bring, according to God's will, remain faithful to him while you are still alive.

Have mercy on me, O Lord,
so that I may remain true to you until the end.

God is never defeated. He may be opposed, attacked, and questioned, but no doubt whatsoever can exist about the outcome. – BROTHER ANDREW

GOD'S LOVING PLAN FOR REDEMPTION

For God so loved the world that he gave his one and only Son, that whoever believes in him shall not perish but have eternal life (Jn 3:16).

John 3:16 is the good news of redemption: the gospel in a nutshell, Billy Graham calls it. It is God's perfect redemption plan for a lost world. God loves us as individuals whom he knows by name. He has a perfect redemption plan for every person. He does not want anyone to be lost, but that all people are saved.

FOOD FROM THE WORD OF GOD
John 3:1-30; Isaiah 49:6-7; 59:12-17.

The most astonishing revelation of God's love for us is the death of his Son, Jesus Christ, on the cross at Calvary. People rejected Christ as the Son of God; they accused him falsely; they sentenced him to death; they stoned him, crowned him with thorns, spat at him, and ridiculed him; and then they crucified him alongside criminals. While they were doing this, he prayed for them, forgave them, and paid the price for their sins by dying in their place. Moreover, he did it not only for them. He also did it for you and for me. Yes, for me he was beaten and ridiculed. For me he wore the crown of thorns and carried the cross. For me he was wounded. For me he walked the road to Calvary.

These astonishing events must force us to take to heart the greatness of God's unchanging, incomprehensible, and eternal love. There is no greater proof of love than when someone sacrifices his life for his friends.

I confess anew my sins before you, O gracious God of love, and I praise you constantly for sacrificing yourself for my sins.

We have to wait for God, long and humble, in wind and rain, in thunder and lightning, in cold and dark. Wait – and he will come. – FREDERICK W FABER

DO NOT REJECT GOD

"You do not want to leave too, do you?" Jesus asked the Twelve. Simon Peter answered him, "Lord, to whom shall we go? You have the words of eternal life" (Jn 6:67-68).

As children of God through the redeeming work of Jesus, it is absolutely unimaginable that we blame God for our problems. When we stand before the Creator of the universe, the holy, almighty, all-knowing God who created us in his image, who keeps the universe on its course, who understands all, who has shown his mercy to us by allowing us to come to him unhindered, through the Lamb of God – how dare we then angrily wave our clenched fists in his face; how dare we demand of him, "Why did you do that to me?"

FOOD FROM THE WORD OF GOD
John 6:41-71; Exodus 13:17-18; Numbers 13:17-21; 14:1-4.

We cannot be angry with others when we are caught up in the terrible consequences of our deeds. Our wrong choices are the cause. God is never the cause. Maybe we do not understand our tragic circumstances. Or maybe we feel we can no longer face the world, that we have lost control. Nevertheless, it is not right to blame God.

Under no circumstances should we flee from God while angrily shouting at him. We must run *to* him when we writhe in sorrow or tremble with anxiety. He is our refuge, our help in times of trouble. We find shelter in his arms, far from the clatter of war or thunder. He promised to comfort us, and we may tearfully climb onto his lap like a hurt child looking for solace, and find it!

Jesus, who loves my soul, when the floodwaters come, when the thunder rumbles and groans, let me rest my head upon your shoulder.

Let us still trust God! He alone knows what is best for our mortal as well as immortal joy and welfare.
WOLFGANG A MOZART

TO HONOUR GOD

I am not seeking glory for myself; but there is one who seeks it, and he is the judge (Jn 8:50).

Jesus sacrificed himself to the work of God's redeeming love, a love that triumphs by conquering sin and saving sinners. He spoke of a righteous God whose judgement was not based on sin, but rather on the love that offered himself, to save all who turn away from sin.

Jesus did not only glorify God through acts of obedience or words of confession. By giving himself, he emphasised the holiness of God. Through his love and death of atonement, he established for all time God's law of love. He gave himself in order to demonstrate the Father's love. He showed that God hates the sin, but loves the sinner. No sacrifice was too great for him. Jesus lived and died in order that the honour and glory of God, of his redeeming love, could break through the dark cloud of sin, and free the hearts of his children.

FOOD FROM THE WORD OF GOD
John 8:42-9:12; Numbers 25:1-13; Malachi 2:1-2, 5-6.

If we want to know how to honour God, let us look at Christ anew. He obeyed the Father unconditionally. Let our lives be characterised by simple, childlike obedience. Let us wait humbly and sincerely for God to give us direction. Let us do everything for him according to his holy will. Let us worship God by striving for sanctification. Are you prepared to do this? If so, God will be glorified by your life.

Most holy God, may my life, my deeds, my example, all contribute to the glorification of your great and loving Name.

Deeds are fruit; words are but mere leaves.
MAXIM GORKY

January 9

FOCUS ON THINGS DIVINE

Set your minds on things above, not on earthly things. For you died, and your life is now hidden with Christ in God (Col 3:2-3).

The New Testament clearly states that sanctification is our deepest responsibility. When striving for sanctification, there are certain steps we need to take:

We must put an end to all sinful practices (Rom 8:13). In Colossians 3:5, Paul also expresses this. To put to death the sins of the mortal body is to destroy the power of sin that tries to rule over us.

We have to realise that we cannot renounce ourselves by virtue of our own strength. Renouncement of the self has to happen under the guidance and power of the Holy Spirit. How does one destroy the power and dynamics of sin? If we want to take on this difficult task, we must first be convinced of our own sin. We must feel moved to believe that God wants every Christian to live a holy life.

FOOD FROM THE WORD OF GOD
Colossians 2:20-3:17; Leviticus 19:1-4, 11-18, 37; 20:7-8, 26; Psalm 34:11-14.

We should not only generally develop a holy way of life. We should also be obedient to God in specific areas. We can only do this by exposing ourselves to the Word of God. Obedience is the path to sanctification, but it is only when we know God's road map that we can obey his commands and walk along that path. His Word must be so powerfully imprinted on our minds that it becomes the controlling influence on our thoughts, our attitude, and our deeds. For this reason, we should constantly focus our thoughts on God.

I sincerely want to live in holiness before you, merciful God. Grant to me, through the Holy Spirit, the gift of obedience in all circumstances.

The realisation of God's presence is the only sovereign antidote against temptation.
FRANÇOIS FENELON

January 10

GOD KNOWS OUR HEARTS

I said, "I will watch my ways and keep my tongue from sin; I will put a muzzle on my mouth as long as the wicked are in my presence." But when I was silent and still, not even saying anything good, my anguish increased (Ps 39:1-2).

To make a fair judgement in this world is anything but easy. The rugby coach tries to judge what the opposition's plan of attack is going to be. The tennis player constantly tries to judge where his opponent's next shot is going to land. Sometimes their judgement is accurate, but more often than not, they misjudge completely.

FOOD FROM THE WORD OF GOD
Psalm 139:1-16, 23-24; Luke 16:9-17:14; Hebrews 4:12-13.

We fail because we do not know all the facts. We do not know what our opponent is thinking. The tennis player expects a slam shot, but his opponent sends a slow ball to the sideline. The rugby player expects his opponent to pass the ball, but he runs straight through a gap. And sometimes, even though we know what is going to happen, we react incorrectly, and we are the losers.

To God life is not a guessing game. His judgement is sure, because he knows all the facts. God knows everything about our lives. He knows our thoughts before we have them (Ps 139:1-6). Nobody can escape from his sight (Ps 139:7-12). He even judges our innermost thoughts and intentions (Heb 4:12-13).

God's judgement is always perfect because he has all the facts. Those who think they can get away with something because he does not see it will discover that God knows everything. *The eyes of the Lord are everywhere, keeping watch on the wicked and the good* (Prov 15:3). Our comfort as believers lies in this: God will reward goodness and punish evil, because he, as the righteous Judge, knows our hearts and minds.

Search me, O God, and know my heart; test me and know my anxious thoughts. See if there is any offensive way in me, and lead me in the way everlasting (Ps 139:23-24).

Man sees your deeds, but God sees your motives.
THOMAS á KEMPIS

January 11

EXALT HIS RIGHTEOUSNESS AND FAITHFULNESS

Great and marvellous are your deeds, Lord God Almighty. Just and true are your ways, King of the ages (Rev 15:3b).

Just imagine how worthy of adoration Christ must have been in the eyes of the angels, when a cloud took him from human sight, and he ascended to heaven. Now he is once more within the glory of God that was his from the beginning of time, before the earth was created. There is, however, another glory: that which he earned through his struggle against sin, death, and hell. As Victor, he wears the crown of the Conqueror. He possesses the glory of the Mediator who cannot fail, the Prince who cannot be conquered. He is the Conqueror before whom all shall kneel, and the Lord who enjoys the deep loyalty of all his subjects. Jesus possesses all the glory heaven can give him, which ten thousand times ten thousand angels could bring him.

FOOD FROM THE WORD OF GOD
Revelation 15:1-16:11; Deuteronomy 32:1-6, 23-25, 39-41; Psalm 86:9-10; 111:1-10; 145:17-21; Jeremiah 10:7.

Even someone with the most fertile of imaginations could never imagine the glory of Christ. Yet his glory will be further revealed when he descends from heaven in splendour, power, and authority, surrounded by all the angels. He will sit upon the throne of his glory. O the magnificence of that glory! It will charm the hearts of his children. Moreover, the sounds of it will eternally echo: "Your throne endures for ever and ever!"

Do you want to share in the glory of the hereafter? Then glorify him now in your life. Praise him for his righteousness and faithfulness.

As long as I breathe, Lord, my almighty God, I want to sing your praise with the angels, and honour you as the faithful and just God.

Praise is the result of a singing heart. It is the inner response of humans in gratefulness and joy to their Maker. – BASIL HUME

January 12

GOD SAVES US TO ATTAIN HIS GOALS

Last night an angel of the God whose I am and whom I serve stood beside me and said, "Do not be afraid, Paul. You must stand trial before Caesar; and God has graciously given you the lives of all who sail with you" (Acts 27:23-24).

Job did not understand the trials to which he was subjected. Martha and Maria did not understand why Jesus waited until after Lazarus's death before coming to them (Jn 11:21). The disciples did not understand why Jesus took them through Samaria, nor why he preferred to wait at the well rather than go with them to buy food (Jn 4:8). Now we understand the reasons for all these things, because we know what the results were.

FOOD FROM THE WORD OF GOD
Acts 27:18-28; Job 1:4-5,12, 15, 16; Psalm 107:1-2, 23-32..

Job was tested because Satan alleged that Job loved and served God only to receive his protection and blessing. Job withstood the test and Satan was defeated (Job 42:10-17). After Jesus had raised Lazarus from the dead, Martha and Maria understood how their brother's illness and death had brought glory and honour to God (Jn 11:43-45). By the time that Jesus left Samaria, the disciples understood that an entire city, which would otherwise have been forbidden to him, had heard the gospel and believed in Jesus, because he spoke with the woman at the well (Jn 4:39-41).

When we have trouble in our lives we can rest assured that God has a plan. Perhaps we do not understand everything. Perhaps we are scared. But we can know that God will make all things work together for the good of those who love him and honour his Name in their lives.

Eternal and omniscient God, help me not to become confused or scared when problems arise, but to leave everything in your loving hands, and to find peace in your will.

To believe in the God of heaven is not to flee from life, but to go out and meet it. – J BLINCO

January 13

GOD - THE SOURCE OF OUR JOY

**We wait in hope for the Lord; he is our help and our shield.
In him our hearts rejoice, for we trust in his holy name.
May your unfailing love rest upon us, O Lord,
even as we put our hope in you (Ps 33:20-22).**

During his final days on earth, Jesus prayed for his disciples, and for all his disciples who would follow them. He prayed for unity with the Father, for joy, protection, and usefulness (Jn 17:11-17).

Friendship with Jesus forms the basis of all the qualities that follow. From this loving relationship arises joy. Jesus knew that when his disciples were to truly live in communion with him, and were to reveal to the world the full joy of his gift, they would meet with resistance. Therefore, he prayed for his disciples to be protected from anything that might destroy their joy and union with him. He did not pray for them to be taken out of this world. No, he prayed that they would be *in* this world, but not *of* this world. And, from this dynamic partnership with Jesus, their usefulness would flow forth.

FOOD FROM THE WORD OF GOD
Psalm 33:18-22; 29:11; 97:11-12; 119:40-50; Lamentations 3:21-25; Romans 15:4-29.

Many of us try to achieve this unity with Christ through good deeds. We try to show joy that we do not possess, or we try to earn joy through hard work. However, all the while, this joy and service only sprouts from our friendship with Jesus. The better we know him, the more we experience the infinite joy, which is not dependent upon external circumstances, which belongs to us even in suffering and sorrow. This joy is a motivating power, even in times of confusion and discouragement.

Thank you, Lord Jesus, for the lasting hope and joy that you bring to my life through my friendship with you.

To love God is something far greater than merely knowing him.
St THOMAS AQUINAS

GOD IS A MERCIFUL JUDGE

Keep yourselves in God's love as you wait for the mercy of our Lord Jesus Christ to bring you to eternal life (Jude: 21).

God is righteous. He is never biased. Beyond his grace, his judgement applies to all. Sin is sin, and God revealed its consequences to us: *For the wages of sin is death* (Rom 6:23). Yes, we have a Father who sits in the council-chamber of righteousness and calls all of creation to account.

Yet God still loves when he passes his judgement: *"O Jerusalem, Jerusalem, you who kill the prophets and stone those sent to you, how often I have longed to gather your children together, as a hen gathers her chicks under her wings, but you were not willing!"* (Lk 13:34). Within the same Judge, we find both righteousness and love.

FOOD FROM THE WORD OF GOD
Jude: 14-25; Psalm 86:4-5, 11-14, 16; Jeremiah 9:13-16; 14:13-16; Lamentations 3:22-26.

Because we have complete trust in the Judge, we do not dread God's judgement. The righteous Judge has clean hands. As sinners who well know where to find mercy, we know God as our loving Father, and not as a merciless Judge. One day he will be our final Judge. And he will absolve us because he took our punishment upon himself. He saw to it that justice was done. He paid our dues. Our business with God was settled at Calvary.

God is just. Even though we might not understand it. Moreover, Jesus is our Advocate, our Intercessor with the Judge. Jesus himself will one day be our Judge. We have complete trust in our Lord as our righteous Judge and as our Redeemer. We rest in his love.

Righteous God, being your child through the atonement of your Son, Jesus, my Lord and Saviour, is an unspeakable privilege.

God is a righteous God, who keeps his promises, even when it seems impossible.
COLIN URQUART

January 15

FIND GOODNESS AND WISDOM WITH GOD ALONE

Therefore everyone who hears these words of mine and puts them into practice is like a wise man who built his house on a rock (Mt 7:24).

We have to admit that the primrose path seems attractive, easy, and pleasant. The sun shines down comfortably, and the path is filled with joy. However, a life given over to enjoyment leads to only one end: destruction.

There is a much better path, but it is far too narrow to take along passionate desires: too narrow for pride, pleasure, covetousness, desire, and greed. It is the path of Gethsemane and Calvary. However, it leads to life. The most remarkable thing is that those who expect to get the most out of life by enjoying themselves, miss out on all that is worthwhile; while those who give up their lives to follow Jesus on the narrow path, eventually gain everything. Few people find and walk along the narrow path. Christ himself said this. And he knows, because he knows our hearts. There are so many places we can choose to turn off, that we must constantly remain focused on the Guide and Finisher of our faith. We must take up our cross without complaining, and carry it behind the great Cross-bearer. He will enfold our weak hands in his almighty hand so that he can lead us on the path of righteousness and wisdom, a path that shines brighter every day until it eventually leads to the gates of the eternal city.

FOOD FROM THE WORD OF GOD
Matthew 7:7-8:4; Psalm 1:1-6; 37:23-25; 92:12-15; Ezekiel 33:30-33.

Good things come to those who look for God and who walk along his path. Build your hope on the Rock of ages and by his mercy walk his way, right to the end.

Loving Father, I want only to stay close to you and to walk the path along which your Holy Spirit leads me. It is best for me to be with you – for time and eternity.

No man was ever truly great, good, and wise without a degree of divine inspiration.
MARCUS TULLIUS CICERO

January 16

GOD STEPS IN TO SAVE US

When she recognised Peter's voice, she was so overjoyed she ran back without opening it and exclaimed, "Peter is at the door!" (Acts 12:14).

The book of Daniel begins with the story of the Babylonian invasion of Judah. The Babylonian invasion succeeded, and a number of children of Israel were taken away in captivity, including Daniel and his friends. These young people understood that it was not by coincidence that they were in Babel: God put them there.

FOOD FROM THE WORD OF GOD
Acts 12:1-25; Exodus 14:10-31; Daniel 3:1-30.

God knew what kind of persecution they would experience and what he would have to do to save them from their trials. The sweltering furnace, the intensity of the heat and the wrath of Nebuchadnezzar were all attempts to counter God's will. Nevertheless, God always triumphs. In their darkest hour of need, he sent his Son to save his children. In doing so God paints us a picture of how he operates in our lives. He does not always choose to save us from the scorching furnace, but he remains with us in his omnipotence, while we are in it.

If God could save these young people from the scorching furnace, he can save us too from all distress and disaster. So he sometimes uses desperate circumstances so that we might learn big lessons, and to lead us to repentance and confession of our sins. He can also use our problems to achieve wonderful results in our lives. Therefore trust in God in all circumstances and believe that he has both the desire and the ability to save his children from the most scorching furnace in order to glorify his Name, and that we may grow and become spiritually strong.

Keep me close to you at all times, O Lord, because it is safest for me to be with you. Thank you that I can rely on you, always and in all circumstances.

Christ did not come in order to explain our suffering, but to fill our suffering with his presence.
PAUL CLAUDEL

January 17

THE WISDOM OF GOD

I will destroy the wisdom of the wise; the intelligence of the intelligent I will frustrate (1 Cor 1:19).

The Greeks sought wisdom. They were known for their philosophers and their wide knowledge on many subjects. They literally idolised wisdom. They worshipped at the altar of science and knowledge.

It sounds a lot like the times we live in. There are people who declare, "If you cannot capture it in a test tube or explain it with a scientific theory, we do not believe it." However, one cannot put the cross of Calvary into a test tube. One cannot express faith by means of a formula. The philosopher Pascal once said, "The heart has its reasons of which reason knows nothing and cannot explain."

FOOD FROM THE WORD OF GOD
1 Corinthians 1:1-25; Job 12:12-13, 16-25; Proverbs 1:1, 4-5, 7; Isaiah 44:24-26.

God is too wise to allow us, as mere mortals, to get to know him through our own wisdom. We cannot solve our problems because we do recognise their origin: sin. We can also not see the solution: redemption. God is too wise to allow us as humans to come unto him with our manmade wisdom. For this reason he appointed Jesus Christ as Mediator.

Indeed, 1 Corinthians 3:19 says, *For the wisdom of this world is foolishness in God's sight.* All the wisdom of the entire world is like a thimbleful of folly to God. In addition, Jeremiah states, *The wise will be put to shame; they will be dismayed and trapped. Since they have rejected the word of the Lord, what kind of wisdom do they have?* (Jer 8:9). On the contrary, if you want to come to God, do it like a little child (Mt 18:3).

Wise Saviour, when I lived unaware of sin and had no remorse, I relied on the wisdom of the world. Now the only true wisdom for me is that which I find with you.

The highest and most excellent achievement of this life is to become quiet and to allow God to work and talk through you. – MASTER ECKHARDT

January 18

GOD, THE SOURCE OF TRUE WISDOM

For who has known the mind of the Lord that he may instruct him? (1 Cor 2:16).

All people search for more wisdom, but unfortunately, many pass by the perfect Source of wisdom. The Scriptures, however, clearly show us the way to wisdom, and reveal the most important starting point: *The fear of the Lord is the beginning of wisdom, and knowledge of the Holy One is understanding* (Prov 9:10). With our limited understanding, there is no true wisdom to be found away from God. We allow matters of minor importance to lead us off the right track, and so we do not reach the Source of true wisdom. Satan, too, leads us astray. However, the Word clearly states, *The fear of the Lord – that is wisdom, and to shun evil is understanding* (Job 28:28).

FOOD FROM THE WORD OF GOD
1 Corinthians 1:26-2:16; Job 28:13-27; Proverbs 2:2, 4-6.

And what do so many people do with the Source of wisdom that is within our reach? They ignore him: *... so that men are without excuse. For although they knew God ... their thinking became futile and their hearts were darkened. Although they claim to be wise, they became fools* (Rom 1:20-22).

As God's wisdom is revealed in the Scriptures, it is necessary for us to study the Bible. Unfortunately, many Christians do not put aside enough time for this. As a result, they never get to the Source of wisdom, and many of their decisions and choices are foolish. Therefore, we must cultivate the spiritual discipline to interact regularly with the Word of God so that we can draw from the Source of true wisdom, and live accordingly.

Lord of wisdom and insight, your Word is perfect. It gives life. Your teachings are trustworthy. They give wisdom to the inexperienced. Make me faithful in seeking you in your Word, so that I might find wisdom.

Hand your life over to God: he can do much more with it that you could ever be able to do.
DL MOODY

GOD DEMANDS A HOLY LIFE

It is God's will that you should be sanctified (1 Thess 4:3).

The way we live reflects our faith in Jesus Christ. If we have no desire to live a holy life, the genuineness of our faith in Jesus Christ is questionable. For a Christian to continue living a sinful life is a contradiction of the very essence of being a Christian. Christ died to set us free from our sins; not to let us blithely carry on living sinful lives (Mt 1:21; 1 Jn 1:6-7). What kind of person would sincerely desire to follow Jesus, and then not want to live a holy life as well?

For us as believers, sanctification is therefore not a matter of choice. Paul wrote to Titus: *For the grace of God that brings salvation has appeared to all men. It teaches us to say "No" to ungodliness and worldly passions, and to live self-controlled, upright and godly lives in this present age* (Tit 2:11-12).

FOOD FROM THE WORD OF GOD
1 Thessalonians 2:17-4:12; Leviticus 11:44-45; Psalm 99:5-9; Amos 2:6-7.

Although sanctification is not a prerequisite for redemption, it is certainly a natural outcome of it. We do not become holy to be saved, rather because we have already been saved, we strive for sanctification. We do not perform good deeds so that we might get to heaven, rather we perform them because heaven is already in our hearts and we want to thank God for it.

If we can trust Christ for our redemption, then we can also trust him for our sanctification. The Holy Spirit not only leads us to repentance of our sins, to rebirth, and to redemption; he also awakens in us the desire to live in holiness.

Holy Spirit of God, keep the desire for sanctification blazing and burning in my heart.

Not everyone who speaks with the spirit of a prophet is a prophet, but only those who live in accordance with the pronouncements of the Master. – WILLIAM TEMPLE

GOD IS PATIENT AND COMPASSIONATE

But for that very reason I was shown mercy so that in me, the worst of sinners, Christ Jesus might display his unlimited patience as an example for those who would believe on him and receive eternal life (1 Tim 1:16).

God's mercy is an abundant stream that washes over us each moment. For this reason, we, his redeemed children, can never stop praising, glorifying and thanking him. We are filled with wonder that he did not act against us, as we deserve. All of us experience "bad days" in our spiritual lives, and sometimes disappoint God. However, his mercy and patience remain constant. It is difficult to fathom God's mercy when in our mind's eye we see how he looks down on this world torn apart by sin. How many chances has he not already given us, yet time and again we disappoint him with our rebellion and disobedience. It is only God's mercy that gives us hope and keeps us in a relationship with him.

FOOD FROM THE WORD OF GOD
1 Timothy 1:1-20; Psalm 103:8-14; Isaiah 1:18; 55:7.

It is by the grace of God that we still exist. This forces us to be thankful that he is so merciful to us that he promised to complete that which he has begun in us (Phil 1:6). By his endless grace, he shows mercy towards us in our weakness. Psalm 103:8 says, *The Lord is compassionate and gracious, slow to anger, abounding in love.* He sees us as we truly are, and pours out his grace on us. Let us lift up our hearts to him in thankfulness. In addition, let us strive to be merciful towards everyone in life whom God sends across our path. We receive his mercy to pass it on to others.

Praise the Lord, for he is merciful and compassionate. Lord my God, I am speechless when I think of your mercy.

Mercy is God himself, his loving energy at work in his church and in our souls.
EVELYN UNDERHILL

GOD IS TRUTH

"What is truth?" Pilate asked (Jn 18:38).

What is truth? At some time or another, everybody asks this question in his or her heart. I have often wondered in what way Pilate asked this question. What was his tone of voice? What was his facial expression? Did he ask the question mockingly? We do not know the answers to these questions. If, at that point in his quest for truth, Pilate were sincere, his frame of mind would quickly have changed to one of compliance. If he truly wanted to discover the truth, he did not really care to carry it out. Declaring one moment that Jesus is without guilt, and the very next moment handing him over to a bloodthirsty crowd, was a violation of the truth. He sentenced the Truth to death. He allowed the Truth to be stoned. He ridiculed the Truth. He allowed the Truth to be crucified.

FOOD FROM THE WORD OF GOD
John 18:19-19:13; Psalm 31:1, 5; 33:4-5; 117:1-2; 119:137-142; Isaiah 45:18-19, 21.

The irony is that, at the precise moment that he asked this question, he was looking at the purest personification of truth: Jesus Christ. The One who is truth incarnate, had just told him, *Everyone on the side of truth listens to me* (Jn 18:37). Pilate did not hear these words. He was so close to the God of truth, yet he could not understand truth. Pray that you may always stay close to God, and place your trust in his truth.

Lord Jesus, keep me close to you so that I may know and love the Truth, and that it may find practical expression in my life.

God is the truth without which we cannot live.
LEO TOLSTOY

January 22

GOD GIVES COMFORT IN TIMES OF HARDSHIP

Praise be to the God and Father of our Lord Jesus Christ, the Father of compassion and the God of all comfort, who comforts us in all our troubles (2 Cor 1:3-4a).

People often say that earthly problems are heavenly discipline. However, problems are even better than discipline. Problems are God's vehicles for carrying our souls to greater heights of triumph. God uses everything that happens to us to shape us, if only we would see it. However, we can also choose to make even the smallest problem into a bulldozer that destroys our vehicles and drives us to misery and despair. We have to decide for ourselves what our problems will mean to us.

FOOD FROM THE WORD OF GOD
2 Corinthians 1:1-17; Psalm 56:1-4; 119:64-80.

No matter how bad your problems may seem to you, view them as God's vehicles to carry your soul and mind to higher spiritual achievement. To your surprise, you will find that your problems are wrapped in God's love, so that your life will not fall apart. When God sent his Son to save us, he used his heavenly vehicles; and nothing has changed today. When God controls the vehicle, it always leads to redemption. He even turns the thunderclouds into his vehicles and rides on the eye of the storm.

Therefore, know that the storms that gather ominously over your life, and darken your skies, are God's victories: his vehicles in which you can rise up and triumph over all darkness. Simply trust in God's comfort and together with him change your problems into victory. Think of the God that Paul describes in 1 Corinthians 1:3. You can be a winner in Christ.

Because I trust in you, almighty God, I will sing my song of victory even in the darkest night: Praise the Lord, for he is good; his love is everlasting.

We sleep peacefully in the arms of God when we surrender ourselves completely to his protection.
FRANÇOIS FENELON

DO YOU KNOW GOD'S POWER TO SAVE?

I am not ashamed of the gospel, because it is the power of God for the salvation of everyone who believes (Rom 1:16).

There are people who read every Bible reading that they can get hold of. Unfortunately, there are also many people who have little or no desire to read the Bible and to learn precious things from it.

We must read the Bible more often than any other book. The Bible is like an inexhaustible goldmine that keeps on giving increasingly while we interact with it. We must read it calmly and then fall silently to prayer. We must digest the Bible verse by verse and make it a part of our lives. We must compare one section to another, contemplate it, and consume it as we do food. We must fill our thoughts with it until we find the Spirit of God talks to us from the pages and encourages us to obey his Word. The Holy Spirit reveals the Word to us so that we may understand it and make it a part of our lives. The Holy Spirit fulfils the words and enables us to obey the Word of God.

FOOD FROM THE WORD OF GOD
Romans 1:1-17; Deuteronomy 31:24-29; Psalm 19:7-11; 119:105-108.

Are you prepared to lay your heart bare before God and not to leave him until he has filled you with his holy knowledge? Are you prepared to explore the Scriptures and react upon your discoveries? Believers often want to know what they ought to read. Read the Bible! It is more important than any other spiritual book. Why not start right now and seek the wisdom of God in his Word?

While I live in a fragile, transient world, I thank you, my God and Father, for your everlasting Word.

The Bible is a window in this world of captivity through which we can look into eternity.
T DWIGHT

January 24

GOD CARES FOR HIS SCATTERED FLOCK

Then Jesus told them, "This very night you will all fall away on account of me, for it is written: 'I will strike the shepherd, and the sheep of the flock will be scattered.' But after I have risen, I will go ahead of you into Galilee" (Mt 26:31-32).

Lambs tend to dawdle, wander from the flock, and become tired. However, the shepherd protects them with his own strong arm. Jesus does the same for newly born souls. He feeds them until they live dynamically. He changes weak and wrong thoughts that lead to despair. He nurtures them and renews their strength. He gathers all the lambs together because it is the will of his heavenly Father that none of them shall become lost. What sharp and compassionate eyes he has to see them all! What a gentle and loving heart that takes care of all of them! What a far-reaching and powerful arm he has to gather all of them!

FOOD FROM THE WORD OF GOD
Matthew 26:20-46; Psalm 73:1-5; Ezekiel 4:5-6, 11-16; Zechariah 13:7-9.

During his life, Jesus gathered all those who were weak. Now that he is in heaven with the Father, his loving heart still goes out to the weak, the simple and the repentant, the shy and the meek, the frightened and the despairing. How wonderfully lovingly he lifted me up, and joined me to his heart of love, his truth, his blood, and his church. How eternally great his mercy with which he drew me to him. How many times since my rebirth has he not come and taken me from the roaming of my own heart, and enfolded me in his loving arms. Yes, time after time Jesus himself comes to rescue his servant and to save him by leading him back to the flock.

God of lambs who are driven apart, I thank you for your mercy that seeks and cares for me every day. Praise the Lord, for he is good!

Healing has two ingredients: the power of God and the love of God. There is a revelation of both in every healing. – FRANCIS MACNUT

January 25

PAUL SPEAKS OF THE TRUE GOD

Now what you worship as something unknown I am going to proclaim to you (Acts 17:23b).

So as to help the citizens of Rome to receive the good news of Jesus, Paul used their worship of a "foreign god" as a starting point for his testimony, *The God who made the world and everything in it is the Lord of heaven and earth and does not live in temples built by hands* (Acts 17:24).

When I think of this God, I bow to him in worship and proclaim his love and mercy to all people. He is with me and he helps me. He was there from all eternity, and he is now with me every moment. The God whom I serve is everywhere: in heaven, on earth and in the sea. However, he is also exalted above it all because everything lives from him, through him and to him. God created everything, and he maintains all.

FOOD FROM THE WORD OF GOD
Acts 17:16-8:4; Genesis 2:4-7; Job 38:1, 4-7, 22-25, 36; 40:8-14.

I will worship only this one true God. Nothing and nobody can ever separate me from him. His son, Jesus Christ, saved me and his Spirit is my comforter.

Therefore, I worship the triune God: the Father, the Son and the Holy Spirit. To him all praise and thanks to all eternity. With Paul, my heart's desire is to introduce those who do not know him to this true God. Through his Word, we learn to know, understand, trust, and worship him. Our love for him compels us to be his faithful witnesses and to lead others to him.

God of ages and of today, I thank you that I may share your love and mercy with others so that they might also know and love you.

Through them who have suffered with dignity, our world has been blessed the most.
LEO TOLSTOY

January 26

WITH GOD ON OUR SIDE ...

**If the Lord had not been on our side – let Israel say –
if the Lord had not been on our side when
men attacked us, when their anger flared against us,
they would have swallowed us alive ...
(Ps 124:1-3).**

God is a refuge in times of need, a rock that never falters,
though the enemy threatens with death, though his armies storm us.
Let all around us then shiver and tremble;
let mountains tumble down from their foundations into the sea –
we shall neither tremble nor retreat.

FOOD FROM THE WORD OF GOD
Psalm 124:1-8; Nehemiah 4:7-9, 13-15; Proverbs 28:25; Acts 19:23-20:6.

The Lord is there, he keeps watch; and so the darkest hours pass;
he saves when the early day breaks over the mountain tops in golden rays.
In the wild roaring of battles nations have risen up
and kingdoms have sunk: the Lord's voice resounds –
all the world trembles before him!

The battle subsides at his command even in the furthest land;
the weaponry that threatened to crush man, he breaks with his victorious hand.
He stops the warring attacks and breaks the sword and bow
formed in the flames of hatred. He breaks the spear in two
and sets the war crafts on fire.

(Based on a hymn by Martin Luther written in 1528.)

Lord our God, we do not fear the enemy, because with you we are on the winning side. You are our victorious God!

In his death he was a scrifice for our sins, through his resurrection, he was a conqueror.
MARTIN LUTHER

January 27

GOD HELPS HIS CHILDREN

But you, O Lord, are exalted for ever. For surely your enemies, O Lord, surely your enemies will perish; all evildoers will be scattered (Ps 92:8-9).

On whom are you depending, that you rebel against me? (2 Kgs 18:20). This was the challenge the field commander of the Assyrian forces snarled at Hezekiah more than two and a half millennia ago. Little could he imagine that 185 000 of his elite troops would be dead within a few days. The almighty hand of God would strike them down. Hezekiah did not answer the field commander, but despite the hopeless circumstances, his heart was focused on God, the God in whom he trusted completely in every crisis (2 Kgs 18:5). This was the secret of his famous victory.

FOOD FROM THE WORD OF GOD
Psalm 92:9-15; 75:1-10; Acts 22:1-23:22.

To this very day, the distinguishing feature of true Christians is their unconditional faith in God. We trust him completely, as the substitute bearer of our sins, Jesus Christ, through whom we have received redemption of our immortal souls. We trust him continually as our interceding champion through whom we will we taste victory in daily life. As long as we trust in him, we shall triumph. Temper, fear, desire, pride, jealousy and moodiness, impatience and gloominess, worry and anguish: we can triumphantly overcome all these things when we trust in Jesus.

We trust in God also as our watchful provider who meets all our needs (Ps 34:22; Phil 4:19). He does not always use crows to feed his Elijah, but one way or another he cares and provides for us when we trust in him. Keep faith! He will ensure victory!

Thank you Lord, my almighty God, for helping me and supporting me when I have to be brave for your sake.

God's help is just a prayer away from you.
WILLIAM BENHAM

January 28

GOD EXPECTS US TO DO THE RIGHT THING

Did not your father have food and drink? He did what was right and just, so all went well with him (Jer 22:15).

To serve God faithfully and to please him, is not just an activity or a pious set of theories or creeds. It should be a steadfast way of life.

Thirty years ago people asked, "Is God alive? Is he not dead? Has he not withdrawn himself from this evil world?" Nowadays they ask, "What difference does God make?" The answer of too many people is, "Not much." Even to many people who possess an impressive knowledge of the Bible, God makes little difference. The way they live from day to day confirms this.

FOOD FROM THE WORD OF GOD
Jeremiah 22:15-16; Genesis 18:18-19; 1 Samuel 12:20-24; 2 Kings 18:5-6; 2 Chronicles 17:3-6; 31:20-21; Acts 23:23-24.

If Christ makes no difference to our system of values or ethics – especially in our daily workplace; if he does not influence our words and attitudes towards our colleagues, if he makes no difference whatsoever to the way we live and work, tell me honestly: What difference *does* he make? Whatever is the use of playing a religious game that consists solely of words, and requires no deeds?

We have to take obedience seriously as a Christian way of life. It is a challenge to our Christianity. Every time you are exposed to his Word, ask yourself, How can I apply this to my daily life? What practical steps can I take to make it obvious in my attitude, character and actions? Where do I need to make changes in my obedience to the Word of God? This requires commitment to a transformed way of life.

I dedicate myself to you completely, O Lord, to seek and do your will and to obey your Word.

There are thousands of ways of pleasing God, but none is possible without faith.
WALTER MAIER

29 January

THE CREATION TESTIFIES

**The heavens declare the glory of God;
the skies proclaim the work of his hands (Ps 19:1).**

This is God's world. He created it and is in complete control of it. We find assurance in the knowledge that his almighty hand created the rocks and the trees, the clouds and the ocean, and that he maintains it from day to day.

This is God's world. At daybreak the morning light, the snow-white lily and the birds proclaim his glory. All those who want to see are moved by the wonders of his hand. All those who want to listen, hear how creation sings God's praises, and how he talks to us: in the roaring of thunder; in the wind among the trees. Yes, everywhere and always in nature God is speaking to us. Psalm 104 says,

FOOD FROM THE WORD OF GOD
Psalm 19:1-4; 50:1-6; 97:1-6; 119:89-91; Romans 1:1-27.

O Lord my God, you are very great …
he stretches out the heavens like a tent …
He makes the clouds his chariot and rides on the wings of the wind …
He set the earth on its foundation; it can never be moved …
He makes the springs pour water into the ravines;
it flows between the mountains.
The moon marks off the seasons,
and the sun knows when to go down.
You bring darkness, it becomes night …
How many are your works, O Lord!
In wisdom you made them all.

This is God's world. We must not forget it. Though evil might sometimes seem to be very strong, God is in control. The battle is not over, but Jesus will triumph, and heaven and earth will be one under his authority.

I praise and thank you, God the Creator, for reminding me through nature that you are in control; also of my insignificant life.

Our God delights in impossibilities.
ANDREW MURRAY

NOTHING CAN SEPARATE US FROM THE LOVE OF GOD

For I am convinced that neither death nor life, neither angels nor demons, neither the present nor the future, nor any powers, neither height nor depth, nor anything else in all creation, will be able to separate us from the love of God that is in Christ Jesus our Lord (Rom 8:38-39).

In life, we soon discover that in order to receive love, we first have to give love. In some way or another, we must show others that we are worth loving. We must convince them that we are worthy of their love. It is such a pity that people so often do not succeed in doing this. And then the invisible circle of love is broken.

FOOD FROM THE WORD OF GOD
Romans 8:18-39; Psalm 136:1-3, 23-25; Isaiah 59:12-17, 21.

As astonishing as it might sound, the love of God does not work this way. God's love for us depends in no way whatsoever on our merits. We do not therefore need to be worthy of his love. We cannot be worthy of God's love. We do not need to earn his love. He gives it to us as an act of his grace. Praise God, for he is good!

The Scriptures repeat this theme again and again, as in the well-known parable of the prodigal son which Jesus himself told. Such is the love of our God! His father apparently died a thousand deaths when his son left home. Yet, his loving, compassionate, and totally selfless attitude never changed. He wanted only to be reunited with his son. His caring concern for his son's welfare never decreased.

Such is the love of our God!

God of love, I kneel before you in speechless wonder at your immeasurable love. And I thank you for it with my reciprocal love. Lord, you know everything; you know that I love you.

Christianity is not a religion; it is a love affair.
DR THIEME

DO NOT REJECT THE KINGDOM OF GOD

To what can I compare this generation? They are like children sitting in the market-places and calling out to others: "We played the flute for you, and you did not dance; we sang a dirge, and you did not mourn!" (Mt 11:16-17).

The kingdom of God is synonymous with the sovereignty of God. Those who chose to live in his kingdom chose to live under his authority, though they are still on this earth.

The kingdom of God is that invisible area where God rules with utter supremacy. Naturally, this is good news that is of great help to us. The bad news is that, because of our sinful nature, we do not want God to rule over us. We prefer to please ourselves.

FOOD FROM THE WORD OF GOD
Matthew 10:41-11:24; Proverbs 1:22-31; Isaiah 55:3, 6-7; Malachi 3:1.

To be honest: We do not want anybody to rule over us except ourselves. We have a lot in common with the people in the story Jesus once told. They said, "We don't want this man to be our king" (Lk 19:14).

Only once we have been spiritually reborn, will we be prepared to subject our hearts and souls to the Lord.

So piously we pray, "May thy kingdom come," while his kingdom has not yet come in our hearts. We add to that, "Let thy will be done," while our own will is done in our lives. There is a high price to pay for the foolishness of rejecting the kingdom of God. However, those who accept the supremacy of God experience radical change in their lives. Has your life already changed in such a way that you joyfully accept the kingdom of God?

It gives me great joy, heavenly Father, to subject myself to your absolute authority. I praise and worship you as the King of my heart and life, and thank you that I may be your servant.

Man can gather knowledge, but wisdom is a gift that comes from God alone.
BOB JONES

February

Prayer for February

1. God hears and answers our prayers
2. Name of all names
3. Flee from all evil
4. Trust in God; do not fear people
5. Christ, the foundation of our faith
6. Jesus sets us free for ever from sin
7. God demonstrates his omnipotence
8. God keeps his promises
9. God comes to live with us and renews everything
10. When we believe, God does great things
11. God gives eternal life to those who believe
12. You choose either for or against Christ
13. Jesus opens the eyes of believers
14. God will faithfully protect you
15. Sorrow leads to repentance
16. Accept God's discipline
17. God grants wisdom to those who ask
18. Guard your tongue
19. Stand firm in your faith
20. Christ is coming! Satan will be defeated!
21. A pure life is important
22. God's people are hospitable
23. God protects those who rely on him
24. Let God's values be your values
25. God's people care about one another
26. Cast yourself on God's mercy
27. God saves and honours his followers
28. Jesus has astonishing authority
29. Here I am, Lord!

Prayer for February

Faithful Guide and heavenly Leader,
I worship you as the Road I want to walk,
as the Truth I want to know intimately,
as the Life you give me in abundance.
Without you I cannot venture onto unknown paths.
When success and achievement come to me,
protect me from pride;
when I suffer sadness and disappointment;
protect me from despair;
when sunlight caresses my face,
may I not forget by whose grace I live;
when menacing clouds gather above me,
may I never forget that you are my shelter.
Keep me, Lord Jesus, from neglect
and disobedience to your will.
Help me to carry out the instructions of
your Word with enthusiasm.
Talk to me regularly
and grant me grace to listen to your voice.
Make me sensitive to your will.
May your love, through my words and actions,
become a concrete reality in this world.
I pray this in the Name of all names:
the Name before whom every knee shall bend
and every tongue confess,
Christ is Lord!
To the glory of God the Father!

Amen

GOD HEARS AND ANSWERS OUR PRAYERS

I have heard your prayer and plea you have made before me; I have consecrated this temple, which you have built, by putting my Name there for ever. My eyes and my heart will always be there (1 Kgs 9:3).

The God of the universe, the Creator and Maintainer of all things, invites us to bring our petitions before him. Jesus said we do not have because we do not ask. James tells us that the genuine prayer of the believer is powerful. Time and again, the Bible tells us that prayer is an effective instrument to implement God's power.

FOOD FROM THE WORD OF GOD
1 Kings 9:1-3; 8:28-30; Psalm 25:1-13; Acts 9:36-10:23.

Prayer, as with all other things in the life of a Christian, is firstly to the glory of God, and then for our own benefit. This sequence may not be switched around. Everything God does and permits is ultimately to his glory. It is, however, also true that God wants his glory to remain in the most important position. Humans always benefit when God is glorified. Therefore, our prayers are primarily to glorify God, but we also receive the benefits of prayer from him.

One of the foremost themes of the Reformation was the idea that we must live our entire lives under God's authority, to his glory and in his presence. Prayer is a dialogue between God and us. In prayer, we open our whole lives to him. He knows what we are thinking, but we still have the privilege to tell him what we think and what we want to do. He says, "Come, talk to me. Make your most intimate requests known to me." Therefore, we pray to know God better, and to be known by him.

Our Father in heaven, may your Name also be hallowed by my prayers. Thank you for the privilege of being able to speak to you intimately.

Prayer is the unconditional requirement for everything God wants to establish in this world.
ANDREW MURRAY

NAME OF ALL NAMES

He (Christ) is the image of the invisible God, the firstborn over all creation (Col 1:15).

The Old Testament clearly shows that God is in control of human history, to the benefit of his people. The climax will be reached when he establishes his kingdom through the Messiah, God's anointed King. The New Testament shows that Jesus of Nazareth is the Messiah. His role is that of king, priest, and prophet.

As prophet, Jesus spoke in the Name of God; as priest, he gave himself as sacrifice for the sins of mankind; as king, he rose triumphantly from the dead and reigns to all eternity at God's right hand. Jesus said to his disciples, *All authority in heaven and on earth has been given to me* (Mt 28:18).

FOOD FROM THE WORD OF GOD
Colossians 1:1-23; Psalm 102:12, 15-22, 25-27; Isaiah 41:2-4; Amos 4:13.

As Christians, we know that Christ reigns, and that he will subject everything to his authority. We are living in the final days, in the period between his first coming to bring salvation and establish his kingdom, and his second coming to complete the work of his kingdom in final triumph and fair judgement.

As the history of mankind progresses, there is more and more chaos and confusion. However, as Christians we can find stability and hope in Jesus, the sovereign King of history. Hebrews 1:8 puts it like this, *But about the Son he says, "Your throne, O God, will last for ever and ever, and righteousness will be the sceptre of your kingdom."* In addition, God will never forget his promises.

The kingdom of the world has become the kingdom of our Lord and of his Christ, and he will reign for ever and ever (Rev 11:15).

I have a great need for Christ; I have a great Christ to meet my needs.
CHARLES H SPURGEON

FLEE FROM ALL EVIL

But he left his cloak in her hand and ran out of the house (Gen 39:12).

Repentance and confession is to firmly turn away from every thought, word, deed, or habit that is wrong. It is not enough to just feel the pains of regret and to apologise to God. Repentance and confession are more than just a matter of emotions. They are inner change in thought and attitude that completely change the pattern of your life.

In this, we may not compromise at all. There might be sins in our lives that we think we will never be able to give up, but we must be willing to give them up while we call on God to release us from them. If you hesitate about what is right or wrong, what you should keep, and what you should give up, do not allow yourself to be influenced by the habits of Christians you do not know well. Live according to the pure statements of the Bible and according to the voice of your conscience. Christ will lead you forth on the path of righteousness.

FOOD FROM THE WORD OF GOD
Genesis 39:6-12; 2 Kings 15:12-16; Proverbs 5:7-9; Malachi 9:38-10:16

When, through the Holy Spirit, he shows you what is wrong in your life, flee from it. It may be a bad relationship or a dangerous pastime, literature that you read, an attitude of pride, jealousy, hate or unforgiving. Jesus told his followers to gouge out their eyes and to cut off their hands and feet if these body parts caused them to sin. This serious imagery calls on us to deal ruthlessly with all temptations that enter our lives.

Lead me not into temptation, Lord Jesus, but when I am tempted, may your Holy Spirit help me and deliver me from the evil one.

All God's giants of the faith were weak people who did great things for God, because they knew that they could rely on him. – HUDSON TAYLOR

February 4

TRUST IN GOD; DO NOT FEAR PEOPLE

**Fear of man will prove to be a snare,
but whoever trusts in the Lord is kept safe (Prov 29:25).**

Many of us have forgotten what it means to fear the Lord. We have lost our wonder of his character. We allow God to mean less and less, and ourselves to mean more and more. As we progress, improve, and thrive intellectually, technologically, and scientifically, we think that we do not need God quite so much.

What then does it mean to fear the Lord? How can we accomplish it? To fear God is both positive and negative. The positive side is to love what God loves: wisdom. Proverbs 2:1-2, 5-6 says, *If you accept my words and store up my commands within you, turning your ear to wisdom and applying your heart to understanding ... then you will understand the fear of the Lord and find the knowledge of God. For the Lord gives wisdom...*

FOOD FROM THE WORD OF GOD
Proverbs 29:25; 2:1-2, 5-6; Psalm 56:3-4; Isaiah 51:7-8, 12-16; Luke 11:37-12:7.

The negative side is to hate what God hates: evil. *To fear the Lord is to hate evil* (Prov 8:13). *Through the fear of the Lord a man avoids evil* (Prov 16:6). *"The fear of the Lord – that is wisdom, and to shun evil is understanding* (Job 28:28).

People who have been gripped by fear of the Lord cannot tolerate evil, because God does not tolerate it. They are reformers, not isolated hermits. Their loathing of evil allows for no opportunity in their lives to be seduced by it. They constantly yearn for the wisdom of the Lord.

*I fear you, Lord my God, with all the love in my heart.
I love what you love, and hate what you hate.
Help me to remain faithful to you.*

I fear God, but I am not afraid of him.
SIR THOMAS BROWNE

February 5

CHRIST, THE FOUNDATION OF OUR FAITH

For no one can lay any foundation other than the one already laid, which is Jesus Christ (1 Cor 3:11).

What does it mean to build your house on a rock or to dig deeply and lay a firm foundation? It means to build on Jesus Christ himself, to live by his words, to believe he is who he says he is, and to turn away from sin and to follow him loyally and faithfully as your Saviour and Leader.

Listen to what Isaiah writes, *So this is what the Sovereign Lord says: "See, I lay a stone in Zion, a tested stone, a precious cornerstone for a sure foundation; the one who trusts will never be dismayed"* (28:16). In Ephesians 2:20 Paul declares, *(You are) built on the foundation of the apostles and prophets, with Christ Jesus himself as the chief cornerstone.* And this hymn puts it wonderfully into words:

FOOD FROM THE WORD OF GOD
1 Corinthians 3:1-4:5; Psalm 118:22; Isaiah 9:7; Zechariah 10:2-6; 13: 8-9.

My hope is built on nothing less than Jesus' blood and righteousness;
I dare not trust the sweetest frame but wholly lean on Jesus' Name.
On Christ, the solid rock, I stand; all other ground is sinking sand.

A life built on Christ and on his teachings, will stand up to trials, assaults and tests, and will remain standing eternally. Jesus says that, though the rains may fall, the floodwaters advance and the storm winds rage, the life that is built on him will endure for eternity. On what foundation have you built your life and your mission in life? Will they be able to stand the test?

Rock of ages cleft for me, grant that my handiwork might endure, and honour you.

Christian religion is a religion of miracles and the miracle of Christ's resurrection is the epicentre and foundation of the Christian faith. – ALAN RICHARDSON

JESUS SETS US FREE FOR EVER FROM SIN

He did not enter by means of the blood of goats and calves; but he entered the Most Holy Place once for all by his own blood, having obtained eternal redemption (Heb 9:12).

John tells us what to do when we have sinned: Confess your sins before God and admit that you need forgiveness. *If we confess our sins, he is faithful and just and will forgive us our sins and purify us from all unrighteousness* (1 Jn 1:9).

God promises to forgive us when we confess our sins. He forgives us once and for all and completely restores our relationship with him. The cross of Christ Jesus always stands at the centre of his forgiveness. Without his body on the cross, forgiveness would not have been possible. Forgiveness therefore never comes cheaply – it was bought at the high price of our Saviour's blood. There can be no forgiveness without tears, without paying a personal price. There can be no forgiveness without the sacrifice of Christ. Because of Christ's sacrifice, we need no longer be prisoners of sin. Therefore, we are no longer losers, but victors in Christ.

FOOD FROM THE WORD OF GOD
Hebrews 8:7-9:12; Psalm 103:8-12; 111:7-9; Isaiah 43:19, 22-25; 53:10-11.

Even though we cannot erase the temptations of sin, we are not without help. God is on our side, Jesus is our counsel, and the Holy Spirit is our teacher and guide. He guides us to our shelter: Jesus Christ. How can we thank God enough for the blood of Jesus that washed away our sins for ever? Let us never forget the price he had to pay to make it possible for us.

Saviour and Friend, I can never thank you enough for the wonderful deliverance from sin that you have brought into my life. May the Holy Spirit always keep me sensitive to the difference between right and wrong.

Jesus became what we are, in order to make us what he is.
ATHANASIUS

GOD DEMONSTRATES HIS OMNIPOTENCE

Who is this? Even the wind and the waves obey him! (Mk 4:41).

What has God's omnipotence thus far accomplished in your life? Think seriously about this, and ask the Holy Spirit to help you.

God has the power to destroy, but also the power to create and re-create. The latter brings life, joy, and peace. It leads to freedom, not slavery; to life, not death; to reform, not stagnation. The power that creates and re-creates, repairs broken relationships, and gives the gift of a full life and of healing to all who accept it. It is a spiritual power emanating from God himself, and revealed by Jesus Christ.

FOOD FROM THE WORD OF GOD
Mark 4:21-5:10; Psalm 29:1-10; 77:11-19.

The power that creates attained its highest point at the crucifixion. There it was that Satan used all the might at his disposal to try to destroy Jesus. However, God used the crucifixion as final proof of his creative omnipotence. The price for our sins has been paid, the righteousness of God complied with, and our relationship with God restored.

Christ died for our sins and in his death we see the power that creates and re-creates. We respond to this almighty act of power with gratitude. This love is so great and indescribable, that it exceeds all earthly love. We can only thank and praise God constantly for the omnipotence that he demonstrated through Jesus Christ. In addition, the Lord used his omnipotence to draw you closer to him. Do you thank him every day for his redeeming omnipotence?

Saviour and Regenerator, you have shown your omnipotence in my life also, and have drawn me closer to you with bonds of love. I shall, without end, praise you and be thankful.

The righteousness of Jesus is the righteousness of a divinely directed relationship of trust, joy, dependence, and receptiveness – MICHAEL RAMSAY

GOD KEEPS HIS PROMISES

God did this so that, by two unchangeable things in which it is impossible for God to lie, we who have fled to take hold of the hope offered to us may be greatly encouraged (Heb 6:18).

The Bible is full of God's promises. Some people like to say, "If God said he would do it, I believe him. And that's the end of the story, whether you believe it or not." Others will question this, "How can I be sure that God really said it? How can I be certain of the meaning of what he said?"

FOOD FROM THE WORD OF GOD
Hebrews 6:9-7:10; Psalm 89:20, 26-27; Isaiah 23:4-6, 14-16.

It is important for us to interpret each of God's promises in its proper context, but we may also claim for ourselves those promises that are applicable to our specific situation, and thus activate the truth of it in our lives.

In Hebrews 4:3 we read an astounding truth: *And yet his work has been finished since the creation of the world.* In other words: at the creation of the world God already provided for all the needs of your life and heart. With his divine omniscience and prescience, he looked down the corridors of time, saw your future problems, and provided what you would need.

Think about the majesty and greatness of God. Focus on the promises he gives you in his Word. Prepare yourself to make his goal for your life a reality. Live every day in the certainty that God is wholly in charge of every situation. Then you can relax because you have nothing to fear or to be anxious about. God cares for you and he keeps the promises given in his Word.

Holy and omniscient God, I worship you for always keeping your promises, in my life too. Through Jesus Christ, you provide for every need in eternal faith to your promises.

The Bible is an inexhaustible fountain of truth. The existence of the Bible is the greatest blessing mankind has ever experienced. – IMMANUEL KANT

GOD COMES TO LIVE WITH US AND RENEWS EVERYTHING

Now the dwelling of God is with men, and he will live with them … He who was seated on the throne said, "I am making everything new!" (Rev 21:3, 5).

The yearning of every believer's heart for the glorious city of God can be traced back to the patriarchs of the Old Testament. The author of Hebrews says Abraham already had such a yearning. *For he (Abraham) was looking forward to the city with foundations, whose architect and builder is God* (Heb 11:10). Moreover, Paul speaks of his people who are in slavery, *But the Jerusalem that is above is free …* (Gal 4:26).

FOOD FROM THE WORD OF GOD
Revelation 21:1-27;
Isaiah 60:18-19; 65:17-19, 22-24;
Zechariah 2:10-13.

The "New Jerusalem" (Rev 3:12, 21:2) is only one of many names for this future city of God. It is also called: the Holy City, the heavenly Jerusalem, and Zion. And it will be a holy and beautiful place.

At this moment Jesus is busy preparing places for us there. He says, *In my Father's house are many rooms; if it were not so, I would have told you. I am going there to prepare a place for you* (Jn 14:2). O, what blessed splendour to be able to sit down at the banquet of the Lamb in God's New Jerusalem! There God's light will shine forever upon us. We shall be with God and God will live with us. *He will wipe every tear from (our) eyes. There will be no more death or mourning or crying or pain …* (Rev 21:4). God will be with us in all eternity and we shall see and know him. How happy are we who have been saved by Christ. We are on our way home.

Holy Spirit of God, keep hope burning in my heart so that I may one day be with God in the new Jerusalem where all around me will be new.

God is with us always; why should we not always be with God?
WILLIAM ULLATHORNE

February 10

WHEN WE BELIEVE, GOD DOES GREAT THINGS

The man took Jesus at his word and departed. While he was still on the way, his servants met him with the news that his boy was living (Jn 4:50-51).

In Joshua 3, we read that the Israelites camped on the banks of the river Jordan. Canaan, the Promised Land, is within sight, but they have a tremendous problem: There is a river in their way and they have no way of getting across or around it. To make matters worse, it is the rainy season. The river is in flood. The water is deep, roaring and menacing.

FOOD FROM THE WORD OF GOD
John 4:27-54;
2 Chronicles 20:12-17, 20-24.

So, what does God do to help them? He gives Joshua strange orders, which he must convey to the Israelites. When Joshua commanded the priests to take up the Ark of the Covenant and go and stand next to the river, they obeyed him. So, what happened? When the feet of the priests who carried the ark touched the shallow waters, the water flowing from upstream stood still. It heaped up … the water flowing down to the Sea of the Arabah (the Salt Sea) from the Jordan Valley was completely cut off. The people crossed over opposite Jericho. The priests who carried the ark of the covenant of the Lord stood firmly on dry ground, while all of Israel walked over the dry river bed until the entire nation had crossed the Jordan (Josh 3:15-17).

God gave them no guarantee that the water would dry up. He did nothing until they had stepped into the water. Only then did God's miracle occur. In the same way, God will give us faith to move mountains when we hold his hand on our road of pilgrimage.

Lord my God, strengthen my weak faith while I closely walk with you. Make me obedient to the instructions of your Holy Spirit.

Were it not for miracles, I would not be a Christian.
St AUGUSTINE

February 11

GOD GIVES ETERNAL LIFE TO THOSE WHO BELIEVE

I tell you the truth, whoever hears my word and believes him who sent me has eternal life and will not be condemned; he has crossed over from death to life (Jn 5:24).

The New Testament does not teach us that everyone will have eternal life, but that those who come to God by faith in Jesus Christ receive eternal life as a gift of mercy from God.

The rebirth – to be born of the Spirit – is to possess the life that God has given us (Jn 3:1-13). Not everyone is born of the Spirit. On the contrary, the Bible tells us that human beings, in their natural state, are "dead to God", and that rebirth – an act of the Holy Spirit – is necessary in order to transplant God's "life" into a human being.

FOOD FROM THE WORD OF GOD
John 5:1-29; Psalm 16:1-2, 9-11; 27:1; 34:21-22; 36:1-9.

The fact that the gift from God is eternal life does not imply that our lives continue unhindered. It does means that we are part of the character of God, and God is eternal! Therefore, his life is being lived in our bodies. This is what eternal life means. Eternal life does not begin after we die – it begins while we are still alive. Eternal life begins with faith in God through Jesus, the living Christ.

Eternal life belongs to those who believe in the Son of man, he who died on the cross. That act of obedience to his Father, his sacrificial death, ensures salvation for all who believe in him. It belongs to those who share in Christ's victory of resurrection.

I praise and thank you, my eternal Father, for having also begun eternal life in my heart when the Holy Spirit led me to you after my repentance and rebirth.

A true Christian is somebody who does not forget for a moment what God did for him through Jesus Christ. His whole attitude and all his activities are rooted in this feeling of thankfulness. – JOHN BAILLIE

YOU CHOOSE EITHER FOR OR AGAINST CHRIST

You diligently study the Scriptures because you think that by them you possess eternal life. These are the Scriptures that testify about me, yet you refuse to come to me to have life (Jn 5:39-40).

What God has done, makes complete sense. It makes sense that God used the Law to teach Israel about their profound need for mercy. It makes sense that Jesus would be our sacrifice because a sacrifice was needed to restore man's relationship with God. It makes sense that Jesus is our High Priest. Yes, that which God has done makes complete sense.

FOOD FROM THE WORD OF GOD
John 5:30-6:15; Genesis 3:14-15; Deuteronomy 18:15-22; 30:19-20.

Yet, why God did it, is totally incomprehensible. If we look beyond the method and study the motive, the building blocks of sense and logic begin to fall to pieces. God's love is not logical: It cannot be neatly rationalised in a sermon or answered in an examination paper. Even after people had spat in his holy face, he still loved them. After he was stripped and disfigured, he died for them out of love. Even today, after billions of people have chosen to forsake him in favour of wealth, fame and status, he waits lovingly for them to return to him.

It is totally inexplicable. It is devoid of all traces of logic, of reason. Bloodstained majesty. A tearful God. A Creator with a tender heart. God has become the laughing stock of the world in order to save his children. He abundantly and unconditionally shares his love with ungrateful people. The only thing that is more absurd than God's actions is our stubborn reluctance to choose his love.

Loving Father, I believe and trust your love, and unconditionally choose you as the King of my heart and life.

It is only through the mystery of self-sacrifice that one can find oneself anew.
CARL GUSTAV JUNG

February 13

JESUS OPENS THE EYES OF BELIEVERS

He replied, "Whether he is a sinner or not, I don't know. One thing I do now: I was blind but now I see!" (Jn 9:25).

God normally does things differently from humans. The Bible tells us of at least four times that he healed blind people. Moreover, each time he did it in a different, creative way. The Lord treats each of us as an individual. Each of us is exceptional and special to him. Each of us is an unique object of his mercy and care. He is a loyal God who never abandons his creation. Even if you were the only human on earth, and even though you are one of many billions, his personal interest in you remains sincere and limitless.

FOOD FROM THE WORD OF GOD
John 9:13-41; Psalm 119:17-24; 146:5-10; Isaiah 42:18-21.

Jesus took mud and put it on the blind man's eyes. This act required two important things from the blind man: faith and obedience. As soon as he obeyed the Master, he was healed of his blindness. Redemption is always the direct result of obedience.

To follow Christ means not to grapple in the dark. This man had never seen the light of day, or a flower, or a mountain, or a tree. He had lived all his life in darkness. How thankful we should be that our Saviour is the light of the world! He can enter any heart of darkness and open our eyes to God's wonderful light. The moment you open your heart to him, his light shines into your life. Through faith and obedience, there is no longer a need for anyone to walk in darkness.

I pray, Lord Jesus, that you will teach me through the Holy Spirit how to believe in you sincerely and how to trust you completely in all circumstances.

Heaven waits to help those who have discovered the will of God in their lives, and who obey it.
J ROBERT ASHCROFT

February 14

GOD WILL FAITHFULLY PROTECT YOU

So then he (Jesus) told them plainly, "Lazarus is dead, and for your sake I am glad I was not there, so that you may believe. But let us go to him" (Jn 11:14-15).

A number of physicists and botanists were searching the Alps for a unique and extraordinary flower. One day they saw through their binoculars a flower of exceptional beauty. However, it was in a rift valley with vertical rock faces on either side. They would have had to lower someone over the edge of the precipice to reach this very rare and sought-after flower.

FOOD FROM THE WORD OF GOD
John 10:34-11:27; Psalm 40:1-5; 91:14-16; Isaiah 25:1, 8-9.

They told a local boy, who had been watching them, "We'll pay you five pounds if you will let us lower you down the rock-face to go and pick the flower." The boy looked down at the rift valley, and then said, "I'll go over the edge and down the rock face, if this man who's with me holds the rope. He's my dad." Have you yet learned to trust God like this boy trusted his father?

Sometimes we put our trust in people. We rely upon what we think they can do for us. People can, however, disappoint us, but God never will! We may be in great distress, but we can always look up and place our trust in our omniscient and loving Father God. He will make everything work together for our good, because he loves us. We can entrust the rope of our circumstances to his care. People may become tired and let go of the rope; their attention may be distracted; or they may grow impatient. However, God never grows weary of holding the rope and of protecting us. We can leave it with absolute confidence in his almighty hands.

Lord Jesus, I trust you every day of my life and I will keep a good heart through the darkest night, because your faithfulness remains firm and true. You provide for me and protect me.

Faith is believing what you cannot see, and seeing what you cannot believe.
MARTIN LUTHER

SORROW LEADS TO REPENTANCE

Yet now I am happy, not because you were made sorry, but because your sorrow led you to repentance (2 Cor 7:9).

Repentance actually means "to think again" – to turn your thoughts around. As when you discover that you are on the wrong road and turn around, searching until you find the place where you turned off the right road. When this word points to evangelical repentance it does not simply mean a turn-about in your thoughts, but a radical change in your goals; a total transformation of your desires and attitudes.

Repentance implies the conviction that sin is an offence against God. Without this conviction, there can be no question of repentance. The transgressor must be completely honest with God. He or she must honestly admit to the truth of the sin in his or her life, and especially acknowledge God's rights, that he or she is God's property in body, soul, and spirit.

FOOD FROM THE WORD OF GOD
2 Corinthians 7:8-8:15; Ezra 10:1-5, 9-17.

Repentance implies that you transform your whole life. Repentant people turn their backs on every form of sin, because they do not tolerate it in their lives. All sins are abruptly laid down. This does not imply that repentant people will never again, and not even for a second, fall back into sin, but that they will purposefully and with assurance declare themselves to be opposed to sin, with all the earnestness of their souls, and will actively fight against it so as to triumph in the Name of the living Christ.

I thank you, O Holy Spirit, for having brought about repentance and conversion in my life, and that I may rest assured in the knowledge that sin no longer rules over me.

Conversion is much more than just repentance for sins: it encompasses a change of character that fits in with heaven. – LEON WALLACE

ACCEPT GOD'S DISCIPLINE

No discipline seams pleasant at the time, but painful. Later on, however, it produces a harvest of righteousness and peace for those who have been trained by it (Heb 12:11).

In the same way that a good father disciplines and educates his children, so God disciplines us in a loving way. We are living in a world of mysticism and riddles. Therefore, it is not at all surprising that these elements infiltrate the religious spheres of our lives. Indeed, the living Christ said that it would be so: *You do not realise now what I am doing, but later you will understand* (Jn 13:7).

FOOD FROM THE WORD OF GOD
Hebrews 12:7-29; 2 Samuel 24:1-4, 8-15, 17-19, 25.

If we want to experience peace and calm in this riotous, chaotic world we will have to get a firmer grasp on the sovereignty of God and trust his love, even though we cannot understand, discern or identify it. We must remember that the hands that model the clay, the hands of the Master Potter, carry the scars of the nails. God's sovereignty will never conflict with his Fatherhood and love. Remember Isaiah's words, *Yet, O Lord, you are our Father. We are the clay, you are the potter; we are all the work of your hand* (Is 64:8). Therefore, you must never play God's righteousness and discipline against his love. Indeed, discipline is based on love.

If we want to enjoy a growing closeness to God, we must respond to his providence and care in a spiritual way, even when it is unfathomable. God's actions with us may take on different guises, but it is always planned with love so that we may know him still better and love him more.

I accept your discipline, holy God and loving Father, because I know from experience that you make all things work together of the good for those who love you.

Still be content to be his child and let the Father daily mete out to you light, power, exercise, problems, fears, virtues, peace and temptation, as he sees fit. – I PENNINGTON

GOD GRANTS WISDOM TO THOSE WHO ASK

If any of you lacks wisdom, he should ask God, who gives generously to all without finding fault; and it will be given to him (Jas 1:5).

Someone once said the wisest man in the world is the one who knows he does not know. In the midst of trials and temptations, we have all said, "Had I only known what to do." Alternatively, "I don't know which way to turn or what to do."

However, God promises to give us his wisdom. Read today's scripture again, attentively. Everything is written there: the whole recipe for receiving wisdom. "Ask" and "give" are the two operative words. If we ask God for it in prayer, he will give it to us.

FOOD FROM THE WORD OF GOD
James 1:1-27; 1 Kings 3:4-14; Daniel 2:18-20, 22-23.

But we should not merely *ask* God for wisdom, we must also ask in faith: *But when he asks, he must believe and not doubt, because he who doubts is like a wave of the sea, blown and tossed by the sea. That man should not think he will receive anything from the Lord; he is a double-minded man, unstable in all he does* (Jas 1:6-8).

If we believe when we pray to God for wisdom, God will give it to us in abundance. Ask him for the wisdom to deal with the crises in your life calmly. Pray for wisdom that you may successfully cope with every situation in life in his Name and to his glory. Then trust God.

I need your wisdom in so many areas of my life, O Lord. Grant it to me generously in answer to my believing prayers.

The wise man prays to God in the storm, not for safety from danger, but for freedom from fear. It is the storm from within that endangers us, not the storm from without. – RALPH WALDO EMERSON

February 18

GUARD YOUR TONGUE

If anyone is never at fault in what he says, he is a perfect man, able to keep his whole body in check (Jas 3:2b).

When your tongue gets out of control, it is a sure sign that you must examine your heart. But, says James, no one can tame the tongue. However, the Word of God encourages us to discover that the Holy Spirit can recreate our tongues too, and can help us to control them.

Constantly fill your heart with good things from the Word of God, so that you are able to keep your tongue under control. Also believe that, with the help of the Holy Spirit, you can successfully control your tongue. When James describes the tongue as a bit in the horse's mouth so that man can control it, he probably purposefully omits to say the rider must control the horse's bit, as the pilot must control the ship's rudder. Through his Holy Spirit, God wants to be the rider or the pilot who controls your tongue.

FOOD FROM THE WORD OF GOD
James 3:1-4:10; Psalm 141:1-4; Proverbs 10:11, 31-32; 12:18-19; 13:3; 18:20-21; Song of Songs 10:12.

Who is in control of your tongue? If you struggle to control your tongue, pray that God through his Holy Spirit will put the desire in your heart to give total control of your tongue to him. When you give up control of your tongue to him, you will quickly discover that you have the power to speak only friendly and constructive words.

Holy Spirit of God, may my tongue always reveal your presence in my life. Take charge of my tongue so that I may use it only to glorify you.

Anger is silenced by a gentle word, just as fire is extinguished by water.
JEAN PIERRE CAMUS

February 19

STAND FIRM IN YOUR FAITH

So then, just as you received Christ Jesus as Lord, continue to live in him, rooted and built up in him, strengthened in the faith as you were taught, and overflowing with thankfulness (Col 2:6-7).

Many poplar trees stood very close to one another. One day when a violent storm broke, they were all blown down. Why? They leaned too much on each other and depended on one another to stay upright. By standing so close together, they kept one another upright, but at the same time prevented each other from developing a sturdy root system and becoming big trees. When the storm winds uprooted the first group of trees, the rest followed one after the other. Very close to these trees, a solitary tree stood on an open plain. It grew to be strong. Even though the storm winds lashed at it as well, it could withstand the full violence without being sheltered by other trees. Why? Because this tree's roots were anchored very firmly in the good earth.

FOOD FROM THE WORD OF GOD
Colossians 1:24-2:15; 2 Chronicles 20:20-21; Psalm 40:1-4; Proverbs 4:3-15; Isaiah 50:10-11.

Christians do not stand alone. They stand together and help one another to grow in faith. However, if we do not have a permanent and solid root system, we will collapse while we sit in our neat, snug rows in church. When the storms break around us, when crises befall us, we will be blown over if we lack faith. Every Christian ought to grow in Christ independently, firmly rooted in his love and in our faith in him by using every means of grace that God makes available to us. Then even if the most violent storm were to break, it could still be said of our faith, "They were not shaken!"

Eternal and unchanging God, keep the roots of my faith firmly anchored in you, so that I will remain standing when storms break around me.

Every person must do two things for himself: he must believe for himself … and die for himself.
MARTIN LUTHER

CHRIST IS COMING! SATAN WILL BE DEFEATED!

***Now have come the salvation and the power and kingdom of our God, and the authority of his Christ. For the accuser of our brothers, who accuses them before our God day and night, has been hurled down* (Rev 12:10).**

When will this heavenly conflict end? That it was Michael who led God's angels to victory, is significant, because Michael is associated with the nation of Israel. Apparently, Satan's intense hate of Israel drove him to make one final assault on the throne of God. Nevertheless, Michael and the heavenly host will defeat him.

FOOD FROM THE WORD OF GOD
Revelation 11:15-12:12; Psalm 2:1-9; Daniel 7:13-18, 21-22.

What bearing has this future war on the church of today? The same dragon that in heaven accuses the believers, also commits fraud. He seduces nations into believing that God's people are dangerous; that they deceive and destroy. God's people must expect strong opposition, but the church will always be able to defeat the armies of the enemy by remaining true to the living God. Satan is by no means a match for God. He is not omnipresent, omniscient, and omnipotent. His power is limited and his offensive tactics fail – as long as God's people trust in the power of the blood of the Lamb and in the Word.

As believers we can rejoice in the victory despite all the bad experiences in our lives. The Word of God encourages us: *Finally, be strong in the Lord and in his mighty power. Put on the full armor of God so that you can take your stand against the devil's schemes* (Eph 6:10-11).

My God and Father, thank you that I may, through Jesus Christ, be on your side and that I therefore need not fear Satan and all his schemes.

I firmly believe in Godly protection. Without it, the world would have become a maze with no hope.
WOODROW WILSON

A PURE LIFE IS IMPORTANT

Rather, as servants of God we commend ourselves in every way ... in the Holy Spirit and in sincere love; in truthful speech and in the power of God; with weapons of righteousness in the right hand and in the left ... (2 Cor 6:4a, 6b-7).

Someone said, "Faith is something that you possess; conviction is something that possesses you." Conviction is not really conviction unless it entails the commitment that enables you to live according to what you say that you believe. A conviction is not an oath, but a determined purpose to live according to the Word of God.

FOOD FROM THE WORD OF GOD
2 Corinthians 6:3-7:7; Deuteronomy 7:1-4; Psalm 18:21-26; 119:1-3, 9-11; Proverbs 4:14-15.

First, we need to be committed to sanctification as a way of life. We must decide that sanctification is so important to God, that it should enjoy priority in our lives. We must commit ourselves to obeying all of God's commandments. We cannot obey some and ignore others, depending on our personal values and preferences. A little bit of trickery with your income tax is just as big a sin as theft; an unforgiving spirit is just as big a sin as murder. God finds all sin insulting and offensive. Not only does it harm the sanctity and majesty of God, but it also has a negative effect on us and on those close to us.

Sin is of grave concern to God. Therefore, we must try our utmost to keep sin out of our lives. Every sin, no matter how small, is an expression of disrespect towards the sovereignty of God. The psalmist realised the gravity of sin when he said: *You have laid down precepts that are to be fully obeyed* (Ps 119:4). We must obey God's instructions completely if we want to live pure lives dedicated to him.

Holy Spirit of God, cleanse my heart of every sin and make me sensitive to the instructions of my heavenly Father.

It is always easier to fight for one's principles than to live up to them.
ALFRED ADLER

GOD'S PEOPLE ARE HOSPITABLE

There we found some brothers who invited us to spend a week with them (Acts 28:14).

The Word not only tells us of believers who were hospitable, it also instructs us to lovingly pay attention to others. In his letters to Timothy and Titus, Paul considers hospitality as one of the duties of the elders in the community. He combines hospitality and encouragement as important Christian characteristics (Tit 1:8-9).

Paul's instructions in Romans 12:9-13 emphasise that this love-in-action is not only the duty of the elders, but that it must be an attribute of all Christian believers. The Oxford Dictionary of Current English defines "hospitality" as "friendly and generous reception and entertainment of guests or strangers". These words paint a picture of an atmosphere of love and encouragement.

FOOD FROM THE WORD OF GOD
Acts 28:11-31; Genesis 24:17-32.

When we carry out the Bible's instruction to be hospitable, the emphasis must not fall on how many things we can give. The Bible does not instruct us as to how long we must provide accommodation for guests or how many meals we must prepare. We need not have a sprawling, modern mansion in order to invite others. Exotic food and drink is not required when breaking bread together. It has nothing to do with how much money we spend, but the time that we are prepared to give others, how much of ourselves we are prepared to give. Focus on people and not on preparations and quantities. In the hands of God, a few loaves of bread and fishes can do miracles; and he wants to use your home to do this.

I make myself available, Lord Jesus, to practise hospitality to the glory of your Name and the strengthening of your kingdom.

When I give of my possessions, I give but little. It is when I give of myself that I begin to understand what giving really means. – KAHLIL GIBRAN

February 23

GOD PROTECTS THOSE WHO RELY ON HIM

**Blessed are you who are poor,
for yours is the kingdom of God (Lk 6:20).**

In the Bible, the gates or gateway to the New Jerusalem are used metaphorically to describe the splendour of the heavenly home where believers will live in the hereafter. We are allowed to set our eyes on the glorious city which God himself has designed and built. We are allowed to see the holy inner sanctum where multitudes worship and praise God without end. We see their white clothing, we hear the psalms of triumph that they sing incessantly, we see the shining joy on their faces, and experience the inexpressible blessedness of their hearts.

FOOD FROM THE WORD OF GOD
Luke 5:36-6:23; Psalm 17:6-9, 13-15; 37:7-13.

However, when the veil is lifted, we see the other side. We find ourselves on the threshold of doom in order to see what is happening there. Whereas everything on the other side was glorious and magnificent, here all is terrifying and dreadful. The Bible describes the final judgement of the wicked as terrifying. Living souls are cast into a bottomless pit. They sink further and further … down and down into the awful pit that has no bottom. There is great weeping and pleading while the souls sink. One hears the groans because they echo against the walls of the pool in terrible ways.

Those who trusted in God are destined for the former scene, that of glory. Because they put their trust in God, death does not frighten them. Indeed, God cares for those who put their trust in him.

God of love and mercy, deliver me from evil so that I may enter into your splendour and be with you until all eternity.

No disappointment awaits those whose will is buried in the will of God.
FREDERIK W FABER

LET GOD'S VALUES BE YOUR VALUES

If anyone would come after me, he must deny himself and take up his cross and follow me (Mk 8:34).

We read in Psalm 85:8, *I will listen to what God the Lord will say; he promises peace to his people, his saints.* Blessed are those who hear the voice of the Lord speaking to their hearts. Blessed are those who find comfort and strength in his Word. Blessed are the ears of those that hear God's whispered words, rather than the flattery of this world (Mt 13:16-17).

FOOD FROM THE WORD OF GOD
Mark 8:27-9:13; 1 Samuel 7:3-14; 16:6-7; Psalm 119:33-37; Song of Songs 2:10-11; 12:13-14.

Blessed are the ears that do not listen to the voice that reverberates on the streets, but to the teachings of God's voice. Blessed are the eyes that are blind to worldly things, but are fixed on the world of faith revealed by God in his Word. Blessed are they who have penetrated this world of wonders, and prepare themselves increasingly to discover heavenly secrets and to get to know and implement God's values. Blessed are they who take the time to get closer to God and overcome all earthly obstructions in order to achieve this purpose.

Contemplate what awaits us in heaven. Firmly close the door on everything that distracts your attention so that you can hear what the Lord your God wants to say to you (Ps 85:7-8). He assures us of redemption through Jesus Christ. Peace and life in abundance can only be found with him. Separate yourself from all temporary things and look for that which is everlasting. If you leave God, life loses all meaning. Remain faithful to him and he will surely bless you.

Holy God and – through Jesus Christ – our heavenly Father, grant that your values may also be mine and that my priorities will be pure, so that I may receive your blessing.

The ability to distinguish between good and evil is within everyone's reach.
ORIGEN of ALEXANDRIA

GOD'S PEOPLE CARE ABOUT ONE ANOTHER

The disciples, each according to his ability, decided to provide help for the brothers living in Judea (Acts 11:29).

Jesus commanded us to be compassionate – not that we may choose to whom we want to show compassion. However, every person is inclined to choose to whom he or she will reach out. Maybe this was also the problem with the priest and the Levite in the parable of the Good Samaritan. Jesus mixed with all kinds of people: the rich and the poor; the socially acceptable and the social outcasts; the simple as well as the educated.

However, our willingness to reach out to others costs us something. The poet Michael Quest pinpointed our dilemma:

FOOD FROM THE WORD OF GOD
Acts 11:1-30; Deuteronomy 15:4-11; Job 29:11-16; Proverbs 22:9.

Lord, why did You tell me to love all men as my brothers?
I have tried, but I come back to You frightened.
Lord, I was so peaceful at home, so comfortably settled.
It was well furnished, and I felt so cosy.
I was alone; I was at peace.
Sheltered from the wind and rain, kept clean.

God wants to tear us away from our comfortable surroundings so that we can go out and help our neighbours in need. That is what Jesus did. We, his followers, may do no less. We often shrink from having to comply with this command. To show compassion to all in need is, however, to follow the example Jesus set – always willing to give of yourself and make sacrifices.

Compassionate Leader and Example, grant me a heart that will reach out joyously, that will sacrifice and give, and so follow the example you set for me.

When the Lord sends you down stony paths, he will provide you with tough shoes.
CORRIE TEN BOOM

CAST YOURSELF ON GOD'S MERCY

"Even now," declares the Lord, "return to me with all your heart, with fasting and weeping and mourning." Rend your heart and not your garments. Return to the Lord your God, for he is gracious and compassionate, slow to anger and abounding in love, and he relents from sending calamity (Joel 2:12-13).

FOOD FROM THE WORD OF GOD
Joel 2:1-3, 6, 10-13; Jeremiah 18:11-12; Revelation 9:1-10:4.

Seeing a hurricane approach is a terrible experience; it is awful to know that destruction is on the way: the birds of the heavens fold their wings; every animal down below looks for shelter; menacing black clouds gather in the sky; the sun makes way for pitch-black darkness. Nature frowns and threatens.

Though few people realise it, this is a very apt depiction of the situation of a sinner before our righteous God. No burning coals have yet fallen from heaven, but a fiery storm is coming. Hurricane winds do not yet howl around you but, in his anger, God is getting his weapons ready for action.

Up until now, the floods have been kept back by mercy, but the floodgates will be opened shortly. God's bolts of lightning are still in his storerooms, but behold! The storm is approaching! And it will be an unbearable moment when God – shrouded in vengeance and anger – appears on the scene. Where, o where, poor sinner, will you hide from the vengeance of God? Where will you flee?

Now is the time that Christ's redeeming hand wants to lead you to God. Let him take your hand in his almighty hand. His broken body is the rock of ages where you can safely hide. You know your distress, your need for salvation. Therefore, believe in God, cast yourself on his mercy – and the storm will pass you by, without harming you.

Thank you, my Saviour and Friend, that you are my Shelter and my Rock, now as well as on the day when God's judgement will burst forth and his wrath against evil will ignite.

Jesus Christ lived so that he may die, and he died so that we may live for ever.
MATTHEW ARNOLD

February 27

GOD SAVES AND HONOURS HIS FOLLOWERS

Him who overcomes I will make a pillar in the temple of my God. Never will he leave it. I will write on him the name of my God and the name of the city of my God, the new Jerusalem, which is coming down out of heaven from my God; I will also write on him my new name (Rev 3:12).

A couple had for many years done missionary work amongst the heathens in Africa, and were on their way back to New York to retire there. Without a pension and in failing health, they were dejected and scared of the future. They were booked on the same ship as President Roosevelt of the United States. The President was on his way home from a big game hunting safari. Naturally, all the passengers tried to get a glimpse of him.

FOOD FROM THE WORD OF GOD
Revelation 3:7-4:5;
Psalm 91:14-16;
Isaiah 22:20-25; Daniel 12:1-3;
Zephaniah 1:14-16.

When they arrived in New York a band and welcoming committee waited on the quay to welcome Roosevelt home. The missionary couple went ashore unnoticed.

That evening, in a cheap flat, the man's spirit cracked. He told his wife, "I cannot take it any more. God isn't treating us fairly." His wife suggested he go to the bedroom and tell God in prayer how he felt. A short while later he appeared from the room, his appearance totally altered. His wife asked him what had happened. "God put the matter straight. I told him how bitter I felt when the president got such an overwhelming homecoming, and that no one was there to meet us. When I had finished praying, it felt as if God put his hand on my shoulder and said to me, 'But you have not yet come home!' "

Loving God, your redemption, love and protection are important to me. Thank you that I can believe in and trust you for all time and eternity.

Your whole life is filled with meaning the moment that you accept Christ as your Saviour.
STEPHAN NEILL

February 28

JESUS HAS ASTONISHING AUTHORITY

The men were amazed and asked, "What kind of man is this? Even the winds and the waves obey him!" (Mt 8:27).

While he was on earth, Jesus showed extraordinary power and authority. He raised Lazarus from the dead. He gave sight to the blind, made cripples walk, gave hearing to the deaf, and healed the sick. His contemporaries experienced an aspect of Jesus' power that we often overlook: the power of his words. The gospel writers contend that Jesus did not speak like the teachers of the law and the Pharisees, but as one with authority (Mt 7:29).

FOOD FROM THE WORD OF GOD
Matthew 8:5-27; Psalm 65:5-8; 104:1-9, 24-33.

When Jesus spoke "as one who had authority", his words were never meaningless or hollow. In contrast to the teachers of the law and the Pharisees, Jesus' teachings were meaningful, rich, and powerful.

The authority of the living Christ is backed by God's omnipotence. God is the powerful source of Jesus' authority. The word "authority" is related to the word "authorship". God is the almighty Author of his creation and the mighty Saviour of his creation. He is the omnipresent authority over his creation.

Jesus himself said, *All authority in heaven and on earth has been given to me* (Mt 28:18). God himself granted this authority to him. Therefore, it is little wonder that his contemporaries referred to him as the "one who had spoken with authority".

Redeemer and Saviour, being under your authority is an indescribable privilege. It comforts me to know that your Father has given all authority in heaven and on earth to you.

Jesus acts with the authority of God. He is the creative word of God. In him, we see God's purpose in the creation of mankind. – WILLIAM TEMPLE

February 29

HERE I AM, LORD!

In Damascus there was a disciple named Ananias. The Lord called to him in a vision, "Ananias!" "Yes, Lord," he answered (Acts 9:10).

Joyful are those who have unfailing faith in Jesus Christ; who are filled with sincere love for their Redeemer. These believers are enthralled by Jesus' character, and rejoice in his coming to a world torn apart by sin. They are completely engrossed in the tender love that he revealed. This is why it is impossible for them not to trust him. They admire and trust him to the utmost. They are also the ones who, together with Simon Peter, whisper the declaration of love: *Lord, you know all things; you know that I love you* (Jn 21:17).

FOOD FROM THE WORD OF GOD
Acts 9:10-35; 1 Samuel 16:1-13

We love God because he loved us first. Therefore, we confidently place our whole lives in his care and under his sovereignty. We accept his instructions and do what he tells us. We know that nothing can go wrong while he is the pilot of our lifeboat. When a captain trusts the harbour pilot to take his vessel into the harbour, he handles his ship according to the harbour pilot's instructions and directions. When a traveller trusts a guide to lead him along a hazardous mountain trail, he carefully follows the trail which the guide points out to him. When a patient trusts his doctor, he painstakingly adheres to his prescriptions and advice.

Faith, which refuses to obey the commands of the Saviour, is not true faith. When we say, "Here I am, Lord," we must be willing to obey and to bear the consequences of our words.

Use me, living Christ, where you think best. I declare myself willing to carefully abide by your instructions through the power of the Holy Spirit.

There is no nobler religion than service to the living God, and it is tangibly expressed in your service to your fellow men. – ALBERT SCHWEITZER

March

Prayer for March

1. Trust in God's promises
2. God is merciful
3. Obedience proves our love for God
4. God's witnesses are empowered
5. Those who sin are hated
6. Believe in the God of miracles
7. Christ's relationship with his Father
8. God rewards our faith
9. Live to please God
10. God answers our prayers
11. God's wrath will flare up
12. The testimony of a pure life
13. Evil emanates from within us
14. God wants to teach us to walk on his path
15. Watch out for false prophets
16. God will judge our actions
17. Honour God in your body
18. Glorify God in everything you do
19. The righteous are rewarded
20. Labour ennobles
21. Even though people see God's miracles …
22. God takes care of those who serve him
23. God expects obedience
24. God speaks to us in dreams
25. God's Word brings joy
26. God demands unwavering loyalty
27. Our redemption is rooted in faith in God
28. Serving God is a matter of choice
29. Focus on matters of God
30. Carry God's light into the world
31. Entrust your needs to God

Prayer for March

Holy Lord Jesus,
this month we again recall the way of the cross:
the Via Dolorosa you walked for our sake.
It was your Father's will that you should suffer and die
on behalf of a world torn apart by sin.
God took the initiative for our redemption
and in obedience to his will, you were incarnated.
You were like us in every way – except that you were without sin.
Therefore, you could pay for our sins.
Saviour and Redeemer, it was not only for mankind,
but also for me!
Yes, for me he was wounded;
for me he wore the crown of thorns.
For me he stood there; for me he walked the bitter road.
So in these times when we follow you on your path of sorrow,
grant that this refrain may continually sound from our hearts:
See the Saviour on the cross, the King of heavens, despised, reviled –
how he let himself be hanged, yet I am driven by self-interest alone.
Grant that we may answer your perfect love
with the purest love of our hearts.
Bless us in this Passion tide.

Amen

March 1

TRUST IN GOD'S PROMISES

(The angel) said, "Do not be afraid, Paul. You must stand trial before Caesar; and God has graciously given you the lives of all who sail with you." So keep your courage, men, for I have faith in God that it will happen just as he told me (Acts 27:24-25).

The story of how the Israelites took Jericho is a striking example of how God keeps his promises. When, on the seventh day, they marched around the city for the seventh time, all the Israelites shouted as one and the city walls collapsed. The leaders of Israel took the city without striking one single blow. They destroyed everything in the city, except for the household of Rahab. Because the Israelites obeyed the Lord, they witnessed that day the fulfilment of two of God's promises: the city of Jericho, the mightiest stronghold of the Canaanites, was completely destroyed, just as God had promised. And Rahab and her family were saved from retribution, just as God had promised.

FOOD FROM THE WORD OF GOD
Acts 27:1-26; Numbers 23:19; Joshua 1:1-9; 1 Kings 8: 22-24, 56.

There is, however, another promise that God made that we must recognise in the conquest of Jericho. To show that God means what he says when he makes a promise, Joshua cursed any man who might try to rebuild the destroyed city of Jericho. During the reign of king Ahab, in the year 925 BC, this curse was fulfilled in the fate of Hiel of Bethel when he rebuilt the city of Jericho. Hiel's firstborn son Abiram died while the foundations of the city were being laid. His youngest son Segub died while the city gates were being set up (1 Kgs 16:34). What God promises, he does.

We dare not ever take God's promises lightly. We can depend on this: what God promises, he will do.

Holy and righteous God, I trust that your promises are "Yes" and "Amen". Help me to trust steadfastly in you.

God's promises are like the stars:the darker the night, the brighter they shine.
DAVID NICHOLAS

GOD IS MERCIFUL

Yet, he was merciful; he forgave their iniquities and did not destroy them. Time after time, he restrained his anger and did not stir up his full wrath (Ps 78:38).

God is merciful, even to those who do not understand him. Through Christ, God has shown all of us his mercy; even though we do not deserve it and cannot earn it, God loves us.

In the fifth beatitude, Jesus invites us to share in his attributes of mercy and charity. However, we must give away this mercy in order to live in the fullness of it. The test of the greatness of what God wants to give us is being charitable towards those who are uncharitable to us. When we suffer disappointment, injustice or pain, we do not become resentful, but act kindly and show mercy. It is not easy – until we remember how merciful Christ is towards us. We are called to be a channel of his Godly grace and mercy. Christ wants to make us an instrument of his grace so that his mercy can flow through us.

FOOD FROM THE WORD OF GOD
Psalm 78:10-16, 32-39; Mark 6:45-7:13.

Christ's mercy reaches out even to those who do not understand nor answer his love. He waits patiently for them to acknowledge and accept him as their Saviour. This patience is not everlasting, but we find ourselves still in the time of mercy and still have the opportunity to be born again in the Lord and to become heirs of his mercy.

Merciful and forgiving God and Father, I thank you for the abundant stream of mercy which flows from your loving heart to me. Make me willing and worthy to accept it.

No athlete is permitted to take part in the race of chastity unless he has first been washed of the stains of sin and blessed with the gift of heavenly mercy. – AMBROSIUS

OBEDIENCE PROVES OUR LOVE FOR GOD

Jesus replied, "If anyone loves me, he will obey my teaching. My Father will love him, and we will come to him and make our home with him. He who does not love me will not obey my teaching" (Jn 14:23-24).

The Master has revealed himself to you and he expects your total surrender to him. Perhaps you are hesitating or even trying to avoid it. You are prepared to surrender yourself to him to a certain extent. However, total surrender without any reservations and unconditionally is asking a bit too much of you. You are scared of it. It overwhelms you and the risks seem far too great.

FOOD FROM THE WORD OF GOD
John 13:36-14:26; Deuteronomy 11:1-15, 22-23, 26-28.

Read today's scripture again, prayerfully. Christ loves you with a love much greater than that of friendship. He gives you his all and asks you for your all in return. The smallest reservation will hurt and dismay his heart. He did not hold back of himself. How can you even consider keeping any part of yourself from him?

Therefore, give yourself abundantly over to Christ. Meet his immeasurable commitment to you with your immeasurable commitment and surrender to him. Lay all that you are at his feet as a sacrifice. Give yourself unconditionally to him, so that nothing can separate you from him. The responsibilities of this love will be a sweet privilege and an overwhelming reward. It will lift you up to splendour, because the joy that results from complete obedience, will descend upon you and you will realise what Jesus meant when he said, *My food is to do the will of him who sent me and to finish his work* (Jn 4:34).

I happily and lovingly bow to your will, my Father, and it gives me great joy to be completely obedient to your will.

Obedience to God is the indisputable evidence of a perfect and sincere love for him.
NATHANAEL EMMONS

GOD'S WITNESSES ARE EMPOWERED

But after the three and a half days a breath of life from God entered them, and they stood on their feet, and terror struck those who saw them (Rev 11:11).

During the darkest periods in the history of mankind there are people who were called upon to witness against the corruption of their times, especially against corruption in the faithless church. Their opponents tried to silence their voices by casting suspicion on them, but God always justified them and gave them life through death.

FOOD FROM THE WORD OF GOD
Revelation 10:1-11:14; Exodus 7:20-21; 1 Kings 17:1; 18:1-2; Daniel 12:5-9; Zechariah 4:11-14.

Every time the enemies of the truth boasted about their victory, the witnesses of the gospel responded with a mighty revival. A few years before Martin Luther appeared on the scene, a coin was minted to commemorate the end of the so-called heresies and false doctrines.

The analogy in Zechariah underscores the fact that this power of testimony is fed from Jesus' heart. He is the beginning of the great line of martyrs whose blood was the seed of the church. His Spirit is the lifeblood of his testimony. Through all the ages, people who called themselves Christians have acted in decidedly unchristian ways. Yet, there has been an unbroken succession of believers who have stood by their Redeemer Jesus Christ to the death.

May we have the courage to stand up with them for the concerns of our Master, so that he will not be ashamed of us at his second coming. Our testimonies are the power of the Holy Spirit that brings growth to the gospel and keeps the church alive.

Mighty Saviour, with Isaiah I want to exclaim, "Here I am, Lord. Send me!" I trust you to give me, through the Holy Spirit, power to be your faithful witness.

The world is far more willing to receive the gospel than Christians are prepared to share it.
GEORGE W PETERS

March 5

THOSE WHO SIN ARE HATED

The world cannot hate you, but it hates me because I testify that what it does is evil (Jn 7:7).

A successful professional golfer was once invited to play golf with the president of America, Gerald Ford, Jack Nicklaus and Billy Graham. After the game, another professional player asked him what it was like playing with Ford and Graham. He let loose torrents of swear words, then said, "I don't need Billy Graham forcing religion down my throat on the golf course."

FOOD FROM THE WORD OF GOD
John 7:1-31; 1 Kings 22:7-8.

Astonishingly Billy Graham never once mentioned God, Jesus Christ or religion. How can we then explain this man's behaviour? It is not difficult: Graham did not need to say a single word in order to make this man feel uncomfortable. He identifies so much with religion, with divine matters that his mere presence was enough to make this wicked man flee, though no one pursued him (Prov 28:1).

Luther was quite right when he remarked, "An evil man shudders at the rustling of leaves. He can feel the breath of the dogs of heaven on his neck. He feels overawed by the holiness, even when it is revealed by an imperfect yet saved human being." Yes, holiness elicits hate. The irony is that there is no greater love than Jesus' love for us, and yet it his love that elicits the hate of people. His love is so majestic that evil people cannot tolerate it, responding with hate.

Grant me great mercy, faithful Lord, to respond to hatred and vengeance with love by always following the holy example you set.

We hate what we fear, and where there is hatred, fear lurks.
CYRIL CONOLLY

BELIEVE IN THE GOD OF MIRACLES

When they had rowed five or six kilometres, they saw Jesus approaching the boat, walking on the water; and they were terrified (Jn 6:19).

"Mom, I need new trainers!" Nicky announced after school. "The teacher told me it's dangerous to run around in the gym with your toes sticking out of the trainers." His mother looked down at his trainers. "You are right, Nicky," she said, "but you will have to wait till the end of the month."

FOOD FROM THE WORD OF GOD
John 6:16-40; 1 Chronicles 16:8-12; Psalm 66:1-7; 114:1-8.

"But, Mom," Nicky protested, "I need the trainers now!" His mom carefully explained to him how a budget works. "That's how your dad and I control our money, Nicky. Trainers are not budgeted for this month. Next month we'll include them."

"Then I'll have to pray for trainers," Nicky said firmly. "I will tell God that we need the money tomorrow." As he left for school the following morning, the trainers were still the only thing on his mind. "Can we go and buy the trainers this afternoon? You'll get the money today because I prayed for it."

"We'll see," his mother said and kissed him goodbye. There was no time to explain again. But it never was necessary to explain because Nicky soon got his answer. An outstanding payment for a story his mother had written for a magazine arrived through the post that day, with the publisher's apologies. The money more than covered Nicky's trainers – an example of a child's trust. Nicky's eyes sparkled, "See Mom, I told you the money would come!"

What a testimony of the essence of faith!

Wondrous Father, your miracles – also in my own life – fill me with humility and astonishment.

Were it not for miracles, I would not be a Christian.
St AUGUSTINE

March 7

CHRIST'S RELATIONSHIP WITH HIS FATHER

"You do not know me or my Father," Jesus replied. "If you knew me, you would know my Father also" (Jn 8:19).

We must think seriously about the life of Christ in the Father. They are ONE: ONE in life and ONE in love. Despite the fact that he lived here on earth, Jesus knew that he was ONE with the Father, that the Father's life was in him and that they were ONE in their love.

The Son is not afraid to hand everything over to his Father. He knows that the Father loves him, that he has no interests besides his beloved Son. He knows that the dependence of his heart is just as perfect as the communication from his Father's side. This is why Jesus said, *I tell you the truth, the Son can do nothing by himself; he can do only what he sees his Father doing, because whatever the Father does the Son also does* (Jn 5:19).

FOOD FROM THE WORD OF GOD
John 8:12-41; Psalm 2:2-12; 110:1-3

Think for a moment about the majesty of this life of Christ in the Father's love. Because he surrendered himself completely to his Father's will, his Father crowned him with honour and splendour. God acknowledges him as his sole representative, makes him a partner in his power and authority, and lifts him up to share in the throne of God.

Christ is the revelation of God. He could never have been this, had there not been perfect unity and perfect communication between him and his Father. He could do it because his Father loves him, and because he dwells in this love.

Holy Spirit of God, thank you for convincing me that Jesus Christ is the Son of God. I dedicate myself anew to you, Father, Son and Holy Spirit.

If Jesus Christ is not truly God, then how CAN he help us? If he were not truly human, how can he help US? – DIETRICH BONHOEFFER

GOD REWARDS OUR FAITH

Then Jesus said, "Did I not tell you that if you believed, you would see the glory of God?" (Jn 11:40).

Faith is the human reaction to God's love and mercy. When you realise that faith is your response to what God says or does, the pressure will be off your shoulders. Maybe you ask, "How much faith do I have?" Look up to God and ask, "What does my Father tell me? What does he want me to do?" When Jesus noticed the faith of various people, he usually spoke of tangible deeds through which someone responded to him.

FOOD FROM THE WORD OF GOD
John 11:28-51; 1 Kings 17:12-24.

If you understand that, you will also discover the measure of your faith. Then Jesus' parable of the mustard seed starts to make sense to you. How much faith did Martha need to bring Lazarus back from the dead? Very little, according to John 11:38-40. If we must measure our faith according to an emotional state, it would appear that Martha had no faith at all. No, what she needed – and precisely what she had – was just enough faith to give the command for the stone to be rolled away from the entrance to the cave, despite the doubts in her heart. And Lazarus was raised from the dead!

Faith is a personal decision of yours to respond to God's words. This decision may be revealed by an external or an internal action, such as entrusting your eternal salvation to Jesus. Gradually this decision develops into an attitude, the attitude of always reacting positively to the Word of God.

Jesus, my Saviour, may my faith be revealed through obedience to your Word, at all times and in all circumstances.

Faith is not necessarily synonymous with piety.
KARL BARTH

LIVE TO PLEASE GOD

(May the God of peace) equip you with everything good for doing his will, and may he work in us what is pleasing to him, through Jesus Christ, to whom be glory for ever and ever (Heb 13:21).

The phrase "cheap mercy" often pops up these days. Unfortunately, it describes the thoughts of many Christians. They have accepted Jesus Christ as their Saviour, but do not practically live out their faith in him. It seems if they only accepted him as a way of getting to heaven one day, or of receiving his help with their problems. They do not commit themselves to him completely. They do not trust him with their lives and they do not obey and glorify him in everything that they do. Their faith has not yet become a way of life for them.

FOOD FROM THE WORD OF GOD
Hebrews 13:1-25; Deuteronomy 10:12-21; Job 31:5-6, 9-11, 16, 16-19, 24, 32.

Our Lord and Master does not want us only to be his casual acquaintances. He asks us to be his disciples, fully committed to following him and glorifying his Name in the world. When we accept Jesus as our Lord, we confirm that he will be our life-long Master and that we will honour and glorify him. Our innermost desire must be to do what he wants us to do. We do not seek his guidance for our own benefit, but only to glorify him. We discipline ourselves by studying and obeying his Word. We proclaim his love to the world around us. We try to think, speak, and act in ways that will draw other people to him.

Indeed, a Christian's life is much more than just an escape from the dangers of destruction. It is a life of surrender, dedication and obedience, that leads to joy and triumph.

I want to dedicate myself to you anew, Lord Jesus, to a life of surrender, commitment, and obedience so that I may taste the fruits of a life that is triumphant and filled with joy.

Mercy is God himself, his loving energy working within the church and in our hearts.
EVELYN UNDERHILL

March 10

GOD ANSWERS OUR PRAYERS

The prayer of a righteous man is powerful and effective (Jas 5:16b).

God hears our prayers. He longs to demonstrate his omnipotence when the skies above us are dark with menacing storm clouds, but also in the pinpricks of our little everyday problems. Huge problems are never too big for his almighty power, and miniature problems are never too insignificant for his love.

God is capable of answering our prayers because he is all-powerful. He controls global events as well as our personal lives. He is willing and able to act on our request and to intervene to our benefit – for his honour and the expansion of his kingdom.

FOOD FROM THE WORD OF GOD
James 4:11-5:20; 2 Kings 20:1-6; Esther 8:8-16.

God determined that prayer is the channel through which we will obtain his help and set his almighty hand in motion. Therefore, even in sickness, failure, rejection and financial distress, we can pray and experience his peace that passes all understanding. Through prayer, we open a window through which God's love and omnipotence can shine in our lives. We can open our hands and receive his wealth. We can open our hearts and his presence will fill and empower us. Through prayer, God provides for our needs. He shows that prayer is very important to him and us alike.

God's answers are not always in agreement with our desires, but are always to our benefit and spiritual salvation. Is your belief in the miraculous power of prayer so strong that you would, like Esther, stake your life on it?

I honour and thank you as the Hearer of and Responder to prayer, heavenly Father. Teach me through your Holy Spirit to pray in truth so that you may perform wonders through me.

Prayer is the breath of the reborn soul, and there can be no Christian life without it.
ROWLAND HILL

GOD'S WRATH WILL FLARE UP

The angel swung his sickle on the earth, gathered its grapes and threw them into the great wine press of God's wrath (Rev 14:19).

The "peace" of the wicked is like the frightening silence in the Alps just before an avalanche. There is absolute quiet. The birds stop singing. They fly low, shrinking with fear when they land. The bees amongst the flowers become silent. A terrifying silence reigns over nature as if death itself has silenced all life with the sceptre which he wields over all that lives.

The storm gathers momentum. Soon lightning will glare across the heavens and shoot out flames of fire. The earth will be shaken by thunderbolts, and granite mountaintops will crumble. All of nature will tremble under the violence and anger of the storm. This is the peace that the wicked experience. They should not rejoice in it, because the storm of God's judgement is approaching. The hurricanes of disaster, which will sweep them from the earth and destroy them, are on the way.

FOOD FROM THE WORD OF GOD
Revelation 14:1-20; Psalm 75:7-8; Isaiah 63:2-3, 6; Jeremiah 25:15-17; Joel 3:12-13.

Saved people, however, find true peace and rest in the mercy of God. He will protect his children during the storm. Yes, awaiting his faithful children is a new life on a new earth, where they shall be with God for eternity. This is how perfect God's love is for sinful people. What will your choice be today: "the peace" of the wicked, or the peace of God that passes all understanding?

I chose you as my Father, O God, through Jesus Christ, my Saviour who will give me true peace and rest. I praise and thank you for it.

The judgement of God occurs wherever the Word of God is preached: people judge themselves by their acceptance or rejection of the gospel. – ALAN RICHARDSON

THE TESTIMONY OF A PURE LIFE

The Lord has dealt with me according to my righteousness; according to the cleanness of my hands he has rewarded me. For I have kept the ways of the Lord; I have not done evil by turning from my God (2 Sam 22:21-22).

As Christians, we must show this gentile world what it means to live in peace with yourself, and to truly love other people. The surest way of drawing them nearer to Christ and to the Christian way of life is to live a guilt-free and abundant life, and to enjoy it so much that others will want to live in the same way. We must be credible examples of true Christianity.

FOOD FROM THE WORD OF GOD
2 Samuel 22:21-25; Job 1:1; 2:3; Psalm 37:17-19, 30-33, 39-40; Acts 25:13-26:8.

Most people argue that it is very difficult nowadays to distinguish true Christians from unbelievers, because there is no difference in the way in which they live. They say that the only difference is that Christians are more religious. They are unable to see that religion alters the essence of Christians' thoughts and life-styles. All that the world sees is that Christians go to church and participate in church activities.

In order to convince a hardened, blunted, cynical world that we are not only different, but also that we are happy as a result of our difference, we must allow them to see how we keep on getting better at the struggle of life because of our relationship with Jesus Christ. Paul's testimony before Agrippa would have fundamentally differed had his way of life not been to the glory of God. Is it of the utmost importance to you to live the way God expects of you, and in a way that pleases him? Then you will be a powerful witness for him in a degenerate world.

Help me, Lord, to make a fundamental difference in the world in which I live, precisely because I belong to you.

If our lives were radiant, it would scarcely be necessary to preach dogma. If we behaved as true Christians, there would be no heathens. – POPE JOHN XXIII

EVIL EMANATES FROM WITHIN US

Nothing outside a man can make him "unclean" by going into him. Rather, it is what comes out of a man that makes him "unclean" (Mk 7:15).

A friend of mine received a coveted award. I cannot recall ever in my life having struggled with jealousy, but on that day, I was dragged along by a torrent of jealousy. I drove home in a state of absolute shock and shame. Where did this attitude come from all of a sudden? There must be a leakage somewhere in my Christian character, for it must have emanated from my heart.

The Holy Spirit instils the example and power of Jesus into every Christian. The minute we resist the Holy Spirit, our sinful nature will come to the fore. Our inclination to sin fills our character with sieve holes, and thus it is important to live a triumphant life in Christ. He promised to enable us to do this through his Spirit.

FOOD FROM THE WORD OF GOD
Mark 7:14-37; Psalm 36:1-4; Proverbs 4:14-17; 6:12-19; Isaiah 59:2-3; Jeremiah 4:14; 17:9.

When we assume that we are good and without the inclination to sin because we are Christians, we fail to notice a vital point. Jesus Christ shed his blood for the forgiveness of our sins, but he did not take away our inclination to commit sin. We still have a sinful nature that requires of us always to be alert in our thoughts and deeds. We must station a guard at the door to our hearts. When I knelt down, confessed my sins before God, and begged forgiveness, I was able to be truly glad about the award my friend had won.

Restore to me the joy of your salvation and grant me a willing spirit, to sustain me (Ps 51:12).

Recklessness towards evil is more treacherous than evil itself: it is more universal, more contagious, and more dangerous. – ABRAHAM JESCHEL

March 14

GOD WANTS TO TEACH US TO WALK ON HIS PATH

I will instruct you and teach you in the way you should go; I will counsel you and watch over you (Ps 32:8).

Our heavenly Father is so interested in his children on earth and so wants our lives to be in accordance with his will and love, that he is prepared to guide, without fail, our lives on earth. He well knows that we are by nature prone to evil, and can only do what is holy when he enables us to do it. Consequently, even his instructions become promises of what he will do for us, his children. He guards over us and guides us every hour of every day.

FOOD FROM THE WORD OF GOD
Psalm 32:8; Exodus 33:7-11; Job 33:31-33; Micah 4:1-2; Mark 9:14-37.

We can depend on him to teach us his ways and to give us direction. Not only in times of trials or difficulties, but also in our everyday lives. For those who patiently await him, it becomes delightful to walk day by day in the joy of the guiding light of God.

There is, however, one thing we need to help us find such a life: true knowledge of God and faith in him as the only Source of wisdom and goodness, always ready to be everything to us and to provide what we need. When we have this knowledge and faith, God will teach us his way, and we will be able to walk it. God so much wants to instruct us through his Word and lead us in the right way. Follow him and experience what it means to live a happy life.

Heavenly Father, I praise your Name because you have poured your immeasurable love over me as well.
May I, with the help of the Holy Spirit, always be sensitive to your voice of wisdom, and so always keep on the right path.

Two kinds of people give God great joy: those who serve him with all their heart because they know him, and those who seek him with all their heart because they do not know him. – PANIN

March 15

WATCH OUT FOR FALSE PROPHETS

I urge you, brothers, to watch out for those who cause divisions and put obstacles in your way that are contrary to the teaching you have learned. Keep away from them (Rom 16:17).

Our Bible reading for today adds: *For such people are not serving our Lord Christ, but their own appetites. By smooth talk and flattery they deceive the minds of naïve people* (Rom 16:18).

In the past decades there have been teachers of theology on whom Satan has focused his attention. We thank God for theologians and ministers who guide our youth on the right path.

FOOD FROM THE WORD OF GOD
Romans 15:30-16:27; Deuteronomy 13:1-10; Ezekiel 13:3, 7-8.

Satan also has his ministers, and there are many of them who present themselves as teachers of truth and righteousness. But this is not who they really are: they have never had a Godly calling. Modern-day heresy is directed towards the infallible Word of God and the infallible Christ. The reality of man's sins, the word of the cross and the Holy Spirit are not appreciated. All aspects of Chirstian faith are questioned.

Fully aware that he is defeated by the living Christ's death and resurrection, Satan provokes religious teachers to question the virgin birth, the fact that Christ was without sin, his reconciliatory death, and his resurrection and ascension to heaven. Postmodernism enables Satan to rob the church of her power.

We pray for spiritual perceptiveness so that we can recognise this questioning in the preaching from our pulpits and in the lecture rooms of our theological schools.

Holy God, teach me to guard against the deception of false prophets. Send to us men and women who have truly been touched by the Holy Spirit, true to the gospel because of their calling.

Conviction is the eye of the fountain of action, the driving force of life. What someone practises, are his or her convictions. – FRANCIS C KELLY

March 16

GOD WILL JUDGE OUR ACTIONS

So then, each of us will give an account of himself to God (Rom 14:12).

When we live in a way that pleases God, we experience peace. We do not try to do dozens of things to please everybody around us. No, we have only one purpose: to please God by doing his holy will.

When we try to please others and ourselves, matters easily get out of hand and we loose the essential balance of the Christian life. Too many people get too involved in various matters that are dear to them and subsequently loose perspective. When this happens, our priorities are no longer determined by God, but by all the voices we hear around us. Many of the things we do are good, but we forget that our main purpose is to please God. Therefore, the Holy Spirit must teach us all over again to focus firstly on God.

FOOD FROM THE WORD OF GOD
Romans 14:1-15:3; Ecclesiastes 12:13-14; Isaiah 43:17; Ezekiel 36:17-23.

As believers whose main aim is to satisfy God, we can live and work with certainty and conviction. We no longer look at life and all its problems through a human perspective. We live our lives with the long-term assurance that stems only from God's eternal perspective.

For whom do you live and die? How does this influence your life-style? What do you use as a guideline so that your life pleases God? Is Jesus Christ your role model for this life-style? Your answers to these questions will determine how God will judge your life.

Faithful Leader and Master, thank you for setting me the example of how to live a life that pleases God. Help me, through your Holy Spirit, to follow your example.

It may be that the day of reckoning comes tomorrow; at that moment we will joyfully stop working towards a better future. But not before that happens! – DIETRICH BONHOEFFER

March 17

HONOUR GOD IN YOUR BODY

Do you not know that your body is a temple of the Holy Spirit, who is in you, who you have received from God? You are not your own; you were bought at a price. Therefore, honour God with your body (1 Cor 6:19-20).

It is often alleged that people "fall" into immorality. This statement is revealing as well as flawed and dangerous. The word "fall" indicates the mentality of a victim. It sounds as if we were walking down the street when someone tripped us or kicked our feet from under us. It implies that moral decay appears out of the blue and that there is very little or nothing that we can do to prevent it.

FOOD FROM THE WORD OF GOD
1 Corinthians 5:9-6:20; Numbers 25:1-3, 6-13; Job 31:9-12; Proverbs 6:26-29.

We do not "fall" into immorality. We walk consciously and with open eyes into it. Indeed, sometimes we run into it, head over heels. Immorality is a choice that we make. It is not something that just happens to us. Sexual sins do not come to us out of the blue. It is often the culmination of a long process in which lustful thoughts are turned into action in an unguarded moment.

Sow a thought and you reap a deed; sow a deed and you reap a habit; sow a habit and you reap a character; sow a character and you reap your eternal destiny. Our thoughts are the fabric with which our characters and our eternal destinies are woven. Therefore, actively fight against impure thoughts.

How do I do this, you may ask. It is not as simple as saying, "I will not covet, I will not covet." No, in your mind and in your heart you must cultivate thoughts that are pure and pleasing to God. These pure and noble thoughts will replace those that are impure (Phil 4:8).

Keep guard over my thoughts, Lord, and help me to cherish positive and pure thoughts. Grant me in this the indispensable help of the Holy Spirit.

If you want others to respect you, your most important duty is to respect yourself.
FEODOR DOSTOYEVSKY

GLORIFY GOD IN EVERYTHING YOU DO

So whether you eat or drink or whatever you do, do it all for the glory of God (1 Cor 10:31).

All creation came about through the omnipotence of God and to his glory and honour. This also includes everyday things. Do you have a good job? Do it and enjoy it for God. Are you well paid? Appreciate it and invest it for him. Do you enjoy good health? Use it to his honour. Are you a member of a happy family? Your family members are there to his honour. Are you planning a change? Let it be to God's glory and in accordance with his will.

FOOD FROM THE WORD OF GOD
1 Corinthians 10:23-11:22;
1 Samuel 2:12, 17, 22-25, 27-33.

God is the Ruler of his universe. He is Lord. That is our confession of faith. He has the right to determine our decisions, so that they will honour him. If God enjoys top priority in your life, you will make decisions in accordance with his standards and demands. There will be reliability in all that you do. You will stay away from all that does not fall within your search for his kingdom and righteousness. Christ will hold the number one position in everything that affects your life and existence. If you are serious about your spiritual life, you will give Christ top priority in your life.

Christ commands us to love God and our neighbour as ourselves. By doing so, we honour God in a special way with our whole lives: not only within the safe confines of the church, but also in the course of our everyday lives.

Almighty Father, I want to honour you first in everything I do. Enable me, through your Holy Spirit, to have the right perspective on life.

The highest and very best achievement in this life is to be quiet before God and to glorify him in your life.
MASTER ECKHARDT

March 19

THE RIGHTEOUS ARE REWARDED

I tell you, on that night two people will be in one bed; one will be taken and the other left (Lk 17:34).

John's vision gives one an inkling of the horror of the last judgement of those who do not believe in God. Imagine it for a moment. The Lamb carefully opens the sixth seal (Rev 6:12-17). Suddenly great chaos grips the universe. John says: *There was a great earthquake. The sun turned black like sackcloth made of goat hair, the whole moon turned blood red, and the stars in the sky fell to earth, as late figs drop from a fig tree when shaken by a strong wind* (Rev 6:12-14).

FOOD FROM THE WORD OF GOD
Luke 17:5-38; Genesis 18:20-21; 19:1-3, 12-17, 24-25.

The earth trembles with fear. The great cities are reduced to rubble. John sees kings, princes, generals, the rich and mighty, slaves and free men running to escape the terror of God's final judgement. They flee to the mountains, hiding in caves, among the rocks and in crevices. However, there is no escape. In desperation they call out: *Fall on us and hide us from the face of him who sits on the throne and from the wrath of the Lamb! For the great day of their wrath has come, and who can stand?* (Rev 6:16-17).

There will come a day of reckoning when God will close his books, and the time will come when all men will be judged: those who are still alive as well as the dead. The righteous will enter into the splendour of the Lord. The wicked shall be cast out into outer darkness.

Lord, all-knowing God, may I never forget that you, who know all about me, will one day pass judgement over my life.
May I live in such a way that I need not fear that day.

When God's judgement is over, the earth will cease to exist and there will be a new heaven and a new earth.
St AUGUSTINE

March 20

LABOUR ENNOBLES

If a man will not work, he shall not eat (2 Thess 3:10).

We often talk of people who were "called to the ministry". But we can also talk of carpenters, architects, lawyers, teachers and cleaners who were "called" to their tasks. No matter what our career, we must glorify God through it and do our job for him, as if he has called us to it.

We must always remember that God mapped out our path of life in his all-knowing discretion. Nothing happens to us that is not God's will. The incidents that tire us and are seemingly unnecessary are meant to give us the opportunity to develop stronger characters. We are called upon to be faithful in the task with which we have been entrusted. For being faithful in the smallest task is, in the eyes of God, just as much of an achievement as being faithful in the biggest task.

FOOD FROM THE WORD OF GOD
2 Thessalonians 2:13-3:18; Proverbs 31:10-31; Ecclesiastes 2:26.

Let us take our tasks in life seriously, we who from day to day do our jobs, whatever they may be. Let us do them with brave hearts, while looking up to him who performed his daily task in the carpenter shop. Never loose sight of Jesus. He first worked in the humble carpenter shop before he started preaching. Do everything to make him smile with approval. Look for opportunities to cheer up your colleagues. Let your heart rise up from your task to God, your Creator, your Savior and Friend. Thus, the humblest of tasks will turn into a holy calling that will ennoble your character.

Holy Father, make me hardworking and true in my daily task so that through it, I might honour you.

Work is love made visible.
KAHLIL GIBRAN

March 21

EVEN THOUGH PEOPLE SEE GOD'S MIRACLES ...

Even after Jesus had done all these miraculous signs in their presence, they still would not believe in him (Jn 12:37).

At times we find it difficult to trust in Jesus and to believe in him unconditionally. Even Moses experienced this. Everyday we see his miraculous deeds which should help us to believe in him, as a well known Afrikaans hymn (freely translated) states so clearly:

If I, O heavenly Father, could rejoice in your glory with thousands of tongues – how I would bring my song of praise to you, O Lord!

I would exalt your honour and glory, your countless deeds of wonder!

If only I could sing your praises to where the sun describes its course, and the stars, high above, silently point out your splendour!

May everything on this earth: mountains, forests, sea and more, exalt my inadequate praises to your glory!

We will all rejoice in your goodness; show our gratefulness to you!
Accept, O Lord, my humble thanks, and hear my prayers.
One day I, a wanderer, will take my place among the heavenly hosts.
Then will I rejoice, O Lord, with songs of praise!

FOOD FROM THE WORD OF GOD
John 12:37-50; Exodus 3:1-6; 10:21-23; Numbers 11:10-16, 18, 21-23.

And Dr Heugh of Glascow once said, "I find nothing worse than the criminality of unbelief that does not want to trust Jesus.

Thank you, Lord, for your miracles around me, in me, and for me. I can only mutter in amazement: How great thou art!

Knowledge is truth preserved in the mind; faith is a fire in the heart.
JOSEPH NEWTON

March 22

GOD TAKES CARE OF THOSE WHO SERVE HIM

Delight yourself in the Lord and do good; dwell in the land and enjoy safe pasture. Delight yourself in the Lord and he will give you the desires of your heart (Ps 37:3-4).

You wake up in the intensive care unit to a machine bleeping in your ear. Reality breaks through and shouts at you, "You're scared of growing old; you're going to die. You are absolutely powerless to do anything about your situation."

It is in times like these that Jesus is closest to us. The moment the realities of life sink in, Truth comes to the fore. He takes us by the hand and challenges us not to sweep the facts under the carpet, but to confront them with him by our side. There is no problem that we cannot solve with the help of Jesus.

FOOD FROM THE WORD OF GOD
Psalm 37:3-6; 27:11-14; Proverbs 15:29; Isaiah 40:27-31; John 16:1-28.

Growing older? It is merely a process that serves as our thoroughfare to a better life. Death? It is merely the entrance hall through which we walk to the brightly lit splendour we call heaven. Funerals, divorces, illness, and hospitalisation: during these times, we cannot deny the truth of life. Maybe this is the very reason why Jesus is with us in these times.

The next time you find yourself alone in a dark alleyway and you are confronted by all the awful realities of life, do not deny or ignore them; do not turn up the volume on the television and try to convince yourself that these truths do not exist. Rather come to a stop, whisper Jesus' Name in amazement and honour and listen carefully; he is nearer to you than you could ever imagine!

Loving Master, you care for me and comfort me every day because you love me. That fills my heart with thankfulness and joy.

The kingdom of God is a kingdom of love, and love is never a stagnant pool in which nothing happens.
HENRY W DU BOSE

GOD EXPECTS OBEDIENCE

Consider therefore the kindness and sternness of God: sternness to those who fell, but kindness to you, provided that you continue in his kindness. Otherwise, you also will be cut off (Rom 11:22).

Man wants to understand, not just blindly obey. We try to understand what is impossible to understand instead of simply obeying. We try to understand God's works instead of obeying him. Do we want to understand God, or do we want to trust and obey him? If we were to understand God, he would no longer be God. It is only when we obey him that we will understand who he is and what he does.

FOOD FROM THE WORD OF GOD
Romans 11:22-12:8; 1 Samuel 15:13-23; Psalm 4:3-5.

Instead of obeying the Lord of life immediately, we try to plan our own redemption with our inadequate mental powers. Instead of doing the will of God every day in a simple and childlike way, we postpone placing our feet on the only step that can lead us to wisdom: obedience.

For the sake of our longing to know and understand, we postpone the only thing that can help us to know and understand – obedience – and create for ourselves substitutes that convince us that it is possible to understand without being obedient. We do not want to accept that unconditionally obeying God and Jesus Christ is one of the greatest privileges of mankind.

However, daybreak smiles over those who do his will. The Morning Star shines in their lives and hearts. Obedience is, after all, the very essence of knowledge.

Your will be done, Lord.
Make me obedient so that I may understand.

We must obey. There is guidance for each of us, and by listening humbly, we will hear the right word.
RALPH WALDO EMERSON

GOD SPEAKS TO US IN DREAMS

While Pilate was sitting on the judge's seat, his wife sent him this message: "Don't have anything to do with that innocent man, for I have suffered a great deal today in a dream because of him" (Mt 27:19).

St Theresa of Avila tells of an amazing experience: "I was praying when I had a vision in which I saw how all things exist in God. I cannot explain precisely what I saw, but what I did see, remains with me vividly to this day. It is engraved deeply in my soul. It was a great act of God's mercy to give me that vision. It shames me indescribably when I recall this magnificent visage, for then I involuntarily think of my sins. I firmly believe that, had the Lord sent that vision earlier in my life, it would have kept me from committing many sins.

FOOD FROM THE WORD OF GOD
Matthew 26:29-27:20; Genesis 20:3-11, 14-15; Daniel 4:18-27.

"In order to explain the vision, I shall use the following illustration: Imagine God as an enormous lamp, larger than the world, and that all our actions and deeds are seen in that light. I saw all my most dreadful deeds reflected back to me from the world of God's light. It was the saddest and most pitiful scene to behold. I knew not where to hide, for that shining light in which there was no darkness whatsoever, kept within it all of the world and the universe.

"O, if only all people could see this vision. It is dreadful committing sin in the presence of such awe-inspiring Majesty!"

God is indeed capable of using all dreams and visions to his honour and the glorification of his name.

Holy God of majesty and authority, you are constantly sending visions to your children in many ways. Keep me from ignoring you.

We have the capacity for virtuousness, but at the same time the capacity for immorality that can make your blood run cold. – RALPH WALDO EMERSON

GOD'S WORD BRINGS JOY

Then Philip began with that very passage of Scripture and told him the good news about Jesus ... When they came up out of the water, the Spirit of the Lord suddenly took Philip away, and the eunuch did not see him again, but went on his way with rejoicing (Acts 8:35, 39).

God ordered Philip to go to a quiet road, which led from Jerusalem to Gaza, so that he could explain the Word of God to an Ethiopian. Philip immediately obeyed and ran to the chariot on which the important official in the service of the Ethiopian queen travelled, on his way back home in a heathen land. After Philip had told him the good news of Jesus Christ, he baptised the Ethiopian as a born-again child of God. Philip's task had been completed, and the Ethiopian journeyed on with the Scripture in his hand and great joy in his heart because he had met his Saviour, Jesus Christ.

FOOD FROM THE WORD OF GOD
Acts 8:26-9:9; Nehemiah 8:1-13; Psalm 119:33-35, 162-168.

The Word of God is indeed a source of great joy for Christians. It is hard to find a genuine Christian who continually studies the Word of God and is not joyful. The purpose of Bible study is to look past the words to the One who inspired them. Of all the good habits that Christians can cultivate, this is one of the most blessed and beneficial.

The Bible is the only book that rewards those who read it with increasing insight as they allow the Word to flow through them and purify them; that can purify the lives of those who read it and allow them to grow spiritually. Other books might impart knowledge, but only the Word of God can reform and inspire in a way that brings nothing but pure joy.

Happy tiding, source of inner gladness – Word of the gospel! Word of light and life, direct our aim as Word of deliverance.

If you study the Word of God in earnest, you will know that it is the Word of God, because you will find in it the key to your own heart, your own joy, and your own duty. – WOODROW WILSON

GOD DEMANDS UNWAVERING LOYALTY

Then Paul answered, "Why are you weeping and breaking my heart? I am ready not only to be bound, but also to die in Jerusalem for the name of the Lord Jesus" (Acts 21:13).

Sometimes King Saul was with the prophets, and then we suddenly find him once again with the witches. Sometimes he was here, then again there, but never pure in what he did. Unfortunately, there are also such people in every Christian congregation, people who easily make compromises. They have loving personalities and probably sensitive consciences. However, their consciences are so sensitive that they easily give in to the opinions of others and never take their own stand on a matter. You can influence these people any which way you like. They are so pliable that you can achieve any purpose with them, because they are not firm and steadfast of character.

FOOD FROM THE WORD OF GOD
Acts 21:1-25; Exodus 32:1-4, 7-8, 26-35.

We must pray seriously to God that in these times he will send to our world people with pluck. People who, when they know that something is right, will not turn away from it or try to avoid it; people who will increasingly persevere precisely because there are problems that must be dealt with and enemies who must be defeated; people who are unshakeably true to their Lord in spite of opposition; people who grow more passionate about their cause the more they are thrown into the fire of affliction. These are people who are like a bow: the further the string is pulled back, the stronger the arrows are that shoot forward; the more they are trampled on, the stronger they become in their struggle for truth against lies.

Holy God, you are my heavenly Father through Jesus Christ. Make me so sure of my faithful trust in you, that I will risk my life for it.

I do not simply want to possess faith; I want faith to possess me.
CHARLES KINGSLEY

March 27

OUR REDEMPTION IS ROOTED IN FAITH IN GOD

For we maintain that a man is justified by faith apart from observing the law (Rom 3:28).

Faith is believing that Jesus Christ is who he says he is and that he will do everything he has promised to do. The Scriptures refer to Jesus the man as perfect in character, as a sacrifice for our sins, as someone who carried our sins in his body to the cross. The Bible also tells us: *That he (Christ) was buried, that he was raised on the third day according to the Scriptures* (1 Cor 15:4). The author of Hebrews wrote: *But because Jesus lives for ever, he has a permanent priesthood. Therefore he is able to save completely those who come to God through him, because he always lives to intercede for them* (Heb 7:24-25). And Psalm 98:9 tells us that he will come again: *For he comes to judge the earth. He will judge the world in righteousness and the people with equity.*

FOOD FROM THE WORD OF GOD
Romans 3:19-4:12; Genesis 15:1-6; Psalm 20:6-8; 32:10-11; 147:7-11.

Jesus is what the Scriptures say he is; he will do what he said he would do. Therefore, we can trust in him, and say, "To me he will be what he said he would be, and he will do for me what he promised to do. I give myself into his hands, for he has saved me. I rest in his promises." This is redeeming faith and those who have this faith have eternal life. No matter what the dangers or problems, and whatever our weaknesses and sins, we who believe in Jesus Christ will never perish.

I praise your holy name, Lord Jesus, for your love has found me and saved me.

Nobody is saved except by undeserved grace, and nobody is judged except by deserved judgement.
St AUGUSTINE

March 28

SERVING GOD IS A MATTER OF CHOICE

So I find this law at work: When I want to do good, evil is right there with me (Rom 7:21).

The Bible talks to us about what is right and what is wrong. What is written in the Bible is therefore the basis for the choices we make. And the Bible talks so clearly about right and wrong, we need not fear that we will make the wrong choices.

Through Joshua, God challenged the Israelites to choose: either the gods of the Amorites, or the true God, Yahweh. Elijah, too, on Mount Carmel put a choice before the people: *If the Lord is God, follow him; but if Baal is God, follow him* (1 Kgs 18:21). Moreover, he made the difference between them very clear.

FOOD FROM THE WORD OF GOD
Romans 7:14-8:17; Joshua 24:1, 14-27.

Choices are very important to each of us. Deuteronomy 30:19b declares: *Now choose life, so that you and your children may live.* There are, however, moments of crisis in our lives when we are tempted to make wrong choices. So, hold on tightly to what the Word of God tells you.

Whom do you irrevocably choose today as the King of your heart? Remember that you are not choosing for yourself alone. Choose today who you want to serve and your choice will influence the next generation, and the next. Choices never affect only one person. The results will touch other people's lives because you are a part of history, and your choices become part of history. Therefore, it is very important to choose irrevocably and finally between God and sin. A great deal depends on your choice.

Lord Jesus, my heart chooses you for ever as its King.

In darkness, there is no choice. The light enables us to see the difference between things. And it is Christ who is our light. – AUGUSTUS W HARE

FOCUS ON MATTERS OF GOD

He who is not with me is against me, and he who does not gather with me, scatters (Lk 11:23).

The perfect example for the life of a Christian is Christ's life on earth. However, we cannot simply imitate him. We cannot merely have an intellectual opinion of Christ. Our Christianity cannot only be a cult or a system of thoughts. We might try for years and years to imitate Christ, our opinions of him might be theologically correct, we might acknowledge his omnipotence, and yet not be Christians.

Yes, it is possible to admire Christ and to try to follow him, without really knowing him ever. It is possible to believe in his divinity, in his redeeming work, and, more importantly, in the need for redemption, without ever submitting to his authority, without ever personally sharing in his work of reconciliation, or ever experiencing rebirth.

FOOD FROM THE WORD OF GOD
Luke 11:14-36; Numbers 15:37-41; Psalm 18:26-30; 119:17-19; Proverbs 4:18:27.

It is only when Christ enters your life that he makes you a Christian. As long as Jesus remains an external force in your life, there will be many times when the world will not be able to see or hear him in your life and so know that you belong to him. However, when Christ is in your life, when he reigns over your life, and you obey him, there will never be a moment when the truth of your Christianity will not be visible. When Christ is in you, you cannot hide him. When the light is within you, it will simply shine.

O Holy Spirit, fill me with the light of Jesus, and keep my eyes focused on him as the Leader and Finisher of my faith.

Faith reveals itself in the total personality.
MARTYN LLOYD-JONES

March 30

CARRY GOD'S LIGHT INTO THE WORLD

You are the light of the world.
A city on a hill cannot be hidden (Mt 5:14).

What does it mean to be the light of the world and the salt of the earth? What should your life-style be in order to shine like a light and to show the people of this world the road that leads to salvation? Is it perhaps necessary for you and me to radically alter our lives in order to be the light of the world and the salt of the earth? To be what God intended us to be?

FOOD FROM THE WORD OF GOD
Matthew 5:13-37; Psalm 18:29; 49:11-15; 97:10-11; Isaiah 49:1-3, 6.

Nowhere in the Scriptures are we commanded to bring unbelievers into the church so that they might be saved. There is not one instance in the Bible where someone was converted in a church or synagogue. In Luke 19, we do not read that Jesus asked Zacchaeus to meet him on the Sabbath in the synagogue. No, he went to Zacchaeus's house. The misconception of our time is that heathens must come and listen, whereas the Bible says we must go out and tell (Mt 28:19).

If we want to be the salt of the earth and the light of the world, we must go to where the lost ones are. It might mean inviting them into your house for dinner, or going to their houses to visit them, meeting them on the golf course, or at a ladies' tea. When they see Christ in our lives, the Holy Spirit will start working in them, and they will wonder why we are so "different". Only then will the salt and the light start working wonders.

Holy Spirit of God, help me to accept the responsibility of reflecting Jesus' light in this world.

The Spirit of Christ is the missionary Spirit, and the more we read about him, the more missionary conscious we will become. – HENRY MATIJA

March 31

ENTRUST YOUR NEEDS TO GOD

And he directed the people to sit down on the grass. Taking the five loaves and the two fish and looking up to heaven, he gave thanks and broke the loaves (Mt 14:19).

We live in a time when many fears are touching our lives. We fear poverty, illness, loneliness and death. We fear the dangers of the night and the stresses of every day. We fear for our children, our finances, our age, and our marriage …

David teaches us that the only way to rid ourselves of fear is to trust God, and to focus on him: *Then my enemies will turn back when I call for help. By this I will know that God is for me. In God, whose word I praise, in the Lord, whose word I praise – in God I trust; I will not be afraid. What can man do to me?* (Ps 56:9-11).

FOOD FROM THE WORD OF GOD
Matthew 14:13-36; Psalm 11:1-5; 116:1-9; Isaiah 26:3-4; 41:8-10; Haggai 2:4-5.

Indeed, trust and faith in God drive away fear. We might be helpless against fear, but God is not. When we trust in him, there is nothing to fear. Faith is much more than believing in what God can do. It is trust in the Person of God himself.

A father once came across his son who had climbed up a rotten tree and the branches started breaking under the boy's weight. He stretched out his arms and called to the boy, "Jump! I'll catch you!" The boy thought about the offer for a moment, and then heard more branches snapping under him. He asked, "Should I let go of everything, Dad, and trust you?" Yes! Our heavenly Father wants us to let go of everything and trust in him.

I praise and thank you, Lord my God, for your faithfulness, which protects me. Grant that I might everywhere and always trust in you with a calm mind.

He who trusts in himself, is lost. For him who trusts in God, all things are possible.
ALPHONSUS LIQUORI

April

Prayer for April

1. Everyone has sinned against God
2. Jesus is our good shepherd
3. The lives of believers glorify God
4. Fight Satan with endurance and faith
5. God affirms his holiness
6. God calls us to walk in his light
7. Those who believe are joyful
8. Remain steadfast in temptation
9. God rewards the righteous
10. The wicked versus the righteous
11. All power is given by God
12. The pain of friends' betrayal
13. Do not be afraid
14. Service to God is important
15. God holds you responsible
16. Is God unjust?
17. God puts words into our mouths
18. Deception causes great sorrow
19. God guides and protects us
20. The wonder of God's forgiveness
21. The price of following Jesus
22. A warning against hypocrisy
23. God, judge of false leaders
24. The rules of the Sabbath
25. A servant of God
26. Kneel before God in prayer
27. Obedience leads to faith and blessing
28. God meets us in our grief
29. Pride comes before a fall
30. God fills his children with his Spirit

Prayer for April

Give thanks to the Lord, for he is good.
His love endures for ever (Ps 136:1).
Sing to the Lord a new song,
his praise in the assembly of the saints.
For the Lord takes delight in his people;
he crowns the humble with salvation.
May the praise of the Lord be in their mouths ...
This is the glory of all the saints (Ps 149:1, 4, 6, 9).
Praise the Lord. Praise God in his sanctuary;
praise him in his mighty heavens!
Praise him for his acts of power;
praise him for his surpassing greatness! (Ps 150:1-2).
How good it is to sing praises to our God,
how pleasant and fitting to praise him!
Sing to the Lord with thanksgiving;
make music to our God on the harp (Ps 147:1, 7).
Praise the Lord, O my soul. I will praise the Lord all my life;
I will sing praise to my God as long as I live (Ps 146:1, 2).
They will speak of the glorious splendor of your majesty,
and I will tell of the power of your awesome works.
They will tell of the power of your awesome works,
and I will proclaim your great deeds.
They will celebrate your abundant goodness
and joyfully sing of your righteousness (Ps 145:5-7).
Give thanks to the Lord, for he is good.
His love endures for ever (Psalm 136:1)

Amen

EVERYONE HAS SINNED AGAINST GOD

If anyone of you is without sin, let him be the first to throw a stone at her (Jn 8:7).

We are born into a wrong relationship with God. The sin that Adam committed plunged all of humanity into sin. Nobody is immune to sin. No human achievement can erase the blemish that separates us from God. Because Adam sinned, we have all sinned. Therefore we all require urgent help; we need forgiveness; we need a Saviour.

How do we escape from the crisis in which we find ourselves? Read the following two Bible verses carefully and prayerfully: *Consequently, just as the result of one trespass was condemnation for all men, so also the result of one act of righteousness was justification that brings life for all men. For just as through the disobedience of the one man the many were made sinners, so also through the obedience of the one man the many will be made righteous* (Rom 5:18-19).

FOOD FROM THE WORD OF GOD
John 7:32-8:11; Job 15:14-16; Psalm 7:20; 14:1-3; Proverbs 20:9; Ecclesiastes 7:20; Isaiah 64:5-7.

What a splendid and wonderful assurance! By believing in Jesus Christ, you receive eternal life from God. You sins are forgiven and your ultimate destination is heaven. You get all of this and much more, not through something that you do, but through what Christ has already done for you. This is what the Scriptures teach us. And it is called: GRACE. God in his mercy offers you salvation and blessedness – not through the works of man, their efforts, or achievements, but through the work of his Son.

Amazing grace, how sweet the sound that saved a wretch like me.
I once was lost, but now am found;
was blind, but now I see (Carmichael).

Awareness of sin is the beginning of salvation.
EPICURUS

JESUS IS OUR GOOD SHEPHERD

I am the good shepherd. The good shepherd lays down his life for the sheep (Jn 10:11).

Are you in need of guidance on your path of life? Look up to Jesus. When you lose sight of him for a moment, stand still and quietly wait for his image to reappear and to experience his presence once again. Entrust the control of your life to him and allow him to execute his plan for your life.

Sometimes Christ leads us to the tranquility of green pastures and still waters. He carries us in loving hands through months and years of happiness and prosperity. We grow spiritually and increasingly serve him in love. However, at other times he leads us to barren fields, to steep hills, and even to mountain peaks of temptation. This, too, is good. The pastures cannot always be green and the waters always quiet. When we then climb over the treacherous heights, we have a panoramic view, and the air that we breathe is refreshing and pure.

FOOD FROM THE WORD OF GOD
John 10:1-33; Psalm 23:1-6; 100:1-5; Isaiah 40:11; Jeremiah 31:10.

Late in the afternoon, the Shepherd brings his flock back to the valleys. He leads us through the dark forests where wild animals lurk. But we know that he has his rod and his staff in his all-knowing hand and will ward off any attack on us. He will not let us enter a shadowy forest on our own. Neither darkness, nor grief, nor death is proof that he is not with us. It does not show that we have chosen the wrong path. Therefore, trust in him in these times, too. Ask for faith that can resist trials, and reach the other side purified.

Good Shepherd, there is no shadowy depth that I will not enter in your presence. I know that I am safe in your hands.

Its piety and poverty are equal, its sweetness and spirituality are unsurpassed.
SPURGEON, ON PSALM 23

April 8

THE LIVES OF BELIEVERS GLORIFY GOD

But you are a chosen people, a royal priesthood, a holy nation, a people belonging to God, that you may declare the praises of him who called you out of darkness into his wonderful light (1 Pet 2:9).

God is glorified when we, his children, grow spiritually. He is glorified when our virtues shine so brightly that everyone around us can see them and can know that we are his children and that we all share in his Holy Spirit.

Our spiritual growth and piety glorify God. When we show mercy towards others and grow spiritually, it contributes to his glory. The fruits of righteousness, which the lives of his children bear, glorify God. Christ himself said: *This is to my Father's glory, that you bear much fruit, showing yourselves to be my disciples* (Jn 15:8).

FOOD FROM THE WORD OF GOD
1 Peter 1:22-2:17; 1 Samuel 7:22-24; Daniel 3:16-20, 26-29.

Members and ministers of the church of Christ must be fruitful for his kingdom. We must bear the fruits of the Spirit in the church, in our lives, through the power of our faith and through our works of love (Gal 5:22-23). We ought never to doubt that God is deeply interested in all of these things. His sincere desire is that we may bear fruit to his glory. His words in Matthew 7:7 prove it: *Ask and it will be given to you; seek and you will find; knock and the door will be opened to you.*

We were created for the purpose of glorifying God through our lives. Therefore, study his Word, so that you will discover the revealed will of God for your life. Also pray, for prayer is the breath of the soul that seeks to glorify and honour God.

Holy God, recreate our lives, and let the good seed grow in us; make us holy in our thoughts, words and deeds.

In our times the road to salvation necessarily runs through the road of action.
DAG HAMMERSKJÖLD

FIGHT SATAN WITH ENDURANCE AND FAITH

This calls for patient endurance and faithfulness on the part of the saints (Rev 13:10b).

During the final days, the children of God will experience terrible onslaughts from Evil. Thus, we will have to be able to launch a counterattack. Therefore, we must believe in the omnipotence of God. We must get our energy from him, and then persevere to the very end. We could never manage this alone.

FOOD FROM THE WORD OF GOD
Revelation 12:13-13:18; Daniel 7:23-27; 11:29-35.

In our battle against the Evil, God provides us with weapons of outstanding quality and efficiency. *Put on the full armour of God so that you can take your stand against the devil's schemes* (Eph 6:11). *Stand firm then, with the belt of truth buckled around your waist, with the breastplate of righteousness in place, and with your feet fitted with the readiness that comes from the gospel of peace. In addition to all this, take up the shield of faith, with which you can extinguish all the flaming arrows of the evil one* (Eph 6:14-17). Furthermore, we must be alert and continually pray for one another.

In the Christian struggle against our cunning enemy God provides us with the entire armour that we need. He gives us his power, and an invincible position. We must put on this armour in faith and take up our positions, and then keep on fighting against injustice and sin. Only then will we be victorious in his name over a sly enemy.

Lord my God, purify my faith, and strengthen my perseverance for the battle of faith that I must undertake.

Satan works through confusion and lies. Put the truth before him and he flees.
PAUL MATLOCK

GOD AFFIRMS HIS HOLINESS

Behold, I come like a thief! Blessed is he who stays awake and keeps his clothes with him, so that he may not go naked and be shamefully exposed (Rev 16:15).

FOOD FROM THE WORD OF GOD
Revelation 16:12-17:8; Ezekiel 13:8-14; 38:18-23.

For people who do not want to subject themselves to the love of God and be changed for the better by his grace, there is no escaping his wrath. Either the fire of God's Holy Spirit purifies us, or the fire of God's wrath devours us. Every human being is faced with this choice.

Rank and station, status or man's esteem will safeguard no one on that terrible day of God's wrath. John's list includes monarchs, high officials, generals, the rich and mighty, slaves as well as free men (Rev 6:15). The question we must ask has been asked in Revelation 6:17: *For the great day of their wrath has come, and who can stand?*

We are so used to emphasising the gentleness and humility of Jesus (Mt 11:28-30) that we forget about his holiness and righteousness. We may not play off the love of Christ against his righteousness. The same Jesus who in the temple took the children in his arms and blessed them, drove the merchants and the moneychangers out of the temple. God's wrath is not like a child's temper tantrum or like the punishment a parent metes out. God's wrath is proof of his divine love of everything that is right and his divine hatred of everything that is evil. Indeed, we worship a God who wants to act fairly against the sin and wickedness of the world.

Holy and loving Father, grant me greater insight into your perfect divinity every day, so that I may joyfully do your perfect will.

The firmness of God is friendlier than the gentleness of people and his coercion is our liberation.
CS LEWIS

GOD CALLS US TO WALK IN HIS LIGHT

He who overcomes will, like them, be dressed in white. I will never blot out his name from the book of life, but will acknowledge his name before my Father and his angels (Rev 3:5).

The older I grow and the better I get to know Christ, the more I become aware of his insistence upon holiness. It appears to me that this is a matter about which there cannot be even the slightest negotiation. There are people who say that Christ is too inflexible in the matters of righteousness and holiness. They claim that in their lives they have made great compromises to God. Can Christ not then make an exception of a single small sin? Is there no room for compromises? Can I not be accommodated? Allow me three percent darkness, and I will walk 97 percent in the light.

FOOD FORM THE WORD OF GOD
Revelation 2:18-3:6;
Deuteronomy 10:12; 13:1-5; 17:2, 5-7; 22:22; 26:17-18;
Psalm 7:10-13.

Be warned: God will not yield even one millimetre on this issue. The truth is that anyone wishing to be a close friend of Jesus must develop a triumph-over-sin outlook; must not try running up an account with God; must refuse to allow long-cherished sins to carry on day after day, week after week and year after year, without any confession and repentance.

The day must come when the church, as a body and as individuals who form a union with Christ in earnestness and honesty, reaches out to holiness. In prayer, we must ask God for the resoluteness needed to conquer sin and wickedness. We must understand that we will never experience the overwhelming feeling of the presence of the living Christ, unless we strive to walk completely in his light.

Lead me, friendly Light, through earthly darkness, lead me forward.

There is no true holiness without humility.
THOMAS FULLER

THOSE WHO BELIEVE ARE JOYFUL

And the disciples were filled with joy and with the Holy Spirit (Acts 13:52).

I am convinced that happiness and joy are the products of faith and knowledge. When we begin to acquaint ourselves with the basic truths of an intellectual discipline, we are overwhelmed by what we do not know. Nevertheless, step by step we become more accustomed to the facts and theories. Then suddenly one day we realise that we have mastered the topic; that we know how to apply our new knowledge. And that brings joy.

The enjoyment of our faith grows in the same way. Initially God seems far away and high above us. Biblical and theological terms sound like a foreign language. Our prayers are tense. Then, with the touch of the Father's hand and the work of the Holy Spirit, we discover how much he loves us and how much he wants us to get to know him personally. Theories of his existence are replaced by an intimate relationship with him. We begin to enjoy God, and this makes us happy.

FOOD FORM THE WORD OF GOD
Acts 13:26:52; Psalm 30:4-6; 11-13; 92:1-8; Isaiah 61:10; Jeremiah 15:16.

Saying that we enjoy God is just another way of saying that we glorify him. We glorify him when we worship him as Creator, Maintainer, Saviour, and Lord of everyone and everything. We glorify him when we worship him for his charity, goodness, love and mercy. Our worship becomes intimate when we joyfully discover and enjoy the character of God. From this joy emanates our desire to obey and serve him. Our obedience and service then become a joyous reaction to his love.

I delight greatly in the Lord; my soul rejoices in my God. For he has clothed me with garments of salvation and arrayed me in a robe of righteousness (Is 61:10).

Happiness and joy are the indisputable signs of the presence of God.
LEON BLOY

REMAIN STEADFAST IN TEMPTATION

Be self-controlled and alert. Your enemy the devil prowls around like a roaring lion looking for someone to devour. Resist him, standing firm in the faith, because you know that your brothers throughout the world are undergoing the same kind of sufferings (1 Pet 5:8-9).

A trial is something that the Lord brings into your life in order to bring out the best in you. A temptation is something that the devil brings into your life in order to bring out the worst in you. We usually see temptations in a negative light, but a temptation is not only an opportunity to do wrong. It is also an ideal opportunity to do what is right.

FOOD FROM THE WORD OF GOOD
1 Peter 5:1-11; Genesis 3:1-6; 39:11-12; Job 2:3-10; 1 Corinthians 9:19-10:22.

Satan did the worst he could to Job and yet we read: *In all this, Job did not sin by charging God with wrongdoing* (Job 1:22). Moreover, if in life we have yet to learn to say "No", our circumstances become life's workshop where we can achieve that goal. Saying "No" when you would like to say "Yes", makes you stronger, cultivates perseverance and builds your Christian character.

When a spark falls onto ice, it causes negligible damage; but when it falls on gunpowder, the consequences are disastrous. "Yes" is a precipice down which millions have already fallen. "No" is a shield that carries the marks of millions of spears of temptation. "Yes" is like a city that throws open its gates to the enemy. Once the enemy is inside, you will never taste freedom again. "No" is like a competent swordsman whom nobody wants to take on. Those who say "No" to evil and without hesitation say "Yes" to good, have progressed far along the road that leads to spiritual maturity.

Holy Spirit of God, may I take every warning against temptation seriously, so that I do not become the prey of Evil.

Every moment of resistance against temptation is a victory.
FREDERICK W FABER

GOD REWARDS THE RIGHTEOUS

I tell you that to everyone who has, more will be given, but as for the one who has nothing, even what he has will be taken away (Lk 19:26).

How do forgiveness and righteousness through faith concur with God's judgement of deeds? Firstly, the gift of sanctification is not a shield that protects believers from judgement and banishment from the presence of God because they have sinned. This is evident from the vision of judgement in Revelation 20:11-15, where we read that, alongside "the books" in which every person's deeds are recorded, "the book of life" is opened. Those believers whose names are recorded in that book, will not be thrown into the "lake of fire".

FOOD FROM THE WORD OF GOD
Luke 19:11-40; Psalm 37:27-28; Proverbs 12:14; 24:12; Isaiah 3:10-11.

Secondly, the gift of sanctification does not offer believers protection against the requirement for the genuineness of our Christianity. We will lose the good that others enjoy if it becomes evident that we were indolent, sinful, and destructive. This is illustrated by Paul's warning to the Corinthians to be careful of what kind of lifestyle they build on the true foundation, Christ: *If what he has built survives, he will receive his reward. If it is burned up, he will suffer loss; he himself will be saved, but only as one escaping through the flames* (1 Cor 3:14-15).

Reward and punishment are indicative of an enriched or an impoverished relationship with God. God expects his children to keep on doing good while they are waiting for the second coming. What kind of servant would you like to be for your Master? Only when the Holy Spirit is able to work in your life and make your faith grow, can you be a better servant.

Help me, O Spirit of God, to always grow in faith and obedience, so that I will better love and serve my Master.

God himself does not intend to judge man before the end of his life.
SAMUEL JOHNSON

THE WICKED VERSUS THE RIGHTEOUS

So the chief priests made plans to kill Lazarus as well, for on account of him many of the Jews were going over to Jesus and putting their faith in him (Jn 12:10-11).

Charles Haddon Spurgeon was known as the prince of preachers. He was one of the most gifted and colourful preachers in the history of the church. Every Sunday the New Tabernacle Church was filled to capacity. People came from all over to listen to him preaching the Word of God. His audience was challenged, encouraged, nourished, and edified in faith. He was truly an exceptional man. Consequently and inevitably, he became the target of malicious criticism by the media, other ministers, influential Londoners, and petty parishioners.

FOOD FROM THE WORD OF GOD
John 12:1-26; Psalm 10:1-16; Matthew 5:10-12.

It is said that his wife, who observed with dismay the consequences of these verbal attacks on her husband, decided to actively assist him in regaining his powerful status in the pulpit. She had Matthew 5:11-12 printed on a large sheet of paper. She then nailed it to the ceiling above their bed: *Blessed are you when people insult you, persecute you and falsely say all kinds of evil against you because of me. Rejoice and be glad, because great is your reward in heaven, for in the same way they persecuted the prophets who were before you.*

This story should help us, the servants of the Lord, to avoid organising a party of self-pity for ourselves. We are not alone; believers have been persecuted and insulted for centuries. And it will keep on happening until the Lord comes again.

Help me, Lord Jesus, to keep my eyes on you and not to sink into self-pity when the world wants to undermine the credibility of my faith. May I then especially trust in you.

The final test of a leader is that he will instil in those around him the conviction that he will persevere.
WALTER LIPPMANN

ALL POWER IS GIVEN BY GOD

Jesus answered, "You should have no power over me if it were not given to you from above ..." (Jn 19:11).

God has complete control over his universe. His sovereign omnipotence means that he is absolutely independent. He is subject to no one and can be influenced by no one. Despite the suffering, violence and horrors of this world, God remains in control, whether we acknowledge him as God or not. Even before the beginning of time, God was in control. Then he created all that there is and he still reigns with sovereign power.

FOOD FROM THE WORD OF GOD
John 19:4-27; 2 Chronicles 20:5-6; 32:6-8; Jeremiah 27:4-7; Daniel 28:33.

The Israelites must have wondered if God was in control when they spent 400 years in slavery in Egypt. Driven daily by cruel slave masters, they must undoubtedly have asked, "If there is a God, where is he?" So too the Jews on their way to the gas chambers in Nazi Germany must have asked, "If there is a God, where is he?"

They must surely have reasoned that there was either no God, or that he did not have the power to put an end to their suffering. But what happened? The almighty God who controls every circumstance, led the Israelites out of Egypt in a mighty demonstration of his supreme power. The state of Israel was re-established and the Jews who were dispersed all over the world have a home once again.

Israel never forgot God's acts of salvation and their redemption. Nations trembled before a confrontation with God's chosen people. True power belongs only to God, and woe to those who think their strength is vested in themselves.

Anew, almighty God, I subject my life, my spirit, my soul, and my body to your supreme power and authority.

We are the conducting wire; God is the stream. We only have power when his stream flows through us.
CARLO CARETTO

THE PAIN OF A FRIEND'S BETRAYAL

Now the betrayer had arranged a signal with them: "The one I kiss is the man; arrest him" (Mt 26:48).

When Judas agreed to betray Jesus, he might just as well have hammered in the nails that would later rip through Jesus' hands on the cross. We ask ourselves how it was possible that a disciple who experienced Jesus' miracles, teachings and love could deliver him into the hands of the enemy for thirty silver coins. We know that Judas was a greedy and dishonest man with a great love of money. Nevertheless, how could he go as far as betraying Jesus?

FOOD FROM THE WORD OF GOD
Matthew 26:47-68; Genesis 40:14-15, 23; Judges 7:2-3; Job 19:13-21; Psalm 55:12-14, 21-22.

Judas was, however, by no means the only one who betrayed Jesus. Even after they had seen his miraculous deeds and heard his words, many people still refused to believe in him. These people might just as well have collected the thirty pieces of silver from the priests. To this very day, there are those people who, despite irrefutable evidence, refuse to believe in Christ, and continue to betray him.

We can choose the world with its bright lights and pleasures, or we can choose Jesus. And this is not a choice that we make only once in a lifetime. Every time that Judas in his heart betrayed Jesus, it was a new betrayal. The same applies to the people who have seen his miraculous deeds and who have heard his words, and yet do not believe. We, too, sometimes say that we believe in Jesus Christ, but we live as if we do not know him. This is betrayal of the highest love. Will today be a day of faith or of betrayal for you?

Lord Jesus, you know our hearts. Purify my heart through your Holy Spirit so that I may never betray you.

Still, as of old, man by himself is priced; for thirty silver pieces, Judas sold himself, not Christ.
WILLIAM BLANE

DO NOT BE AFRAID

One night the Lord spoke to Paul in a vision: "Do not be afraid; keep on speaking, do not be silent. For I am with you ..." (Acts 18:9-10).

How tenderly God comforts us and banishes our fear: *So do not fear, for I am with you; do not be dismayed, for I am your God. I will strengthen you and help you; I will uphold you with my righteous right hand* (Is 41:10). *For I am the Lord, your God, who takes hold of your right hand and says to you, Do not fear; I will help you* (Is 41:13). And he daily repeats these encouraging promises to us.

FOOD FROM THE WORD OF GOD
Acts 18:5-28; Genesis 28:15; Deuteronomy 7:17-21; Psalm 46:2-4, 8; 121:5-8; Isaiah 41:10-13.

We are daily inundated by thousands of fears storming thunderously down on us, distressing our hearts. Since the time that Adam admitted: *I heard you in the garden, and I was afraid ...* (Gen 3:10), man has been terrified. In order to conquer our fears, we require faith in the living and almighty God. Indeed, all fear is slavery and Jesus came specifically to set us free from slavery.

Our Lord Jesus sends us an all-encompassing message of eternal comfort, as he did for the disciples of Galilee: *Why are you so afraid? Do you still have no faith?* (Mk 4:40). Christ is the solution to all the terrifying problems in our lives. He is our salvation. As his followers, we can therefore rise above our fear. Keep your eyes on Jesus; abide *in* Him; believe that he is stronger than your anxiety. Inseparably hold on to Christ, and fears will no longer plague you.

Gracious God, help me, through your Holy Spirit, to always hold on to Jesus so that fear will not invade my life.

Fear is never a good advisor, and triumph over fear is a Christian's first spiritual obligation.
NICOLAI BERDYAEV

SERVICE TO GOD IS IMPORTANT

And now, compelled by the Spirit, I am going to Jerusalem, not knowing what will happen to me there (Acts 20:22).

David Brainard, a missionary working amongst the Indians of the United States, was so filled with passion for the magnificence of Jesus Christ and the salvation of lost souls that he said, "I didn't care where or how I lived, or which trials I had to endure, if I could only save souls for Jesus Christ."

Paul was a passionate man, even before his conversion. Though his goal at first had been to wipe the Name of Jesus Christ from the face of the earth and to eradicate the early church, his only aim after his conversion was to glorify Christ and to establish the church. The driving force behind his newly found enthusiasm and ambition was the glorification of the Master and the growth of his kingdom.

FOOD FROM THE WORD OF GOD
Acts 20:7-38; 1 Kings 18:40; 19:1-10, 15-16, 19.

Our Saviour himself was gripped by an ambition that permeated his whole life: *Then I said, "Here I am – it is written about me in the scroll – I have come to do your will, O God"* (Heb 10:7). When, near the end of his earthly life he prayed his pontifical prayer, he could confirm that he had achieved his goal completely: *I have brought you glory on earth by completing the work you gave me to do* (Jn 17:4).

Serving God, no matter where, is of the utmost importance, even if we have to risk our lives for it. We dare not ask, "What is in it for me?" No, we must ask, "What of my best, my most precious, and my noblest can I put in – my life?"

Heavenly Guide, help me to be faithful in your service right to the end, whatever it may cost me.

Service to God that matters is service that costs you something.
HOWARD HENDRICKS

GOD HOLDS YOU RESPONSIBLE

*God will give to each person according to what he has done.
To those who by persistence in doing good
seek glory, honour, and immortality, he will give eternal life.
But for those who are self-seeking and who reject
the truth and follow evil, there will be wrath and anger (Rom 2:6-8).*

The information that the Bible gives us about God's work as Judge is part of the Scriptures' testimony of his character. It confirms what is said everywhere in the Scriptures about his perfection, his righteousness and fairness, his wisdom, omniscience and omnipresence. It also shows that the essence of God's righteousness is recompense: he judges people fairly in accordance with what they deserve.

FOOD FROM THE WORD OF GOD
Romans 1:28-2:16; Psalm 94:1-15; Proverbs 5:21-23; 15:9-11.

Returning good for good and evil for evil is completely natural to God. When the New Testament talks about the final judgement, it is also presented in terms of recompense. *The dead were judged according to what they had done as recorded in the books* (Rev 20:12; see also Mt 16:27). Paul confirms this when he says, *God will give to each person according to what he has done. To those who by persistence in doing good seek glory, honour, and immortality, he will give eternal life. But for those who are self-seeking and who reject the truth and follow evil, there will be wrath and anger … For God does not show favouritism* (Rom 2:6-11).

God has determined that he will reward each according to his deeds. Recompense is the inescapable moral code of creation: God will see to it that every person gets what he or she deserves – if not here, then in the hereafter.

Righteous Judge and loving Father, may your Holy Spirit lead me so that one day I may hear from your holy mouth, "Well done, my good and loyal servant."

The Christian demand for justice does not come from Karl Marx. It comes from Jesus Christ and the Hebrew prophets. – BRONLEY OXNAM

IS GOD UNJUST?

What then shall we say? Is God unjust? Not at all! For he says to Moses, "I will have mercy on whom I have mercy, and I will have compassion on whom I have compassion." It does not, therefore, depend on man's desire or effort, but on God's mercy (Rom 9:14-16).

There is no need for the children of God to try and understand him. We only need to love and obey him. We do not need to understand him in order to open our thoughts and lives to him. We have not been called to understand him. We have been chosen and called to love him, to glorify him, to serve and obey him.

FOOD FROM THE WORD OF GOD
Romans 9:1-29; Joshua 10:22-23; Job 40:1-7; Isaiah 1:9; 45:6-7, 9; Hosea 1:10; 2:1-2, 22.

Sometimes God enters our lives like a hurricane, as was the case with Job. At other times, God appears to us in a form that we have never seen before and in sounds that we have never heard before. It sometimes makes us wonder whether God's signals have not perhaps become mixed up. At times, he takes us southward in order to get us in a northerly position. Sometimes it appears to us as if God has placed us, as reasonable creatures, in an unreasonable world. We do not understand everything, because he is God and we are insignificant human beings.

We dare not forget or eliminate the distance between God and ourselves. We are human and mortal; he is divine and eternal. We have a need for love; God is gladdened by love and *is* love. We must learn to understand; God understands perfectly. We look for reasons; God is above all reason. We feel battered by stormy winds; God creates the winds and controls their intensity. But, God is fair in everything, he loves us with an eternal love and holds us safely in his hands.

Eternal God who is love, in humble submission I accept your love as you give it to me. I praise and thank you for it.

God is not an idea or a definition that is imprinted on our memories. God is a presence that we accept in our hearts. – LOUIS EVELEY

GOD PUTS WORDS INTO OUR MOUTHS

For I will give you words and wisdom that none of your adversaries will be able to resist or contradict (Lk 21:15).

Every child of God is sometimes confronted with the challenge of having to say something important, and many of us then wonder, "What on earth should I say?"

In Luke 21 Jesus speaks of our uncertainties about what we should say when we have to be witnesses for him in circumstances that are hostile to the Christian faith. He assures us that the Holy Spirit will give us the ideas, the words and the courage we need, but so often lack. There may be times when you are hesitant about sharing your faith in Christ with other people, or when your faith is challenged by unbelievers. Trust that God is also the Creator of your thoughts and the Source of your words, especially at such times.

FOOD FROM THE WORD OF GOD
Luke 21:1-28; Exodus 4:10-16; Numbers 23:5-12.

Lloyd Ogilvie said, "Your only task is to open your thoughts calmly to wisdom far beyond your ability. We are never of ourselves equal to being sufficient. It is when we think that we can depend on ourselves that we land in trouble. A Christian is not someone who works for the Lord, but someone in whom and through whom the Lord works. We are not expected to speak for God, but to put our tongues in his control so that we can speak the thoughts that he places within us."

Listen, therefore, to the Lord before you speak. Once you have heard what he is telling you, you will be able to speak confidently.

Lord, all-knowing God, give me a willing spirit and help me to trust you to convey your message through me to the world.

Witnessing is to remove the various obstacles of our self-love, so that we can allow Christ, who dwells within us, to reveal himself to our neighbours. – PAUL FROST

April 18

DECEPTION CAUSES GREAT SORROW

And he (Peter) went outside and wept bitterly (Lk 22:62).

The truth was a holy matter to the Jews of the Old Testament. To them truth meant recognising reality, but also far more than that: for them there was an intimately personal dimension to truth, as well as ethical and emotional dimensions.

Trust is a by-product of truth and personal relationships are, after all, built on trust. Therefore, truth is a special ingredient of any close relationship between two people. We trust people who have shown over a period of time that they love the truth. Moreover, someone who is trustworthy is someone who sticks to the truth. We do not in any way trust people who have shown themselves to be habitual liars. Satan is the father of lies and likes to twist and destroy the truth. The Scriptures tell us that Satan was a liar from the start.

FOOD FROM THE WORD OF GOD
Luke 22:54-23:12; Genesis 27:2-10, 30-37, 41.

It is extremely painful for anyone to carry a lie in his or her heart. A broken truth normally means a broken heart. Consequently we feel hurt when people do not keep their promises or when they tell us stories that later turn out to be lies. We become disillusioned and sometimes embittered. Our trust has been broken. And deeply seated trust takes years to develop but can be destroyed within a matter of seconds. So, take care to always keep to the truth. Ask God to assist you in this through his Spirit.

Saviour and Leader, you are the way, the truth and the life, because you never betray our trust. May I, through your Holy Spirit who dwells in me, everyday keep to the truth.

Does being deceived hurt you? Then never deceive someone else.
JOHANNES CHRYSOSTOM

April 19

GOD GUIDES AND PROTECTS US

And having been warned in a dream not to go back to Herod, they returned to their country by another route (Mt 2:12).

Few things in the Bible are clearer than God's guarantee that he will give guidance to whoever in faith asks it of him. Every day of your life can be planned and guided by God: every day, every moment and every step. God wants to be the Guide of your life and it pleases him to see his will being done in your life.

History proves that God actively guides people's lives. When each of us looks back over his or her life, we see how wonderfully and lovingly God has guided us. Abraham's slave testifies in Genesis 24:27: *Praise be to the Lord, the God of my master Abraham, who has not abandoned his kindness and faithfulness to my master. As for me, the Lord has led me on the journey to the house of my master's relatives.*

FOOD FROM THE WORD OF GOD
Matthew 2:1-23; Psalm 57:1-11; Micah 5:1-5.

God will lead you. The Scriptures teach us this and give us examples of how he led believers. Yes, right now God is leading you, because he promised to lead you when you want his guidance in your life. In addition, he always keeps his promises. Even when we think about the future, when we think of times of trouble that might still arise, we can know and declare with certainty that God will lead us.

Thank God for his guidance in your life. By having faith in his reliability, you may know that he will also lead you in the future. Praise him for it. Every day God guides us. Believe it, and rest assured in this knowledge. It gives you peace and serenity.

Faithful Guide, I praise your holy Name because you lead me on your path from day to day. Keep me from wandering off onto pathways planned by my own unseeing heart.

We are all chords in God's concert of joy.
JAKOB BOEHME

April 20

THE WONDER OF GOD'S FORGIVENESS

Forgive us our debts,
as we also have forgiven our debtors (Mt 6:12).

Believers are not always done with sin after their conversions. Yes, we know the joy that forgiveness brings. We are gladdened by the assurance that our debt has been paid. However, nowhere do the Scriptures promise that we will be exempted from temptation and seduction, from the possibility of sinning again. Evil thoughts, immorality, theft, murder, adultery, greed, malice, fraud, debauchery, envy, slander, pride and frivolity come from within, from the heart of man.

FOOD FROM THE WORD OF GOD
Matthew 5:38-6:15; Psalm 25:1-22

How is it possible that a God who hates sin and demands purity, a God who expects growing faith from his children, would occupy himself with believers who are inclined to sin? The answer is that he, through the act of his Son, made provision for purification that runs so deep, and which is so radical and continuous, that we can dwell in uninterrupted communion with him.

The Scriptures unambiguously state: the forgiveness of sins is proclaimed to us through Jesus, through whom everyone who believes is justified from everything we could not be justified from by the law of Moses (Acts 13:38-39). God forgives us our wickedness, and then forgets our sins (Heb 8:12). Because Jesus carried our sins and sentences on the cross, we will never again fall under the judgement, regardless of whether we still commit sin after our conversion. The blood of Jesus purifies us from all sin (1 Jn 1:7), but only in answer to our genuine repentance and confession (1 Jn 1:9). How merciful and loving is the God we serve!

Holy God, through the blood of the Lamb purify my heart of all sin, and give me a pure heart once again.

Forgiveness is man's greatest need and his greatest achievement.
HORACE BUSHNELL

THE PRICE OF FOLLOWING JESUS

Anyone who does not take up his cross and follow me is not worthy of me (Mt 10:38).

During the Sermon on the Mount Jesus said, *Blessed are you when people insult you, persecute you and falsely say all kinds of evil against you because of me. Rejoice and be glad, because great is your reward in heaven* (Mt 5:11-12b). The chosen ones who are maltreated, robbed and abused shall all be rewarded for their suffering.

God knows when you are unfairly subjected to suffering for the sake of his Name. God has not abandoned you and delivered you into the hands of people who are more powerful. He knows when you, his child and follower, are not promoted because of your faith. He knows when less qualified people are appointed above you because you refuse to make moral compromises.

FOOD FROM THE WORD OF GOD
Matthew 10:11-40; Psalm 71:7-16; 119:41-48; Jeremiah 20:7-9.

God knows about everything that happens in our lives. He has already put his judicial system into place: prosecutor, attorney, jury and judge, and all of these in the Person of Jesus, our Saviour. On his appointed day for the hearing, he will see to it that justice is done for his chosen people. In the meantime, you and I must stoop under our crosses without complaint, carrying them joyfully behind the great Bearer of the cross.

How intensely does the need to testify for Jesus burn in your heart? (Jer 20:9). What price are you willing to pay in order to follow him? What comforts you when you follow him faithfully in difficult circumstances? Answer these questions truthfully and receive your rewards from his hand.

Almighty and gracious God, may I never complain about the cross that you impose upon me. May your Holy Spirit continue to make it possible for me to follow you and obey you faithfully.

There are no bearers of crowns in heaven who were not bearers of crosses on earth.
CHARLES H SPURGEON

A WARNING AGAINST HYPOCRISY

You hypocrites! Isaiah was right when he prophesied about you: "These people honour me with their lips, but their hearts are far from me" (Mt 15:7-8).

The *Oxford Advanced Learner's Dictionary of Current English* (Oxford: Oxford University Press 1995) explains the word "hypocrite" as follows: "A person who pretends to have standards or opinions which he or she does not have, or to be what he or she is not." In the ancient Greek dramas and comedies, actors were called *hupokrites* on stage, they pretended to be someone that they in reality were not.

FOOD FROM THE WORD OF GOD
Matthew 15:1-31; Proverbs 26:24-26; Isaiah 29:13-14.

In the same way, there are many people who go through life as actors. They pretend to be what they are not. They are hypocrites, impostors. The masks that they wear, however, fool nobody but themselves. God knows who and what they are.

Through the centuries millions of people died and were buried without Christ by their side, eternally damned, because they were hypocrites. They pretended to be Christians, but never were. It is said that Thomas K Beecher could not tolerate any form of hypocrisy. When he discovered that his church clock was always running too fast or too slow, he had a poster put up on the wall next to the clock, with these words written on it: "Do not blame my arms; the problem lies deeper!"

Do not make the mistake of trying to be a better Christian all by yourself. The problem lies too deep. Only Christ can heal you of hypocrisy. And he will do it when you give yourself to him in true repentance and with sincere faith and seek his forgiveness.

God of truth, keep me sincere and honest and protect me,
through the work of the Holy Spirit,
from every form of pretence and hypocrisy.

The old hypocrite was someone who pretended to be better than he or she actually was; the modern hypocrite tries to look worse than he or she really is. – CHARLES TEMPLETON

GOD, JUDGE OF FALSE LEADERS

Woe to you, teachers of the law and Pharisees, you hypocrites! You clean the outside of the cup and dish, but inside they are full of greed and self-indulgence. Blind Pharisee! First clean the inside of the cup and dish, and then the outside also will be clean (Mt 23:25-26).

Our church runs the risk of falling into a superficial theology that would not even be capable of turning the wheels of a toy car, let alone motivate the disciples of Jesus Christ in the merciless world of today.

FOOD FROM THE WORD OF GOD
Matthew 22:41-23:36; Jeremiah 5:30-31; Ezekiel 13:8-16.

Already there is a growing lack of true spirituality. And this when there is currently only one aspect left in which our country can be outstanding: the power of our faith. In a post-modern secular world, we are still one of the religious countries. There are, however, indications that this will not be the case much longer. The church must start making an effort to work at its credibility, integrity and effectiveness in this new millennium.

We boast of full churches, but the congregations listen to empty sermons. There are exceptions, but people mostly leave our churches spiritually unnourished or undernourished, returning to a cynical world against which the sermon offered them no defence. The problem is not only heresy, false teachings, or unbelief. The problem is that what is said does not carry the mark of God's blessing. Jeremiah attacked the false prophets with these damning words. *But which of them has stood in the council of the Lord ...? Who has listened and heard his word?* (Jer 23:18). Are God's standards too high for us? In that case, we must keep away from the pulpits.

Lord, your word is like a fire, like a hammer that hacks stones. May your Holy Spirit help me to hear what you want to say to and through me.

My main aim with preaching is to break the hardest heart and to heal the broken heart. – JOHN NEWTON

THE RULES OF THE SABBATH

Then he said to them, "The Sabbath was made for man, not man for the Sabbath. So the Son of man is Lord even of the Sabbath" (Mk 2:27-28).

Sabbath rest means worshipping with the Christian community. In sincere worship, we discover all the components that lead to rest in our own private world. We shall look back, we shall look up, and we shall look ahead. This kind of worship is not negotiable for those who have committed themselves to a meaningful, Godly way of life.

Sabbath rest means conscious acceptance of personal rest: rest for our souls and peace of mind in our lives. Sabbath rest means a rest that brings peace and serenity to our personal world. In the same way that Christ calmed a storm, brought peace into the life of someone who was possessed by many evil spirits, restored health to a sick woman, and raised a friend from the dead, he wants to bring peace and rest to the storm-torn lives of people who are weak under pressure from an ungodly world. We may accept this peace as a gift from him, and make it our own.

FOOD FROM THE WORD OF GOD
Mark 2:23-3:30; Exodus 29:31-34; 1 Samuel 21:1-6; Isaiah 56:1-2.

True worship does not necessarily need an altar, a pulpit, a minister, or a prescribed prayer – only a sincere and grateful heart. And God, who knows us better than anybody else and who tells us more than anyone ever could, gave us the Sabbath to lead us on the path of worship and to help us. How do you think he will feel about the way you observe the Sabbath?

All-knowing God, who knows my heart, thank you for the true Sabbath rest that you make possible for me.

It is only once you start worshipping that you start to grow spiritually.
CALVIN COOLIDGE

April 25

A SERVANT OF GOD

For even the Son of Man did not come to be served, but to serve, and to give his life as a ransom for many (Mk 10:45).

Unfortunately, we find the thought of service distasteful, except if it is temporary and beneficial to ourselves. Being forced to accept a lower status is bad enough; but choosing it is unheard of. To be a washer of feet by choice is unimaginable.

In our everyday language words like "obedience", "submission", "service" and even worse, "know one's place" leave a bad taste in the mouth. They are usually met with challenges from people who are obsessed with their "rights". Of course, there is nothing wrong with rights and it is fitting to have legislation protecting the rights of people. The problem is that legislation can only protect us against the bad; it cannot bring the good in us to the fore. Moreover, it can definitely not convince us of the value of giving up our rights for the sake of someone or something else.

FOOD FROM THE WORD OF GOD
Mark 10:35-45; Genesis 12:1-4; 22:1-2, 10-12; 24:34-37; 26:3-5, 23-25.

The cross is telling proof that there is much more to love than to justice; that there is much more to right than to rights. Someone who wins a public dispute for human rights has done a good thing. However, someone who wins a personal struggle, forsaking human rights in the interest of human responsibilities, has done something far better. People will often label this sincere attitude of service as humiliating and ludicrous, but is this not what was said of the cross?

Jesus Christ, Servant of God and holy Example, enable me to be a servant of yours and my fellow men without counting the cost or feeling sorry for myself.

Service is God's way of liberating individuals; servitude is man's way of destroying individuals.
MICHAEL HARPER

KNEEL BEFORE GOD IN PRAYER

They went to a place called Gethsemane, and Jesus said to his disciples, "Sit here while I pray" (Mk 14:32).

Holy God, and through Jesus Christ also my heavenly Father,

when I kneel before you, I am seized by the reality that, before you, I am stripped of all pretence and that I purely come to beg forgiveness.

You accept no great names as references, no recommendations regarding quality and character. You accept no mitigating circumstances. All my excuses crumble to dust and ashes in the court of your appeal. I am never forgiven on the grounds of hereditary inclinations, emotional instability, or uncontrollable weaknesses. I cannot plead the corrupt environment in which I grew up, or the eccentric twists of life that happened to me, or my own incredible stupidity.

FOOD FROM THE WORD OF GOD
Mark 14:26-52; 1 Kings 8:54-61; Ezra 9:1-15; Daniel 6:11.

In the end I have only one defence; only one – but, thank God! – always one: Forgive me, O Father, for Jesus' sake!

Like a song without end, the chorus resounds:

I am forgiven!
I am purified!
I am a child of God!
For Jesus' sake!

Amen

Holy God, you are my heavenly Father through Jesus Christ. Make me so sure of my faithful trust in you, that I will risk my life for it.

Prayer is the most important thing in my life. Were I to neglect it for a single day, I would lose a great deal of the fire of my faith. – MARTIN LUTHER

OBEDIENCE LEADS TO FAITH AND BLESSING

"Put out into deep water, and let down the nets for a catch." When they had done so, they caught such a large number of fish that their nets began to break (Lk 5:4b, 6).

John Henry Sammis (1846-1919) wrote a well-known and loved hymn. The first verse and chorus are:

When we walk with the Lord in the light of his Word,
what a glory He sheds on our way!
When we do his good will, He abides with us still,
and with all who will trust and obey!
Trust and obey, trust and obey, for there's no other way
to be happy in Jesus but to trust and obey.

FOOD FROM THE WORD OF GOD
Luke 4:31-5:11; 2 Kings 5:1-15.

These words say precisely what the Bible teaches us: The key to spiritual happiness and blessing is faith in God and obedience to Christ and the Holy Spirit.

Lack of faith and disobedience not only end in unhappiness, they also have serious repercussions on our lives. However, steadfast faith and absolute obedience lead to happiness and blessing. In quite a few places, the Bible tells us this (for example Ps 119). The lives of many Biblical figures also illustrate this truth (for example the life of Jacob).

Can you honestly say that you believe and trust, or must you confess that you also sometimes try to negotiate with God? He does not ask you to question him, to try to change his will or to compromise with him. His command is that you trust and obey him. That is the only way in which your faith is strengthened and the only way in which you will receive his rich blessings.

Father God, I want to give you nothing less than total obedience and trust. Help me, by the power of the Holy Spirit, to do this.

Obedience is the fruit of faith; patience is the blossom of the fruit.
CHRISTINA ROSETTI

April 28

GOD MEETS US IN OUR GRIEF

Meanwhile, all the people were wailing and mourning for her. "Stop wailing," Jesus said. "She is not dead but asleep" (Lk 8:52).

The symbol that the living Christ left behind in the world is the cross. It is unmistakable proof that God cares about us in our suffering, pain and sorrow. At any moment, Jesus could have summoned an army of angels to free him from the cross, but for our sake, he did not do so. *For God so loved the world that he gave his one and only Son, that whoever believes in him shall not perish but have eternal life* (Jn 3:16).

FOOD FROM THE WORD OF GOD
Luke 8:22-56; Exodus 3:7-10; Psalm 9:9-11; 33:18-22; 34:16-20.

This is why the cross is the cornerstone of our faith. Yes, for our sake he chose the Via Dolorosa, the way of sorrow. And in spite of suffering such a cruel death, he won the greatest victory in history. He connected mankind inseparably to God once more. Thereby, God made only good come from that terrible day of suffering and sorrow.

Jesus' followers also suffer hardships and experience crises. God never promised that he would make the hurricanes pass by our houses, or that deadly germs and pests would flee the bodies of Christians. Peter tells the suffering Christendom: *To this you were called, because Christ suffered for you, leaving you an example, that you should follow in his steps* (1 Pet 2:21). However, it is actually in our moments of deepest sorrow that we draw closest to God's fatherly heart and that we get to know him better and love him more.

I praise and thank you, my Saviour and Sanctifier, that on the cross you not only relieved my pain, but that you also took my greatest sorrow – my sins – upon yourself.

The strangest truth of the gospel is that suffering brings about redemption.
MILO L CHAPMAN

April 29

PRIDE COMES BEFORE A FALL

For everyone who exalts himself will be humbled, and he who humbles himself will be exalted (Lk 14:11).

God does not despise pride in the positive sense of the word. The Bible shows in many ways that a quiet self-confidence forms the basis of our doing what we can and must. The apostle Paul's ministry was founded on the knowledge that Christ would help him to finish what he had started in his Name. We must cultivate this kind of pride at all costs and thank God for it and glorify him through it.

However, pride in the sense of arrogance, self-righteousness and dictatorial behaviour that belittles others brings out the worst in one, and that is a threat to healthy personal relationships. This conceit is in no way the answer to our human problems. All the main causes of disasters and suffering – fear, desire, greed, cruelty, lust and unbelief – can be traced back to pride.

FOOD FROM THE WORD OF GOD
Luke 13:22-14:14; Proverbs 3:11-12; 15:33; 18:12; Isaiah 2:12-17.

You know the state of your own heart; your yardstick is the Word of God. Have you made peace with God? Is your conscience clean? Are you filled with the Holy Spirit? Then you will not be conceited. Instead, your life will be filled with a humble, open, adoring, loving attitude before God and your fellow men. You will reflect something of a creature who dwells in the presence of his or her Creator, and returns with the radiance of his splendour to everyday life.

My Redeemer and Saviour, you set us an example of perfect humility. May your Holy Spirit give me the power to follow your example honestly.

Pride is the soil from which all sins grow; the parent out of whom all other sins are born.
WILLIAM BARCLAY

GOD FILLS HIS CHILDREN WITH HIS SPIRIT

All of them were filled with the Holy Spirit and began to speak in other tongues as the Spirit enabled them (Acts 2:4).

The preacher Lloyd Ogilvie tells of an experience he had: "One day we were travelling on sailboats when the wind dropped and the sea became calm and as flat as a mirror. All we could do was to sit and wait for the wind to come up again. As we waited, we drifted past another sailboat that was also floating about aimlessly. These people waved to us and with hand signals showed us that the sea was flat. One stood by the sails and blew against them. I contemplated this gesture for quite some time. It is like many Christians and far too many churches: human breath blowing against sails. Little wonder that we make no progress."

FOOD FROM THE WORD OF GOD
Acts 2:1-28; Isaiah 44:1-8.

The Hebrew word for the Spirit of God is *ruach*, which means breath or wind. At Pentecost, the power of the Holy Spirit was like a mighty wind. The Spirit filled the disciples, inspiring them for the gospel. What we need is a powerful display of this Wind, the fresh and driving wind of a new Pentecost.

Therefore, stop blowing your own breath against the sails of your life and those of the church. Ask God to fill the sails with his Wind, because without the Holy Spirit we will drift around aimlessly and perish on the calm sea.

Holy God, anchor me in your truth through the coming of the Holy Spirit into my life. Reveal and confirm to me that which I do not know; perfect in me that which I lack. Keep me pure in your service through the mighty work of your Holy Spirit.

Every time that we confess, "I believe in the Holy Spirit," we mean that we believe there is a living God who is willing to penetrate people's lives and personalities, and to change them for the better. – JB PHILLIPS

May

Prayer for May

1. God's love in Christ
2. Be humble
3. God will provide
4. Our attitude towards wealth
5. The Scriptures reveal God's will
6. All people are precious to God
7. God himself will judge his children
8. Live in peace
9. Add knowledge to your faith
10. God's children love one another
11. The price of discipleship
12. Thomas was not alone
13. Christ's witnesses should not fear
14. God is faithful to his followers
15 Live with a clear conscience
16. God's strength is within us
17. Christ sets us free
18. God is merciful to us
19. Jesus can forgive
20. The power of faith
21. The righteous are rewarded
22. Pray with conviction
23. Be strong in the last days
24. Innocent before God
25. God uses messengers
26. Do to others as God does to you
27. Show true regret for your sins
28. God is in total control
29. Christ is coming again
30. Jerusalem honours Jesus as King
31. The most important commandment

Prayer for May

Holy God, our heavenly Father,
we worship you in your majesty and righteousness,
but also in your unfathomable love and immeasurable grace.
We praise you for the privilege, as your children,
of sharing in this love and grace.
It makes us grateful as well as humble,
and enables us to share your love with other people.
Because we are your children and
have a special relationship with you,
we know that you will provide for our needs
and lead us safely in your way.
We thank you for your Word, which you want to reveal in our lives,
and which helps us to walk in your ways.
We rejoice because we are precious to you and you care for us;
because you love us despite knowing everything about us.
Help us to live in peace with you and our neighbours.
We plead, through the Holy Spirit: add knowledge to our faith.
Thank you for considering us worthy of being your fearless witnesses.
Help us to make you, and not ourselves,
the focus of our witness.
May we jubilantly testify to your splendour and majesty,
your uninterrupted love and steadfast mercy.
We praise you as a faithful God who keeps his word.
May your power every day be fulfilled in our weaknesses.
We thank you sincerely for forgiveness of sins and trespasses
through the blood of Jesus Christ.
Daily strengthen our faith and our prayer life.
With longing and excitement we look forward to the second coming
of your Son, Jesus Christ, our Saviour.
We worship you as the God who is always in control
of your creation, and of our lives.
Help us to live and work in commitment to you.
We pray this in your name and for the sake of
Jesus, our Saviour.

Amen

GOD'S LOVE IN CHRIST

I pray that you ... may have power, together with all the saints, to grasp how wide and long and high and deep is the love of Christ, and to know this love that surpasses knowledge – that you may be filled to the measure of all the fullness of God (Eph 3:17-19).

The love of God through Jesus Christ in all its fullness, faithfulness, tenderness and goodness is unfathomable to the human brain. Where will we find the words to describe his incomparable and unequalled love for the human beings he has created? Words fail to even scratch the surface, while the depths remain untouched.

FOOD FROM THE WORD OF GOD
Ephesians 3:7-4:13; 1 Chronicles 16:28-29, 34, 39-41; Psalm 136:1, 4-9, 26.

Before we can have any conception of the love of God through Jesus Christ, we must understand his splendour and majesty, and his incarnation. But who can describe to us the heavenly majesty of Christ? When he sat on the throne in the highest heaven, he was true God from true God; through him the heavens and everything in them, on them, and under them were created. His own almighty hand maintained the universe, and he was constantly surrounded by the angels' songs of praise. He was the Supreme Ruler over all of his creation; God of everything and everyone. Who can describe this magnificence of Christ?

And who can describe how deeply he descended to us for the sake of his love for us? To become human was humiliating in itself; to become a Man of sorrow so much more; to bleed and die, that was the worst. To die on a cross, deserted by his Father ... This is a love that makes our minds grow dizzy and which can never, ever be put into words.

Lord Jesus, may your love fill my heart with adulating gratefulness, and lead me, through your Holy Spirit, to a practical revelation of the power of your love.

Christ never loved humanity. He never said that he loved humanity. He loves humans.

GK CHESTERTON

BE HUMBLE

Do nothing out of selfish ambition or vain conceit, but in humility consider others better than yourselves (Phil 2:3)

The proud have a very high opinion of their own wisdom, power, or righteousness and are too self-assured. The meek, on the other hand, trust in God and rejoice in submitting themselves completely to God. God is their refuge, their righteousness, and their strength.

The meek will lay down all the honour and things they have done, and give it to God as a sacrifice. They will not glorify themselves or seek praise for their achievements. The attitude of the meek is to dedicate themselves completely to God, and to give him the honour. Their hearts do not rebel against doing exactly this.

FOOD FROM THE WORD OF GOD
Philippians 1:1-2:4; 1 Samuel 18:7-19; Proverbs 22:4; 27:2; Isaiah 57:14-19; Micah 6:8.

The meek are resigned to subjecting themselves to the instructions and laws of God, because they see it as fitting and right that the creatures should be subordinate to their Creator. They want to give to God the honour that is his alone, which is to rule over them and make them subject to certain laws and rules that are intended to be in their best interests.

Humility prevents an unnatural and dangerous desire for wealth and authority. The meek avoid unhealthy ambition that harms their fellow humans. They accept the position that God has given them amongst other people. They do not long for misplaced honour. For them the maxim of life is: "Soli Deo Gloria!" – to God be all the glory!

Loving God, by being humble I can demonstrate your love in my immediate environment. May the Holy Spirit assist me in this and make me genuinely humble.

Later on I was so humble that I was proud of my humility.
CJ LANGENHOVEN

GOD WILL PROVIDE

And my God will meet all your needs according to his glorious riches in Christ Jesus (Phil 4:19).

When I was at university, there were many students whose parents had lived through the Great Depression. It was a struggle to survive, let alone talk of supporting a student at university. But time and again we saw how miraculously God had provided for them and their children's needs. Many of the children of those believing parents are today active in the ministry – believing children of believing parents who held on to faith in God in the darkest circumstances. And he met all their needs.

FOOD FROM THE WORD OF GOD
Philippians 4:1-23; Psalm 37:3-5; 55:23; 68:4; 97:10-12; 105:1-5; Proverbs 16:1-9.

It is with this kind of trust that Paul writes to the believers in Philippi that his God will meet all their needs. Those Christians needed the encouragement, because they were by no means wealthy (2 Cor 8:1-5). Nevertheless, out of their meagre belongings they sent a sacrificial gift to Paul in Rome (Phil 4:14-18). And Paul assured them that God would reward them, because God's affairs were dear to their hearts.

There are two important details regarding this promise that we should remember. First of all, God will meet every *need*, not vain desire. God may see our needs totally differently from the way that we see them. Second of all, God wants to meet our needs *according to his glorious riches in Christ Jesus.* And *he is able to do immeasurably more than all we ask or imagine* (Eph 3:20). Trust God to meet your needs, too, and live in the expectation that he will keep his promises.

God, the Provider, thank you for allowing me to bring my needs before you, and that I can trust that you will care for me.

Allow temporary things to serve their purpose in your life, but let eternal things be the object of your desires.
THOMAS á KEMPIS

OUR ATTITUDE TOWARDS WEALTH

Command those who are rich in this present world not to be arrogant nor to put their hope in wealth, which is so uncertain, but to put their hope in God, who richly provides us with everything for our enjoyment (1 Tim 6:17).

There is a difference between a rich person who loves his wealth passionately, and a poor person who continues to live in poverty. When he dies, the rich person's heart will still be burdened with worldly matters and the joy that they gave to him. But the heart of the poor person will be free from sadness and the yearning for wealth.

FOOD FROM THE WORD OF GOD
1 Timothy 6:1-21; Deuteronomy 8:11-14, 17-18; Ecclesiastes 5:10-19.

However, if the rich person held on to his earthly possessions loosely, not allowing it to make a home in his heart, and used his wealth as a channel and not a storage tank, at any time parting with his riches, he will enter into eternity just as the person who accepted his poverty, and who did not despise it with bitterness. Both will rejoice, "I am free!"

God often allows people to accumulate riches and possessions to give them the opportunity to further his cause of truth and justice in our world. Confessing Christians view themselves as only stewards of God's riches, and sincerely believe that everything that they own belongs to God. Consequently, their possessions are at his disposal. The question is: Are the actions of rich people in accordance with what they confess? God often tests them to determine whether they are hypocritical or not. God is the source of all riches and happiness. Therefore, cultivate a Godly attitude towards wealth.

Merciful God, thank you for that which you lend to me in my life. Give me the grace to spend it correctly, and to your honour.

Wealth is a good servant, but a merciless disciplinarian.
FRANCIS BACON

THE SCRIPTURES REVEAL GOD'S WILL

All Scripture is God-breathed and is useful for teaching, rebuking, correcting and training in righteousness (2 Tim 3:16).

Few joys in life can surpass that of a sudden and exciting discovery. Instantly the pain and cost of the search are forgotten; the bygone hours and frustrations; the sacrifices and the despair that at times ate away at one's courage. Bowled over by the ecstasy of the discovery, it feels as if time has come to a standstill. Your heart is filled with joyous gratefulness, and a new and brighter future unfolds before you.

FOOD FROM THE WORD OF GOD
1 Timothy 3:12-4:22; Nehemiah 8:1-3, 14-18

However, Solomon told of the greatest discovery of all: *My son, if you accept my words and store up my commands within you, turning your ear to wisdom and applying your heart to understanding, and if you call out for insight and cry aloud for understanding, and if you look for it as for silver and search for it as for hidden treasure, then you will understand the fear of the Lord and find the knowledge of God. For the Lord gives wisdom, and from his mouth come knowledge and understanding* (Prov 2:1-6).

Talk about the greatest discovery! There are numerous chambers and vaults filled with the holy words that lie buried in the Scriptures. They lie there quietly, difficult to find, and difficult to spot when you go over them too hastily. But they are there, just waiting to be discovered. God's Word is like an infinitely deep mine that stands ready to reveal its treasures. Are you willing to delve?

Word incarnate, may the Holy Spirit show me the riches of your Word, day by day so that I may discover the treasures therein and use them to your glorification.

The Bible lives, it speaks to me; it has feet, it runs after me; it has hands, it takes possession of me.
MARTIN LUTHER

ALL PEOPLE ARE PRECIOUS TO GOD

Your love has given me great joy and encouragement, because you, brother, have refreshed the hearts of the saints (Phil: 7).

Are you doing everything in your power to gain acceptance and self-respect? Do you do it uninterruptedly like a Namaqualand donkey that walks round and round the bucket pump to supply others with water fresh as a daisy, while you yourself get very little of it?

Then believe this: You have immeasurable worth. You are accepted exactly as you are. Maybe not by all people, but definitely by God himself. When people reject you – as Paul tells about the slave Onesimus – because you do not fit in with their clique, remember: You are not alone. The same happened to Jesus Christ, but he never went around with his head drooping. How did he manage to keep his head high – always? He knew that feelings were not what counted, but what you know. And Jesus knew that God accepted him and loved him very much.

FOOD FROM THE WORD OF GOD
Philemon verses 1-25; Genesis 41:39-40, 42-45; 45:4-5, 9-12, 14-17.

God is your Creator. He is intensely interested in your well-being and cares deeply about you. Moreover, he loves you dearly. *For God so loved the world that he gave his one and only Son, that whoever believes in him shall not perish but have eternal life* (Jn 3:16). Where "the world" is written, you can freely fill in your own name, for you are an important part of God's world. You can *know* that God loves you. Therefore, you can accept yourself as a new person who lives in and through him, just as the Father accepts you and lives in you through his Spirit.

Loving Creator, thank you that there is no need for me to doubt myself, or to struggle to improve my self-image before you, because I am your child who lives from your love.

What other people think of me is becoming less and less important to me.
What they think about Jesus because of my behaviour is of paramount importance. – CLIFF RICHARD

May 7

GOD HIMSELF WILL JUDGE HIS CHILDREN

For we know him who said, "It is mine to avenge; I will repay," and again, "The Lord will judge his people" (Heb 10:30).

Without order in the universe, there could have been no science. A great deal of the genial knowledge of the space programmes is due to the discovery of the most accurate knowledge of this order. Ignoring this order would lead to disastrous consequences. Thousands of hours of work, the most sophisticated technology and the latest developments in space science are all useless and hopeless without an ordered universe to rely on and trust in.

FOOD FROM THE WORD OF GOD
Hebrews 10:11-39; Isaiah 66:14-16; Amos 5:4-7, 14-15.

God, who determined and created the order, also established spiritual and moral order. A life lived in accordance with this order guarantees fulfilment. Disobedience paves the way to disaster. You can reject God's absolutes, but never get rid of them. The law of sin and death is just as indisputable as the law of gravitation. Morality is not arbitrary, but part of the natural laws of the universe. God's law remains, whether we like it or not.

We ignore this fact at our peril. To ignore God's scientific laws is destructive. But to disobey his moral laws, has eternal consequences for us. When we pay no attention to God's moral laws, we diverge from the social order. If we refuse to turn to God for mercy, we willingly subject ourselves to his unchanging righteousness and judgement, because God cannot be untrue to himself.

Gracious God, give me the courage to live the way you expect of me.

God delays the decline and destruction of the universe for the sake of the Christian seed, which he knows is the reason in nature for the preservation of the universe. – JUSTIN MARTYN

8 May

LIVE IN PEACE

He must turn from evil and do good; he must seek peace and pursue it (1 Pet 3:11).

When you open your life to the presence of the risen Christ, he enters your life with the quiet footstep of peace, in the same way that he repeatedly came to his helpless and bewildered disciples, praying for them, *Peace be with you!* (Jn 20:21).

Christ enters our lives in peace in order to invoke a new love. His own life, which was characterised by peace, is born *within* us. When he penetrates your experiences; when he enters your personality; when he becomes sovereign of your spirit, you become a person of peace. That is when you start to understand what living in peace with God, with yourself, and with your neighbours means. Increasingly you hand over control of your life to him, and your character, behaviour and conversations radically change. Peace, goodwill, joy, serenity and composure replace hostility, bitterness, jealousy, ill temper, strife and unhealthy rivalry.

FOOD FROM THE WORD OF GOD
1 Peter 2:18-3:12; Genesis 26:26-31; 1 Samuel 24:8-12; Zechariah 8:13, 16-19.

God's peace brings about healing. It dresses wounds, pours out the oil of comfort, creates quiet and peacefulness, makes the turbulent soul calm down, and calms the anxious spirit. This peace only comes from Christ Jesus: *Peace I leave with you; my peace I give you. I do not give to you as the world gives. Do not let your hearts be troubled and do not be afraid* (Jn 14:27). The peace of Christ is one of the irrefutable signs that God is present in your life.

God of peace, give me an ever expanding and improving understanding of your peace, and may it beneficially affect every aspect of my life.

The foundation of peace is God and the secret of peace is trust in God.
JB FIGGIS

ADD KNOWLEDGE TO YOUR FAITH

For this very reason, make every effort to add to your faith goodness; and to goodness, knowledge (2 Pet 1:5).

Each of us has been called to be spiritually self-sufficient. We cannot only rely on ministers and other Christians to keep our faith going. Therefore, we must devote ourselves to increasing our faith, knowledge, self-control, perseverance and love.

Some Christians start off the week geared for action, but by Saturday they are exhausted. They barely manage to drag themselves to church on Sunday to be equipped for the new week ahead. In 1 Corinthians 3:2, Paul talks about nourishment from the milk of God's Word. Babies need someone to feed them milk, and in the same way new Christians need someone to help them understand biblical truths. But believers who are mature in faith must also be able to feed themselves with the Word of God.

FOOD FROM THE WORD OF GOD
2 Peter 1:1-21; 2 Chronicles 1:7-12; Proverbs 1:1-7; 2:3-6; 8:9-10.

Unfortunately, many Christians do not do everything in their power to enrich their faith. Prayer and Bible study are of the utmost importance for growing in faith and knowledge. God reveals himself to us in the Bible, and through prayer we have direct access to him. When Bible study and prayer become permanent features of our spiritual lives, we reap the benefits of a mature and stable relationship with God.

God desires that we should grow to maturity in faith, that we should feed ourselves spiritually, and develop the ability to stand firm in the face of adversity. We will only be able to achieve this when our faith is supplemented by knowledge from his Word.

Holy Spirit of God, strengthen my faith and knowledge so that I may reach spiritual maturity through Christ.

Spiritual maturity is not achieved through erudition, but by conforming to the well-known will of God. – DW LAMBERT

GOD'S CHILDREN LOVE ONE ANOTHER

Dear friends, since God so loved us, we also ought to love one another (1 Jn 4:11).

Being a Christian entails much more than accepting certain dogmas and having a particular lifestyle. Being a Christian means that God is a living reality in your life. A Christian is someone of whom Christ has taken possession so completely, that feelings, thoughts and attitudes are radically altered.

For a Christian, love becomes a necessity, because God is love, and the Christian knows: *Whoever does not love does not know God, because God is love* (1 Jn 4:8). God wants to dwell in you and influence you. But above all, his desire is to reach other people through you. He expects you to be a channel for his love.

FOOD FROM THE WORD OF GOD
1 John 3:11-4:21; 2 Samuel 9:3-11; Esther 2:7; Zechariah 7:9-10.

When you earnestly plead in prayer for God to become a reality in your life, when you in obedience live according to his will in all matters, he will enter your life and influence and reform your whole way of life. The most important principle is to treat other people the way Jesus would have treated them. With excitement you will discover that being a Christian essentially means treating other people with love – as Christ himself would have treated them. Then you will dedicate yourself to it with all your heart and your whole life.

If you sincerely want to become a more loving person, surrender yourself unconditionally and completely to Christ. He has always made sinful people more loving.

Lord Jesus, I could never fathom your love, but I so much want to love as you love. I will strive every day to lead people to you through love.

Love heals people: those who give it, as well as those who receive it.
CARL MENNINGER

May 11

THE PRICE OF DISCIPLESHIP

And anyone who does not carry his cross and follow me cannot be my disciple (Lk 14:27).

Shadrach, Meshach and Abednego (Dan 3) were prepared to pay the highest price in order to be God's followers. What is the price that you must pay to follow God? Are you prepared to pay that price?

Christ repeatedly said that we must deny ourselves, take up our cross, and follow him. By that he meant that it is not easy to be his faithful servants in this world. The apostle Paul also warns: *Everyone who wants to live a godly life in Christ Jesus will be persecuted* (2 Tim 3:12).

FOOD FROM THE WORD OF GOD
Luke 14:15-15:10; Daniel 3:8-12, 16-20, 26-30.

A Christian's faith does indeed sometimes bring about blood, sweat and tears. But when we accept Christ's challenge to become his disciples, he takes away our burdens: the burden of sin, of guilt, of a life far removed from God and without hope. And he says to us, *Take my yoke upon you and learn from me, for I am gentle and humble in heart, and you will find rest for your souls* (Mt 11:29). This yoke is never too heavy for us to bear, because Christ bears it with us. He promises, *My yoke is easy and my burden is light* (Mt 11:29).

Christ calls us to follow him without considering what price we might have to pay. He never promised that the road would always be easy, but in the midst of trials, temptations and even suffering, his peace, joy, and fellowship will be ours. In each of life's circumstances, he gives us inner peace that we could never experience, except in him.

Crucified Saviour, you paid on the cross for my salvation, therefore I will willingly and gratefully carry my cross. Thank you for carrying the heaviest part of my cross yourself.

When God sends you down stony paths, he will provide you with tough shoes.
CORRIE TEN BOOM

May 12

THOMAS WAS NOT ALONE

So the other disciples told him, "We have seen the Lord!" But he said to them, "Unless I see the nail marks in his hands and put my finger where the nails where, and put my hand into his side, I will not believe it" (Jn 20:25).

How tenderly God works with doubters! Just think of Gideon, Mary Magdalene and Peter. And how wonderfully they responded to the love of God! Let this be your comfort and encouragement when you are struggling against doubt.

FOOD FROM THE WORD OF GOD
John 20:11-31; Judges 6:12-22, 36-40.

Surrender yourself completely to God, without holding anything back or doubting. He will reveal himself to you and, through Jesus Christ, make you the person who is acceptable to him. Follow his paths as you come to know them through the Scriptures, as you learn about them through nature. Always do what is right in the eyes of the Lord. Walk along his paths as the Holy Spirit indicates them to you and leads you. Moreover, do not allow your faith to become fixed in your senses – in feeling and in seeing.

Do not even consider waiting for God to reveal himself to you as long as you are following a path mapped out by your own blind heart. No matter how weak you may feel, always be prepared to do his will, and he who brought about this desire within you, will enable you, through his power, to do his will. Come to him with every temptation, every thought of reluctance, inattentiveness, unbelief, disloyalty, and everything that leads you to self-condemnation. Place your powerlessness in his all-powerfulness, and find your salvation by waiting for God and believing in him.

I believe, Lord. Help me with my unbelief.
Help me to believe unconditionally, like a child.

Nobody is an unbeliever except if he wants to be; and not everybody is an unbeliever because God's mercy only conquers some and ties them inseparably to Christ. – STEPHAN CHARNOCK

CHRIST'S WITNESSES SHOULD NOT FEAR

When they saw the courage of Peter and John and realised they were unschooled, ordinary men, they were astonished and took note that these men had been with Jesus (Acts 4:13).

The people in today's two Scripture readings were God's fearless witnesses. Does your spiritual heritage encourage you also to proclaim bravely God's truths in all places? After all, Christians are the redeemed who have been saved in order to proclaim redemption to others. God's Word instructs us to tell others that they live in slavery of sin, and that it would please God to set them free from this cruel life-style.

FOOD FROM THE WORD OF GOD
Acts 4:13-37; Isaiah 43:1-7, 10-13.

Sometimes the task that we have been given is discouraging. The people to whom we go perhaps do not want us to tell them how they can be saved. Moses knew this scenario all too well (Ex 2:13-14). It could also be life-threatening. We may perhaps not lose our lives, but we could lose our popularity, our friends and even our jobs.

However, despite all of this, witnessing is a rewarding and focused task, and Christ himself is our hope for triumph. To know in moments of danger and disappointment that our instruction comes from God, spurs us on in our task. The inner excitement of knowing that God has invited us to be his fellow workers rids our work of all fear and worry. Then we are people who are busy doing God's work. He will show us what to do, and how to do it; and all the time we fall under the protection of his hand.

Lord Jesus, help me through your Holy Spirit to be your fearless witness. Thank you that in your service I have nothing to fear.

Keep a good heart! God is stronger than the devil. We are on the winning side.
JOHN CHAPMAN

GOD IS FAITHFUL TO HIS FOLLOWERS

As the time drew near for God to fulfil his promise to Abraham, the number of people in Egypt greatly increased (Acts 7:17).

Faithful God through all the ages, I want to sing a song of praise about your faithfulness. You are great in your faithfulness, from generation to generation you are faithful. Every dawn announces new grace from your loving hand.

You have provided in every pressing need, with compassion and love. You are great in your faithfulness to every one of your followers. With you, there is no shadow of unfaithfulness. You never change. We can always rely on your compassion. As you ever were, so you are now and will be for all eternity.

FOOD FROM THE WORD OF GOD
Acts 7:17-42; Psalm 105:24-45.

Nature proclaims your unchanging faithfulness to your children: summer and winter, spring and autumn, sun, moon and stars in their silent orbits join all creation as innumerable witnesses to your eternal faithfulness, your immeasurable love and your infinite mercy. Forgiveness of sins and heavenly peace that pass all understanding; your loving presence that guides us and gladdens our hearts; strength and hope for every new morning; abundant blessings: all mine.

You are great in your faithfulness, O God, from generation to generation you are faithful. Every dawn announces new grace from your loving hand. You have provided in every pressing need, with compassion and love.

You are great in your faithfulness to every one of your followers. Praise the Lord, for he is good. His love knows no end.

Faithful God, the firmament would have been too small a page, and all the oceans would not have been able to hold enough ink to testify to your faithful deeds.

Religion is the first and the last thing, and until man has found God and been found by God, he has no beginning and works towards no end. – HG WELLS

LIVE WITH A CLEAR CONSCIENCE

So I strive always to keep my conscience clear before God and man (Acts 24:16).

Serving God in faith should become a way of life. God must become such an integral part of our lives that he makes a difference in all areas of our lives.

If we believe in Christ, but he makes no difference to our values and to how we behave towards other people, at work, in our married life, on the playing field, or in our business activities; if he makes no difference whatsoever in the way we live, work, and play, then our faith is not sincere. There is no purpose in having a religion to which we confess with our mouths, but which does not become a reality in our lives.

FOOD FROM THE WORD OF GOD
Acts 23:23-24:23; Genesis 18:18-19; 1 Samuel 12:20-24; 2 Kings 18:5-6; 2 Chronicles 17:3-6; 31:20-21.

We must take God's instruction of obedience as a practical deed seriously. It is a challenge that the Scriptures put to us repeatedly. Every time that you are exposed to the Scriptures, you must ask yourself: How can I apply in my life what I have just read here? What practical steps can I take to enable this truth to take root in my attitude, character and behaviour? Where in my life can these words of God make a difference?

Undertake in earnest to change your life in accordance to God's will. After all, Jesus Christ's warning still applies to our lives, *Not everyone who says to me, "Lord, Lord," will enter the kingdom of heaven, but only he who does the will of my Father who is in heaven* (Mt 7:21).

Loving Father, I commit myself anew to being obedient to you. May this obedience characterise my life as a practical testimony.

Obedience is commanded everywhere in the Gospels. The pliability of an obedient heart ought to be the correct adjustment of our will that pervades our deeds. – CATHERINE MARSHALL

GOD'S STRENGTH IS WITHIN US

My grace is sufficient for you, for my power is made perfect in weakness (2 Cor 12:9).

Three times Paul went to God, begging him to remove the thorn in his flesh, but all God gave him was the words of today's Bible verse. However, when you study the life of Paul, you discover that he was anything but a weakling.

He confronted the apostles of Christ over the issue of whether Gentiles could also be saved – and won! He devoted his life to preaching God's Word, and often found himself caught up in the most hostile of situations. He established numerous churches, and trained the ministers, elders and deacons of the first congregations. Moreover, he single-handedly wrote almost a third of the New Testament. To me, this does not sound like the work of a weakling. He was a man of dynamic action who set Christians in motion everywhere.

FOOD FROM THE WORD OF GOD
1 Corinthians 12:1-13:14; Exodus 14:6-14; 1 Samuel 30:1-8, 17-18.

How then, do we explain Paul's admission that he is weak? The secret lies in one sentence he uttered, *For when I am weak, then I am strong* (2 Cor 12:10b). By this he meant, "When I, Paul, am weak in my own strength, I am trusting in the strength of God that is in me. His power strengthens me, enables me to do what he asks of me, filled with energy and enthusiasm to do his will."

Does that tell you something about the times when you doubt yourself, and feel weak in his glorious service?

I praise and thank you, Lord my God, for providing so wonderfully for the needs of weak people and filling them with your strength. Always keep me aware of my weakness and of your omnipotence.

Admitting our weakness is the first step towards regaining our strength.
THOMAS á KEMPIS

May 17

CHRIST SETS US FREE

It is for freedom that Christ has set us free. Stand firm, then, and do not let yourself be burdened again by a yoke of slavery (Gal 5:1).

In the Scriptures of the Old Testament that we read today, we see the difference between the children of a slave-woman and those of a free woman. This freedom comes from God alone. Freedom is the privilege of those who are obedient to him, but it also involves responsibilities.

FOOD FROM THE WORD OF GOD
Galatians 4:21-5:15; Genesis 15:1-4; 16:1-4; 21:5-14.

Jesus said, *If you hold to my teaching ... you will know the truth, and the truth will set you free* (Jn 8:32). The truth sets us free because it gives us understanding. Understanding helps us to accept the necessary conditions, limitations and discipline required of us before we can know true freedom. Accepting the truth of God's Word sets us free from the slavery of sinful habits and desires that do us damage, and from behaviour that brings shame to God. Freedom results from obedience to God. And disobedience implies the loss of freedom.

True freedom is controlled by love. Freedom to do what you want, without considering other people's feelings and the consequences for them, is destructive and leads to immorality. But Christian freedom is freedom to love and serve others.

True freedom is serving God with love. When our minds are focused on Jesus Christ and his expectations, egocentric habits are excluded from our lives. We live happy lives when we surrender to God through Jesus Christ, for his yoke is easy and his burden is light (Mt 11:30).

Lord Jesus, my heart is overflowing with thankfulness for the freedom to love and serve, a freedom that has been established for me through your sacrifice. Prevent me from abusing this freedom.

There are two kinds of freedom: false freedom, where man is free to do what he wants to do, and true freedom, where man is free to do what he ought to do. – CHARLES KINGSLEY

May 18

GOD IS MERCIFUL TO US

For it is by grace you have been saved, through faith – and this not from yourselves, it is the gift of God (Eph 2:8).

Our lives are exceptionally enriched and deeply touched by the compassion and grace of those people who take time to try to understand us; people who care enough to forgive our weaknesses and shortcomings, and who take the trouble to build a friendship with us.

These are often the very people towards whom you have shown no special friendship. Their compassion and grace towards you were totally unexpected and undeserved. Therefore, you experience twice the joy. What is more, it is a tremendous inspiration that challenges you to respond to it in a way that you never dreamt possible.

FOOD FROM THE WORD OF GOD
Ephesians 2:4-3:6; Isaiah 57:16-19; Daniel 9:17-18; Micah 7:18-19.

This is exactly what grace does to people. It makes them excited and gives them hope. It assures them that life is beautiful and worth living. It convinces them that there is sufficient reason to reach out to better things, because other people care so much about them. It affirms that, if someone has shown grace to them, they in their turn can show grace to other people.

In order to discover the true Source of inner inspiration for this kind of behaviour, we must look to the grace and compassion of God, our loving Father. Nothing else in the world will make us feel as humble. Nothing else will soften our rock hard attitudes. Nothing else will compel us so forcefully to do the right thing, and to show grace to our fellow men at all times.

Merciful and compassionate God, I bow before you in worship on account of the wonder of your mercy to me.
Enable me to be a carrier of your grace.

A state of mind that sees God in everything, is proof of the growth of his grace in a grateful heart.
CHARLES F FINNEY

May 19

JESUS CAN FORGIVE

When Jesus saw their faith, he said to the paralytic, "Son, your sins have been forgiven" (Mk 2:5).

In Isaiah 53 the prophet predicts that the Servant of the Lord *will justify many, and he will bear their iniquities* (Is 53:11). Therefore, it is not surprising that Jesus forgave so many people their sins when he was on earth. The question to you is whether *your* spirit has been healed by Christ who forgave your sins?

Forgiveness is one of the first and most splendid blessings that we receive from God's merciful hand. For us, it is the transition from the old life to a new life that is dedicated to God. It is the sign and guarantee of God's unfathomable love. Along with it, we receive all the spiritual gifts that have been prepared for us in Christ.

FOOD FROM THE WORD OF GOD
Mark 2:1-22; Isaiah 43:22-25; 53:10-12; Jeremiah 31:33-34.

Believers never dare to forget the splendid truth that they are sinners who have been forgiven. Nothing else causes our love and gratefulness to flare up and awakens our love as does the sure knowledge that we always experience God's forgiving love. It strengthens and encourages us. Each new day from the hand of God, every new thought of him reminds us that everything we are or have is due to God's forgiving mercy.

This forgiving love is one of the greatest revelations of the character of God. In it is hidden God's glory and holiness, and he wants to share it through Jesus Christ with his lost children. Praise the Lord, for he is good; his love is everlasting!

O happy day on which my soul was purified by Jesus' blood. I rejoice, while I gratefully kneel before Jesus who is my Saviour!

Nothing in this lost world carries the sign of the Son of God as surely as forgiveness.
ALICE CAREY

May 20

THE POWER OF FAITH

He said to her, "Daughter, your faith has healed you. Go in peace and be freed from your suffering" (Mk 5:34).

The Bible teaches us that Christ saves us through faith, and that we receive the Holy Spirit in our hearts through faith. It is also a faith that works through love. Love, on the other hand, is established and maintained by faith. This interaction is an absolute necessity in the life of a disciple of Jesus.

It is through faith that Christ overwhelmingly defeated the world and evil. It is through faith that we can ward off the fiery arrows of evil. It is through faith that we can clothe ourselves with Jesus, forsaking our old selves with our sinful inclinations. It is through faith that we can remain standing.

FOOD FROM THE WORD OF GOD
Mark 5:21-43; 1 Kings 18:25-46.

It is through faith that we can control the flesh and restrain our desires. It is through faith that we receive the Holy Spirit who works in us to do what is acceptable to God. He pours out his own love into our hearts, also causing our love to flare up.

Nothing but the life and energy of the Holy Spirit of Jesus Christ can save us from sin. When we open the doors of our lives to him in unconditional trust, Jesus enters and dwells in us. He lives in us and is constantly present in our lives. By pouring his love out over us, he stirs harmony with him in our hearts. In this way, and only in this way, he purifies our hearts through faith.

Saviour and Lord, your mercy never ceases to leave me speechless. Help me to share generously with others the love that you have poured out into my redeemed heart.

Faith is the beginning and the end of love and in God the two are combined in unity. After that come all the other things that make us Christians. – IGNATIUS OF ANTIOCH

May 21

THE RIGHTEOUS ARE REWARDED

"I tell you the truth," Jesus replied, "no one who has left home or brothers or sisters or mother or father or children or fields for me and the gospel will fail to receive a hundred times as much in this present age ... and in the age to come, eternal life (Mk 10:29-30).

It is as if the Lord wants to say to us in these Scriptures, "Do not allow problems and trials to get you down. Let my promises comfort and strengthen you at all times. I can reward you far beyond your wildest expectations. You will not work on this earth for long, or always be depressed by sadness. Keep a good heart, and you shall experience a joyous end to your suffering. There will come a time when labour and confusion will come to an end. Short-lived and poor is everything that goes with time. Do what you do for me with dedication; work faithfully in my vineyard (Mt 20:7). I will reward you. Write, read, sing praises, mourn, be quiet, pray and carry your cross with courage. Eternal life is worth all of these things.

FOOD FROM THE WORD OF GOD
Mark 10:17-45; Psalm 58:11-12; 73:24-26; Isaiah 51:11; 58:11, 13-14.

"Peace will come to you on the day that is known only to me, the Father. Then there will be no more daytime or night-time (Zech 14:7). You will no longer ask, *Who will rescue me from this body of death?* (Rom 7:24), or exclaim, *Woe to me that I dwell in Meshech, that I live among the tents of Kedar!* (Ps 120:5). Death will be conquered. There will be salvation, joy and glorious fellowship with me. Lift your eyes to heaven; know that your struggle will pass, that you will be rewarded for your faith and deeds. And you will live with me eternally."

Righteous God, I believe that through grace you will reward my faith far beyond what I am capable of praying or thinking. I praise your Name.

Our God is a God of promise. He keeps his word, even when it seems impossible; even when circumstances want to predict the reverse. – COLIN URQUHART

May 22

PRAY WITH CONVICTION

Therefore I tell you, whatever you ask for in prayer, believe that you have received it, and it will be yours (Mk 11:24).

When the children of Israel were on the brink of entering the promised land, they sent out twelve scouts to spy out the land. Ten of them returned with disturbing news: the cities are huge, the leaders invincible and the people gigantic. Two returned and said, *The Lord has surely given the whole land into our hands; all the people are melting in fear because of us* (Josh 2:24). Ten were blinded by the mountain and became afraid; only two looked to the all-sufficiency of the Mover of mountains, and took courage.

FOOD FROM THE WORD OF GOD
Mark 11:15-12:12; Joshua 10:12-14; Psalm 145:18-19; Jonah 2:7-9.

Every person stands at some time in the shadow of a mountain that seems unconquerable: a detrimental habit; an unhappy marriage; an intolerable situation at work; financial difficulties; physical disabilities. What is your immovable mountain? Have you been standing in its shadow for so long that you have grown accustomed to the darkness of despair? Do you close your prayer time before God with the question, "Is it worth it?"

Today I challenge you to shift the focus of your prayers from the mountain to the One who can move mountains. God knows what your mountain is, so there is no need for you to waste time by describing it to him at length. Rather focus your attention on the Mover of mountains, on his splendour, omnipotence and faithfulness. Walk with him in faith and follow his lead. Your faith will grow, your confidence will increase, and your prayer life will develop dynamic new strength. And you will notice how the mountain moves aside.

Hearer of my prayers, help me in your omnipotence when I stand in my mountain's shadow, and help me to focus on you, and to obey and follow you faithfully.

The purpose of all prayer is to discover God's will and then to make his will our prayer
CATHERINE MARSHALL

BE STRONG IN THE LAST DAYS

Therefore keep watch because you do not know when the owner of the house will come back ... (Mk 13:35).

God's people must be watchful and loyal in the last days. The suffering of these times purifies us for the second coming. But we can be sure that God will save us in these times, and that we will be safe and well. However, God expects us to do certain things in the last days:

We must place our hope in Christ, and build on nothing less than the blood of the living Christ and his righteousness. We dare not trust in anything else for our preservation. Our watchword must be the Name of the Lamb. We must stand on the Rock that is Jesus Christ. Everything else is just quicksand in which we will soon sink away.

FOOD FROM THE WORD OF GOD
Mark 13:11-37; Psalm 11:1-7; Daniel 9:26-27; 11:33-35.

When darkness hides the face of God from us, we must find peace in his unchangeable mercy and his reliable promises. At the centre of every storm and hurricane we must hold on to Jesus Christ, our anchor in trials. He is the eternal Rock who was cleft for us and who will keep our anchors firm.

His oath, his covenant and his blood must be our support and lifeline during the overwhelming flood that is coming. When everything around us comes tumbling down, he is our only hope and salvation. When he comes again with a blare of trumpets, we must be found righteous by him, shrouded in his righteousness, purified by his blood and set free by his mercy. Then we have nothing to fear from the final days. Praise the Lord, for he is good!

Saviour and Master, grant that I may be ready for your second coming; my lamp burning and filled with oil, so that I may enter into the splendour of my Lord.

We are not a post-war generation; we are a pre-peace generation. Jesus is coming again!
CORRIE TEN BOOM

INNOCENT BEFORE GOD

For in the day of trouble he will keep me safe in his dwelling; he will hide me in his tabernacle and set me high upon a rock (Ps 27:5).

Jesus stood in innocence before God, so it was not necessary for him to prove his innocence to his prosecutors. Here we find the secret of spiritual strength that willingly endures injustice, that accepts that everything that happens to you in life is the will of God, regardless of whether a great injustice is committed against you, or an insignificant insult is hurled at you. Before you condemn the person who commits the injustice against you, be quiet and remember that God may use this situation to see whether you will also glorify him under these circumstances. Trials are a part of God's holy will for your life. Submit yourself to his will. Together with the peace that God will grant you, you will receive the wisdom to know how to act in every situation. God has saved you, so you too need not prove your innocence.

FOOD FROM THE WORD OF GOD
Psalms 27:1-6; 26:1-6;
Deuteronomy 19:1-14;
Mark 14:53-15:5

Jesus looked beyond the injustice that was done to him. He was willing to entrust his honour to God's hand, knowing that it would be safe with him. *When they hurled their insults at him, he did not retaliate; when he suffered, he made no threats. Instead he entrusted himself to him who judges justly* (1 Pet 2:23). In the first place it revolves around God's honour. The Father would see to the honour of the Son. Let us follow Christ's example; we shall experience rest and peace. God will watch over us, and see that justice is done to us.

Just Judge, thank you that we are dealing with your omniscient righteousness and mercy, and not with the ignorant mercilessness of humans.

Innocence comes into contact with evil without knowing it; it astounds temptation and is protected where nobody else is protected. – BASIL W MATURIN

GOD USES MESSENGERS

In the sixth month, God sent the angel Gabriel to Nazareth, a town in Galilee (Lk 1:26).

All over the world there are stories of angels appearing to people, serving them, talking to them and then disappearing. They warn people against God's coming judgement, tell of the tenderness of his love, provide in a desperate need and then they disappear. In all of these stories, one thing is clear: The angels never draw attention to themselves, but give all the honour to God. They imprint his message on people's hearts as words that set free, that save and support.

FOOD FROM THE WORD OF GOD
Luke 1:5-45; Judges 13:2-14, 24; Malachi 4:5-6.

Demonic activities and devil worship is on the increase worldwide. The devil is alive and more active at present than at any other time in human history. The Bible teaches us that his activities will become more rigorous because he knows that his time is limited. Through his demonic influence, he succeeds in leading many people away from faith in Jesus Christ. But we can say with certainty that the activities of the devil are neutralised for the children of God by the service of his holy angels. They are keen to set God's inheritors, his saved ones, free from evil.

As believers we must look up to God and take courage. The angels of God are closer to us than we think. God's Word assures us, *For he will command his angels concerning you to guard you in all your ways; they will lift you up in their hands, so that you will not strike your foot against a stone* (Ps 91:11-12).

Almighty God, I pay attention to the messages that you send to me through your angels. Help me, through the work of your Holy Spirit, to understand them correctly and to obey them.

An angel is a spiritual being created without a body by God, for service to Christendom and the church.
MARTIN LUTHER

DO TO OTHERS AS GOD DOES TO YOU

Do to others as you would have them do to you (Lk 6:31).

Mercy means caring for people in need, ministering to the wretched, helping those who hurt, identifying with the suffering of others. Commiseration means putting yourself in someone else's shoes, seeing with his or her eyes, touching with his or her hands and feeling the pain of his or her heart. Stop watching these people from a safe distance. Get in touch with them, get involved with them in their need and offer help that can relieve the pain.

FOOD FROM THE WORD OF GOD
Luke 6:24-45; 2 Samuel 7:8-13, 16-22; Psalm 86:15; Jonah 4:1-2.

There are so many opportunities to get involved with the homeless, with hungry street children or aids orphans, to assist the lonely, the needy elderly; to tell prisoners of the final liberation, to spend time with terminal patients in hospitals, to aid cancer associations in their immense task. Show God's mercy to these people. Identify with their sorrow and their needs. Care and get involved. Offer more than pious words. Give of yourself.

What do compassionate people receive in return for caring? The great compassionate One promises, *Blessed are the merciful, for they will be shown mercy* (Mt 5:7). God rewards our mercy with his mercy. This is exactly what Jesus our Saviour did for us when he came to earth. When he was incarnated he put himself in our shoes and could see the world through our eyes, feel our pain and identify with people in need. He understands. Do you?

Compassionate Lord Jesus, you are my holy example. Constantly reveal your immense mercy to me, and give me, through your Holy Spirit, the desire to show other people mercy.

Lord teach me to experience the needs of others first-hand, and to conceal the mistakes I see. May I show mercy to others as you show mercy to me. – ALEXANDER POPE

May 27

SHOW TRUE REGRET FOR YOUR SINS

Therefore, I tell you, her many sins have been forgiven – for she loved much. But he who has been forgiven little, love little (Lk 7:47).

Isaiah knew from his own experience that one must first be broken of countenance before God before one can rejoice, *Here am I. Send me!* (Is 6:8). Only after he had seen his ugly sins in the white light of God's holiness, could he say, *I am ruined! For I am a man of unclean lips, and I live among a people of unclean lips* (Is 6:5). Isaiah lay broken before God. But God does not break for the sake of breaking. He breaks in order to build up again, *See, this (live coal) has touched your lips; your guilt is taken away and your sin atoned for* (Is 6:7).

FOOD FROM THE WORD OF GOD
Luke 7:36-50; Job 11:4-6, 13-20; Proverbs 26:12; Isaiah 5:20-24; 6:1-8.

We cannot be satisfied with our "goodness" once we have seen the holiness of God. However, our repentance lasts only for a short while, because God himself said, *I, even I, am he who blots out your transgressions, for my own sake, and remembers your sins no more* (Is 43:25). With God you first have to descend into the valley of repentance before you can ascend the mountain peaks of spiritual joy. You must first grow tired of living without Christ before you can look for and find his salvation. You must first reach your end before you can start living in Christ. Blessed are those who grieve over their own unworthiness, helplessness and stupidity, for they will receive God's joyfulness in abundance.

Merciful God and Father, I confess my sins and transgressions anew, so that you can take the burden from me, and allow me to taste my pardon and freedom.

Not to sin anymore is the purest form of repentance.
MARTIN LUTHER

May 28

GOD IS IN TOTAL CONTROL

Taking the five loaves and the two fish and looking up to heaven, he gave thanks and broke them. Then he gave them to the disciples to set before the people. They all ate and were satisfied (Lk 9:16-17a).

God is in total control of his entire creation, not only of planet Earth. There is nothing that falls outside of his control.

My study looks out over beautiful False Bay with its ever-changing appearance. Sunlight and shadows on the water, clouds and clear blue sky make the view change every now and then. Sometimes the rocks of the Hottentots Holland Mountains at Gordon's Bay and the peaks at Cape Point look tender in the light of the morning sun. They glow warmly, embraced by sunshine and tranquillity. Sometimes the sea roars and foams under a bleak sky. The mountains stand ominous in the grey mist. Waves wash high against the sandbars.

FOOD FROM THE WORD OF GOD
Luke 8:49-9:17; Deuteronomy 32:39; 2 Chronicles 4:42-44; Job 12:7-10; Psalm 90:1-6.

In summer and in winter, autumn and spring, the tides ebb and flow and the character of the beach changes. The forces of nature are unremitting, their power immeasurable. In the violence of the storm they are untameable. With amazing precision they move millions of tons of water from place to place. They reflect the gigantic energy of the cosmos that knows no rest, and that never comes to a halt.

In the same overshadowing way the Creator God watches over his children, ensuring that his divine purpose for us materialises. Always and everywhere, he is in total control. *Indeed, he who watches over Israel will neither slumber nor sleep* (Ps 121:4).

Almighty God, I praise and worship you for your sovereignty over creation, because my insignificant life is an important part of your creation.

Change and decay surrounds me. O God who never changes, abide with me.
HENRY FRANCIS LYTE

CHRIST IS COMING AGAIN

Be dressed ready for service and keep your lamps burning, like men waiting for their master to return from a wedding banquet, so that when he comes and knocks they can immediately open the door for him (Lk 12:35-36).

The last promise that the risen Saviour made to his disciples was that he would soon come again. Link this to Paul's admonition to the Thessalonians, and you have a safe rule to live by. Live expectantly and patiently, then you will carry out the will of the Lord until he comes again (1 Thess 5:23; 2 Thess 1:11-12).

FOOD FROM THE WORD OF GOD
Luke 12:35-48; Psalm 24:1-6; Isaiah 26:7-12.

What are those blessings that await believers when Christ comes again? The most important is: We can confidently expect to be rewarded for our faith. There are clear promises in God's Word that assure us that obedient disciples will be rewarded.

When we await Christ's coming with excitement, we will be enfolded by the love of God. Our patience will be rewarded with love, and this love will be at work in our own lives. When the love of God flows through us, we become a channel that brings his love to the people around us. God is love and this love is greater than us. So what flows from God, must flow through us to others. People around us yearn for love because our world is saturated with hate, Satan's legacy since the tragic events in paradise. Let us then, as Christians, spread God's love in a loveless world, while we await the glorious coming of his Son.

Lord Jesus, my heart rejoices for you are coming again. May I be ready to receive you in love and in worship.

Christ has kept the day of his coming a secret from us, so that we can wait anxiously for it, almost like people who are keeping watch. – MARTIN LUTHER

30 *May*

JERUSALEM HONOURS JESUS AS KING

Hosanna to the Son of David! Blessed is he who comes in the name of the Lord! Hosanna in the highest! (Mt 21:9).

In your imagination you can hear the jubilation of the crowd as Jesus slowly enters Jerusalem. From the dusty roads of the earth, where the mouths of children sing his praises, to the throne of God in heaven where hosannas of angels continuously rise, there is one all-encompassing shout of joy, *See, your king comes to you ...* (Mt 21:5b).

Not only on this day, but also all through the ages, Christ triumphantly reigns in the hearts of those who have accepted salvation from his hand. The Pharisees would barely have been able to believe how prophetic their words were when they said that the whole world would follow him. And why would we not follow Jesus? For he leads us to victory. Together with Paul we rejoice, *But thanks be to God, who always leads us in triumphal procession in Christ and through us spreads everywhere the fragrance of the knowledge of him* (2 Cor 2:14).

FOOD FROM THE WORD OF GOD
Matthew 20:20-21:11; Psalm 95:1-3; 118:24-27; Isaiah 62:10-12.

Just as we begin to think that we have more problems than we can handle, Christ reaches out to us and lifts us up so that we may sit on the donkey with him as we enter Jerusalem. Just when we think that nobody cares, that there is no reward for righteousness, Jesus smiles and whispers, "My Father will honour those who honour me." All our pain, our anxiety and our problems will not disappear instantly, but through our faith we will be the children of the triumphant King.

I bow in grateful worship before you, O King of creation, and praise and worship you that I may be a child of the triumphant King.

If God is for us, who can be against us? You can fight with confidence if you are sure of victory. With Christ, and for Christ, victory is certain. – St BERNARD of CLAIRVAUX

THE MOST IMPORTANT COMMANDMENT

Jesus replied, "Love the Lord your God with all your heart and with all your soul and with all your mind. This is the first and greatest commandment" (Mt 22:37-38).

By obeying God, you demonstrate that you love the Lord with your heart, your soul and your mind. You may try to associate yourself with other gods: the god of learning, of success of wealth, of diligence and of labour. You may give yourself over to good deeds. You may try to make a god out of another person. Indeed, you may even give the church most of your time and energy. You can carry any yoke ... But only the easy yoke of Jesus gives you true freedom.

Bow anew under his yoke every day. As the presence of God increasingly dominates the various facets of your life, you will understand more and more clearly that anything or anybody else to whom you turn to bring meaning, purpose and strength to your life, will eventually disappoint and destroy you. Only God can truly give meaning to your life.

God knew that we would never be complete if we did not worship him, the God of love. You may try to fill your life with other people, with enjoyment, with work or the accumulation of wealth, but all this can only satisfy you to a certain extent. That which is empty, cannot satisfy your needs. We must learn to turn away from the empty wells of fame and fortune, success and power, achievement and our own merits, to come to the Fountain from which living waters flow.

FOOD FROM THE WORD OF GOD
Matthew 22:15-40; Deuteronomy 6:4-9; 7:9-11; Joshua 22:2-5; Psalm 31:24; Proverbs 8:17; Jeremiah 7:21-23.

Holy God, because I love you unconditionally, you satisfy my soul with good. May I daily live and work in your love.

Give me such love for God and my fellowmen, that it will erase all hate and bitterness.
DIETRICH BONHOEFFER

June

Prayer for June

1. On marriage and divorce
2. Flee from evil
3. Babylon will be punished
4. It is important to live a pure life
5. God will purify your faith
6. Set your hopes on Christ's coming
7. Called as God's witness
8. God's Spirit brings about understanding
9. Always seek God's guidance
10. The Holy Spirit hands out talents
11. God's chosen people also suffer
12. One finds joy in serving God
13. The value of encouragement
14. God's children are his property
15. God welcomes repentant sinners
16. God forgives and saves
17. The greatness of God's forgiveness
18. Unbelief will be punished
19. Give God what is due to him
20. Envy has no place with God
21. Be generous
22. God blesses those who believe
23. We reap what we sow
24. Guard against greed
25. There is only one God who saves
26. Avoid evil
27. Faith pleases God
28. God will care for you
29. God condemns false teachers
30. Walk in the light

Prayer for June

Almighty God,
we worship you as Creator and Maintainer of your creation.
As long as the earth endures, seedtime and harvest, cold and heat, summer and winter, day and night will never cease (Gen 8:22).
We are amazed by the rhythm and balance of the seasons;
that you predestined them to bless the earth in this way.
Winter has its own unique enchantment:
rain and cold, frost and snow;
bare oaks in their naked beauty.
Winter is a time of rest for nature: a slumbering wait for
a new awakening of scintillating life.
In this winter season, bring rest to my turbulent heart, O Lord!
Winter, too, has its pressing worries:
people who are homeless and starving,
people who are cold and lonely.
Teach me through your Holy Spirit the true meaning of compassion.
During winter, we will have a lot of time to read,
especially in your eternal Word;
to reflect and to meditate;
to prayerfully talk to you and listen to you.
There are so many people we want to commit to your mercy:
the elderly, the sick, the unemployed and the grieving.
Funerals in the winter rain are so much sadder –
give comfort, compassionate God!
Winter is to many a time to take leave, to get away and for family.
Thank you for the excitement of holiday trips
when we are renewed in body and spirit,
so that we can love and serve you better.
We pray this in the Name of Jesus, our risen Saviour,
who creates new life from death.

Amen

ON MARRIAGE AND DIVORCE

Is it lawful for a man to divorce his wife for any and every reason? ... Therefore what God has joined together, let man not separate (Mt 21:3b, 6b).

God instituted marriage to create a new union between two people. In Malachi 2:5 we find a specific point of view of God's purpose with marriage. It is a vital spiritual goal, and being aware of it determines our perception of marriage.

Jesus does not idealise marriage. He does not say that each and every marriage is created in heaven. What he does say is that marriage itself was created in heaven, that it was instituted by God. In answer to the question of whether it is lawful for a man to divorce his wife, Jesus' answer is indeed: No. God decrees that two people become one in marriage, and that man has received no authority to reverse or adjust this decree. Is it wise then to accept Jesus' statements on this matter and to assign legal authority to them? Perhaps not. The problem is that if his words are assigned legal authority, exemption clauses would have to be created for certain cases. Prolonged debates would be conducted on the different situations that should be included or excluded.

FOOD FROM THE WORD OF GOD
Matthew 19:1-16; Genesis 2:18-24; Malachi 2:13-16.

It is probably best to uphold Jesus' statement without compromise, taking it as an ideal for which one should strive. Legislation has to make provision for the hardness of people's hearts, but Jesus shows a way that is superior to our legislation and provides us with the ability to change man's heart and of turning this ideal into a practical reality.

God of love and mercy, may your holy purpose for my marriage be fulfilled through Jesus Christ who lives in me.

A successful marriage is always a triangle: a man, a woman, and God.
CECIL MYERS

June 2

FLEE FROM EVIL

Then I heard another voice from heaven say: "Come out of her, my people, so that you will not share in her sins, so that you will not receive any of her plagues ..." (Rev 18:4).

As God's people, we must do everything in our power to separate ourselves from the sinful world. Through our unity with the living Christ, we have in fact been set free of the domination of sin, but every day we discover that sin is at war to regain supremacy over our lives. Maybe we do not like having to fight this life-long battle against sin, but the sooner we accept it, the better we will be equipped to handle it.

FOOD FROM THE WORD OF GOD
Revelation 17:6-18:10; Genesis 19:12-15; Jeremiah 51:6, 45-47, 49-50.

The Bible says, *The heart is deceitful above all things and beyond cure. Who can understand it? I the Lord search the heart and examine the mind, to reward a man according to his conduct, according to what his deeds deserve* (Jer 17:9-10). Even we as believers do not know the secrets of our own hearts (1 Cor 4:3-5). Knowing that sin occupies our hearts and that our hearts are deceitful and unreliable should make us extremely cautious.

Although sin no longer rules over us, it is still engaged in battle with us. If we are not careful, sin will defeat us. Our only hope for victory in this battle is to act swiftly and firmly against the first indications of sin in our lives. On this earth, our struggle against sin will never end. Jesus rightly remarked, *Watch and pray so that you will not fall into temptation. The spirit is willing, but the body is weak* (Mt 26:41).

Lord of my heart and life, keep me watchful and prayerful, so that I will not be overwhelmed by sin, but will flee from it before it is too late.

Sin is not painful because it is forbidden; it is forbidden because it is painful.
BENJAMIN FRANKLIN

BABYLON WILL BE PUNISHED

Woe! Woe, O great city, dressed in fine linen, purple and scarlet, and glittering with gold, precious stones and pearls! In one hour such great wealth has been brought to ruin! (Rev 18:16-17a).

In spite of what many people think, there *will* be a day of reckoning. God's wrath will be revealed, especially towards the false religions through which millions were tortured and murdered. God's judgement will be executed unwaveringly, and his people will be acquitted.

Babylon is the symbol of sin and false religion and is diametrically opposed to Jerusalem, the city of God on earth. The destruction of Babylon symbolises the victory of God over Satan too, of good over evil, and of true religion over false doctrines.

FOOD FROM THE WORD OF GOD
Revelation 18:11-24; Jeremiah 51:25-26, 36-44.

The woman in our scripture reading is Babylon, and she comes to a terrible fall. The cup of her fury, prepared for the children of God, is poured in full strength into the cup of God's wrath (Rev 14:10). As many believers in our day and age, this woman is convinced that she will never experience the sorrow or suffering that is retaliation for her extravagant lifestyle. She boasts that the kings of the earth are her lovers, but actually, she is lonely because God has deserted her.

Self-glorification and a promiscuous life-style are this woman's character traits. For this she will receive torture and sorrow, along with all who follow her. The yearning for achievement and the accumulation of wealth are still dominant factors in people's lives. The fools of our world are to be found in every business – but the day of reckoning is coming. Then God himself will destroy Babylon and her followers.

Righteous God, grant that I may be ready when you come to judge the world. May I be found true to you through Jesus Christ and the Holy Spirit.

If we judge ourselves in time, we will not be judged by God.
JEAN PIERRE CAMUS

June 4

IT IS IMPORTANT TO LIVE A PURE LIFE

Therefore come out from them and be separate, says the Lord. Touch no unclean thing, and I will receive you. I will be a Father to you, and you will be my sons and daughters, says the Lord Almighty (2 Cor 6:17-18).

A conviction is not really a conviction if it does not include a resolve to live according to what you say you believe. A resolve is not an oath, but a firm decision to live by the Word of God, as he would like to see it in your life.

FOOD FROM THE WORD OF GOD
2 Corinthians 6:3-7:7; Deuteronomy 7:1-4; Psalm 18:21-26; 119:1-3, 9-11; Proverbs 4:14-15.

The most important resolve we can make is to strive for sanctification – in every sphere of our lives. It is so important to God that it must take priority in our daily lives. We must commit ourselves to obeying all of God's commandments. We cannot select according to our own terms and conditions. Large and small sins do not exist. To God, sin is sin, whether it is dishonesty or murder. *All* sin is reprehensible in his eyes. In determining sin, we do not look only at its effect on people around us, but also at whether it is an insult to the holiness of our God. Sin is a serious matter to God, and it becomes serious for us, too, when we realise that all sin is an expression of our disrespect for the authority of God.

The psalmist acknowledges this when he says, *You have laid down precepts that are to be fully obeyed* (Ps 119:4). If we are only partially obedient to God, we are disobedient. Therefore, we must obey God's instructions to the full.

I yearn for purity and sanctification, Lord my God. Help me through your Holy Spirit to have the conviction that this can be realised in my life.

Next to the omnipotence and holiness of God, the serene beauty of a holy life has the strongest influence on this world. – BLAISE PASCAL

June 5

GOD WILL PURIFY YOUR FAITH

But just as he who called you is holy, so be holy in all you do (1 Pet 1:15).

Trials bring you closer to the heart of God. Yes, sorrow can sometimes bring us closer to God than joy. But before sorrow can serve any purpose, we have to bear it triumphantly and with hope, as Jesus Christ did. Only then will sorrow not overwhelm us, but through it we will be strengthened, ennobled, purified and matured to the glory of God.

Through fire, through blows by the anvil, through the hammer that shatters hard rock, God makes you who you are. You were gold in the rock, and God was the Miner who wrenched you free from it. Then you were pulverised and melted so that God could see his face reflected in you. Now you are pure gold, freed from the rock by God's mercy for you. When you look back through the years at the sorrowful experiences on your path of life, and see what they have meant to you; when you think back to what you were and what you are now, you say with a grateful heart: I will not give up what I have learnt through God's process of purification for anything in the world.

FOOD FROM THE WORD OF GOD
1 Peter 1:1-21; Deuteronomy 8:2-3, 5; Job 23:10-12; Isaiah 48:1-2, 8, 10; Zechariah 13:9.

When God comes to you, shining in his sanctity and majesty, you will be able to recognise him and confess gratefully, "I know you as my God. I will not flee from you. I will trust you unconditionally. I took my bitter medicine and have been healed. My sorrow purified me and made me strong. "

Lord God Almighty, thank you that I could go through your process of purification, and that through Jesus Christ and your mercy I could emerge on the other side as a purified disciple.

Pureness means that we, as far as is humanly possible, will reflect the likeness of God.
JOHN CLIMACUS

June 6

SET YOUR HOPES ON CHRIST'S COMING

While we wait for the blessed hope – the glorious appearing of our great God and Saviour, Jesus Christ (Tit 2:13).

When last did you ponder on the words of today's reading? Perhaps most of us have to admit, "Much too long ago!" Many people are inclined to store away these thoughts for times when their lives are touched by death, for example at funerals. But the Bible overflows with promises and encouragement that are relevant to the second coming of our Saviour Jesus Christ.

FOOD FROM THE WORD OF GOD
Titus 2:1-15; Isaiah 40:1-10; Luke 3:1-22.

Critics deny it and cynics laugh about it. Students of the Scriptures ignore it, even though it is mentioned in the Bible 318 times. Liberal theologians try to reason it away with the excuse that they have "rethought" it. Fanatics twist and abuse it. The second coming of Christ will continually be attacked, abused and denied. But it is written, solid as a rock. These words *will* be fulfilled. In the meantime, they give believers hope and comfort in a world of despair and unbelief.

What is expected of us as his disciples, in the interim? Perhaps we should first understand what we must not do. We do not sit around idly waiting for the flourish of trumpets. We do not continually stare up at the heavens in anticipation of his second coming. No, we live! But we live as if every day is our last, and we live it to his honour and glory. We ardently perform our daily tasks at work or at home for his Name's sake. We become the light of the world and the salt of the earth. We remain balanced, cheerful, friendly and stable. And we expect our Saviour and Lord every minute of every day.

Holy Spirit of God, help me to expect, every moment and with excitement, the second coming of my Lord and Master, and to live every day in accordance with his will.

There are three clear comings of the Lord that I know of: it is his coming TO people, his coming IN people, and his coming AGAINST people on the day of reckoning. – St BERNARD of CLAIRVAUX

CALLED AS GOD'S WITNESS

Now get up and stand on your feet. I have appeared to you to appoint you as a servant and as a witness of what you have seen of me and what I will show you (Acts 26:16).

The very best instruments of evangelisation are believers who witness courageously to their faith in Jesus Christ, and who express it in their everyday lives. Perhaps you were once invited by a church member to join them. Perhaps other members received you in friendship, and in this way you chose the Lord. People are often led into a personal relationship with Jesus because there were members of his church who cared enough to guide them lovingly into the kingdom of God.

FOOD FROM THE WORD OF GOD
Acts 26:9-31; Exodus 15:11-14; Deuteronomy 4:5-8; 2 Samuel 7:18-29.

Our life-styles as Christians should bear witness to our message. If we had to be spiritually perfect *before* we could witness for Christ, not one of us would ever qualify. According to Paul, we must share the gospel with others while we are still changing into true Christians and witnesses for our Master. He wanted all believers to realise that if we had to wait to be the people God wants us to be *before* we started witnessing, the task of the gospel would never be completed.

As imperfect people who are inheritors of God's mercy, we are called upon to invite other people to follow Christ with us, to follow in his triumphal procession through the ages, to become increasingly like Christ, and to be his fearless witnesses in the intervening time.

Lord Jesus, inspire me through your Holy Spirit to be your enthusiastic witness every day.

Our task as laypeople is to express our personal fellowship with Christ so intensely that it will be infectious.
PAUL TOURNIER

June 8

GOD'S SPIRIT BRINGS ABOUT UNDERSTANDING

And we, who with unveiled faces all reflect the Lord's glory, are being transformed into his likeness with ever-increasing glory, which comes from the Lord, who is the Spirit (2 Cor 3:18).

What a startling moment it is when one learns and understands what the essence of God is really like. Then when you talk about God's character or traits – of his holiness, love, righteousness, truth and mercy – you talk about the glory of God, and then you understand for the very first time what you are talking about.

FOOD FROM THE WORD OF GOD
2 Corinthians 3:1-4:15;
Job 24:13, 23-24; Proverbs 4:18-19;
Isaiah 5:11-12; Jeremiah 5:18-24.

How is it possible for us to glorify God? It happens every time we reveal his traits in our everyday lives. Every time we share the good news of Jesus Christ with someone, we glorify him. Every time we are patient in times of disturbance and confusion, we glorify God. Every moment people see the character of God revealed in our attitudes and respond to it positively, we glorify God.

The glory of God is not limited to a church of bricks and mortar; it is not reserved for some or other elevated situation. It can shine brightly when you enter a supermarket or a hair salon. It shines every time you are patient in rush-hour traffic, every time you listen to a dispirited person, or when you go to visit someone who is lying in a hospital bed; every time you train children on a sports field. Yes, through you, the glory of God can be revealed anywhere.

Thank you, O Holy Spirit, for opening my mind so that I may live to the glory and honour of God in a broken world.

If the glorification of God means that you must erupt into service, you must be ready to walk out into the night. – M BASILIA SCHLINK

June 9

SEEK GOD'S GUIDANCE ALWAYS

Paul and Barnabas appointed elders for them in each church and, with prayer and fasting, committed them to the Lord, in whom they had put their trust (Acts 14:23).

Before they chose the elders, Paul, Barnabas and the congregation sought the will of God through prayer and fasting. After all, it is impossible to make the right decisions without the guidance of God. Because God is the source of wisdom and because we need wisdom when we have to make decisions, it is essential that we come to the Source in prayer before we make a decision.

FOOD FROM THE WORD OF GOD
Acts 14:1-28; 1 Chronicles 14:8-17; 2 Chronicles 18:3-5; Proverbs 3:5-8.

When you are young and idealistic, you plan your own path and sometimes forget to involve God in your plans. As you become more mature, you realise how uncertain this life is, how limited your own abilities and wisdom are, and how easily evil can mislead you. Then you need a guide to show you the way through the maze of decisions and choices that you have to make every day. Yes, you need a guide who can understand you, and who has your best interests at heart. You need a guide who understands your personality, your talents and abilities, your likes and dislikes and who plans your path for you accordingly.

You have such a Guide! God bends down to you and takes your hand in his almighty hand. He knows and understands you because he is your Creator. He wants to steer your life on the right course. Read and obey his Word. Through prayer and supplication, trust in the guidance of his Holy Spirit. When you do this, you will discover that life becomes an adventure in faith.

All-knowing and all-wise Father, may I through the Holy Spirit, seek your wisdom and guidance in everything so that I may live creatively and adventurously.

God wants us to meet life full of expectations, in the faith that God will be at work in every situation every time that we trust in him. – COLIN URQUHART

THE HOLY SPIRIT HANDS OUT TALENTS

All these are the work of one and the same Spirit, and he gives them each one, just as he determines (1 Cor 12:11).

The gifts of the Spirit are given to different people so that we must all work together as a unit to the glory of God (1 Cor 12:1-13). Sometimes another Christian has to make you aware of a talent that you have received from God through the Holy Spirit. You may humbly say, "I am a person with only one talent." But then someone comes to you saying, "That is not at all true. I know about your writing and the many other things that you do, but the best talent of all is your ability to sit at the side of a sorrowful friend and, without saying a word, bring comfort to him or her."

FOOD FROM THE WORD OF GOD
1 Corinthians 12:1-11; Exodus 31:1-11; Numbers 11:24-25; Deuteronomy 34:9-12; Isaiah 11:1-2.

Yes, you may be using a God-given talent without being aware that the gift was given to you by the Holy Spirit. Perhaps it is true that we sometimes desire to have some or other talent. Perhaps we would even be willing to exchange the talent that we have for another gift that seems more attractive. But our all-wise God gave his gifts to people in accordance to his holy will, and one day he will call us to account for how we have used the talents that he gave us through the Holy Spirit.

If we truly want to be used by our Lord and Master, we must determine through prayer what our special talent or talents are, and then start using them enthusiastically in God's service.

Holy Spirit, Godly Giver of gifts, lead me to use the talents that God gave to me through you, to his honour only.

Father, recreate by your grace my longing heart; make it, through the Holy Spirit, your quiet dwelling so that all my talents will fall under your control. – ANGELUS SILECIUS

June 11

GOD'S CHOSEN PEOPLE ALSO SUFFER

You became imitators of us and of the Lord; in spite of severe suffering, you welcomed the message with the joy given by the Holy Spirit. And so you became a model to all the believers in Macedonia and Achaia (1 Thess 1:6-7).

God loves us sincerely, but this does not safeguard us against suffering. This is why Paul encourages the Thessalonians with his testimony of God's miracles of love in his own life. Maybe someone has encouraged you with the love of God, in your suffering too. This means that you in turn can also encourage someone else by testifying to the power of God's love and grace in your own life.

FOOD FROM THE WORD OF GOD
1 Thessalonians 1:1-2:16; Deuteronomy 7:6-8; Psalm 40:4-17.

If there was one instance when Jesus was a true source of comfort to his followers, it was his handling of his suffering at Gethsemane. Picture him standing in the garden, his heart so filled with love that nothing could stop it from overflowing; so full of sorrow that it had to find expression. Behold the Saviour on the cross as the nails were mercilessly driven through his hands and feet.

All of us are sometimes emotionally overwhelmed. Disappointment and sadness continually wash like waves over our lives. We are flung back and forth like broken shells. Praise God Almighty who does not leave us without comfort in moments like these: our Saviour is a safe harbour for storm-ravished ships, a safe haven for grief-stricken pilgrims. The mercy of our God is far greater than our sins; his love much higher than our thoughts. He is the unchanging Rock where we find shelter against the tide that wants to overwhelm us. Yes, his chosen people also suffer, but he loves us, and cares for us in our trials.

Lord, my merciful God, show me through your Holy Spirit the path of faith, and lead me to your eternal rest and tranquillity.

Christ did not come to reason away or take away our suffering. He came to fill it with his presence.
PAUL CLAUDEL

June 12

ONE FINDS JOY BY SERVING GOD

If you obey my commands, you will remain in my love, just as I have obeyed my Father's commands and remain in his love. I have told you this so that my joy may be in you and that your joy may be complete (Jn 15:10-11).

If someone were to ask, "How can I be a joyful Christian?" our Lord's answer is very simple, "You cannot have my joy without me. Remain in me, and I will remain in you. Then my joy will be in you."

There is no joy like the joy love brings. There is also no joy outside the love of Christ. Jesus spoke to his disciples about the love of his Father for sinners. He remains in his Father's love and loves us with that love (Jn 15:9-17). His joy is the joy of love and he pours it out over every sinner.

FOOD FROM THE WORD OF GOD
John 14:27-15:27; Psalm 33:1-5, 12-22; 35:27-28; 51:10-14.

This is the joy that Jesus wants us to share with other people: the joy of knowing that God loves us, that the living Christ loves us, that we love other people and that we live in love for those around us. Yes, God alone is the source of our joy. He *is* our outstanding joy and the only one who can make us perfectly happy. Therefore, we must possess as much as possible of God: of his will and his fellowship.

Our faith is meant to give indescribable joy to our lives. Why then is it that religion robs so many people of the joy in their lives? It is because they refuse to believe that there is no other joy like the joy of remaining *in* Christ and in his love and to be channels through which his love can spill over to other people.

Holy Spirit, thank you that joy is one of the gifts that you want to give to me, and that I find it by obeying God, my Father through Jesus Christ.

We are all chords in God's concert of joy.
JAKOB BOEHME

THE VALUE OF ENCOURAGEMENT

So the churches were strengthened in the faith and grew daily in numbers (Acts 16:5).

A father passed away and the family received many tokens of comfort and encouragement from neighbours and the community at large. Food, flowers and letters of sympathy and love were heaped upon them. The evening before the memorial service was to take place, their caring neighbour silently came into their house, collected the whole family's shoes and polished them. The following morning when they were getting ready to go to church, they discovered their shiny shoes. The family later witnessed that, of all the tokens of sympathy, this act outshone them all and that they, in turn, would like to practice the service of shoe polishers.

FOOD FROM THE WORD OF GOD
Acts 15:22-16:10; Ruth 2:8-13; 2 Samuel 19:5-8; Job 2:11; Proverbs 25:11.

The greatest encouragement and comfort often do not come from words, but from acts of love. When a beloved colleague of mine lost his wife, I could not find the words to comfort him. For half an hour I just sat with him and held his hand. When I left I felt like a failure. The next morning my friend phoned me to tell me how much my visit and especially my silence had meant to him.

We have been instructed to encourage others. After all, the Word of God is full of the encouraging promises God made to us. And in a world torn apart by sin we all need encouragement. What is your testimony about the encouragement that you have thus far received? Does it help you to encourage others?

Loving Holy Spirit, help me to remain faithful in the ministry of encouragement, out of gratefulness for the encouragement that I receive from God's hand.

No man is so unimportant that he should think that his encouragement would not mean something.
EDWARD CLARENDON

GOD'S CHILDREN ARE HIS PROPERTY

Don't you know that when you offer yourselves to someone to obey him as slaves, you are slaves to the one whom you obey – whether you are slaves to sin, which leads to death, or to obedience, which leads to righteousness? (Rom 6:16).

God has called us to live separate and holy lives. This is what sanctification means. The Greek word for sanctification is *hagios*, which means "separate that which belongs to God". This means that God is our owner and that he says to us, "You belong to me!"

In his letter to the Romans Paul writes in the introduction, *To all in Rome who are loved by God and called to be saints ...* (Rom 1:7). He does not only write to leaders of the church or to spiritually mature people. He writes to all of God's people who stand with him as chosen ones called by God. Therefore, we can also rejoice in our status as beloved people who have received God's forgiveness through Jesus Christ.

FOOD FROM THE WORD OF GOD
Romans 6:15-7:6; Deuteronomy 7:6-8; 10:12, 20-21; Psalm 95:6-7; Jeremiah 11:1-4; Zechariah 8:7-8

However, what is the significance of this in our daily lives? Nothing less than that everything we possess and everything we are belong to God. This includes our thoughts, emotions, desires and bodies. God extends his sovereignty into our lives in order to place the people and the plans in our lives under his control. But it does not end here. Our memories that determine our present lives and the values that shape our futures, our daily tasks and our immediate surroundings where we spend the lion's share of our lives also fall under his sovereignty. Even our money and our possessions belong to God. Being chosen means accepting the sovereignty of God in every aspect of our lives – and this requires surrendering to God unconditionally.

Holy God, through your Son I am no longer a slave to sin, but belong to you. I dedicate myself to you anew.

Sanctity is not an optional extra in the process of rebirth: it is the whole aim of it.
DONALD NICHOLL

GOD WELCOMES REPENTANT SINNERS

Jesus answered him, "I tell you the truth, today you will be with me in paradise" (Lk 23:43).

A woman once went to address the prisoners of the Montinlupa Prison. She told them how she and her family offered refuge to Jews during the Second World War, and how the Gestapo came hammering on their door one icy cold night in February 1944, with warrants for their arrest. They had been betrayed by two of their neighbours. This woman was Corrie ten Boom.

FOOD FROM THE WORD OF GOD
Luke 23:13-43; Isaiah 30:8-15; Jeremiah 36:2-3.

After the war was over, the two Hollanders who had betrayed them were taken prisoner. "My sister Nollie," Corrie related, "heard of the court case against the two men who had handed us over to the Gestapo and wrote to them. She told them that we had forgiven them, and that we were able to do so because Jesus lives in our hearts."

Both men wrote back. One of them wrote, "I have found Jesus as my Saviour. If he gives one the ability to forgive like Corrie ten Boom and her sister, then there is hope even for me. I have laid my sins before the Lord." The other man wrote, "I know what I did to you and your family, that I caused the death of quite a number of those of you who rescued Jews. I also helped to kill hundreds of Jews. My only regret is that I could not murder many more of you."

Corrie challenged the prisoners to accept Jesus and his forgiveness. Would you not also like to entrust your salvation to him?

Just the way I am, I can wait no longer; I come, so soiled, so stained, O Lord, I cast myself at your feet
O Lamb of God, I am coming!

The only true forgiveness that is offered is that which is offered even before the transgressor has apologised and asked for forgiveness. – SØREN KIERKEGAARD

GOD FORGIVES AND SAVES

Some men brought a paralytic, lying on a mat. When Jesus saw their faith, he said to the paralytic, "Take heart, son; your sins are forgiven … Get up, take your mat and go home" (Mt 9:2, 6).

Followers of other faiths give us instructions on how to find favour with God by acting correctly. But we as Christians say that sin has ruined us to such an extent that it is impossible for us to win God's favour. We cannot obey God's commands. We are guilty and totally incapable of saving ourselves.

FOOD FROM THE WORD OF GOD
Matthew 8:28-9:17; Psalm 32:1-7; 103:8-13; Isaiah 43:25.

Other religions tell their followers to adhere to the instructions of their founders. We as Christians proclaim our Founder as the incarnation of God, who died for our sins and triumphantly rose from the dead in order to make forgiveness possible for us. He is the Living and calls on us to trust in him. We worship and serve him alone. Indeed, salvation through the love of the Son of God who took the Father's judgement of our sins upon himself, who rose from the dead and reigns forever, is not to be found in any other religion.

All who in repentance confess their sins and who trust in Jesus are recreated through the Holy Spirit. They are united with Christ in their resurrection. Their nature is changed, so that their deepest longing is to obey God and to serve him only. They proclaim God through Jesus Christ as their heavenly Father. They are born again into a new relationship with Jesus Christ. They have the assurance that their sins have been forgiven and that they are children of God, inheritors of an unconquerable hope and joy. All of this we find only with our God.

O God and Father, you have shown amazing grace to me. Help me to lead sinners to you so that Jesus may save them.

The old primitive sins are not dead, but lurk there in the dark corners of our modern hearts. – CARL GUSTAV JUNG

THE GREATNESS OF GOD'S FORGIVENESS

This is how my heavenly Father will treat each of you unless you forgive your brother from your heart (Mt 18:35).

Today, seriously reflect on the parable of the king and his officials in Matthew 18:21-35. Ask yourself whether the greatness of God's forgiveness serves as a model for you when you have to forgive others.

To receive forgiveness and to be forgiven cannot be separated. By forgiving others, we receive forgiveness. By forgiving, we open ourselves to God's forgiveness. Everyone who loves God will also love his or her neighbour. He or she who hates other people, cannot possibly love God. Love for your neighbour and love of God are inextricably linked. We only learn to love once we start getting to know God. We truly start learning to love God when we start learning to love our neighbour. Someone who is receptive to the love of God, also acts in love towards his or her neighbour. He or she who has received forgiveness from God, will also forgive other people.

FOOD FROM THE WORD OF GOD
Matthew 18:10-35; Psalm 51:1-21; Ezekiel 18:21-23.

God's forgiveness gives us the freedom to love. God's forgiveness gives us the ability to forgive … and to forgive … and to forgive – not only seven times, but seventy times seven. If God has forgiven us the enormous debt we owed him, how can we then refuse to forgive our neighbour who is really only a little indebted to us?

I who have received your forgiveness, O Lord, gratefully sing to you my song of salvation. Help me to lovingly forgive those who trespass against me.

He who cannot forgive others, destroys the bridge over which he himself has to cross, for everybody has a need for forgiveness. – THOMAS FULLER

UNBELIEF WILL BE PUNISHED

Whoever believes and is baptised will be saved, but whoever does not believe will be condemned (Mk 16:16).

People often want to know how it is possible for one to be ruined if God is a God of love. People are ruined because they trample on the love of God instead of accepting and appreciating his love. They ignore his love, hold his love in contempt and close their hearts to it. Many say that they will one day, perhaps, think about it.

The Bible gives us the assurance that there will be a "one day". The day of reckoning. To those who held his love in contempt God will say, "I loved you every day of your life with an eternal love. I loved you with a perfect love. I offered myself to you through my love for you. I put my wisdom at your disposal, as well as my comfort and strength – and my Holy Spirit. I gave myself to you through my beloved Son so that you might be saved. But you trampled on all of this and refused my love. On earth you did as you saw fit, until the end, so now you can continue your unbelief in eternity."

FOOD FROM THE WORD OF GOD
Mark 16:9-20; Numbers 14:1-11, 20-24; Psalm 78:20-22.

Does this description apply to your life? Will you continue to reject and trample on God's love? How you answer this question will determine where you will spend eternity. The good news of the gospel is that we can accept God and his love, that we can be saved by the love of his Son Jesus Christ and can become inheritors of heaven.

Merciful God and Father, keep me from trampling on your love.

To love God is something far greater than merely knowing him.
St THOMAS AQUINAS

GIVE GOD WHAT IS DUE TO HIM

With his wife's full knowledge he kept back part of the money for himself, but brought the rest and put it at the apostles' feet (Acts 5:2).

The sin of Ananias and Sapphira was that they kept for themselves that which belonged to the Lord. Many people make the mistake of thinking that only once they have accumulated enough, they can start calculating how much of it they want to give to God. But in this way we are only robbing ourselves. Is there something in your life that you are keeping back from God? Your heart, your possessions, your talents, your time or your relationships?

A farmer once explained to his pastor, "When I have enough, I will give half of it to the Lord." So the pastor asked him, "If you were to discover a rich gold-vein on 2 000 acres of your land, would you give the income from 1 000 acres to the Lord?" "Definitely," said the farmer, his eyes sparkling greedily. "Anyone can make a living from a rich gold-vein on 1 000 acres!" Then the pastor asked him, "If you had two head of cattle, would you give one to the Lord?" To which the farmer complained, "It's unfair! You know very well I only have two head of cattle!"

We do not wake up one morning and suddenly discover that we have a surplus of time, talents and money to give to the Lord. We begin our offerings to God by giving small quantities. Every day we learn to handle our finances, power, time, relationships and temptations. And one day we will discover that we are capable of managing our entire life and live for God.

FOOD FROM THE WORD OF GOD
Acts 5:1-16; Deuteronomy 23:21-23; Joshua 7:20-21, 24-25; Ecclesiastes 5:1-6; Isaiah 6:18-19.

*I dedicate my spirit, my soul, my body to you, O Lord.
For all eternity I lay myself before you as an offering.*

It is only through the mystery of self-sacrifice that one can find oneself anew.
CARL GUSTAV JUNG

ENVY HAS NO PLACE WITH GOD

Repent of wickedness and pray to the Lord. Perhaps he will forgive you for having such a thought in your heart. For I see that you are full of bitterness and captive to sin (Acts 8:22-23).

In Numbers 16 we learn that God views envy and jealousy of his servants as an insult to him personally, and that he views the sin of envy and jealousy in a very serious light. Therefore, we are called to:

FOOD FROM THE WORD OF GOD
Acts 8:1-25; Numbers 16:1-3, 28-35; Psalm 106:16-18.

- Delight in the spiritual victories of other children of God.
- Delight through Christ Jesus in every triumph of his servants.
- Be glad when the success of a fellow Christian is greater than ours.
- Rejoice when someone receives something we would like to have.
- Stay inwardly peaceful when someone else gets the attention that we think we deserve.
- Do battle against envy and jealousy in earnest.

Today, say to yourself:

- I will not be envious or spiteful.
- I will strive only for the glory of God.
- I will rejoice in the successes and triumphs of others.
- I will not think that others are less important or less talented than I am.
- I will not see my work as more important than that of others.
- I will pray for my rivals.
- I will rejoice in my relationship with the Lord and will not compare it to other people's relationships with him.

May God grant this.

Forgive me, Lord, for any trace of envy or spite that stealthily enters my life. May the Holy Spirit teach me to be humble.

In jealousy there is more self-love than love.
FRANÇOIS DE LA ROCHEFOUCAULD

June 21

BE GENEROUS

Out of the most severe trial, their overflowing joy and their extreme poverty welled up in rich generosity (2 Cor 8:2).

One can compile a long list of all that God promises to those who are generous. God will make them rich in every respect. Our generosity must be of such a standard that it always honours God. We all know how strong the temptations of materialism are and how very easily we can rationalise them. Only by the grace of God and with great effort on our side can we escape the deluge of luxuries that threaten to drown our Christian compassion.

We all struggle with this problem. With the money for the new suit that I did not really need, I could have satisfied a homeless child's hunger for a whole month. Ask yourself honestly: Dare I slavishly follow the latest fashion trends if it limits my ability to render assistance? May I consider any means in order to accumulate wealth, rather than living a Christian lifestyle without compromise?

FOOD FROM THE WORD OF GOD
2 Corinthians 8:1-9:15;
Deuteronomy 14:22-29, 15:10;
Proverbs 21:25-26, 28:7.

We have been brainwashed into thinking that bigger homes, successful businesses and luxury goods are praiseworthy aims in life. Consequently we become entangled in materialism. The more we accumulate, the more we think we need in order to live. We must break this demonic circle because it causes us to overlook our brothers and sisters in need, and thereby we ignore the commandment of our Lord. Eventually it destroys us. But generosity is definitely the path that leads to true life and joy.

Lord Jesus, you came to share everything with me, even your life.
May your holy example inspire me to be
generous every day, to your honour and glory.

No abandonment or desire destroys our nature as much as respectable selfishness.
GEORGE MACDONALD

GOD BLESSES THOSE WHO BELIEVE

Consider Abraham: "He believed God, and it was credited to him as righteousness." So those who have faith are blessed along with Abraham, the man of faith (Gal 3:6, 9).

I need Thee ev'ry hour

I need Thee ev'ry hour, most gracious Lord.
Thy name is my strength; be Thou ever with me,
be Thou ever with me; bless me, bless me, bless me Lord!
I need thee ev'ry hour, in sorrow or in joy,
Thou art my strength and shield now and eternally.
Be Thou ever with me, be Thou ever with me.
Oh! bless me, bless me, bless me, Lord.

I need Thee ev'ry hour, teach me Thy will
and Thy rich promises in me fulfil.
I need Thee, oh I need Thee,
ev'ry hour I need Thee.
Bless me, bless me, bless me Lord.

I need Thee ev'ry hour, most holy One.
Oh, make me Thine indeed, Thou blessed Son.
I need Thee, oh I need Thee,
ev'ry hour I need Thee.
Oh bless me now my Saviour!
I come to Thee, come to Thee!

H Dalle Carbonare

FOOD FROM THE WORD OF GOD
Galatians 3:1-20; Genesis 22:15-18; 1 Kings 2:1-14; Psalm 18:30-36; 23:1-3, 6.

Holy Spirit of God, keep me from lack of faith, superstition, or unbelief, so that I do not miss out on God's rich blessings.

The more we count the blessings we possess, the less we will yearn for luxuries we do not possess.
WILLIAM A WARD

June 23

WE REAP WHAT WE SOW

Do not be deceived: God cannot be mocked. A man reaps what he sows (Gal 6:7).

Our dividends in heaven are determined by what we invest there while we are still on earth. Either we can invest in eternal security, or we can invest in the wind. Someone once wrote, "Sow flowers and wherever you walk, flowers will still seed your path; sow weeds and you will reap weeds. What you sow is exactly what you will reap."

In accordance with the laws of nature, you reap what you sow. If you sow wheat, you will reap wheat. If you sow weeds, you will reap weeds. In our spiritual and moral life the same principle applies as in nature. We must guard against spending too much time, energy and money on recreation, pleasure and other forms of self-enjoyment. We will reap very little from these seeds. Little wonder that John warns young believers, *Dear children, keep yourselves from idols* (1 Jn 5:21). Idols are not only images made from wood or stone, but can be anything that comes between us and the Lord and distracts our minds from our total commitment to God.

FOOD FROM THE WORD OF GOD
Galatians 5:13-6:18; 1 Chronicles 10:3-4; Psalm 37:7-9; Proverbs 3:3-4; 12:20-21; 23:29-32; Ecclesiastes 2:26.

If we invest our lives in the passing and insignificant things of this world, we will reap only insignificant things and our lives are destroyed. If we want to grow optimally, we must continually yearn for the solid diet of the Word of God.

Can you make a list of the positive things that you have sowed? Would it correspond with the fruits of the Spirit in Galatians 5:16-25? Sow now so that you may reap heavenly dividends later.

Holy Spirit, help me to sow only pure seed for eternity so that I may reap God's approval.

Work and study as if everything depends on you, but pray and trust as if everything depends on God.
ELBERT HUBBARD

GUARD AGAINST GREED

For this you can be sure: No immoral, impure or greedy person – such a man is an idolater – has any inheritance in the kingdom of Christ and of God (Eph 5:5).

Someone said, "Our cheque books have a lot more to do with heaven and perdition than our hymn-books." Jesus told the story of the rich man and the poor beggar. The rich man, blinded by his abundant wealth, did not realise his need for salvation and did not prepare himself for the hereafter. Lazarus on the other hand who had only received bad things, crumbs from the rich man's table, was well prepared for eternity. Consequently their lives in the hereafter were completely reversed (Lk 16:19-31).

FOOD FROM THE WORD OF GOD
Ephesians 4:17-5:5; Proverbs 1:10, 15-19; 28:20; 30:15-16; Jeremiah 8:10-12.

Greed is a terrible hindrance to our spiritual growth because if we are greedy we place our trust in earthly things rather than in God. The way we handle our possessions reveals a lot about the quality of our spiritual lives.

Cyprian, the third-century bishop of Carthage, gave an astounding description of people who live in abundance: "Their possessions bind them in chains. Their courage is tied, and their faith is suffocated. Their judgement is adversely affected and their souls are hardened. If they had gathered their treasures in heaven, they would not have an enemy and a thief in their household now. They consider themselves as possessors, but they are the ones who are possessed. They are addicted to their own possessions. They are no longer masters of their money, but slaves to it."

Jesus calls us to a life of responsible stewardship with regard to everything we possess. Greed is a very serious obstacle on our road to spiritual maturity. Guard against it.

Lord Jesus, teach me to guard against any form of greed, which disgraces you.

If you want to outlaw greed, you first have to outlaw her mother: the longing for luxuries.
MARCUS TULLIUS CICERO

June 25

THERE IS ONLY ONE GOD WHO SAVES

For there is one God and mediator between God and men, the man Christ Jesus, who gave himself as a ransom for all men (1 Tim 2:5-6a).

All through the ages, people have stumbled across the simplicity of our salvation. Every sect and cult has its own version of the salvation doctrine and each one undermines the simplicity of the gospel as revealed by the Word of God by thinking that man, through his works and deeds, can achieve his own salvation (2 Cor 11:3).

From the beginning right until the end, the Word of God proves these people wrong. The message of salvation that is interwoven in the 66 books of the Bible written over a period of 1 500 years by more than 40 different authors, forms a wonderful and intangible unit. The message is simple: Through grace God saves repentant sinners who come to him in faith. There is nothing secretive about it, nothing hidden and no complications.

FOOD FROM THE WORD OF GOD
1 Timothy 2:1-3:13; Deuteronomy 4:34-40; Isaiah 43:10-13; 44:8.

God descended from heaven and came to speak to us through his Son (Heb 1:1-2). Jesus is the only source of salvation according to God's perfect plan. Those who do not believe in his Name are condemned and excluded from eternal life. Regardless of how upright or religious a person is, or how involved in charitable work – everyone who wants to be saved must be born again. Only those who forsake sin and in faith turn to him who was crucified so that we should not perish, are promised eternal life. Because he, Christ, is the one and only way to the one and only God.

I praise and thank your holy Name, O God, that I have been called by Jesus Christ to eternal life with you, and have been saved.

There is a natural, basic tendency within our souls that makes us turn to God as naturally as flowers turn to the sun. – RUFUS M JONES

June 26

AVOID EVIL

Everyone who confesses the name of the Lord must turn away from wickedness (2 Tim 2:19).

We must strive for sanctification, because God said, *Be holy, because I am holy* (1 Pet 1:16). Paul underscores the fact that we have been called to live holy lives for this purpose, we have been saved. The Christian who does not strive for sanctification in earnest in every area of his or her life, is going against God's purpose for his or her salvation.

What then is sanctification or sanctity? One of the best definitions we can come up with is: without sin (1 Jn 2:1-2). Most Christians are quite happy with simply sinning as little as possible. John states that our aim should be not to sin at all. Every sin, no matter how small it might seem to us, is an insult to God's authority, rejects his law and scorns his love. Therefore, we ought not to tolerate sin at all.

FOOD FROM THE WORD OF GOD
2 Timothy 2:14-3:11; Psalm 5:4-7; 101:1-5; Proverbs 4:14-17, 20-27.

When Paul was instructing the Christians of Ephesus on the importance of sanctification, he said, *So I tell you this, and insist on it in the Lord, that you must no longer live as the Gentiles do* (Eph 4:17). He demands sanctification of them and does so under the authority of Jesus Christ. Sanctification is not one of various options open to us, but a necessity for every Christian. And we must strive for sanctification in every aspect of our lives. We must rejoice sincerely in innocence and in a holy life. For this purpose God has sent his Holy Spirit to aid us.

Grant me more holiness, O God, more fervour in my heart, more comfort in trials and more sorrow about sin.

All of us can attain the Christian virtue of sanctification, despite the circumstances in our lives and whatever our life's task might be. – Sr FRANCIS DE SALES

FAITH PLEASES GOD

And without faith it is impossible to please God, because anyone who comes to him must believe that he exists and that he rewards those who earnestly seek him (Heb 11:6).

It is essential that we should have a faith that is pleasing to God. Faith is not so much about matters of the past or of the present, but focuses in particular on the future. Faith acts as a catalyst in the lives of the children of God: it causes change without changing itself.

Faith is the purposeful and positive response of our hearts to the goodness that is within God. It makes us willing to act powerfully for his sake. It makes us willing to share every aspect of our lives with him to the best of our ability: our time, strength, attention, talents, possessions, love, energy and acceptance. Faith is a complete commitment which keeps nothing back.

FOOD FROM THE WORD OF GOD
Hebrews 11:1-40; Genesis 6:9-22; 7:10-12; 8:13-22; 9:1-2, 11.

Faith means that we actively and energetically give our best to God without considering our own interests. Faith is not merely idle words but total surrender of all we are to him who is our *summum bonum* (supreme good).

To talk about faith in any other terms than these, is to be preoccupied with your own selfish interests. Superficial spirituality is a great threat to Christianity. Hundreds of thousands of people allege that they believe in God, that they believe in Christ, that they believe in the Holy Spirit, yet their personal lives do not at all testify to it.

God wants us to have dynamic faith. He is waiting for us to respond to him and his love. And when he finds it, he is delighted by it.

Holy God, may my faith always please and delight you.

Faith essentially means to take somebody at his or her word.
DAVID WATSON

GOD WILL CARE FOR YOU

Cast all your anxiety on him because he cares for you (1 Pet 5:7).

Barbara Hyatt worked as a secretary and receptionist at a morgue. One winter morning she sat thinking about her husband who had been retrenched and the fact that she had to work now. She thought about the arrears instalment on the house, about the food she still had to buy, about the children who urgently needed clothes, about Christmas drawing near – and her tears started running freely.

FOOD FROM THE WORD OF GOD
1 Peter 4:12-5:14; 1 Kings 17:2-4, 6-16; Psalm 145:9, 13-14, 18-19.

Suddenly her thoughts were interrupted by a loud bang. She saw that a little bird had flown into the windowpane and now lay half-conscious on the ground. This reminded her of God who says in his Word that he knows about the birds of the air and that he cares for them. How much more will he not care for his children? She felt so encouraged and decided anew to entrust all their needs to God.

The following morning a friend stood at their door and said, "The Lord has sent me to give this money to you." The sum of money was exactly what she needed for the instalment on the house, and to buy groceries. Later she received more money through the post from a dear friend. A note was included with it, "Love in Jesus!" The family were invited to a Christmas dinner. So the children could have a wonderful Christmas.

Barbara ends her testimony with these words, "In this way God assures us, time and again, that we must cast our cares in faith and trust on him: he will provide!"

Faithful God and Guide, teach me the lesson every day of absolute trust in you.

The more we rely on God, the more reliable we find him.
CLIFF RICHARD

June 29

GOD CONDEMNS FALSE TEACHERS

These men are springs without water and mists driven by a storm. Blackest darkness is reserved for them (2 Pet 2:17).

Deception and heresy also occur in the church of Christ. The triune God is questioned cynically and the leaders are often at the forefront. For us as Christians it is sometimes difficult to recognise the deceivers. Jesus spoke of false prophets who perform great and miraculous deeds and who mislead even the believers.

Satan does not want to establish a church here on earth and call it "The First Church of Satan". He would much rather infiltrate the church of Christ: the catechism, the youth ministry, the Christian curriculum, the seminaries and ultimately the pulpit. The apostle Paul warns that many church members will follow false prophets, unaware that they are eating from these people's hands, and that they are ingesting Satan's poison into their spiritual lives.

FOOD FROM THE WORD OF GOD
2 Peter 2:1-22; Isaiah 56:9-12; Hosea 4:6-11.

Many Christians are being deceived horribly every day. False prophets use big theological words and terms that impress people. They are intellectually gifted and cunning. They are skilled at deceiving unthinking and uninformed people. They do it without even having to think about it, and to roars of applause from a hostile world that is bent on destroying the church of Christ.

Blackest darkness is reserved for these false teachers, unless they truly accept Jesus Christ as their Saviour. The best course of action against these false teachers and their deception is for us to keep our eyes firmly fixed on our perfect Teacher, Jesus Christ, so that when the false teachers appear, we will be able to recognise them easily and keep them out of our lives.

Teacher of the truth, O Holy Spirit of God, teach me to know God's truth and help me to live according to it, for the glory of my Saviour.

It seems as if people have an unlimited capacity to deceive themselves into accepting their own lies as the truth. – RD LAING

30 June

WALK IN THE LIGHT

But if you walk in the light, as he is in the light, we have fellowship with one another, and the blood of Jesus, his Son, purifies us from all sin (1 Jn 1:7).

Servants of Christ reflect his light in a community that is lost in darkness. They look strange to those who walk in darkness. But this is exactly what Christ intended to happen. Think about the characteristics of light and apply them to your spiritual testimony in this world which is filled with darkness.

FOOD FROM THE WORD OF GOD
1 John 1:1-2:17; Job 24:13; 38:12-13; Psalm 43:3-4; Proverbs 4:18-19; Isaiah 9:1; 42:6-7; Jeremiah 13:15-16.

Light is toneless and soundless. There is no noise, no racket and no brandishing of banners. Light simply shines. It is like a single lighthouse on a rocky and isolated coast that shines its light and conveys a silent message.

Light silently indicates direction. Jesus says that our light must shine in such a way that other people can see our good deeds and praise God (Mt 5:16).

Light attracts attention. When a light is switched on in a dark room people automatically look at it. If you are the only Christian in a non-Christian neighbourhood, you are automatically a light in that darkness. If you are the only Christian nurse in your ward, the only Christian in your class, the only Christian in your company, or the only Christian salesman in your area, then you are a light that shines in the dark, a servant of God who is involuntarily watched and who sends out a very clear message, often without saying a single word.

Let your light shine because you live in the Light and this eternal Light not only lights your way, but also guides others to the Light. Yes, shine in this way for Christ – the Light of the world – so that you drive away from the darkness.

Lord Jesus Christ, through the Holy Spirit light up every dark corner of my life so that I may lead others to your light.

Light is not polluted, not even when it shines through pollution.
St AUGUSTINE OF HIPPO

July

Prayer for July

1. Alone with God in prayer
2. God forgives all who repent
3. Splendour that surpasses all
4. God's miracles lead us to him
5. God does not tolerate sin
6. The great gift of love
7. The saved people of God *will* live again
8. God's judgement is final
9. God's righteous judgement
10. God protects his children
11. The unity of believers
12. Only owe love
13. Be prepared for opposition
14. Spread the good news
15. God heals body and soul
16. What is true repentance?
17. The unrighteous fear God
18. God changes our hearts and lives
19. God loves us sincerely
20. Believe and be saved
21. Compassion is a virtue
22. Repent and believe
23. To God love is most important
24. Not all who hear, understand
25. Keep God's instructions in your heart
26. Greatness begins with humility
27. Worship God
28. God punishes the persecutors of his messengers
29. God rewards compassion
30. Trust in God to provide
31. Faith is not a spiritual luxury

Prayer for July

Holy God, through Jesus Christ our loving Father,
July is traditionally a holiday month.
Everybody is travelling: visiting family, away hunting,
at the seaside or a game park.
And death mercilessly takes its toll on our roads.
So much unnecessary loss, pain, mutilation and sorrow.
You have given us life – our most precious possession.
Help us to travel with great responsibility,
With respect for life, both for ours and that of others.
Thank you for this intimate time we can spend with family.
Bring us closer to one another and to you, our Saviour.
Thank you for those with whom we can share our holidays,
and for lovely memories that are stored in our hearts;
for the strengthening of ties of friendship.
We pray for those who are working while we rest.
Thank you for the breathtaking beauty of winter landscapes.
Renew our spirits while our bodies are resting.
May we not forget you while we are on holiday.
May we continue with our personal interaction with you
by reading the Bible, praying and contemplating.
Make us the salt of the earth and the light of the world.
In the powerful Name of Jesus our Saviour.

Amen

July 1

ALONE WITH GOD IN PRAYER

But Jesus often withdrew to lonely places and prayed (Lk 5:16).

Jesus needed seclusion because he was also human – the only perfect human that ever lived. He needed to be alone with his Father. He isolated himself in order to heal his loneliness. He needed the silence of eternity, just as a desert-traveller needs water. His need for silence was an expression of his love for his Father.

He, who was the personification of Godly love, also felt a need to give and receive love. His deepest needs could only be satisfied by God, and so can ours. No human being, no matter how much they mean to us, can satisfy our need for love. Jesus needed times of seclusion during which he could bask in the sunshine of his Father's love, be drenched by it and find rest in it. No matter how exhausted he was, this deep-seated, quiet fellowship with his Father revitalised him more than a good night's rest.

FOOD FROM THE WORD OF GOD
Luke 5:12-32; Psalm 5:4-12; 119:145-147.

Human love and friendship do indeed enrich our lives and satisfy our need for love, but never completely. At the centre of human existence, there is a yearning for the love of God. It can only be satisfied when our lonely longing is transformed into quiet fellowship with God. Do you become quiet often enough with your Father so that you can really understand the deeper meaning of your fellowship with him, and make use of it?

Holy and merciful God, I praise and thank you for moments of seclusion and fellowship in prayer with you. May I be strengthened by it every day for the task you have given me.

What is of the utmost importance is that God should become such an intense part of our lives that spontaneous conversation with him becomes second nature. – CLIFF RICHARD

GOD FORGIVES ALL WHO REPENT

Then Peter began to speak, "I now realise how true it is that God does not show favouritism but accepts men from every nation who fear him and do what is right" (Acts 10:34-35).

Many people think about the events on the cross in this way: people were so bad and God was so angry with them, that he could not forgive them unless somebody capable of it could take the punishment for all humanity. But nothing could be further from the truth.

Love, and not anger, led to Jesus' crucifixion. Calvary was the result of God's innermost desire to give and to forgive. Therefore he executed his plan for salvation. What is more, Jesus knew that he could absorb all the wickedness of humanity through his mediating suffering, thus healing, forgiving and saving us. After he had completed this, the greatest of all his deeds, he said, *It is finished* (Jn 19:30). The great act of redemption had been completed. Jesus could return yet again to the light of God's care.

FOOD FROM THE WORD OF GOD
Acts 10:1-48; Exodus 34:6-7;
Psalm 65:1-4, 11-13;
Isaiah 1:18-20; 55:7.

The process of salvation is a great mystery that is hidden in the heart of God's love. But we know that it is true and real. Not only because the Bible tells us so, but also because we can see the influence of it in the lives of people and experience it in our own lives. On these grounds we can know that confession and forgiveness are realities. Without the cross, confession of guilt would have had only therapeutic or psychological value. However, it is so much more. It changes an objective relationship with God into a subjective one. It brings change and healing to our innermost being.

Loving and merciful God, I bow before your love, which found me even before I could confess to my sins. Hold me close with your love every day.

To him who has confessed his sins in earnest, all pretence has ended and reality has begun.
WILLIAM JAMES

SPLENDOUR THAT SURPASSES ALL

For our light and momentary troubles are achieving for us an eternal glory that far outweighs them all (2 Cor 4:17).

Man's place in creation is remarkable. The psalmist witnesses, *You made him a little lower than the heavenly beings and crowned him with glory and honour. You made him ruler over the works of your hands; you put everything under his feet* (Ps 8:5-6).

What we can be when we are restored to the image of God by Christ's work of salvation and the Holy Spirit, what we can be when we become like Jesus, we can scarcely imagine. This mortal body will be clothed with the immortal, and this perishable body will be clothed with the imperishable (1 Cor 15:53-55). Our bodies will be changed into something endlessly more splendid than the bodies we now inhabit. We cannot even begin to imagine how we will be changed through the omnipotence of Christ. There is room for unlimited and exciting expectations for those who live according to the will of God. We can only speculate about the plans of our eternal God who gave his beloved Son in order to make all of this possible for us. Only the very best that heaven can offer is prepared for those of us who love and serve God. Become quiet before God for a few moments; close your eyes. Imagine that you are standing in the temple of God with clean hands and a pure heart. See God as eternal light and splendour and praise him for the indescribable glory that awaits his children.

FOOD FROM THE WORD OF GOD
2 Corinthians 4:16-6:2; Psalm 24:3-10; Isaiah 35:1-2; 60:18-20.

Lord, our Lord, how majestic is your name in all the earth! (Ps 8:9).

He who lives only for this life without preparing for eternity, is wise only for a moment and a fool in all eternity. – JOHN TILLITSON

GOD'S MIRACLES LEAD US TO HIM

When the proconsul saw what had happened, he believed, for he was amazed at the teaching about the Lord (Acts 13:12).

In each of these Scripture readings God makes miracles occur so that he can reveal himself to specific people and thus lead them to faith. God still reveals himself in our lives today through both big and small miracles – if only we would see it! The question is: do we respond to them positively or negatively. What is *your* reaction to God's miracles in your life?

FOOD FROM THE WORD OF GOD
Acts 13:1-25; Exodus 4:28-31; 2 Kings 5:14-17; Psalm 106:8-12.

When Jesus was on earth, he restored sight to a blind man's eyes, which would undoubtedly have been closed by death at some or other stage. He raised Lazarus from the dead, even though he would die again. Whatever he did for the health of the body, he did in the knowledge that the people would not continue living here on earth forever. But eventually he will also give eternal health to our bodies.

Because many people cannot believe in the invisible God, he builds their faith in invisible things by his visible deeds. Yes, God who created heaven and earth never hesitates to do visible miracles. He performs them so that people can "see" him, the invisible God and learn to love and serve him. So do not be sad because God no longer performs such miracles through Jesus in our day and age, and do not forever look back longingly to God's past miracles. He still performs miracles today to invite us to lives of faith in his omnipotence.

God Almighty who works miracles, I praise you for every miracle that you have performed in my life.

All miracles are weak lights like beacons on our path to the harbour where the great light shines, the perfect light of resurrection from the dead. – JACQUES ELLUL

GOD DOES NOT TOLERATE SIN

Therefore let us keep the Festival, not with the old yeast, the yeast of malice and wickedness, but with bread without yeast, the bread of sincerity and truth (1 Cor 5:8).

Can a Christian hide sin? Some people think so, but a thorough investigation points to a different answer. God does not tolerate sin and is never deceived. He may allow sin to rage on for a while, but a day of reckoning always comes.

FOOD FROM THE WORD OF GOD
1 Corinthians 4:6-5:8;
Deuteronomy 17:2-7, 12-13;
Isaiah 1:24-29; 9:18.

Nothing leads to sin more easily than the belief that this world is all there is. People who commit violent crimes, adversely affecting the innocent, usually first convince themselves that there will never come a day of reckoning, of judgement. Even motorists who disobey the speed limits on highways, convince themselves that they will not be fined.

However, Jesus says that people who think they will never be caught, are wrong, *There is nothing concealed that will not be disclosed, or hidden that will not be made known* (Lk 12:2). God is opposed to sin. No one, and especially Christians can sin, thinking that they will get away with it.

The motto of the Royal Canadian Mounted Police is: "We always get our man!" They want to make it clear that no matter where a criminal flees, he *will* be found. The same applies to sin. Try as we may, we cannot hide our sins from God. Regardless of how many good deeds we perform, they will never be able to hide our disobedience before God. Sin will not pass unpunished – not even in the lives of God's children.

Righteous God, may your Holy Spirit protect me against sin and especially from the notion that I can get away with it.

Sin is not painful because it is prohibited; it is prohibited because it is painful.
BENJAMIN FRANKLIN

THE GREAT GIFT OF LOVE

And now these three remain: faith, hope and love. But the greatest of these is love (1 Cor 13:13).

During the approximately 33 years he lived on earth, Christ clearly revealed to us the essence of his love:

Jesus was interested in the families of his followers, their homes and health, physical as well as spiritual.

Jesus was prepared to make time for people in need, even though his ministry took up a lot of his time.

FOOD FROM THE WORD OF GOOD
1 Corinthians 12:12-13:13; Ruth 2:14-20; 1 Samuel 20:4-9.

Jesus offered them loyal support in their spiritual struggles by means of mediating prayer.

Jesus gave complete forgiveness, even though it appeared to be undeserved.

Jesus humbly served his followers and even washed their feet as an example.

Jesus let himself be nailed to the cross out of love for humanity.

Through all these acts of compassion, Jesus set an example of practical love; a love that provided for the deepest needs of people. Calvary summed up his love: the cross dealt decisively with all of our sins, paving the way for us to enjoy all of God's blessings.

If we want to love other people as Jesus asks us to do, we must learn to show practical love. It must be a reflection of the love that we receive from Jesus, which in turn inspires us to show his love in our lives. Would you not like to take up the challenge of expressing Jesus' love in your life?

God of love, purify and sanctify my love, too, through the example of Jesus Christ. I praise and thank you!

God does not love us because we are precious; we are precious because God loves us.
FULTON J SHEEN

THE SAVED PEOPLE OF GOD WILL LIVE AGAIN

For as in Adam all die,
so in Christ all will be made alive (1 Cor 15:22).

When we are so saturated with pain that we cannot even pray, we think that our bodies cause us humiliation. When we are tempted by the desires of the flesh, the word "bestial" comes to mind. Yes, our bodies do keep us humble. Our bodies link us to the dust of the earth. Maybe God actually planned it this way always to keep us humble, we who are often so proud of our bodies.

But our Saviour, Jesus the living Christ, will change this. We, who are connected to him through true faith, have bodies that will be changed to be like his glorious body. Through faith, our souls are reformed and our bodies will undergo a renewal. How soon this glorious change will occur, we cannot say. But the mere thought of it should enable us to resist the temptations of the flesh.

FOOD FROM THE WORD OF GOD
1 Corinthians 15:12-58; Psalm 49:13-16; Isaiah 25:6-8; Daniel 12:1-3; Ezekiel 37:11-14.

One day we will be like Jesus. We will no longer suffer throbbing headaches; no stiff or painful ligaments; no blurred vision or impaired hearing; no unreliable heartbeat. The aged person will no longer be a bundle of incapacity, or the ill person a mass of suffering: *The Lord Jesus Christ, who, by the power that enables him to bring everything under his control, will transform our lowly bodies so that they will be like his glorious body* (Phil 3:20-21). Praise the Lord, for he is good; his love is everlasting!

Risen and glorified Saviour, I thank you and praise you that I may place my hope in you, not only in this present life, but also for a glorious future with you.

Christianity is in essence a religion of resurrection. The concept of resurrection lies at the heart of it. If you take that away, you destroy Christianity. – JOHN RW STOTT

GOD'S JUDGEMENT COMES SUDDENLY

"But the day Lot left Sodom, fire and sulphur rained down from heaven and destroyed them all. It will be just like this on the day the Son of Man is revealed." (Lk 17:29-30)

When God decides that it is time for judgement there is no doubt about what he will do. This knowledge ought to influence our daily lives dramatically. Therefore, listen in earnest to Jesus' pronouncements on the judgement.

FOOD FROM THE WORD OF GOD
Luke 17:11-37; Genesis 18:20-21; 19:1-2, 12-17, 24-25.

Luke helps us especially to understand the sudden coming of the judgement. It will occur on a day when we are all busy with our usual things. In our Scripture reading the destruction of Sodom is used as an example. We read in Luke 17:28: "It was the same in the days of Lot. People were eating and drinking, buying and selling, planting and building."

We do not find anything dramatic here. At that moment, they were not busy with anything terribly sinful, or perhaps they were. The fact of the matter is that it might have been an ordinary Monday morning while we are getting ready for work or to go to school, or a Saturday afternoon while we are busy in and around our homes, or any time while we are buying and selling, eating and drinking. Do we live so focused that we can meet the Lord on any ordinary day? Are you ready for that day of salvation – or damnation?

With my lamp filled and brightly burning,
I await your coming, o Lord.

When Christ comes again on the clouds it will simply be a manifestation of the metamorphosis that was gradually brought about by his influence on the hearts of people. – P TEILHARD DE CHARDIN

GOD'S RIGHTEOUS JUDGEMENT

And then the lawless one will be revealed, whom the Lord Jesus will overthrow with the breath of his mouth and destroy by the splendour of his coming (2 Thess 2:8).

The wages of sin is death (Rom 6:23a). This is what sin deserves. When you work, you have a fair claim to compensation. In this way too, however, people amass a wage when they sin. And God is honour bound to pay people their fair wages.

The Scriptures tell us that in the last moments of the earth, the Judge will sit down and open the books. We will be there so that we can settle our final accounts with God and receive our fair judgements. What will come your way on that last day of reckoning – the wages of sin, or the eternal glory of God because you accepted his mercy through Jesus Christ?

FOOD FROM THE WORD OF GOD
2 Thessalonians 1:1-2:12; Proverbs 1:24-33; Isaiah 1:27-31.

We as sinful people often think of hell, that we might be thrown into it. There the devouring fire and languishing thirst will never end and the suffering will be unbearable. When you think about this, learn from it that the wages of sin is death. Stop committing sin because hell is the outcome for the unsaved person who refuses God's forgiveness. It is a frightening display of the holy justice of the righteous God, of his unbending aim to maintain holiness and joy in his entire kingdom.

Every sinner can now escape from this terrifying judgement. After all, God revealed himself to us in his holy Word – and let Christ die on the cross in order to save us.

Righteous God, your judgement and the certainty of damnation cannot be reasoned away. Thank you that the doors to paradise are open for me who has received eternal life through Jesus Christ.

There are no small sins. No grain of sand is small in the mechanism of a watch.
JEREMY TAYLOR

GOD PROTECTS HIS CHILDREN

Holy Father, protect them by the power of your name – the name you gave me – so that they may be one as we are one (Jn 17:11b).

Psalm 91 has a very positive message for every child of God.

God promises us a shelter, a safe fortress and protection based on the guarantee of the essence of God. Those who claim this promise for themselves and dwell in the shelter of the Most High will find rest in the shadow of the Almighty. God offers us unequalled security by providing us with this unique protection.

FOOD FROM THE WORD OF GOD
John 16:25-17:26; Deuteronomy 33:29; Psalm 91:1-16.

When we choose to dwell in his safe fortress – as the psalmist puts it – God will respond by adopting us as his children. In fact, the Almighty is saying, "If you come and live in my safe fortress, I promise to be your heavenly Host who has the holy responsibility of protecting you and caring for you." When we place our trust in him, he guarantees that he will offer us his safe protection against everything and everybody who might possibly harm us.

However, we will have to struggle through trials. It is simply a part of our lives on earth. But when we live in God's fortress in fellowship with him, we accept the shelter that only he can offer, and we will be safe until the task that he has given us on earth is completed. Yes indeed, our security is based on the fact that we hold on to a God who takes care of all who place their faith and trust in him.

Lord Jesus, when I read your prayer today, I once again became aware of your love and care. I praise and thank you for it.

If man were not created for God, why then is he only happy when he finds God? If man were created for God, why then does he oppose God? – BLAISE PASCAL

THE UNITY OF BELIEVERS

(I pray also) that all of them may be one, Father, just as you are in me and I am in you. May they also be in us so that the world may believe that you have sent me (Jn 17:21).

God is a God of unity. This is why Jesus repeatedly prayed in his pontifical prayer (Jn 17) that "all of them may be one", as the Father and the Son are one. Jesus knew that Satan would try to destroy the church through division. Therefore, he prayed in earnest that the church might be a united body in order that God's work on earth could be done by it.

FOOD FROM THE WORD OF GOD
John 17:21-18:18; Genesis 13:1-9; Psalm 133:1-3; Isaiah 66:19-33.

Because unity is so important to God, a large section of the New Testament gives instructions concerning the maintenance of unity in the church. 1 Corinthians 14:40 instructs the church to do everything *in a fitting and orderly way.* Ephesians 4:3 calls on us to *make every effort to keep the unity of the Spirit through the bond of peace.*

Satan knows the united strength of believers. This is why he is so desperate to disperse believers by continually attacking the church virulently. He is delighted when members of the church choir have a row; when church leaders attack one another; when members of the congregation have heated arguments over petty issues; when married couples live together in discord. And when Satan succeeds, God's people become ineffective.

As believing children of God we must fight against division. When we spot division we must kneel before God, identify the cause and restore unity through God's strength so that he may continue with his work through us.

Holy King of the church, help your church on earth to operate as a united front, so that your kingdom may also be on earth as it is in heaven.

The unity of man with God means the unity of people with each other.
St THOMAS AQUINAS

July 12

ONLY OWE LOVE

Let no debt remain outstanding, except the continuing debt to love one another, for he who loves his fellowman has fulfilled the law (Rom 13:8).

Anyone who has lent money to someone else, especially a fellow Christian, will realise that a barrier immediately goes up between them because of the lender-debtor relationship. This is because lenders and debtors are not really free to love one another. So consider it very seriously before you lend money to a fellow Christian. Also, think very carefully about the consequences before you borrow anything from someone else. You might find that you become the slave of the one from whom you borrowed. And are you then still free to love that person?

FOOD FROM THE WORD OF GOD
Romans 12:9-13:14; Deuteronomy 15:10-11; Psalm 37:21, 26; 112:5-9; Proverbs 6:1-5; 22:7.

Why is so much written in the Bible about debt? I believe that there are three main reasons. Firstly, debt is treacherous. Running into debt is easy; getting out of it is virtually impossible. Secondly, debt leads to enslavement. Moreover, when this enslavement is a part of the system of the world, we are no longer free to be the witnesses that God has called us to be. Thirdly, debt is dishonouring to God when it robs him of the opportunity to work in our lives and to provide for us.

Being in debt is symptomatic of problems that go much deeper: meanness, self-pleasure, impatience, fear, weak self-image, lack of discipline and much more. So when you do find yourself in debt, do not ask how you can get out of it, rather ask how you landed up in it. Then it will be far easier to get out and stay out of debt.

Holy Spirit of God, help me to practise a life-style that will prevent me from running into debt and enable me to give love to my fellowmen.

If you get your relationship with money right, it will contribute to getting almost every other relationship in your life right. – BILLY GRAHAM

BE PREPARED FOR OPPOSITION

But I will stay in Ephesus until Pentecost, because a great door for effective work has opened to me, and there are many who oppose me (1 Cor 16:8-9).

After my conversion and re-birth, I as a young Christian struggled with many divergent questions. I was encouraged by good and loving members of the church and told simply to live a good enough life, to be loving and friendly, and to believe – then the whole world would clasp me to its heart with love. Unfortunately, one only later discovers that it is not as straightforward as this. It is one of the disillusioning shocks that we as mature Christians experience.

If God himself, who is perfect, had to endure the harsh opposition to which he was subjected in the person of Jesus Christ when he lived amongst us on earth, how can we expect to escape it? Jesus was talking about precisely this when he said, *And anyone who does not take his cross and follow me is not worthy of me* (Mt 10:38).

FOOD FROM THE WORD OF GOD
1 Corinthians 15:44-16:24; Ezra 4:1-5; Psalm 35:1, 6-9; Jeremiah 18:18.

Anyone who decides to live for God in righteousness, must expect and endure hardships and opposition: *In fact, everyone who wants to live a godly life in Christ Jesus will be persecuted* (2 Tim 3:12). Unfortunately, the fact of the matter is that the fiercest attacks do not necessarily come from an unrighteous and unsaved world. The fiercest critics are often church people.

Therefore, you dare not allow opposition to cause you to lose enthusiasm for the work of the Lord. Being opposed or persecuted because of your impeccable Christian character and irreproachable conduct is a positive indication that you belong to God.

Help me, Holy Spirit, to remain, as my Master did, faithful to God in the face of all opposition.

In order to evade criticism, you simply have to do nothing, say nothing, and be nothing.
ELBERT HUBBARD

SPREAD THE GOOD NEWS

Therefore go and make disciples of all nations, baptising them in the name of the Father and of the Son and of the Holy Spirit (Mt 28:19).

Is your salvation so genuine that your testimony can comfort the broken hearted and set prisoners free from the web of sin? Is your salvation of such a quality that you cannot but spread the joyous tiding to those who await the good news of the gospel? The spreading of the gospel was more than mere sales talk to the Christians of the early church. Every one of them in his or her own way shared with others what he or she had learnt.

FOOD FROM THE WORD OF GOD
Matthew 28:11-Mark 1:20; 1 Chronicles 16:23-28; Isaiah 6:1-8; 61:1-7; Jonah 3:1-5, 10.

Their testimony bore witness to the spontaneous, unquenchable, bubbling enthusiasm of these people who had met the most exceptional man who had ever lived. They testified to their loving relationship with him, Jesus Christ. Only Jesus, the crucified Saviour, can save us. The disciples of the early church were totally possessed of this person. They were followers of the Master and learned from him how to live and die. They were dedicated to their Guide, filled by his Spirit and inspired by him.

They had had a personal meeting with the Saviour and simply could not keep it a secret. They did not testify because they had to, but because they could do nothing else. The Holy Spirit continually taught them how to witness: *But you will receive power when the Holy Spirit comes on you; and you will be my witnesses* (Acts 1:8).

Eternal and merciful God, strengthen me through your Holy Spirit, so that my testimony of Jesus the Saviour will never become silent.

The church survives through witnessing, as fire survives by burning.
EMIL BRUNNER

GOD HEALS BODY AND SOUL

The people were all so amazed that they asked each other, "What is this? A new teaching – and with authority! He even gives orders to evil spirits and they obey him" (Mk 1:27).

Bethlehem, Galilee, and Calvary – Jesus walked these places when he was on earth. In our day, he walks in the main streets of our cities, in the narrow streets of towns and on the gravel roads to farmsteads. His sandals are not dull from the dust of the road to Emmaus, but from the pollution of nature. His face is lit by flickering neon lights. He walks in hidden alleyways where faces are dark and sinister. At airports and railway stations milling crowds push and shove him, but ignore him. Yet he feels how the strength of God flows from his body and in all the faces of the people walking past him, he looks for an honest seeker.

FOOD FROM THE WORD OF GOD
Mark 1:21-45; 2 Kings 20:4-6; Psalm 31:14-16; 145:8-9; Isaiah 30:18; 57:18-19; Jeremiah 17:14; Hosea 6:1-3.

Yes, Christ walks through our streets and plays the leading role in the drama which tells how God's love came to mankind through him, Immanuel – God with us. He is the Broken One, but also the Healer. He was hungry, and yet he is the Bread of life. He had no home, yet it was he who said, *And if I go and prepare a place for you, I will come back and take you to be with me that you also may be where I am* (Jn 14:3). He was the great Bearer of the cross, and yet he said, *Come to me, all you who are weary and burdened, and I will give you rest* (Mt 11:28). He died on the cross, yet he is the only Way to triumphant victory. Isaiah 53:4 says that he has taken *up our infirmities* and yet he is the great Healer of the bodies and souls of people.

Thank you, Lord Jesus, for also having touched my body and soul with you benevolent and healing hand.

In healing, one can concentrate on one of two of God's qualities: his power or his love. Both are manifested in every healing. – FRANCIS MACNUT

July 16

WHAT IS TRUE REPENTANCE?

Many of those who believed now came and openly confessed their evil deeds (Acts 19:18).

As a child I often had to work in the garden before I was allowed to go and play. My foster mother made a list of everything I had to do. Sometimes she would walk with me to see if I had done everything properly. Now and then there would be weeds that I had missed, a plant that had not been watered or a bed that had not been dug up well enough. I immediately set about correcting the error. And I definitely did not make the same mistake again.

FOOD FROM THE WORD OF GOD
Acts 19:1-20; Psalm 51:1-17.

By looking at my work in this way, my foster mother was not loveless or hypercritical. She taught me to do a job well. Once I had corrected my mistakes, she always praised me by saying, "You have done a wonderful job, my child." The relationship between God and us should be the same. We ought to know what things are on our heavenly Father's "list" for us to do. We find his list in his Word. We must also be receptive so that he can show us our mistakes, and we must sincerely confess every day what we have done wrong. When we do this, we can know that we are forgiven instantly and totally (1 Jn 1:9).

Sin enters our lives very subtly, but when we open our lives to Christ, he helps us to ward off sin from our lives. Therefore, open your life to him and place it under the searchlight of God's Word. In his strength, you will notice the sin in your life, repent of it and leave it behind you.

Guard me from allowing sin to sneak into my life, O merciful God.

Sin is a force in our lives: may we clearly understand that it can only be conquered by a greater force.
HENRY DRUMMOND

THE UNRIGHTEOUS FEAR GOD

As Paul discoursed on righteousness, self-control and the judgement to come, Felix was afraid and said, "That's enough for now! You may leave. When I find it convenient, I will send for you" (Acts 24:25).

If it is true that a previous generation overemphasised God's sanctity and his purity at the expense of his love, our generation overemphasises his love at the expense of his sanctity and purity. We say, "God our Father is loving and tender," forgetting that around his throne seraphims and cherubs with covered faces are constantly singing, *Holy, holy, holy is the Lord Almighty; the whole earth is full of his glory* (Is 6:3).

FOOD FROM THE WORD OF GOD
Acts 24:17-25:12; Genesis 3:7-10; Ezekiel 21:1-7; Nahum 1:2, 5-6; 2:10.

We forget so easily that God is the holy and sovereign one who reigns over the earth in righteousness. Consequently, we lose the feeling of wonder, of holy respect and fear of God. We must realise anew that God is a mighty presence. Then we shall once more learn to have respect for him. Believing that there is an almighty God on the throne and that he is applying his holy, perfect and acceptable righteousness, will once again fill the hearts of sinful people with reverence for God.

The Puritans were acutely religious and feared God in a dignified manner. They were afraid to sin against God and viewed him as the One who was present with them at all times, and who knew everything about them. We do not have enough holy seriousness and we lack the realisation that our holy God occupies the throne; our God who actively and unceasingly maintains his dynamic holiness. This fact alone should force us into worship and keep us from ever damaging his holiness.

Holy and Almighty God, convince me of your holiness and righteousness so that I will never play them off against your love.

We must fear God through love and not love him through fear.
JEAN PIERRE CAMUS

GOD CHANGES OUR HEARTS AND LIVES

No, a man is a Jew if he is one inwardly; and circumcision is circumcision of the heart, by the Spirit, not by the written code. Such a man's praise is not from men, but from God (Rom 2:29).

Jesus preached the message of conversion and faith everywhere, *Repent and believe the good news!* (Mk 1:15). And the faith that he preached, requires a living and practical faith that radically alters your life.

FOOD FROM THE WORD OF GOD
Romans 2:17-3:20; Jeremiah 4:4; 7:3-5; 9:25-26; Micah 3:8-12.

The Bible also talks about genuine conversion as well as fake conversion. In 2 Corinthians 7:9-10 Paul writes, *Yet now I am happy, not because you were made sorry, but because your sorrow led you to repentance. For you became sorrowful as God intended and so were not harmed in any way by us. Godly sorrow brings repentance that leads to salvation and leaves no regret, but worldly sorrow brings death.* God-given sorrow leads to true regret and conversion – and that is not really sorrow. You might be filled with sorrow over you sins and yet have no regret, because you are sorrowful for the wrong reasons. Instead of grieving over sins that disappoint and hurt God, you feel bad only because your sins caused you personal pain, or exacted something from you because they were made known. Indeed, if repentance and conversion do not bring about a radical change in your character, heart and life, then the repentance and conversion are not genuine.

The agonising results of false conversion are seen everywhere in our churches. There are no broken hearts, sins are concealed and confessing Christians do not walk in the light of God. But, the fruits of genuine conversion are seen in altered thoughts, hearts, and behaviour.

*Holy Spirit of God, you who lead us to genuine conversion,
convert my thoughts, heart and life in such a way
that I will truly and inseparably belong to God.*

Conversion is something far greater than just repentance of sin:
it includes a change of nature that is pleasing to God. – LEW WALLACE

GOD LOVES US SINCERELY

God has poured out his love into our hearts by the Holy Spirit, whom he has given us (Rom 5:5b).

Jesus said, *No one is good – except God alone* (Lk 18:19b). The glory of God in heaven and on earth is indeed based on the fact that everything he does is good and filled with love. Yes, this God who only wants what is good, is a God of love. He does not seek to further his own interests and does not live for himself alone. He pours out his astonishing love on everything and everyone that he has created. Paul rightly says that love is not self-seeking (1 Cor 13:5). Love sacrifices itself completely for the sake of others. This is why God sacrificed himself for our sake in the person of his Son Jesus Christ. The good news we preach is this, *For God so loved the world that he gave his one and only Son, that whoever believes in him shall not perish but have eternal life* (Jn 3:16).

FOOD FROM THE WORD OF GOD
Romans 4:13-5:11; Psalm 62:6-9; 69:14; Isaiah 38:15-17; 48:9-11; 63:7-9.

Similarly, the Son also sacrificed himself on the cross to prove his love for us and to win our hearts for him. The undying love, with which the Father loves the Son, is the same love with which the Son loves us. This very love of God the Father is the love that Jesus Christ, through the work of the Holy Spirit, poured out into our hearts. The triune God desires that our lives be drenched in the dynamic power of his love, and that this love will flow forth from our lives to touch every other life benevolently.

I praise and thank you, God and Father, for the gift of your unfathomable love for me. Praise the Lord, for he is good; his love is everlasting!

The Name of this immeasurable and boundless source of love – is God.
PAUL TILLICH

BELIEVE AND BE SAVED

That if you confess with your mouth, "Jesus is Lord," and believe in your heart that God raised him from the dead, you will be saved (Rom 10:9).

We cannot follow God in our own way. The right road is very clearly indicated to us: *Christ is the end of the law so that there may be righteousness for everyone who believes* (Rom 10:4). Yes, we are saved only through faith in the act of atonement of the crucified Jesus Christ.

People do not get to know God through personal wisdom. Neither is it through endless theological arguments that people acquire humble hearts. The door that leads to the kingdom of God is as lowly as the entrance to Jesus' birthplace in Bethlehem: first you must bend low in humility – yes, even go on your knees – to enter there.

FOOD FROM THE WORD OF GOD
Romans 9:30-10:21; Leviticus 18:1-5; Deuteronomy 30:19-20; Psalm 19:1-4; Joel 2:28-32.

I have never yet met anyone who is convinced of the kingdom of God purely through intellectual knowledge. But no one can enter the kingdom of God solely through religious experience either. It is knowledge of faith in Jesus Christ, and the experience of it in your life that leads you into the kingdom of the Father. *Jews demand miraculous signs and Greeks look for wisdom, but we preach Christ crucified: a stumblingblock to Jews and foolishness to Gentiles, but to those whom God has called, both Jews and Greeks, Christ is the power of God and the wisdom of God. For the foolishness of God is wiser than man's wisdom, and the weakness of God is stronger than man's strength* (1 Cor 1:22-25).

Holy Spirit, through your mercy, strengthen my faith in Jesus, my Saviour, day after day so that I may be assured of my salvation.

Jesus Christ is everything for man's total need.
RICHARD HALVERSON

July 21

COMPASSION IS A VIRTUE

"Which of these three do you think was a neighbour to the man who fell into the hands of robbers?" The expert in the law replied, "The one who had mercy on him." Jesus told him, "Go and do likewise" (Lk 10:36-38).

Compassion entails doing your best to promote the fortune and welfare of others. Nowadays there are many stories like the one about the Good Samaritan, which prove that when you have compassion for someone who urgently needs your help, even when it is inconvenient to you, you are putting into practice a God-given virtue.

FOOD FROM THE WORD OF GOD
Luke 10:30-11:13; Genesis 39:19b-23; Exodus 2:16-20; Psalm 112:1-5; Proverbs 3:1-4.

The New Testament often refers to the compassion of God. Jesus says that God is even *kind to the ungrateful and the wicked. Be merciful, just as your Father is merciful* (Lk 6:35-36). In Romans 2:4 we read that God's kindness, tolerance and patience seek to lead sinners to repentance. In our utter despair as a result of sin, Paul speaks in Ephesians 2:7 of the immense greatness of God's goodness, which has been proved to us through Jesus Christ.

What can we learn from the compassion and goodness of God? He is good to all people, also to the ungrateful the wicked, those who are totally lost, those without hope, the rebellious … We are inclined to have compassion for those to whom we feel attracted. God shows mercy also to outcasts, the ungrateful and the wicked. He never turns his back on anybody. We as God's followers should therefore cultivate a compassionate attitude, and honestly desire to promote the joy and welfare of others. We must not simply be sensitive to their needs – we must actively do something about it.

God of compassion, I seriously pray that you will show me ways in which I can demonstrate your love and mercy to other people around me.

The best thing that you can do for your heavenly Father is to show compassion to his other children.
HENRY DRUMMOND

REPENT AND BELIEVE

In those days John the Baptist came, preaching in the Desert of Judea and saying, "Repent, for the kingdom of heaven is near" (Mt 3:1-2).

The wood seller of a certain town testified about his re-birth and conversion during a church service. While he was talking, one of the townspeople slipped out of the church. He returned with a bundle of wood that he had bought from the wood seller the day before. "He is truly born again!" the townsman assured the congregation. Everybody knew that the wood seller was dishonest. He always said there were twelve pieces of wood in a bundle, but often there were only eleven, or even ten. He also alleged that every piece of wood was exactly one metre long, whereas they were often quite a few centimetres shorter. The man with the bundle of wood counted the pieces and found that there were exactly twelve. He also measured them: every piece was precisely one metre in length. To all the townsfolk, this was proof enough that the man's heart and life had changed, that he had truly been born again.

FOOD FROM THE WORD OF GOD
Matthew 3:1-4:11; Psalm 34:1-23.

The message of John the Baptist was that people had to change their hearts and lives because the kingdom of God in Jesus Christ was near. It does not differ from the message of the Old Testament, nor does it differ from the message brought by Jesus Christ, *The kingdom of God is near. Repent and believe the good news!* (Mk 1:15). To this very day it is still the message of God's Word to us. Have your heart and life already changed through the mercy of God, so that other people can see and know it?

I thank and praise you, Lord Jesus, for having changed my heart and life through the Holy Spirit, so that I may live for your honour.

Not to sin anymore is the most sincere form of conversion.
MARTIN LUTHER

TO GOD LOVE IS MOST IMPORTANT

I desire mercy, not sacrifice (Mt 12:7b).

"Lord," I said, "I want to be your man, not my own. So to You I give my money, my car – even my home."

Then, smug and content, I whispered to God with a smile, "I bet it's been a while since anyone has given You so much, so freely?"

His answer surprised me. He replied: "Not really. Not a day has gone by since the beginning of time that somebody hasn't offered meagre nickels and dimes. Golden altars and crosses, contributions and penances, stone monuments and steeples: but why not repentance? The money, the statues, the cathedrals you've built, do you really think I need your offerings of guilt? What good is money that's meant only to salve the hurting conscience that so many of you have? Your lips know no prayers. Your eyes no compassion, but you will go to church (when church-going is in fashion). Just give me a tear, a heart ready to mould and I'll give you a mission, a message so bold that a fire will be stirred where there only was death; and your heart will be flamed by my life and my breath."

FOOD FROM THE WORD OF GOD
Matthew 11:25-12:21;
Deuteronomy 10:12-13, 20-21;
Psalm 51:18-19; Micah 6:6-8.

I stuck my hands in my pockets and kicked at the dirt.

It's tough to be corrected (I guess my feelings were hurt).

But it was worth the struggle to realise the thought that the cross isn't for sale and Christ's blood can't be bought!

This quote taken from *God came near* by Max Lucado, gives one something to think about – and it draws one closer to the Lord.

Holy Jesus, may I always remember that the most important thing is not what I give to you, but what you give to me.

Come let us bring to Christ the great universal sacrifice of our love, and worship him with songs of praise and prayers. For he sacrificed his cross to God so that we may all be made rich.– PAUL FROST

July 24

NOT ALL WHO HEAR, UNDERSTAND

This is why I speak to them in parables. Though seeing, they do not see; though hearing, they do not hear or understand (Mt 13:13).

Jesus warned that a person's heart might be damaged by sin to such an extent that it might become totally insensitive to the gospel of salvation. This heart knows no regret, experiences no feelings of guilt and has no interest in God. These people's lives are full of evil thoughts, cherished sins and ungodly actions. They are reckless, unscrupulous, detached and do not become convinced of their sins. This fool is described in Proverbs. Fools despise knowledge, resist teaching and instruction, have contempt for wisdom and say in their hearts that there is no God. They do not want to hear with their ears and their minds are closed. They do not want to be bothered by the gospel's invitation to salvation.

FOOD FROM THE WORD OF GOD
Matthew 12:43-13:17; Psalm 119:97-106; Jeremiah 6:10; 25:4-5, 7; Zechariah 7:11-12.

Many people have such hearts. You can overwhelm them with good seed, but it just lies there without a purpose. It never penetrates the hard shell of their lives in order to start growing. Then it is not long before Satan comes and takes away the good seed completely. Every time you try to testify to such a person, you have to start all over again with the basic truths.

Dry, hard soil at the edge of the ploughed land does not necessarily indicate resistance to religion. However, because sin has already hardened their hearts to such an extent, some people are completely unproductive, and consider themselves not to be responsible to God. They are those who hear the good news without understanding it.

Give me a tender heart, O God, which wants to understand all that you wish to give me out of your mercy.

Let your religion be less of a theory, and more of a love affair.
GK CHESTERTON

July 25

KEEP GOD'S INSTRUCTIONS IN YOUR HEART

I will open my mouth in parables, I will utter things hidden since the creation of the world (Mt 13:35).

William Bucky Hope came from Ireland to Ugie in the Eastern Cape to take up the position of secretary at the local children's home, a calling that he filled for more than 35 years. During all this time, his health was always poor. He was often ill. This exceptional man often opened his worn Bible and explained God's great truths to the orphans in a way that the people of that village had never heard before. I was so impressed and moved by his words that I, as a recently reborn 16-year-old boy, asked him where he had learnt all these things. Did he attend a college or a seminary?

FOOD FROM THE WORD OF GOD
Matthew 13:18-43; Deuteronomy 11:18-21; Psalm 119:10-16, 116-120; Proverbs 2:1-6.

The humble man replied, "My dear young friend, I learnt these things on my knees on the plank floor of a small dilapidated house in Ireland. There, with my Bible open in front of me, I knelt for hours before God, begging his Spirit to reveal Christ to me and to open his Word in my heart. There on my knees he taught me more than I could have learnt in any college or seminary." No wonder then that one morning, we found him in his room, dead on his knees. This was how he had lived and taught.

Jesus also talks to us through the Word of God. We can sit at his feet while we read his Word and the Holy Spirit teaches and guides us. We can talk to him in prayer, and live according to his commands.

Word incarnate, I am prepared to do anything so that I may be able to understand your eternal Word correctly and with all my heart.

The Bible is a window in this prison world through which we can get a glance of eternity.
T DWIGHT

GREATNESS BEGINS WITH HUMILITY

Therefore, whoever humbles himself like this child is the greatest in the kingdom of heaven (Mt 18:4).

Why is humility in the lives of his children so important to Jesus? Because he is the ultimate truth. If we understand and acknowledge that there is no good in us, it makes us humble before him who is truth and has the ability to change us.

May God give us the grace to always be humble. In his divine majesty, he lovingly seeks honest people, but they must be humble in all their deeds, not only trusting in themselves and their own deeds. Humility is the truth that God is looking for in us. *God opposes the proud but gives grace to the humble* (1 Pet 5:5). However, we cannot be humble through our own strength. But Paul writes to the Philippians, *I can do everything through him who gives me strength* (Phil 4:13). God himself enables us to do great things for him and his kingdom. We also find clarity and courage for a life of humility when we think of the words of St Augustine, "Give me, Lord, that which you desire of me, and make your commands my desires."

FOOD FROM THE WORD OF GOD
Matthew 17:14-18:9; 2 Chronicles 33:12-13; Psalm 18:25-27; 138:1-6; Proverbs 29:23; Jeremiah 44:10-11.

It is of vital importance that we understand what humility really means. We must bear in mind that Satan will not cease to do great damage to us. He prevents us who pray from being humble, from treasuring the longing to be like Jesus. But do not allow yourself to be diverted. Walk the road of humility before God until the very end.

Grant, Lord Jesus, that it may remain my sincere desire to be humble.

The reason why God loves humility so much is that he is a great lover of the truth. For indeed humility is nothing but the truth, while pride is nothing but lies. – VINCENT DE PAUL

WORSHIP GOD

"It is written," he said to them, "'My house will be called a house of prayer,' but you are making it a 'den of robbers'" (Mt 21:13).

Worshipping God is more than just a Sunday pastime. It is to constantly think about God's holiness, love and redemption. His purpose with creation was to make people a worshipping community that would sing his praise and honour as a sign of their thankfulness for his redeeming mercy.

When God made a covenant with the people of Israel, they met with him in the first public meeting between God and his people. This meeting with God became the model for worshipping in Israel. For it is through worshipping that God's revelation, salvation and covenant are recalled. It was also handed down from generation to generation as the way in which God should be worshipped in spirit and in truth.

FOOD FROM THE WORD OF GOD
Matthew 21:12-32; Psalm 26:8; 96:1-9; Isaiah 56:6-7; Jeremiah 7:8-15; Ezekiel 8:16-18.

We worship God for what he has done for us in the past, for what he is doing for us now, and for what he will do for us in the future. Our aim must be to worship in a meaningful way. This is why we must prepare our spirits, hearts and minds for that holy moment when we draw close to God and worship him actively and dynamically.

In our day and age, the way we worship is often adapted to people's likes and dislikes. Devotion and seriousness often make way for a concert atmosphere. When we worship, our focus should be the glory of God. Therefore, ask the Holy Spirit to lead you in your worship, and worship God in spirit and in truth.

Holy, holy, holy is the Lord Almighty; the whole earth is full of his glory (Is 6:3).

We can just as little affect the glory of God by refusing to worship him as a lunatic can extinguish the sun by writing "darkness" on the wall of his cell. – CS LEWIS

July 28

GOD PUNISHES THE PERSECUTORS OF HIS MESSENGERS

O Jerusalem, Jerusalem, you who kill the prophets and stone those sent to you, how often I have longed to gather your children together, as a hen gathers her chicks under her wings, but you were not willing. Look, your house is left desolate (Mt 23:37-38).

FOOD FROM THE WORD OF GOD
Matthew 23:29-24:14; Psalm 94:20-23; Jeremiah 2:30; 34-35; 20:1-6.

A young man once went to the American evangelist Dwight Lyman Moody and asked him, "Mr Moody, I want to be a Christian, but do I then have to forsake the world?" In his characteristic manner, Moody answered him, "My young friend, if you live in total dedication to Christ, the world will soon forsake *you*." If we are popular in the world, or if we are not sometimes penalised for our close connection to Christ, then there is good reason to look into our discipleship.

The world persecutes us in various ways. Sometimes it uses the sword, at other times destructive words. Most of us are immune to the sword, but we stumble before malice from the mouths of our enemies. May we always remember that those who persecute us because we are followers of Christ will be penalised. The ungodly who take delight in persecuting God's messengers will receive punishment from God.

Under the old dispensation, God often executed his judgements immediately after a crime was committed against him, so that the connection between the crime and the punishment could clearly be understood. Now the punishment may be postponed, but it is surely coming, and it will be terrible to fall into the hands of the living God. God does not let the persecutors of his messengers remain unpunished.

Holy and righteous God, I praise you for the strength you give me to remain standing as your witness in every persecution.

Nobody becomes a martyr because of rumours and opinions: faith creates martyrs.
JOHN HENRY NEWMAN

GOD REWARDS COMPASSION

The King will reply, "I tell you the truth, whatever you did for one of these brothers of mine, you did for me" (Mt 25:40).

There is a Japanese proverb that says, "One friendly deed can drive away three months of winter cold." Friendly words or deeds really do warm a person's spirit. Friendliness is love in action. Genuine friendship towards others, which proves that we see them as important in the eyes of God and therefore believe that they should be treated with respect and consideration, is the result of God's love in our hearts. It means treating others politely, encouraging them, and offering ourselves and our possessions to those in need.

FOOD FROM THE WORD OF GOD
Matthew 25:14-40; Psalm 41:1-3; 112:5-9; Proverbs 14:31; 19:17; Isaiah 58:7-11.

In the Scriptures that we read today, God views contempt for the poor and oppressed, the homeless and the downhearted in a very serious light. Through them he encourages us to be compassionate, friendly and generous. Is this not precisely how God acts towards us?

In Proverbs we read that love and friendliness are primary character traits of a woman (and also a man) of noble character: *She speaks with wisdom, and faithful instruction is on her tongue* (Prov 31:26). We must all strive to put it into practice. Brighten someone's day with an unexpected word or gesture of friendliness: a member of your family, someone at work, on the sports field, at church. Just think what an impact Christians could have on the world if friendliness and love were to be the criteria for everything we do. And … then we would also have done it to Christ!

Lord, my living Christ, you are the perfect example to me of friendliness towards other people – strangers, the oppressed and sinners. Help me through the Holy Spirit to follow your example.

Friendliness has led more sinners to repentance than zeal, eloquence and learning.
FREDERICK W FABER

TRUST IN GOD TO PROVIDE

Taking the five loaves and the two fish and looking up to heaven, he gave thanks and broke the loaves. Then he gave them to his disciples to set before the people. He also divided the two fish among them all. They all ate and were satisfied (Mk 6:41-42).

FOOD FROM THE WORD OF GOD
Mark 6:17-44; Psalm 69:31-37; 107:8-9; 145:1-7, 14-19.

Trusting in God gives us a clear perspective on life. When we consider doing God's work on earth in order to enrich ourselves through it, we try to serve two masters and therefore our judgement is twisted. Who amongst us has not yet experienced this? We try to determine what the will of God is, or to look at our lives in honesty, but our sense of duty is continually being overshadowed by the thought that once we have chosen a certain course, it can harm our personal interests in another sense.

In this case, our eyes are not focused on Jesus and we walk in darkness. When, however, we get so involved in God's interests that we no longer care about our own interests, everything becomes clear and we follow God's guidance. And he never disappoints us. May we never think that God is selfish or ungenerous in the giving of his gifts. He provides bread as well as fish when he feeds the crowd; colours as well as leaves when he clothes the flowers of the field.

You have become a part of his heavenly family and may call him, "Abba, Father!" This compassion proves the special love he has within his heart for us. Would he then only look after our spiritual needs, ignoring our temporal needs? Surely, the trusting children of God, our loving Father, can rest assured that he will satisfy all our needs.

Father God, along with the psalmist we rejoice, For he satisfies the thirsty and fills the hungry with good things (Ps 107:9).

Leave the past to the grace of God, the present to his love, and the future to his providence.

St AGUSTINE OF HIPPO

July 31

FAITH IS NOT A SPIRITUAL LUXURY

I can do everything through him who gives me strength (Phil 4:13).

Sometimes it feels as if we totally lose control of our circumstances in life. The demands of life simply become too much for us. It appears to us as if our faith is not enough to carry us through. Our circumstances appear increasingly hopeless. We feel so powerless that we want to exclaim along with Paul, *What a wretched man I am! Who will rescue me from this body of death?* (Rom 7:24).

FOOD FROM THE WORD OF GOD
Philippians 4:10-19; 1 Timothy 4:6-16; Hebrews 11:1-6

If you have reached this breaking point, return to the fundamental things in life, those things that strengthen your faith and assure you of the presence of God Almighty – intensive prayer, Bible study and fellowship with other believers. You will find balance again and will see people and events from the right perspective.

God does not want you to break under pressure. He wants to create a living faith within you that has a stabilising effect during stressful times and will help you to experience peace of mind again. A faith like this is not a spiritual luxury, but a necessity for everybody who lives close to his Saviour.

Therefore, go to him with your needs and trust him unconditionally. He will carry you through your hard times. And yet again, you will be able to exclaim along with Paul, only this time words of hope: *Thanks be to God – through Jesus Christ our Lord* (Rom 7:25).

My Father and my God, I know that I cannot do the will of God in my life without faith. Therefore, I pray along with the disciples of old, "Strengthen my weak faith!"

The beginning and the end of faith is love, and God has put these two together in unity.
IGNATIUS OF ANTIOCH

August

Prayer for August

1. God demands generosity
2. Who is equal to God's wrath?
3. Remember to help the poor
4. God empowers his children
5. Your neighbour as yourself …
6. Seek, honour and trust God
7. Marriage – a gift from God
8. To marry or not to marry
9. Do not lead someone astray
10. Desire spiritual gifts
11. The basics of our faith
12. Simply trust in God
13. New heart, new deeds
14. Honour your father and your mother
15. Come and stay with me
16. Wickedness versus righteousness
17. Be brave for the truth
18. Jesus is a patient teacher
19. God is looking for reliable witnesses
20. God alone gives power and wisdom
21. Our words betray our hearts
22. Righteousness in the eyes of God
23. God's kingdom is intended for his children
24. Do the will of God
25. The results of faith
26. The evil one persecutes the righteous
27. Your sacrifice to God
28. God is merciful to us
29. Praise God for his salvation
30. Called to do God's work
31. Build your life on a firm foundation

Prayer for August

Holy God, in Christ Jesus my heavenly Father,
help me to *believe* anew during this month,
as all the heroes of faith in your eternal Word.
Save me from the Thomas syndrome that
requires feeling and seeing in order to believe.
I so want to see and confess the invisible.
"My Lord and my God!"
Help me to safeguard *hope* undamaged in my heart,
the hope that all the noble ideals of my heart will be realised,
that I will grow spiritually to maturity
in love, knowledge, and truth,
so that I will be able to distinguish
the things that really matter.
Keep a spirit of optimism burning in my heart.
Help me to distinguish and express *love*, O Lord.
I so want to be able to say honestly,
"Lord, you know everything, you know that I love you!"
Help me to love my neighbour as myself,
sincerely and unselfishly with a love that breaks down all barriers,
and to make reconciliation a practical reality.
I beg this in the Name of God my Father
and Christ Jesus my Saviour,
through the work of the Holy Spirit.

Amen

August 1

GOD DEMANDS GENEROSITY

Because of the service by which you have proved yourselves, men will praise God for the obedience that accompanies your confession of the Gospel of Christ, and for your generosity in sharing with them and with everyone else (2 Cor 9:13).

We all know how subtle the temptations of materialism are. It is only through great effort as well as the grace of God that we can avoid the deluge of luxuries that is washing away our Christian charitableness. We are all familiar with this problem. We buy what we see and desire, sometimes even when we cannot really afford it. And we conveniently forget about the millions of people worldwide who do not even have dry bread to eat.

FOOD FROM THE WORD OF GOD
2 Corinthians 8:16-9:15; Deuteronomy 14:22-29; Psalm 112:5-9; Proverbs 21:25-26; 28:27.

We ought to ask ourselves honestly: Do we dare buy and buy, and then buy some more while we are not prepared to help our neighbours in need? Is it right to be more concerned about our own financial security and that of our families than about our neighbours who do not even have a roof over their heads?

The thing that is so special about Paul's guidelines to the Corinthians about the giving of gifts is the preparation. He sent people to prepare the thanksgiving offering that the congregation had promised beforehand. How does my generosity work? Do I only give when I am cornered, or do I plan for it? Do I budget a certain portion for giving to the poor? It is a choice that can ultimately bring me great joy in life.

Dear Father, you provide so generously in all my needs. May I never be reckless about the needs of others.

It is a preoccupation with possessions, more than anything else, that prevents one from living a free and noble life. – BERTRAND RUSSEL

August 2

WHO IS EQUAL TO GOD'S WRATH?

They called to the mountains and the rocks, "Fall on us and hide us from the face of him who sits in the throne and from the wrath of the Lamb! For the great day of their wrath has come, and who can stand?" (Rev 6:16-17).

As improbable as it looks and as much as people ignore it, it is a certain fact that there will be a day of reckoning. On that day, the time of mercy will be past and the day of punishment will have come, and who will then be able to save man? Ensure that on that day you will be found loyal so that you need not flee in mortal fear from the face of God.

FOOD FROM THE WORD OF GOD
Revelation 6:1-17; Isaiah 2:12-21; Nahum 1:2-6.

The day of reckoning will bring fear to the hearts of people who did not serve God. Their hearts will be filled with fear, not so much because of revolution, or frightening wars and plagues, but because they will see God sitting on his throne. They will behold the God of love as the God of wrath. They will beg to be hidden from his sight. They will do anything not to have to see their Maker face to face. They will choose to be buried under rocks in the mountains to which they will flee. These people will not return to God in large numbers. For them there will be no repentance or confessions of guilt. They will just flee panic-stricken from God, in order not to have to observe his terrifying wrath on an unrepentant mankind.

On that day, will you be one of the terrified fugitives, or have you found shelter in the Rock of ages, Jesus our Saviour?

Triumphant God and Father, thank you that I may await your day of reckoning with a mind that is at ease because I have found salvation with the living Christ.

Sleep with clean hands, either kept clean through the day by integrity, or washed at night by confession of guilt. – JOHN DONNE

REMEMBER TO HELP THE POOR

All they asked was that we should continue to remember the poor, the very thing I was eager to do (Gal 2:10).

The Bible states in no uncertain terms that we ought to follow God's example by being concerned about the poor and the oppressed. God often reminded his people of their oppression in Egypt when he commanded them to care for the poor.

When Paul was collecting charitable donations for the poor of Jerusalem he pointed out to the Corinthians that Jesus became poor so that they might become rich. *For you know the grace of our Lord Jesus Christ, that though he was rich, yet for your sake he became poor, so that you through his poverty might become rich* (2 Cor 8:9). When John summons us to be charitable, he first refers to the example of Christ: *This is how we know what love is: Jesus Christ laid down his life for us. And we ought to lay down our lives for our brothers. If anyone has material possessions and sees his brother in need but has no pity on him, how can the love of God be in him?* (1 Jn 3:16-17). We ought to follow the example of Jesus' astonishing self-sacrifice in our relationship with the poor and the oppressed.

FOOD FROM THE WORD OF GOD
Galatians 1:22-2:21; Leviticus 25:35-38; Nehemiah 8:1-12; Psalm 72:1-4; 113:5-8; Proverbs 14:31; 21:23.

The Word of God commands us as believers to care for the poor. After all, when God's people really care, they imitate God himself. But furthermore, it teaches us that those who neglect the poor are not really children of God, despite all their religious rituals and confessions.

Lord Jesus, give me a heart as compassionate as your own, so that I will joyfully fulfil my duty towards the poor and the oppressed.

He who shuts his ears and his heart to the poor, will himself call out and not be heard.
ALEXANDER POPE

August 4

GOD EMPOWERS HIS CHILDREN

The weapons we fight with are not the weapons of the world. On the contrary, they have divine power to demolish strongholds (2 Cor 10:4).

Our struggle on earth is not against people, but against spiritual evil. Our struggle is against Satan and the despair that he causes. We are fighting against all the forces of sin: impurity, drunkenness, oppression, unfaithfulness and wickedness. We enter into battle against these things, but not with spears and swords. No, the weapons we have at our disposal are not of this earth.

FOOD FROM THE WORD OF GOD
2 Corinthians 10:1-11:4; 2 Samuel 22:2-7; 2 Chronicles 20:20-22; Psalm 55:17-19; Jeremiah 23:25-29.

Our God despises everything that is evil and sinful. That is why he comes with us to the battlefield in our crusade against the evil one. He will save us, and give us the grace required to fight to the very end – and in his Name we will be able to do it triumphantly. We can depend on it that God Almighty is on our side. With such a powerful ally, there can be no doubt whatsoever about the outcome of the battle. We have God on our side. He is the Almighty, and all power in heaven and on earth has been given to his Son Jesus Christ, and the Holy Spirit confirms and maintains his will amongst us.

Therefore, we, as God and Christ's warriors, must put on the full armour that the Spirit offers us. We must march against the enemy in the Name of Christ the Triumphant and the God of holiness and omnipotence. Through faith, lay your hands firmly on your salvation. Do not allow a single day to pass without achieving a victory in the Name of Jesus.

March onward, Christian soldiers, as to war, with the cross of Jesus going on before.

When we are feeling too brave, may we remember our own weakness. When we are feeling too weak, may we remember the power of God. – SIR THOMAS MOORE

YOUR NEIGHBOUR AS YOURSELF ...

If you really keep the royal law found in the Scripture, "Love your neighbour as yourself," you are doing right (Jas 2:8).

Our lives are deeply touched by people who take the trouble to understand us, who care enough about us to forgive our mistakes and make us their friends. These are often people to whom we have not been at all friendly. It therefore comes as a complete surprise to us that they have befriended us. For this very reason it gives us twice the joy. It also inspires us, and challenges us to treat them the way that they have treated us.

FOOD FROM THE WORD OF GOD
James 2:1-26; Leviticus 19:15-16; Proverbs 21:3; Obadiah 9:11-15.

To discover the true source that inspires this kind of behaviour, we as Christians must look beyond our neighbours and see the immeasurable grace of God. Nothing else on earth humbles us to the same extent. Nothing else softens our stone cold spirits so that we in our turn also show mercy. Nothing else inspires us as powerfully to do the right thing, that is: to show mercy to our neighbours.

God calls on us to be merciful, to be forgiving and compassionate, to be loving. This does not mean that we purposefully overlook evil, or sweep wickedness under the carpet. It means that we care enough to lead other people to God so that they can also share in his perfect mercy. It is he who will purify, recreate and renew us through his compassion and grace. His tender love is infinitely deep and immeasurably large. Praise the Lord, for he is good.

Help me, Holy Spirit, to pass on the love of God, shown to me through Jesus Christ, to others on my path of life in this loveless world.

We never love our neighbours as truly as when our love for them is born out of our love for God.
FRANÇOIS FÈNELON

SEEK, HONOUR AND TRUST GOD

But seek first his kingdom and his righteousness, and all these things will be given to you as well (Mt 6:33).

So often we test God instead of trusting him unconditionally. We negotiate with him instead of believing in his omnipotence. We are like children who test the ice before skating on it, even though they can see that thousands are skating on it without hesitation. Rather than walking in trust where God leads us, we constantly question God's road, and make excuses as to why we cannot walk his road in trust.

FOOD FROM THE WORD OF GOD
Matthew 6:16-7:6; Nehemiah 9:1-3; Isaiah 58:3-5; Joel 2:12-13, Zechariah 7:1-6.

What is the value or quality of our faith if we do not want to trust God completely? Trusting ourselves is totally natural. We trust in our own strength, our own abilities, and our own talents. But we refuse to trust God to instruct us and to show us the right way.

Give God the most important position in your life and let his will be done in everything that you undertake, plan and do. Then you glorify God. And this is the secret of progress in your life: simple trust in God, unconditional surrender to his will and unshakeable obedience to his commands. That is how you glorify God. St Augustine said, "Be careful of despairing of yourself; you are instructed to place your trust in God, and not in yourself."

Are you seeking the will of God in your life? How do you honour God in your life? What is the quality of your faith and trust in God? That will determine how strong the spiritual power in your life is.

Lord my God and Father, I want to seek, honour and trust you, in earnest, day by day. Grant me guidance through the Holy Spirit so that I may succeed in this.

Human reasoning is weak and can be deceived; but faith cannot be deceived.
THOMAS á KEMPIS

MARRIAGE - A GIFT FROM GOD

The husband should fulfil his marital duty to his wife, and likewise the wife to her husband (1 Cor 7:3).

In this Scripture reading Paul specifically highlights one fact: marriage is inviolable and lasting. When you get married, he says, it is for life. A wife must not separate from her husband (1 Cor 7:10), and likewise a husband must not separate from his wife (v 11). The husband may not send the wife away (v 12), and the wife may not send the husband away (v 13). Writing it once might have been enough. Twice would have stressed it greatly. Three times would have been more than enough. But four times! Clearly, Paul is very serious about this matter.

FOOD FROM THE WORD OF GOD
1 Corinthians 7:1-24; Genesis 2:23-24; 24:1-8; Proverbs 18:22; Malachi 3:15-16.

Married couples must delete the word "divorce" from their vocabularies. We may not even use it to threaten one another during arguments. So what then does it take to remain permanently surrendered to one another despite problems?

Grace. The grace to negotiate our way through the minefields of differences. The grace to forgive one another and to carry on in the knowledge that love always prevails. The grace to persevere even though the same problems arise again and again. A marriage that is grounded in grace is permanent, durable and indestructible. In the eyes of God, marriage is a serious matter. This is why our thoughts about it must be pure, biblically founded and divinely inspired. Are you prepared to change your thoughts on marriage for the sake of one of God's most valuable gifts to you?

Creator God, you ordained marriage, and I plead with you that I may achieve your holy and loving purpose with my marriage.

Success in marriage is not so much about finding the right person, but rather about being the right person.
BR BRICKNER

TO MARRY OR NOT TO MARRY

Are you married? Do not seek a divorce. Are you unmarried? Do not look for a wife (1 Cor 7:27).

Some people are specially called by God to work for him as individuals – this is what Jesus, Paul and Jeremiah teach us. These people have a unique and special contribution to make to the kingdom of God. Jesus himself said that there are people who remain unmarried for the sake of the kingdom of God: *... and others have renounced marriage because of the kingdom of heaven. Let him who can accept this teaching do so* (Mt 19:12).

FOOD FROM THE WORD OF GOD
1 Corinthians 7:25-8:8;
Deuteronomy 17:14-15, 17;
1 Kings 11:2-6; Proverbs 31:10, 31; Jeremiah 1:4-10, 16:1-2.

Paul builds on this foundation by suggesting that unmarried people can focus their energies on the work of God in a manner that married people cannot do (1 Cor 7:32-35). Many people take offence to Paul's recommendation of unmarried life. But in fact his words are charged with practical wisdom from life itself. He is not opposed to marriage. On the contrary, his huge contribution to Christian theology is precisely the way in which he linked the union between a man and a woman in marriage to the union between Christ (the Bridegroom) and his church (the bride).

But Paul stresses the point that we must know that nobody should enter the covenant of marriage without realising what a great deal of time and energy it takes to make a success of the relationship. We ought to be prepared to work at our marriages, making them part of our service to God. We must pray that we will be faithful to his calling, be it in our marriages, or in his service.

Eternal and holy God, make my marriage pleasing to you, and keep me from playing off my marriage against my service to you.

A successful marriage is an edifice that must be rebuilt every day..
ANDRÈ MAUROIS

DO NOT LEAD SOMEONE ASTRAY

Be careful, however, that the exercise of freedom does not become a stumbling block to the weak (1 Cor 8:9).

No one would dispute the fact that we as Christians must renounce all things that are wrong in our lives. But not all of us would concede that, for the sake of the gospel, a disciple of Christ sometimes has to give up certain things that are good and right.

In 1 Corinthians 9, Paul confirms his rights in the gospel four times. Three times he says that he refrains from exercising these rights for the greater good of the preaching of the gospel. He declares that he is prepared to give up any right out of love for Christ, and so that the gospel may spread.

FOOD FROM THE WORD OF GOD
1 Corinthians 8:9-9:18; Numbers 6:1-8; Amos 2:11-16; Malachi 2:7-9.

Oswald Chambers said about this, "If we are only prepared to sacrifice wrong things for Jesus' sake, we should never say that we love him totally. Anybody would forsake things that are wrong, if only he knows how. But are we also prepared to sacrifice our very best for Jesus? The only right Christians have, is the right to give up their rights. If we want to give our best to God, there has to be victory in the area of justified interests as much as in the area of unjustified enjoyment."

Yes, we must choose our priorities carefully, even concerning things that are right. If we are aiming for the highest in spiritual experience, the challenge to renounce some of our rights will always be there. Are we prepared to do this for the sake of our neighbours?

Holy Spirit of truth, help me to be prepared to renounce my rights for the sake of the spreading of the gospel and for the glory of God.

God does not force anybody, because love never forces. So service to God is a matter of absolute freedom.
HANS DENK

DESIRE SPIRITUAL GIFTS

Follow the way of love and eagerly desire spiritual gifts, especially the gift of prophesy (1 Cor 14:1).

God gives to us the gifts of the Spirit. He decides what gifts should be entrusted to whom. We are responsible for using the gifts he gives us, but we have no responsibility towards gifts that he has not given to us. We also must not desire the gifts that have been given to someone else.

We may, however, yearn in good spirit for certain gifts, and we may even pray for them, but if it is not the will of the Holy Spirit, we will not be given what we ask for. If we are dissatisfied because the Holy Spirit has denied us certain gifts, we are committing a sin. Paul says the purpose of these spiritual gifts is *to prepare God's people for works of service, so that the body of Christ may be built up* (Eph 4:12). So God has entrusted to each of us a specific task, and has also given us the gifts to equip us for those tasks.

FOOD FROM THE WORD OF GOD
1 Corinthians 14:1-25; 1 Kings 13:1-3; 16:34; 2 Kings 23:13-16; Isaiah 6:26-27.

In 1 Corinthians 12:7 Paul says that the purpose of these spiritual gifts is given to the benefit of all. This is why we may not use them selfishly. Actually, we must use our gifts to help one another and to be of service to God. He also created these gifts in order to unite the body of Christ (1 Cor 12:12-31). The gifts of the Spirit should therefore never tear the body of Christ apart. They should in fact be used to unite us to the glory of his Name.

Holy God and Father, may I use the spiritual gifts that you give me through the Holy Spirit to your honour and glory.

The Holy Spirit of God first accords us love; then he inspires us with hope; then he gives us freedom; and freedom is just about the last thing present in most of our churches. – DWIGHT L MOODY

THE BASICS OF OUR FAITH

For what I received I passed on to you as of first importance: that Christ died for our sins according to the Scriptures (1 Cor 15:3).

Jesus Christ was born in the image of a person; he lived and worked, was crucified, and was triumphantly raised from the dead and ascended to his former glory with the Father. He never sinned. He lived in perfection and died in perfection in order to save all people through all ages from sin.

Each of us can rightly say: It was I that caused him the pain and scorn. For *me* he wore the crown of thorns and carried the cross. Those wounds were for *me*. He had to walk the way of sorrow for *me*. He has paid for *my* sins. He bled and died for *me*. He took *my* sins upon him so that I can be free. Through his death, *I* have received righteousness and salvation.

FOOD FROM THE WORD OF GOD
1 Corinthians 14:26-15:11; Psalm 47:5-10; Isaiah 53:1-10.

God himself took my sins upon him in Jesus Christ and granted me his mercy. This is why I kneel down in amazement, and worship the God who works with sinners in this way. I look away from myself and see his sacrifice for my salvation. And I realise that he has made me whole. He has enfolded me in righteousness. He has adopted me as his child. He is my Lord and Saviour. He is my Father God.

I am filled with joy. I used to be downhearted, despairing and full of sin. Now my spirit testifies along with his Spirit that I am his child. I look up to him with thanks, calling out, "Abba, Father!" This is the core of the Christian faith.

God my Father, grant that my faith may remain strong and keep on growing in love and knowledge of your incomprehensible plan of salvation.

Salvation does not only look back to Calvary; it also looks ahead to the freedom in which the redeemed stand. Exactly because they were saved at such a high price, believers must be God's people. – LEON MORRIS

SIMPLY TRUST IN GOD

And will not God bring about justice for his chosen ones, who cry out to him day and night? Will he keep putting them off? I tell you, he will see that they get justice, and quickly. However, when the Son of Man comes, will he find faith on earth? (Lk 18:7-8).

The late Afrikaans singer and songwriter Koos du Plessis says in one of his songs, "All that I am, is only grace; all that I have, is only borrowed." Seeing what you have as a gift from God is the first sign of an attitude of simplicity and humility. We work, but when it comes to our daily bread, we know that we live by grace. What we own, is not a result of our work, but of God's care.

FOOD FROM THE WORD OF GOD
Luke 18:1-30; Job 36:18-19; Psalm 49:1-12; Jeremiah 9:23-24.

Knowing that what we own has been lent to us by God is the second sign of an attitude of simplicity and humility. Only God can protect our possessions. We can trust him with them. And this not only applies to our possessions, but also includes other things such as our reputation and jobs. Humility means that we are free to trust God with all things in our lives.

Making our possessions available to other people is the third sign of an attitude of simplicity and humility. Sometimes we hold on to our possessions so tightly because we are scared of the future. But we need not be scared. God is our omnipotent Creator and loving Father. We can share our possessions with others, because he will care for us.

Do you seek the kingdom of God in earnest? If so, these attitudes will dominate your life. It is the sum total of Christian faith and trust.

Lord my God, I want to entrust all that I am and have completely to you. May your Holy Spirit guide me in this.

Everything we have is qualified by what we are.
JOHN LANCASTER SPALDING

August 13

NEW HEART, NEW DEEDS

But Zacchaeus stood up and said to the Lord, "Look, Lord! Here and now I give half of my possessions to the poor, and if I have cheated anybody out of anything, I will pay back four times the amount" (Lk 19:8).

True repentance and confession occur when we realise how sin grieves and saddens God. Maybe the thought that sin makes God sad is new to you. Genesis 6:5-6 does, however, say, *The Lord saw how great man's wickedness on the earth had become, and that every inclination of the thoughts of his heart was only evil all the time. The Lord grieved that he had made man on the earth, and his heart was filled with pain.*

FOOD FROM THE WORD OF GOD
Luke 18:35-19:10; 2 Chronicles 31:1; Jonah 3:1-10.

Jesus, too, was deeply saddened when he wept about Jerusalem: *O Jerusalem, Jerusalem, you who kill the prophets and stone those sent to you, how often I have longed to gather your children together, as a hen gathers her chicks under her wings, but you were not willing!* (Lk 13:34).

God's heart is torn by our sins and that alienates us from him and from our fellow-believers. If we want to overcome sin, we must surrender ourselves unconditionally to God. We must look at our sins from his perspective. He created us, and gave us his Son to re-create us. Ask God to show you what sin does to him. Once you see and comprehend how great his love for us is – despite our sins – you will want to turn away from sin. Ask the Lord to change your heart, because only then will you succeed in turning away from sin.

Holy and loving Father, may I never forget how deeply sin agonises you. Purify my life and deeds through the work of the Holy Spirit.

As long as we collaborate with sin, we will never see the loving face of God clearly.
JULIA NORWICH

HONOUR YOUR FATHER AND YOUR MOTHER

Children, obey your parents in everything, for this pleases the Lord (Col 3:20).

Much is said and written these days about caring for the aged, but what is being done to allay their fears about the future? These fears include financial concerns in a time of rising costs and dwindling incomes, and fears of illness without anyone to care for them because their relatives live too far away.

Each of us, regardless of our age, must remind ourselves that we are of great value in the eyes of God, and that he has a plan for each of us. When the psalmist talks about the righteous, he writes, *They will still bear fruit in their old age, they will stay fresh and green ...* (Ps 91:14).

FOOD FROM THE WORD OF GOD
Colossians 3:18-4:18; Leviticus 20:9; Deuteronomy 5:16; 21:18-21; Proverbs 6:20-23; 17:25; 23:22-25.

It is ironic that many of the countries to which we send missionaries with the message of the gospel can teach us a lot about honouring fathers and mothers. A pagan woman once said to a missionary, "My sister, who is much wealthier than I, arranged for herself to have the honour of looking after our elderly mother. But as the youngest daughter, it is my duty and privilege."

God knows our hearts and our intentions. When we treat the aged in our midst with love and care, we are obedient to the fifth commandment. And obedience has a reward all of its own. Jesus himself set the example for us. In his suffering on the cross, he thought of his mother and entrusted her to the care of John, the apostle of love (Jn 19:26-27).

Lord Jesus, thank you for broadening my outlook, and that you have taught me that by caring for the aged I honour my own parents.

Caring for the aged is a calling just as delicate as caring for the youth.
JAMES DOUGLAS

COME AND STAY WITH ME

When she and the members of her household were baptised, she invited us to her home. "If you consider me a believer in the Lord," she said, "come and stay at my house." And she persuaded us (Acts 16:15).

With the increase in unemployment and the growing numbers of vagrants and street children around us, we are challenged to ask God how we can serve him in this. Ruth Calkin once wrote *There is room* about this subject:

FOOD FROM THE WORD OF GOD
Acts 16:11-34; Genesis 18:1-8; Judges 19:16-21; 2 Kings 4:8-10.

You know how it happened, Lord:
She said: "May I live with you just a little while? I have no place to go. I'm lonely and afraid."
I hastily glanced at the small room.
I thought of other rooms smaller and extremely crowded.
I said: "You see my small house, there is really no room.
But I have room in my heart for caring, for praying.
I'll make phone calls – there must be a family somewhere ..."
That was this morning, Lord. All day long I prayed, I called, I waited ...
Then You accomplished what I cannot explain.
Through the hours You pushed back the walls – until suddenly, tonight, there is room for her in my house, as well as in my heart.
You are indeed a Master Builder!

(From: *Tell me again, Lord, I forget* 1974.)

Prayerfully read today's readings on hospitality again. Pray that the Lord may show you how you can use your house and your heart.

Lord Jesus, there was no place for you at the inn. Keep me from making the same mistake.

Hospitality is one of the forms of worship.
TERESA of AVILA

WICKEDNESS VERSUS RIGHTEOUSNESS

"What shall I do, then, with this Jesus who is called the Christ?" Pilate asked. They all answered, "Crucify him!" "Why? What crime has he committed?" asked Pilate. But they shouted all the louder, "Crucify him!" (Mt 27:22-23).

Once, while Francis Xavier was preaching in one of the large Japanese cities, a man approached him as if he wanted to tell him something in private. When the missionary bent forward to hear what the man wanted to say, the man spat in his face. Without saying a word and without showing any sign of being upset, Xavier took out his handkerchief, wiped off his face and continued with his sermon, as though nothing had happened. The derision of the audience suddenly turned into admiration.

FOOD FROM THE WORD OF GOD
Matthew 27:21-44; Psalm 22:6-8; 42:1-4; 44:13-16; Isaiah 53:1-5.

The city's most highly educated physician happened to be there and said, "A religion that teaches one such virtue and inspires one with so much courage, that gives one so much control over oneself, cannot but come from the true God."

The Holy Spirit makes this kind of behaviour possible for every believing follower of Jesus Christ. Acting in this way will also do more to lead unbelievers to repent than hundreds of thousands of words. With the living Christ as our example, with love as our motivation, and with humility as our clothing, may we trust in God the Holy Spirit for the wisdom and strength to react to insults and persecution in a manner that is worthy of Christ. Only then are we in a position to reflect the honour and attitude of our Master.

Lord, my God and Father, grant me the grace to overcome and endure the pain and insults that I encounter for your sake along my path; without self-pity, but with dignity.

We multiply when we are cut down: the blood of Christ is the seed.
QUINTUS TERTULLIAN

BE BRAVE FOR THE TRUTH

Then the Lord said to me, "Go; I will send you far away to the Gentiles" (Acts 22:21).

A student friend of mine who was highly gifted and outstanding, an attractive young man with a healthy body, could have had an easy ministry in our own country or one of the surrounding mission fields. But comfort and convenience were not his aims in life. He chose to take the gospel to the faraway then Sudan, to go and do evangelistic work amongst the Bedouins on the edge of a barren desert.

FOOD FROM THE WORD OF GOD
Acts 21:27-22:21; Ezekiel 2:1-7; 3:4-11.

My friend worked at a remote oasis and enticed travellers by supplying them with meals, clothes and first aid, and of course, he preached the good news of salvation through Jesus Christ while they were there. From the Bedouins he learned that it is worse than murder to know of a source of water without telling those you encounter where it is.

Few of us will ever live in a wilderness as he did. Few of us will preach salvation through Jesus Christ to nomads. However, all around us are thirsty people: our neighbour, the petrol attendant, the paper delivery boy, the secretary who types your letters, or the distant relative who sometimes comes to visit you. If these people do not know Christ, they are going to die from thirst. You know about the Source of living water. Do not keep it from someone who is thirsty. And it is not only a matter of hospitality, but also a matter of life or death.

Holy Spirit of God, grant me the courage to always be a powerful witness of the message of salvation through Jesus Christ.

If Christ is within us and controls our personality, we will leave pure impressions on the lives we touch, not because of our exceptional characters, but because of his. – EUGENIA PRICE

JESUS IS A PATIENT TEACHER

When morning came, he called his disciples to him and chose twelve of them, whom he also designated apostles (Lk 6:13).

In Luke 6, Jesus elects his disciples. He calls them personally and binds them to him with the intimate ties of love that have withstood the test of time. In this way, Jesus chose to share his life on earth with these twelve fallible people.

They were neither theologians nor political leaders – just ordinary men who had became extraordinary in the forming hand of the Master Potter. That makes their election all the more noteworthy. Their weaknesses and flaws were painfully visible, but that did not exclude them from his friendship or from fellowship with him. If God were to demand perfection before he allows us into the circle of his disciples, who amongst us will be able to qualify?

FOOD FROM THE WORD OF GOD
Luke 6:12-16; 9:18-43; Nehemiah 9:18-21, 26-31.

Their shortcomings did not disqualify them; otherwise Paul, with his impetuous personality, would not have been included. Nor would James and John with their selfishness and racism have been accepted. Thomas's doubt would have placed him, too, outside this intimate circle. But Jesus welcomed them all to share in his love and fellowship.

Describe your own spiritual pilgrimage with Jesus, as Nehemiah wrote the story of God's dealings with the children of Israel. How does God, as a patient, wise and gracious Teacher, assist you? Do you praise and thank him for it?

Father God, thank you for allowing me to be your pupil through Jesus Christ and the Holy Spirit. I praise your name for the path on which you lead me.

Do not try to reach God with your mind. It is impossible! Reach him through love – that is possible! – CARLO CARETTO

GOD IS LOOKING FOR RELIABLE WITNESSES

He (Jesus) told them, "The harvest is plentiful, but the workers are few. Ask the Lord of the harvest, therefore, to send out workers into his harvest field" (Lk 10:2).

As far as we know, Abraham lived a comfortable, carefree life until he started to pray. Through prayer he heard God's message that he had to gather all his belongings, leave his land and embark on a road to an unknown destination. Then his life became difficult and dangerous.

FOOD FROM THE WORD OF GOD
Luke 9:44-10:16; 2 Samuel 22:21-30; 2 Kings 18:3, 5-8; 2 Chronicles 16:7-10.

Prayer was the point of departure for Moses too. He was tending the flock of his father-in-law Jethro. He had enjoyed a peaceful and carefree life, but when Moses started to pray, things changed radically for him. It all started with the burning bush in the desert, where God spoke to him and set him a humanly impossible task: to lead the Israelites out of Egypt. This must surely have been the last peaceful and comfortable day in Moses' life.

Peter, John, James and Andrew were thriving businessmen, well established and respected in their communities, until they spoke to Jesus of Nazareth. Their earlier lives came to an end when they responded positively to his invitation, "Follow me!" They received intensive training for three years, and then carried out Jesus' command, *Therefore go and make disciples of all nations* (Mt 28:19). They carried out this command despite opposition and persecution.

This is the danger as well as the glory of prayer. When we start talking to God and listening to his voice, our lives may very well never be the same again.

Thank you, Lord my God, that you see me also as fit to be called into your service. May I follow you faithfully until the very end.

Missionary work will never happen unless the church goes beyond the borders of her own life and becomes actively involved in the immediate vicinity. – DAVID SHEPPARD

GOD ALONE GIVES POWER AND WISDOM

At that time Jesus, full of joy through the Holy Spirit, said, "I praise you, Father, Lord of heaven and earth, because you have hidden these things from the wise and learned, and revealed them to little children" (Lk 10:21a).

Unfortunately, many Christians do not believe Christ's promise that he will surround the church with spiritual power. They doubt whether his promise applies to every believer. Consequently, they lack the faith required to make the power that Jesus offers their own.

FOOD FROM THE WORD OF GOD
Luke 10:17-37; 1 Kings 3:28; 4:29-34; Daniel 5:10-14.

Another shortcoming of many Christians is that they refuse to wait prayerfully for the promises that God made to us in his Scriptures. People give up, instead of persevering. Consequently, they are not spiritually empowered. The church, too, has for the most part lost sight of strength from above. Everybody talks about our dependence on the Holy Spirit, but precious little of this dependence ever materialises. Christians, and even ministers, set about their tasks with almost no spiritual power at all. It is very sad to have to say that amongst the ranks of the ministers of the Word of God, we find people who do not possess the power of the Holy Spirit.

May God have mercy on us, his church on earth. We as Christians, as the church of God, as ministers, must do something about this matter right away. The source of wisdom and strength for believers is none other that God himself. No one else can give us this strength. Our God is also our greatest reason for exceptional joy. But where do you find your joy if the Spirit of God cannot work powerfully within you?

Father, God of mercy, you are the source of all true wisdom, knowledge and power. May your Holy Spirit still renew and strengthen me with wisdom and knowledge.

No one can do the work of God if he is not first enveloped in the power of the Holy Spirit. It is impossible to preach the gospel outside of the Holy Spirit. – G CAMPBELL MORGAN

August 21

OUR WORDS BETRAY OUR HEARTS

The good man brings good things out of the good stored up in him, and the evil man brings evil things out of the evil stored up in him (Mt 12:35).

Are you not sometimes overwhelmed by the thought that one day you will be called to account before God for every word that has come out of your mouth? Listen attentively to your own words today and write down what they reveal about the state of your heart. Then pray to God, asking him to help you so that your words might be proof of your innocence before him.

FOOD FROM THE WORD OF GOD
Matthew 12:22-42; Psalm 15:1-5; 40:9-10; Proverbs 10:19-21; 15: 1-4, 26.

The tongue betrays the true person. That which we constantly talk about is, after all, that to which we apply our hearts. The words that we use, as well as the words that we do not use, confirm what we think, feel and are. As Christians, we must learn the ability to do thorough and serious self-examination regularly. If we want to understand who we really are, we need to be honest about what our words say about us. We must listen carefully to the whisperings of the Holy Spirit. He will make us aware of words we use which are wrong.

When we become aware that our words do not reflect who we would really like to be, we must confess it and ask God's forgiveness. And then we must take a dose of his medicine: we must read sections from God's Word that underscore the fact that we should only speak kind and uplifting words. These words will purify our mouths and hearts. Then we can get up and live our lives with renewed power to speak words of truth, wisdom, and life.

May the words from my mouth be pleasing to you, my Rock and my Salvation.

Our words are a reliable index to the state of our souls.
St FRANCIS DE SALES

RIGHTEOUSNESS IN THE EYES OF GOD

So the last will be first, and the first will be last (Mt 20:16).

The moral of the parable in Matthew 20:1-16 is that the revolution of God that was brought about by Jesus Christ is an exceptionally just revolution. It offers a full place and a full reward to everyone, even the latecomers and outsiders.

In this parable, the people who had worked all day complained about the landowner's unfair charity. But to those who were in need, the work they performed at the last minute, as well as the landowner's charity, were good news. God's revolution is indeed an equalising revolution, but it is not a revolution that pulls everyone down. No, it is a revolution in which even those who arrive at the last minute are welcomed by God's astonishing mercy and compassion, and given a full day's wage.

FOOD FROM THE WORD OF GOD
Matthew 19:27-20:16; 1 Samuel 2:1-10; Nehemiah 9:16-17.

Entry into the kingdom of God is only possible through the mercy of God for sinners. There is no entrance fee that we can pay, because no one will enter into the kingdom of God on his own merits, but only on the grounds of God's immeasurable mercy and goodness. On the day of reckoning, everyone will be called to account, and will receive according to how they responded to God's mercy and charity.

Today, think seriously about God's mercy and righteousness, and ask yourself whether there might not lurk some envy in your heart because of his mercy to other people. Pray for a better understanding of his goodness and righteousness, and be charitable towards others as well, as God is charitable towards you.

God of goodness and grace, thank you for every undeserved display of your generosity towards me. Your loving treatment of my neighbours gives me great joy.

Righteousness is truth in action.
BENJAMIN DISRAELI

August 23

GOD'S KINGDOM IS INTENDED FOR HIS CHILDREN

"Therefore I tell you that the kingdom of God will be taken away from you and given to a people who will produce its fruit (Mt 21:43).

Who can become a citizen of the kingdom of God? Anybody can! *The Spirit and the bride say, "Come!" And let him who hears say, "Come." Whoever is thirsty, let him take the free gift of the water of life* (Rev 22:17). An open invitation to the wedding banquet of the Lamb has been extended to everyone (Mt 22:9). All people who place their trust in God and who are obedient to him can become part of his kingdom.

FOOD FROM THE WORD OF GOD
Matthew 21:33-22:14; Psalm 103:15-22; Isaiah 45:22-23; 56:3-7.

Unfortunately, not everyone wants to surrender his or her life to God. Some people stubbornly continue to walk their own path, and do not want to subject their own will to the loving will of God. *Whoever believes in the Son has eternal life, but whoever rejects the Son will not see life, for God's wrath remains on him* (Jn 3:36). These people will not enjoy the salvation that God has brought about for mankind. *Yet to all who received him, to those who believed in his name, he gave the right to become children of God* (Jn 1:12).

Who can become a citizen of the kingdom of God? Anybody can! God's mercy excludes no one. His mercy knows no limits. Jesus Christ, our Advocate, *is the atoning sacrifice for our sins, and not only for ours but also for the sins of the whole world* (1 Jn 2:2). His salvation is so broad that it can include all people of all times, including you and me, today!

I want to obey you conscientiously, my Saviour God, so that I may always be part of your kingdom.

Wherever God reigns as king in a human heart is where the kingdom of God is established.
PAUL W HARRISON

August 24

DO THE WILL OF GOD

Whoever does God's will is my brother and sister and mother (Mk 3:35).

The key to Christ's triumphant victory over evil and the secret of his power rest in his obedience to the will of his Father. Unfortunately, many Christians are forever looking for pleasure and self-gratification. They have not yet learned that only obedient children are happy children. It is only obedience to God that brings true and lasting happiness to our lives. There is one thing that assures you of a healthy spirit: obedience to God.

FOOD FROM THE WORD OF GOD
Mark 3:31-4:20; Exodus 19:4-6; Deuteronomy 26:16-19; 28:1-12.

Why are there so many people who are uncertain of their salvation? Why are there so many people who do not understand what is meant by the peace of God that passes all understanding? God himself provides us with the answer in Isaiah 48:18: *If only you had paid attention to my commands, your peace would have been like a river, your righteousness like the waves of the sea.* People like to say, "I need faith." Or else, "I have too little faith. That is why I am not sure of my salvation, and do not have peace in my heart." But in most instances it is not faith that is lacking, because even with trembling and uncertain hands we can receive God's wonderful gifts.

No, what is lacking is obedience. Someone who is disobedient to God cannot have faith and trust in him. Trust and faith are the spiritual results of obedience to God, and this is the one thing that God expects of his children.

Holy Spirit, Guide and Teacher, make me faithful to the demands of my Father so that I may be assured that I can find my faith and peace in him as my father.

Blessed are the obedient, for God will never let them go astray.
FRANCIS DE SALIS

August 25

THE RESULTS OF FAITH

So Herodias nursed a grudge against John and wanted to kill him. But she was not able to, because Herod feared John and protected him, knowing him to be a righteous and holy man (Mk 6:19-20a).

When we trust in God, we have a clear perspective on life. But when we consider only partially doing God's will and his work on earth, while partially serving our own interests, we cannot focus on what really matters in life. Then we try to serve two masters and our priorities are distorted.

FOOD FROM THE WORD OF GOD
Mark 6:17-44; Psalm 69:30-34; 107:8-9; 145:1-7, 13-8.

Have you ever tried to determine what God's will for your life is, but were afraid that when you do his will, you will be sent in a direction that could adversely affect your own interests? If this is so you did not focus on one aim: the will of God for your life. And when you do not focus on God's will, you necessarily walk in darkness. But when you get so involved in the affairs of God that your own interests become insignificant, everything in your life becomes crystal clear, and you leave your worries with him.

God is not miserly with the giving of his gifts. He has adopted you as his child. You are a member of his family. This act of love is proof of exceptional grace to you from him. He will reward your faith in and your obedience to him. Unbelievers worry about life sustenance, but the child of God can be sure that he will provide in every need.

God who provides, I praise and thank you for meeting all my spiritual as well as my physical needs from the wealth of your grace.

We sleep peacefully in the arms of God when we surrender ourselves to his providence.
FRANÇOIS FÈNELON

August 26

THE EVIL ONE PERSECUTES THE RIGHTEOUS

Later on they sent some of the Pharisees and Herodians to Jesus to catch him in his words (Mk 12:13).

The scorn and suffering that Christ had to endure from the evil world is symptomatic of an inborn resentment of man against all that is Godly and righteous. This is the cross Christians have to bear, and the reason why Christians are so frequently persecuted. Let us not, however, forget that there is blessing and joy in persecution. Through persecution and trials we grow into worthy followers of Christ, who have joyful hearts despite our suffering.

FOOD FROM THE WORD OF GOD
Mark 12:13-27; Psalm 7:2-3, 14-18; 64:2-5; 140:1-10; Proverbs 28:10.

Our Master commands those who are insulted and persecuted to *rejoice and be glad, because great is your reward in heaven, for in the same way they persecuted the prophets who were before you* (Mt 5:12). The phrase "Christian gladness" has almost entirely disappeared from our vocabulary. One of the reasons for this is that people think joy and happiness are only to be found in comfort, wealth and a life of luxury. James did not say that you should be glad when all is going well for you, but *whenever you face trials of many kinds, because you know that the testing of your faith develops perseverance* (Jas 1:2-3).

Those who are persecuted are fortunate, because they are being prepared for heaven. For persecution is to a Christian what growth pains are to a child: No pain means no development. No suffering means no splendour. No struggle means no victory. No persecution means no reward. Ask God to give you the strength to stand firm against evil.

Loving Father, help me to bear all persecution for your sake with dignity, so that I may experience the consequent joy.

The martyrs were tied up, imprisoned, stoned, burnt, and tortured on the rack – and yet they multiplied. – St AUGUSTINE of HIPPO

YOUR SACRIFICE TO GOD

Calling his disciples to him, Jesus said, "I tell you the truth, this poor widow has put more into the treasury than all the others. They all gave out of their wealth; but she, out of her poverty, put in everything – all she had to live on" (Mk 12:43-44).

God promises that he will give in abundance to those who make charitable offerings to him. However, those who do not do this, will lose even that which they have. Can you imagine anybody these days giving so much to the Lord that an order would be given for him or her to stop making offerings? (Ex 36:6-7).

FOOD FROM THE WORD OF GOD
Mark 12:38-13:13; Exodus 35:4-9; 36:2-7; Proverbs 3:9-10; Malachi 3:8-12.

Many children of the Lord rob themselves of all his splendid blessings by not acting as his stewards and giving back what he has entrusted to them. They act as though everything they have belongs to them alone, as though they already possess an everlasting inheritance. They forget that they have nothing at all which is their own; that they have been bought by the blood of Jesus Christ; that everything they own – physical strength, time, livelihood, eyes, hands and feet – belongs to Christ because he bought them with his precious blood.

God wants to use us in his kingdom. And as we give back to him that which he entrusts to us, he trusts us ever more with his gifts. If you know that you are making too few offerings to God, start by putting aside a small percentage, however little, for him. He will bless you. And as he blesses you, you will be able to make ever-growing offerings to him. In this way you will be faithful to God, and your heart will be tuned in more and more to being a true steward of God and to stand before him as his thankful servant.

God who provides, make me faithful in my stewardship of that which you have given to me through grace.

The two things that bring the greatest blessing when placed under God's control are our time and our money.
WILLIAM LOUW

August 28

GOD IS MERCIFUL TO US

Praise be to the Lord, the God of Israel, because he has come and has redeemed his people (Lk 1:68).

When we read the song of praise of Maria and the song of Zechariah in Luke 1, we become aware of God's endless grace towards them and all other people. How thankful we should be towards this God who shows mercy and forgiveness towards everybody who repents and confesses his or her sins.

The Israelites were forever worshipping the foreign gods of the pagans around them, despite the pleas and warnings of the prophets. Time and again they were guilty of this sin. In many places in the Scriptures, the Holy Spirit takes over the refrain to ensure that God's people do not relapse.

FOOD FROM THE WORD OF GOD
Luke 1:46-79; Jeremiah 3:12, 19-20, 22; Lamentations 3:21-33; Micah 7:18-20.

To this very day, when people turn away from God in rebellion, revolt and pride, but return to him in humility, Gods still shows mercy to them. We all have our own golden calf that we want to put in the place of the living God. There are things in our lives that are more important to us than God, because they provide us with instant gratification. We are also discouraged in the desert by a life of routine without any immediate or significant results. In order to banish our feelings of emptiness and being lost in this secular world, we seek satisfaction from lesser gods. But God patiently waits for the day when we will abandon these false gods. He may discipline us from time to time, but in his endless mercy he will never leave us nor forsake us (Heb 13:5).

Eternal God, every day you prove your incomprehensible mercy to me. May I never take your mercy for granted.

A spiritual attitude that sees God in everything is proof of growth in mercy and a thankful heart.
CHARLES G FINNEY

PRAISE GOD FOR HIS SALVATION

... because of the tender mercy of our God, by which the rising sun will come to us from heaven to shine on those living in darkness and in the shadow of death, to guide our feet into the path of peace (Lk 1:78-79).

In his holiness and righteousness, God could not leave sin unpunished. Therefore, out of mercy and grace he sent his own Son (Jn 3:16). In the Person of Jesus Christ he came down to earth and paid the full price of the sins of all people of all times. On the cross, God revealed his heart to us. He despises and condemns sin, and yet, through the power of the cross he forgives sinners, people like you and me. Praise the Lord, for he is good. His love is everlasting.

FOOD FROM THE WORD OF GOD
Luke 1:76-2:20; Psalm 146:1-10; 147:1-11; 148:1-11; 148:13-14; Isaiah 12:1-6.

We all trespass by not obeying God's commands. We do not obey Jesus' law of love. We bring hurt, pain and suffering to ourselves and to others by what we do or say, or by what we refuse to do, to say or to be. In doing so, we tear God's heart apart. But even before we ask, he forgives us our transgressions. He reconciles us with himself. He restores us in honour as his children. He enfolds us in his love and heals us through his forgiveness.

The same voice that called from Calvary, "Father, forgive them!" to this very day still says with the power of his pierced hands, "The ransom for all times and for all people has been paid. Now is the time for forgiveness – for you. You can be forgiven and set free." O, the wonder of God's mercy! Do not reject it.

God of love, I rejoice in your mercy, and endlessly praise and glorify your holy Name.

People will never take evil seriously nor see the necessity of putting God's mercy to the test, until they join in the redeeming purpose of his love. – JB PHILLIPS

30 August

CALLED TO DO GOD'S WORK

And the child grew and became strong; he was filled with wisdom, and the grace of God was upon him (Lk 2:40).

Many people wrongly believe that God only calls ministers and missionaries to his service. But God has a calling and a task for each of his children. The people who have been called, equipped and sent out by God are often ordinary, everyday dedicated people like you and me.

Yes, God called a man with a speech impediment to talk on his behalf, namely Moses. God made him the greatest leader of the Old Testament. God called David, the shepherd boy, away from his flock to become the greatest king that has ever ruled in Israel.

FOOD FROM THE WORD OF GOD
Luke 2:25-52; 1 Samuel 3:4-10, 19, 10.

Somebody once said, "It does not take a special kind of person to become a Christian, it just takes all of that person." God takes the weak, the sick and the handicapped to put the strong to shame. Jonathan Edwards was one of the greatest revival preachers in America, and in the world. He suffered from asthma. While he was preaching, he constantly coughed and cleared his throat. He was a thin, fragile man. His eyes were very weak. But his sermons lead crowds to true repentance and rebirth.

The people who are chosen and used by God, God's very own superstars, are not necessarily people who possess outstanding abilities. But they are people who are available, and who have learnt the secret of giving all the honour and glory to God. When you use your life to the honour of God, God will use your life to his honour.

Father God, I make myself available anew, so that you can use me as you wish and to your honour alone.

Do not fear that your life will come to an end; rather fear that it will never begin.
JOHN HENRY NEWMAN

August 31

BUILD YOUR LIFE ON A FIRM FOUNDATION

He is like a man building a house, who dug deep and laid the foundation on rock (Lk 6:48).

Imagine that there was a builder who knew only one season: summer. And imagine that this builder is asked to erect a building. All his material would be light, because he does not know the violence of the wind. The water pipes would be above ground, because he does not know the force of frost. The weakest roof would be sufficient for him, because he knows nothing about pouring rain. But if you were to tell this builder that the winds will become stormy, that the rivers will freeze, that the windows will be covered with snow, and that the rain will fall on his roof, he would, if he were a wise man, say, "I must not build only for one season, but for all seasons. I must not only build for sunny days, but also for stormy days."

FOOD FROM THE WORD OF GOD
Luke 6:46-7:17; Psalm 18:1-6, 16-25, 47.

So, why then would we be foolish when building our own characters and spiritual lives? We build our homes for sunshine as well as rain, why would we build our characters with any less care? If we think about winter during the summer, why then would we not think about misfortune in times of fortune? If we think about autumn during spring, why then would we not think about God's judgement in times of joy?

Just as it would be foolish for a builder not to consider the elements of nature, so it would be foolish for those who build their characters not to keep in mind the fire with which God tests every building.

Eternal Architect, grant me the mercy to build up my life in a way that will place your stamp of approval on the work of my hands.

God has placed good and evil within our power, and has given us freedom of choice. He does not hold back those who are unwilling, but enfolds the willing in his love. – JOHN CHRYSTOSTOM

September

Prayer for September

1. Faith is more important than miracles
2. God requires obedience
3. Come to the living waters
4. A reward awaits us
5. You must repent
6. God accepts those who come to him
7. Jesus warns against deceitfulness
8. To follow Jesus
9. Signs of the end of time
10. Jesus understands our hearts
11. Where is your treasure?
12. Bear good fruit
13. God receives everyone
14. We need a keeper
15. Change your heart – God forgives
16. The will of God cannot be stopped
17. Make God's deeds known
18. Do not silence God's message
19. God's great mercy and goodness
20. The healing power of forgiveness
21. God's blessing comes from suffering
22. God plans our lives
23. We are God's children
24. Pray for one another
25. Mutual love in marriage
26. We are fighting a spiritual struggle
27. Stop complaining and arguing
28. Your life – an example
29. Strive for achievement for God
30. We are responsible for one another

Prayer for September

God the Creator and Father,
we praise and thank you for being the Maintainer of your creation.
We thank you for the multicoloured splendour of spring;
for new life awakening all around us;
for trees that are spreading out their floral beauty
like gigantic bouquets against the sky.
Youthful green in countless shades
unfurls all over your creation.
Lord, our Lord, it is as if you have just
spoken the words that set creation in motion.
The earth awakes and rejoices with new life:
winter is something of the past –
the time for singing has dawned.
May all of us – farmers, poets, painters,
economists, learners and teachers,
see your artist's hands in everything,
and know in amazement:
You have visited our land.
Our Regenerator and Saviour,
touch our lives;
bring about new growth in our barren hearts.
May the grain of wheat that fell on the soil and died
now sprout, grow powerfully, and bear a splendid harvest.
May a spring song of joy then rise up
from our hearts with propulsive joy:
Praise the Lord, for he is good.
His love is everlasting.

Amen

FAITH IS MORE IMPORTANT THAN MIRACLES

The Pharisees came and began to question Jesus. To test him, they asked him for a sign from heaven (Mk 8:11).

For three years Judas spent every day in the company of Jesus. He saw the miracles Jesus performed; he heard the Master's words of wisdom; he even participated in his ministry. No one ever questioned Judas's faith. He enjoyed exactly the same status as all the other disciples. Only Christ himself knew the sinister thoughts of Judas's heart. No one else would have been able to believe that this man would betray Jesus.

While the other disciples were developing into apostles, Judas became an instrument in the hands of Satan. His faith was not sincere. His heart hardened until he became the treacherous man who would betray his Master for a couple of silver coins. Jesus warned Judas at every possible opportunity and encouraged him to open his heart to God, begging of him to become a good person. But Judas let every opportunity that was offered to him pass him by, and followed his own path instead. He heard the gospel of salvation from Jesus' own mouth, and yet he refused to abandon his selfishness. The words of Jesus to Judas in John 13 represent Jesus' final appeal to this man. Eventually, Jesus' merciful and loving pleas to Judas would do nothing but confirm the betrayer's condemnation.

FOOD FROM THE WORD OF GOD
Mark 8:1-26; Psalm 78:40-59.

Who saw more miracles performed than the Israelites or the people who walked on earth with Jesus? But faith in God is much more important than miracles.

Miracle-working God, thank you for all the magnificent miracles you perform, but help me to believe unconditionally.

Jesus himself was the one and convincing miracle of God.
IAN MACLAREN

GOD REQUIRES OBEDIENCE

As has just been said: "Today, if you hear his voice, do not harden your hearts as you did in the rebellion" (Heb 3:15).

There is a direct link between faith and obedience. This is why unbelief always leads to disobedience. When our life on earth is passed, we will have to account before God for our deeds. Only if we persevere in faith until the very end will God say to us: *Well done, good and faithful servant! You have been faithful with a few things; I will put you in charge of many things. Come and share your master's happiness!* (Mt 25:23). Are you ready to give full account of your faithfulness and your obedience to God?

FOOD FROM THE WORD OF GOD
Hebrews 3:7-4:13; Numbers 14:2-3, 6-9, 20-23; Daniel 9:2-6, 9-11.

How do we find God, and how do we grow in obedience to him? Jesus very clearly states that we must obey God's commands. We must convert the knowledge we have into practical obedience. He was forever telling people to leave their fishing nets, to sell all they had and to follow him obediently.

Yes, Jesus prescribed a theology of obedience. He called people to responsibility to God – whether they were believers, sceptics, or searchers. He did after all say, *Why do you call me, "Lord, Lord," and do not do what I say?* (Lk 6:46). Jesus knew that obedience to his own words and the words of his Father would result in faith. This is why his command to us is to obediently do what he asks us to do.

Holy Spirit of God, continually teach me the lesson of absolute obedience to my Master.

We are all born as subjects and obedience means perfect freedom. He who does this, will be free, safe, and happy. – SENECA

September 3

COME TO THE LIVING WATERS

The Spirit and the bride say, "Come!" And let him who hears say, "Come." Whoever is thirsty, let him come; and whoever wishes, let him take the free gift of the water of life (Rev 22:17).

Let us rejoice in the living water that flows for us from an inexhaustible Source. Let us come closer and put our roots down in the good earth of God's love and mercy. Then every day will be a new birth, and the richness of life through God's immeasurable goodness will be our portion.

Every morning we will wait excitedly for the sunrise. We will get to know God better every day and have the desire to love him in earnest. We will live in the joyful certainty of his presence in our lives. And we will contemplate God's love for us as it is now, and as it will be on that day when we enter into the New Jerusalem, the place that Jesus himself has prepared for us (Jn 14:1-3). We will count the hours until we are able sit down at the wedding banquet of the Lamb (Rev 19:5-8). On that day, Christ will call us by a new name. We will be called a crown of magnificence in his hand. He will delight in us and we will delight in him.

FOOD FROM THE WORD OF GOD
Revelation 22:1-22; Psalm 46:5-6; Isaiah 55:1-3; Ezekiel 37:1, 7-12.

Come to the water and take deep draughts of his love. Let it flow through you and give you a foretaste of the day on which the water of life will flow for you through the New Jerusalem. Forget your fears and relax in his love. Here, at the source of living water, you will find daily renewal until the Master comes again.

Thank you, Lord my God, that I have through your grace found the source of living water, and that I may daily be enriched and strengthened by it, and grow spiritually.

Growth is the only guarantee of life.
JOHN HENRY NEWMAN

A REWARD AWAITS US

And he said, "These are they who have come out of the great tribulation; they have washed their robes and made them white in the blood of the Lamb" (Rev 7:14).

Much is written in the Scriptures about the achievements of people. But time and again their achievements are traced back to the power of the blood of Christ.

By the power of his blood, peace is brought about between God and man. By the power of his blood, all who place their faith and trust in God may receive forgiveness of sins as well as eternal life. By the power of the blood of Jesus, the power of evil is defeated. By his power, we are continually cleansed of all our sins. By the power of his blood, we are given the ability to serve God righteously. By the unstoppable power of his blood in the eyes of God, even the least worthy of us now has the freedom to enter God's sanctuary and to live and receive strength there every day.

FOOD FROM THE WORD OF GOD
Revelation 7:9-8:13; Isaiah 4:3-6; 25:6-9; 51:6-9; 61:10.

The precious blood of Jesus was given the power of victory by the attitude of the lamb of the One who spilled his blood. Jesus, the living Christ, is the pure Lamb of God who cleanses the sins of mankind with his own blood. Yes, Jesus is so often given the title of "the Lamb" in the Scriptures because it so aptly describes his work: to be a sacrifice for our sins. But this title also has a deeper meaning: it describes Jesus' character. He is tender and humble, and constantly offers himself to God for the sake of the salvation of people like you and me.

Lamb of God, purify me with your blood, every day, and help me through your Holy Spirit to live a pure life.

In Christ's life, he was an example of how we should live; through his death, he was a sacrifice for our sins; he was a conqueror; he was a king; and because of his intercession for us, he is a high priest. – MARTIN LUTHER

September 5

YOU MUST REPENT

Yet I hold this against you: You have forsaken your first love. Remember the height from which you have fallen! Repent and do the things you did at first. If you do not repent, I will come to you and remove your lampstand from its place (Rev 2:4-5).

Alexander Solzhenitsyn once gave the annual inaugural address at Harvard University. He spoke about the problems of both capitalism and Marxism. The problem with these systems, he argued, is that neither of them takes God into consideration. But forgetting about God is not a sin peculiar to economy-driven governments, but can also be the sin of religion. Religious people "forget" God by placing religious structures above him.

FOOD FROM THE WORD OF GOD
Revelation 2:1-17; Jeremiah 2:1-9.

In Acts 7, Stephen revolts against such a system. He alleged that religion in Jerusalem had become rotten. The elders of the city were furious with him and first banished him from the city, then had him stoned. His sincere faith threatened their clinical, structured faith.

We are all inclined to drift away from God. Therefore, the Bible repeatedly calls on us to be alert, to pray and to remember, to turn back to God, to repent, to draw closer to God and to surrender ourselves anew to him. We, too, must hear what Stephen was trying to put across to the Sanhedrin, *However, the Most High does not live in houses made by men* (Acts 7:48a). He is God the Creator, the Alpha and the Omega, and he longs for a personal, living relationship with each of us. He does not look for structures, systems, or a religion that is dead. He wants *you*, *your* heart and *your* love. He wants to be *your* God and *your* Friend.

Holy Spirit who brings life, I praise you for leading me to repentance and conversion. Help me to grow in my living relationship with my God and Father.

We ought to love God because he is God, and the measure of our love for him ought to be immeasurable.
St BERNARD of CLAIRVAUX

GOD ACCEPTS THOSE WHO COME TO HIM

It is my judgement, therefore, that we should not make it difficult for the Gentiles who are turning to God (Acts 15:19).

God himself gave us the law. But not one of us can keep his law. In Romans 5:20 it is explained to us in the following way: *The law was added so that the trespass might increase. But where sin increased, grace increased all the more.* Law is the instigator of sin, but can never destroy sin. How can this vicious circle be stopped? The answer can be found in the word "mercy".

FOOD FROM THE WORD OF GOD
Acts 15:1-21; Psalm 22:27-28; 67:1-8; Isaiah 45:22; 56:6-8; Jeremiah 12:13-14.

Let us give an even clearer definition of this biblical term. Where sin grows and multiplies rapidly, mercy flows in. Where there is a noticeable increase in sin, mercy multiplies incomprehensibly. Where sin is limited, mercy knows no bounds. Where sin is great, mercy is overwhelming. Where sin seemingly reigns supreme, mercy always surpasses it. The sins that the law identifies, could not put an end to the massive outpouring of God's mercy. Jesus' death on the cross was sufficient payment for our sins and allowed God's grace to grow anew – and God's grace is not merely sufficient; it is abundant and generous.

In his unfathomable mercy, God offers you forgiveness of your sins. Accept it and make it your own. Once you have accepted his forgiveness, you will be given the power to resist sin and to triumph over it. But never forget: this forgiveness and salvation does not become yours because of something that you have done, but solely because of the mercy of God. Yes, God gives it to you out of his mercy.

The mercy that you show me, O God, fills me with speechless wonder. Help me, Spirit of God, to live by this mercy every day.

Mercy cannot be sought, bought, or fabricated. It is a gift from a merciful God to humankind in need.

BILLY GRAHAM

September 7

JESUS WARNS AGAINST DECEITFULNESS

Beware of the teachers of the law. They like to walk round in flowing robes and love to be greeted in the marketplaces and have the most important seats in the synagogues and the places of honour at banquets (Lk 20:46).

Maybe it is time for us to ask ourselves: How many types of sin are still multiplying in our hearts, in our congregations, without our being rebuked? Do we not perhaps excuse ourselves by merely preaching about sin, without mentioning the particular sins that we continue to commit? Do we not preach against sin in general, while refusing to refer to the terrible details? Or have our consciences been blunted to such an extent that we fail to spot anything that looks like sin?

FOOD FROM THE WORD OF GOD
Luke 20:20-47; Ezekiel 34:1-4, 7-10; Micah 2:1-3.

Preachers often preach against sin without explaining exactly what constitutes sin. They talk about sin in general, but seldom do they highlight a specific sin that prevails in our lives. They condemn all sin, but do not concern themselves with the details of the sins in their own hearts and the sins of the people entrusted to their spiritual care.

It is difficult to grasp how people who love God's law and try to follow it so sincerely, can still be involved in so many forms of trespassing his law, without any signs of repentance or self-reproach. The church of Christ dare not deceive herself over this issue. It is of the utmost importance that we should continually pray for a sensitive conscience, and that we should at all times guard against violating our own consciences by committing sin. We must be honest with ourselves and with those around us about the sin within us. By doing so, we keep our consciences RECEPTIVE AND AWAKE.

Holy Lord Jesus, open my spiritual eyes so that I may notice the sin in my life, and conquer it through your power.

Most of us follow our consciences in the same way that we push a wheelbarrow: we push it ahead of us in the direction we would like to go. – BILLY GRAHAM

September 8

TO FOLLOW JESUS

"Come, follow me," Jesus said, "and I will make you fishers of men" (Mt 4:19).

The essence of Jesus' words to his disciples was, "Follow me!" He invited them to learn from him, to obey him and to associate themselves with his cause. And they put their own affairs aside, because Jesus demands loyalty and faithfulness from each of his disciples.

Jesus' call has not changed. He still extends the invitation, "Follow me!" And he still demands that we lay down our own lives. These days, however, it does not necessarily mean that we should leave our jobs, our families and our homes as the disciples did back in biblical times. Rather, it implies an inner surrender of our whole lives to Christ, and a refusal to allow our jobs, our families, or our homes to cause a rift between Christ and ourselves.

FOOD FROM THE WORD OF GOD
Matthew 4:12-5:12; Genesis 12:1-4; Isaiah 6:1-8.

What is it, then, that we must lay down? Firstly, sin. We must repent of our sins and turn to Christ. Repentance and conversion are inseparably linked. We cannot follow Jesus if we have not yet made a clean break from sin.

Secondly, we must remove the "I" from the throne of our lives, because following Christ means giving him the right of ownership to our lives. It means worshipping him as the King of our lives. Following Jesus means renouncing ourselves, losing ourselves in him, crucifying ourselves. Yes, Christ calls us to surrender ourselves to him. He calls us to make him the Lord and Master of every aspect of our lives.

My spirit, my soul, my body I dedicate to you, my Lord.
I lay myself down as an eternal offering before you.

Happy are they who know that discipleship simply means that you live through mercy and that mercy simply means discipleship. – DIETRICH BONHOEFFER

September 9

SIGNS OF THE END OF TIME

Now learn this lesson from the fig tree: As soon as its twigs get tender and its leaves come out, you know that summer is near (Mt 24:32).

Our generation is witnessing the fulfilment of many prophecies. Many of the wondrous signs that Jesus said would precede his second coming are taking place before our very eyes.

There is the evangelical sign: *And this gospel of the kingdom will be preached in the whole world as a testimony to all nations, and then the end will come* (Mt 24:14). In our day, there is not a single continent on earth where Christian religion has not taken root due to the preaching of the gospel.

FOOD FROM THE WORD OF GOD
Matthew 24:9-35; Isaiah 13:9-10; 34:1-4; Daniel 7:13-14; Micah 7:4-6.

Then there is also the religious sign: *Don't let anyone deceive you in any way, for [that day will not come] until the rebellion occurs and the man of lawlessness is revealed, the man doomed to destruction* (2 Thess 2:3). This sign we see around us every day. Crime, manslaughter, lawlessness, hate and murder are increasing all the time.

The political signs of the end of time are also in abundance. Can the current conditions in the world possibly be described more accurately than in the words of the Master? *There will be signs in the sun, moon and stars. On the earth, nations will be in anguish and perplexity at the roaring and tossing of the sea. Men will faint from terror, apprehensive of what is coming on the world, for the heavenly bodies will be shaken* (Lk 21:25-26).

Lastly, there is also the Jewish sign: *Jerusalem will be trampled on by the Gentiles until the times of the Gentiles are fulfilled* (Lk 21:24b). Whatever point of view we recognise regarding the second coming of Jesus, history is fast moving in this direction.

Amen. Come, Lord Jesus! (Rev 22:20).

Our Lord will come in order to finally break through all man's undertakings so that the free course of his Word can be assured. – JOHN CALVIN

September 10

JESUS UNDERSTANDS OUR HEARTS

For there is nothing hidden that will not be disclosed, and nothing concealed that will not be known or brought out into the open (Lk 8:17).

The first kind of soil in the parable of the sower describes the hardened hearts of which there were just as many in the time of Jesus as there are today. What is it that makes a person's heart hard? There can only be one answer, namely sin. Sin hardens the heart and those who have hard hearts, only sin more.

FOOD FROM THE WORD OF GOD
Luke 8:1-21; Psalm 78:1-4; Isaiah 1:2-3; 6:9-10; Jeremiah 6:9-10.

These kinds of people are described in Romans 1. They suppress the truth about God to which creation testifies (v 18-20); they inevitably deteriorate into spiritual ignorance and moral decay (v 21-31); eventually, they not only practise these sins, but also approve of them (v 32). Here we see that sin leads people to reject God and his truth, and that rejection of God and his truth only leads to more sin.

What causes people to reject the truth of God? All God's characteristics – his supremacy, holiness, omnipresence, omniscience and omnipotence, his holy love – all are causes of annoyance to sinful people. Instead of repenting our sins and turning to God for his mercy, we suppress the knowledge that we have, and we refuse to look for the knowledge that can lead to our salvation.

When Christ came to proclaim the kingdom of God, he proclaimed God's right to reign in the heart and mind of every person. Pray that Jesus, who knows your thoughts, will soften your heart, making it receptive for the seed of God's love and mercy.

Holy God and King of my heart and life, thank you for the difference that your Word and your mercy through Jesus Christ make in my life.

Desiring what God wants and always wanting it, on all occasions and without exception, this is the kingdom of God that is everything within us. – FRANÇOIS FÈNELON

WHERE IS YOUR TREASURE?

For where your treasure is, there your heart will be also (Lk 12:34).

The Bible talks in no uncertain terms about the slavery that is inherent in wealth. Jesus himself revealed the iron grip that wealth has on our lives. That is why he warned his followers, *Do not store up for yourselves treasures on earth, where moth and rust destroy, and where thieves break in and steal* (Mt 6:19). He challenged the rich young man not only to give up his wealth internally, but also literally to get rid of his possessions in order to enter the kingdom of God (Mt 19:16-22). Jesus gave people who were seeking God the following advice, *Sell your possessions and give to the poor. Provide purses for yourselves that will not wear out, a treasure in heaven that will not be exhausted, where no thief comes near and no moth destroys* (Lk 12:33). He told them about the rich farmer whose passion in life was to gather riches. We would have called him wise, yet Jesus calls him a fool (Lk 12:16-21).

FOOD FROM THE WORD OF GOD
Luke 12:8-34; Job 20:20-23; 31:24-28; Proverbs 30:7-9; Ecclesiastes 5:10-11.

Jesus says that when we sincerely desire the kingdom of God, we must do what a merchant in search of fine pearls does: we must be prepared to sell everything we own in order to get hold of the pearl (Mt 13:45-46). He calls on everyone who wants to follow him to have an attitude free from care about earthly possessions: *Give to everyone who asks you, and if anyone takes what belongs to you, do not demand it back* (Lk 6:30). Who of us, except by the mercy of God, can obey this condition?

Teach me, O Holy Spirit, that everything I own belongs to God, and that it has only been lent to me so that I may glorify him through it.

What I am is only mercy; what I have is only lent to me.
KOOS DU PLESSIS

September 12

BEAR GOOD FRUIT

If it bears fruit next year, fine! If not, then cut it down (Lk 13:9).

Fruit is the produce of a tree that was planted and nurtured in order to yield fruit with which to feed humans. The fruit is not there for the benefit of the tree or branches, but for those who enjoy the fruit. As soon as the fruit is ripe, the tree gives it up and starts its cycle again, so that it will produce fruit in the new season. A tree that bears fruit does not live for itself, but for those to whom the fruit brings nourishment and refreshment. The purpose of the fruit tree is to bear fruit that will delight the farmer. This is its glory, its reason for existence and its security.

FOOD FROM THE WORD OF GOD
Luke 12:57-13:21; Isaiah 5:1-7, 13-17.

This is a striking illustration of believing children of God remaining *in* Christ, the true Vine. Not only do they increase in strength, but their bond with the Vine also grows stronger, surer and firmer all the time. They also bear fruit, and in abundance. They have the privilege of giving it to others so that they, too, can live from it and flourish. The children of God become like a life-giving tree from which others can eat, through which they may be satisfied and refreshed. In their immediate surroundings they become a focal point of life and blessing. All of this because they remain *in* Christ and receive from him the Spirit and life that they, in their turn, share with others. You, too, must be a blessing to others by remaining *in* Christ all the time. God will use you to be a blessing to others.

Lord Jesus, may I bear the fruit that you expect of my life in you.
I want to remain in you so that you
may feed and bless my neighbours through me.

Do not be scared of growing slowly; only be scared of stagnating and dying.
ANDREW MURRAY

GOD RECEIVES EVERYONE

But while he was still a long way off, his father saw him and was filled with compassion for him; he ran to his son, threw his arms around him and kissed him (Lk 15:20b).

One of the most difficult and painful acts is admitting your guilt to God before him; admitting with genuine sadness that you have made a mistake. The Bible uses the word "conversion" for this act.

Conversion implies that you have moved in one direction, but then, suddenly, you turn around and move in the opposite direction. Both John the Baptist and Jesus the living Christ made conversion the point of departure of their preaching because they were ministering to a generation whose personal lives were shattered.

FOOD FROM THE WORD OF GOD
Luke 15:11-31; Proverbs 28:13; Jeremiah 18:1-10; Ezekiel 33:10-16.

Conversion is activated by the act of repentance before God – an admission that you have sinned and are in desperate need of forgiveness. The Scriptures place conversion as a high priority, because through it we reveal the secrets of our hearts. And the reconstruction of a shattered life cannot begin until our hearts open voluntarily.

Before our lives can be repaired, we must first look at the damage that has been done to a broken world. We must assess our broken relationships and heal them. We must ask God for forgiveness; likewise we must forgive others. In order to achieve this it is important that we should come together, showing mercy to one another as God has shown mercy to us. It is not easy, but reconciliation is one of the unique features of a Christian community. Reconciliation can neither be earned nor demanded. It has to be given freely, as God freely shows his mercy to those who ask him for it.

Restore to me the joy of your salvation and grant me a willing spirit, to sustain me (Ps 51:12).

For them who still reside in this world, it is never too late to repent. Entry into God's mercy is open and easy for those who seek and find the truth. – St CYPRIAN

September 14

WE NEED A KEEPER

Feed my sheep (Jn 21:17c).

The shepherd stands at the centre of his flock's existence. He provides in their every need. Sheep that are scared do not easily lie down, but as soon as the shepherd appears and walks amongst them, the restlessness of the flock dissipates and calmness sets in. Our good Shepherd appears amongst us in the same way, saying, *So do not fear, for I am with you* (Is 41:10). His presence in our time of need dispels all fear and anxiety, and gives us rest.

FOOD FROM THE WORD OF GOD
John 21:14-25; Numbers 27:15-17; 2 Samuel 5:1-2; Psalm 78:70-72; Ezekiel 34:1-5, 11-12, 30-31.

Sheep are also restless when they are hungry. The shepherd looks for the best possible grazing for them. Our good Shepherd knows what we need in order to find inner satisfaction. He provides nourishment for our souls in the green pastures of his Word. Once fed by his promises, we can lay ourselves down, satisfied, content and carefree.

Sometimes the shepherd has to force his sheep to go and lie down. Likewise, our good Shepherd sometimes makes us lie down due to illness, loneliness, or sorrow that comes over our lives. But always the Shepherd leads his sheep to the green pastures of spiritual nourishment, to quiet and peaceful waters. There he restores our souls, because the good Shepherd likes to see his flock relaxed, refreshed and contented in their relationship with him.

Are you a member of the flock of Jesus Christ, our good Shepherd? Then lead others to him who do not yet belong to his flock. This is what he commanded us.

Lord Jesus, you are my shepherd in life, in death, and until eternity. I praise and worship your holy Name for this.

The world around us will recognise us as disciples of Jesus when they see that our prayers for their sake are answered. – COLIN URQUHART

CHANGE YOUR HEART - GOD FORGIVES

Peter replied, "Repent and be baptised, every one of you, in the name of Jesus Christ for the forgiveness of your sins. And you will receive the gift of the Holy Spirit" (Acts 2:38).

When Peter's audience listened to his striking words on Pentecost, they responded positively to the truth concerning the living Christ. He asked them to change their hearts and assured them that, if they did this, God would forgive them and grant them the Holy Spirit as their guide. Today, Peter's message is still as valid as it was on that first day of the Pentecost.

FOOD FROM THE WORD OF GOD
Acts 2:29-3:10; Psalm 130:1-8; Hosea 6:1-6.

Jesus desires that we should *live*. He has come that we *may have life, and have it to the full* (Jn 10:10). Are there any remaining hidden sins in your life? God knows about them. He wants you to confess them before him and turn away from them. He wants you to live rightly: *You do not delight in sacrifice, or I would bring it; you do not take pleasure in burnt offerings. The sacrifices of God are a broken spirit; a broken and contrite heart, O God, you will not despise* (Ps 51:16-17). God demands a repentant, humble heart that has been renewed by the Holy Spirit.

It is then that we see our sins from God's perspective for the very first time; then that we pray that God will shine the light of his Holy Spirit into the darkest recesses of our hearts; then that we pray for consciences that are sensitive, and that we may abhor sin; then that we ask God in prayer to help us to cultivate the right attitude. And we fall before him in worship and gratitude.

Your mercy and forgiveness overwhelm me, O God. I dedicate myself anew and with gratefulness to you.

It only takes a few minutes to commit a sin, but it does not even take that long to receive God's forgiveness. Repentance and confession ought to be a lifelong action. – HUBERT VON ZELLER

September 16

THE WILL OF GOD CANNOT BE STOPPED

But if it is from God, you will not be able to stop these men; you will only find yourselves fighting against God (Acts 5:39).

Romans 8:28 assures us, *And we know that in all things God works for the good of those who love him, who have been called according to his purpose.* We can only see the beginning, while God from the beginning sees the end. Not only does he know what he is doing, but he also knows the outcome of his mighty deeds.

FOOD FROM THE WORD OF GOD
Acts 5:26-6:7; Job 23:13-16; Psalm 127:1; Ecclesiastes 3:14-15; Isaiah 46:8-13.

God not only sees the pain and sadness, he also sees the future benefits and joy that they will bring forth. He knows how the good earth is torn open by the sharpness of the plough, but he also knows how the ploughed earth will soon be covered in a golden harvest of corn. He sees the consequences of trials and he remembers every painful experience so that he may bless it later on with joy and peace. May this be our comfort when are heavily burdened by pain and sorrow, loss and trials.

Now we only see rough granite. We see small pieces being chiselled away; we feel the sharp point of the chisel; we know the weight of the hammer, and our emotions and memories are overwhelmed by all these things. If only we could see the great Artist's sculpture after he has finished it off, we would have better understood the chisel and the mallet, as well as the Master Artist. But no matter what happens in our lives it is all part of God's divine plan to lead us to his magnificent focal point. In all things God works for the good of us who love him.

Our Father in heaven, hallowed be your name, your kingdom come, your will be done on earth as it is in heaven (Mt 6:9-10).

The first degree of humility is obedience without delay.
BENEDICT

MAKE GOD'S DEEDS KNOWN

"Leave your country and your people," God said, "and go to the land I will show you" (Acts 7:3).

Stephen was a powerful witness for God. And so was Sofie Lichtenfels, the "charwoman".

Sofie witnessed by means of her calloused hands and knees, and the music of a washbasin and scrubbing brush. Her witness was quite simple, "God has called me to scrub and to preach. I am a born preacher, but because I am poor, I have to work. My work is thorough and I can be trusted, so I am much in demand. But when they take me into their service, they must hear me preach. No sermon, no work. I scrub as if for the Lord, and I preach to everybody in the household. When I do not have any work I tell it to my Father. He is the best employment agent, and you do not have to wait a long time for him or pay.

FOOD FROM THE WORD OF GOD
Acts 6:8-7:16; Psalm 105:1-23.

"We sometimes pray so foolishly. For 12 years, I prayed that the Lord would make me a missionary in a foreign country. One day I was praying like this again, when the Lord said to me, 'Sofie, where were you born?' 'In Germany,' I replied. 'And where are you now?' 'In America, Lord.' 'So, are you not already a missionary in a foreign country? Who lives on the storey above you? A family from Sweden. And above them, Swiss. In your backyard are Italians and Chinese. You have never spoken to them about me. Do you really think I should send you thousands of kilometres away while you have foreigners, and even heathens, on your doorstep?'"

Holy God, grant that I may faithfully deliver the message you have given to me where you have placed me.

A woman on a farm can milk cows to the glory of God.
MARTIN LUTHER

September 18

DO NOT SILENCE GOD'S MESSAGE

You stiff-necked people, with uncircumcised hearts and ears! You are just like your fathers: You always resist the Holy Spirit! (Acts 7:51).

In his remarkable sermon Stephen gave an accurate interpretation of the history of the Jews and showed how it is connected to the new faith that he had adopted, his faith in the living Christ. He got the better of his adversaries and declared them the guilty party. He rejected all their accusations. He gave an overview of their history since the time of Abraham and through it he proved how the eternal God cannot be confined to an earthly temple.

FOOD FROM THE WORD OF GOD
Acts 7:43-8:3; 2 Chronicles 24:17-22; 36:11-17.

Stephen reminded them of God's presence with Jacob, even when he was in Egypt. He reminded them that they – as a nation – were the messengers of God, yet they were constantly disloyal to that message. He pointed out how Joseph's brothers were disloyal to him and maltreated him, while God would rescue them through none other than him. They rebelled against Moses and rejected his message. They stoned the prophets and desecrated the temple. They boasted about the authority of the law, yet they did not keep it.

When Stephen delivered his final, searing judgement, he did it on purpose. He knew very well what the reaction of his audience would be, and told them that they were stiff-necked and had uncircumcised hearts and ears, murderers and traitors of the Righteous One (Acts 7:51-52). Stephen was killed because they wanted to silence God's voice and did not want to hear his message. And what about you? What are you doing with God's message?

Word incarnate, make me unconditionally obedient to your message so that I will not sin against you.

The only way that religious truth can be affirmed, is through martyrdom.
SAMUEL JOHNSON

September 19

GOD'S GREAT MERCY AND GOODNESS

Consider therefore the kindness and sternness of God: sternness to those who fell, but kindness to you, provided that you continue in his kindness. Otherwise, you will also be cut off (Rom 11:22).

Being good without also being merciful is impossible. Mercy, therefore, also means being good. It implies caring deeply and sincerely about the needs of others. And this concern leads to compassion and grace.

FOOD FROM THE WORD OF GOD
Romans 11:1-24; Psalm 85:7-13; 86:8-10; Isaiah 45:22-24; 52:10; Ezekiel 18:21-23.

The goodness and mercy of God runs through the entire Scriptures like a powerful theme. The goodness of God draws us towards him with ties of love stronger than steel. The mercy of God makes us his grateful children. The goodness of God as expressed through Jesus Christ and revealed by the Holy Spirit, assures us of our salvation. The mercy of God in Jesus, who laid down his life for us, brings us forgiveness of sin. God's goodness seeks and finds us, welcoming us as members of his family, as his beloved children.

The mercy and goodness of God enable us to stand before him as the redeemed who have been declared righteous by the blood of the Lamb. God's mercy erases our debts. We are united with him, while living in peace with others. The goodness of God reforms and recreates us in his image. His goodness gives meaning and dignity to this life, and endless joy and peace in the life hereafter.

This steady, sustained, certain goodness and mercy of God bring us joy both now and in all eternity. Do you experience it in your life?

Do not keep your goodness and mercy from me for a single moment, O God of love. May they continually radiate to your honour in my life.

Mercy is love that cares and bows down and saves.
JOHN RW STOTT

September 20

THE HEALING POWER OF FORGIVENESS

Now instead, you ought to forgive and comfort him, so that he will not be overwhelmed by excessive sorrow. I urge you, therefore, to reaffirm your love for him (2 Cor 2:7-8).

Forgiveness of sins is a gift of mercy from God. In his unfathomable mercy, God sets sinners free and receives us back in his favour and love. When we have received forgiveness, we are free to talk to God in prayer. Then we are grateful every day, because we have been set free and there are no obstacles that separate us from God. With the door open to him, God desires that we should spend quality time with him by having fellowship with him and his Word every day, by living in the light that is reflected from his face.

FOOD FROM THE WORD OF GOD
2 Corinthians 1:18-3:3; Genesis 32:6-10; 50:15-21; Psalm 32:1-7.

It is important that you honestly ask yourself whether this miracle of God's forgiveness has already occurred in your life. God wants this certainty to influence your relationships with those who are close to you. Someone to whom forgiveness has been given, has the freedom to forgive someone else in turn. If you find it difficult to forgive, you need to remind yourself how freely and generously God forgives all your trespasses. The result of an unforgiving heart is that you yourself will not receive God's forgiveness.

Is there anyone in your life who wants and needs your forgiveness urgently? If this is the case, remember: As you need God's forgiveness every day, you must be prepared to forgive others. If you refuse to forgive, you are burning the bridge you yourself have to cross in order to be forgiven.

Merciful God, may I always follow your example of merciful forgiveness.

"I can forgive, but I cannot forget" is just another way of saying, "I do not want to forgive."
HENRY WARD BEECHER

September 21

GOD'S BLESSING COMES FROM SUFFERING

And we know that in all things God works for the good of those who love him, who have been called according to his purpose (Rom 8:28).

In his Word, God tells us that he can make everything that happens to us work to our good. Through hardship and suffering, he reveals things to us, which we would not have understood if we had not been in that specific situation. Though we may not know what an accident, a fire, an earthquake or a storm has brought about in our lives, our only assurance as believing children of God is that he is powerful enough to bring about beauty from ashes and to let the oil of gladness flow from our sorrow and pain (Is 61:3). Through this, he trains and purifies us so that we may become precious and steadfast in our relationship with him, as well as in our dealings with other people.

FOOD FROM THE WORD OF GOD
Romans 8:18-39; Exodus 2:1-3, 7-14, 22.

When we turn to God in trials, seeking his help, he does not allow our sorrow to be wasted. As he protected Job, he will give to us the mercy required to emerge from our suffering unharmed. But God will see to it that we do much more than simply make it through trials unhurt. He will ensure that we hold ever more firmly onto our trust in him and our love for him. He will ensure that we conquer our circumstances. Yes, in times of trouble we are indeed given the ability to discard more and more of the obstacles that negatively influence the beauty and reality of our love, joy, peace, tolerance and humility. Praise the Lord, for he is good!

Holy Spirit, help me to trust in the love and mercy of God when I experience trials and hardship.

A Christian is someone who shares the suffering of God in this world.
DIETRICH BONHOEFFER

September 22

GOD PLANS OUR LIVES

But when God, who set me apart from birth and called me by his grace, was pleased to reveal his Son in me so that I might preach him among the Gentiles, I did not consult any man (Gal 1:15-16).

Not knowing what the future has in store for us – especially for each of us individually – is definitely for the better. If we could know the future we would often have ruined or tried to change God's plan for our lives. If we could see into the future and what problems it holds for us, we would have tried to avoid them, while the problems in our lives are actually God's paths to new experiences and blessings.

FOOD FROM THE WORD OF GOD
Galatians 1:1-24; 1 Samuel 9: 14-17; 1 Chronicles 17:7-11; Psalm 139:13-17.

God's plans and intentions for us are always plans and intentions of love and goodness. They always further our spiritual growth. But the road that takes us to the mountain tops sometimes passes through dark valleys and rough terrain. By avoiding the difficult part of the road you will not succeed in reaching the mountain top. You will never see the sight that would have opened up before you.

Walk in faith with your hand in God's hand, instead of trying to walk the road that your blind heart plans according to your own foolish choices. He plans your life as he planned the lives of David, Samuel, Saul and Paul.

Have you sought God's plan for your life? Are you prepared to test yourself to determine whether you are carrying out God's plan for your life? Remember: his plan for your life involves your existence; his road for you is best.

Lead me, friendly Light, through earthly darkness. Please lead me ahead! Black is the night where I am a wanderer. Please lead me ahead! Light my way, not because I desire to see far ahead, just step by step, O Lord!

A leader is someone who knows the road, who has been there, and who can lead you there.
JOHN ERSKINE

September 23

WE ARE GOD'S CHILDREN

But when the time had fully come, God sent his Son, born of a woman, born under law, to redeem those under law, that we might receive the full rights of sons (Gal 4:4-5).

We must think seriously about the implications and responsibilities of being a child of God. It means that we must live as children of a holy God. Just as a couple adopt a child because they choose to and not because they are forced to, so God adopts us. He chooses to do so. He is under no obligation to do it. On the contrary, he could easily have punished us for our sins deservedly. But he loves us. He has saved and redeemed us. He offers us his forgiveness and gives himself to us to be our heavenly Father.

God's mercy does not end with this great initial deed, just as earthly parents' love does not end as soon as the adoption papers have been signed. That is only the beginning of the process of establishing the child's status as a member of the family. The real work is still to come: establishing real family bonds between them as the adoptive parents and the adopted child, and gaining the child's love by loving him or her. For goodwill and love awake goodwill and love.

The same applies to God. Right through our present lives and in all eternity, he will, ever more and more, show his love to us in some or other way. But in return, he expects that our love for him should increase daily. What does you life look like? Can you exclaim joyously, "God is my Father, I am his child"?

FOOD FROM THE WORD OF GOD
Galatians 3:21-4:20;
Deuteronomy 14:2; 32:5-10;
Isaiah 64:8-9; Hosea 1:10-12.

My God and Father, may I live and love as a child of God and not a child of the world.

Our heavenly Father never takes anything from his children unless he intends to give them something better in return. – GEORGE MULLER

September 24

PRAY FOR ONE ANOTHER

I have not stopped giving thanks for you, remembering you in my prayers. I keep asking that the God of our Lord Jesus Christ, the glorious Father, may give you the Spirit of wisdom and revelation, so that you may know him better (Eph 1:16-17).

The story of the paralysed man who was brought on a mat to Jesus demonstrates the powerful effect of interceding love. We "carry" the people for whom we pray to Jesus in order that he may meet them in their need, touch their lives, heal them and give to them the joy of healing and being healthy.

FOOD FROM THE WORD OF GOD
Ephesians 1:1-23; Deuteronomy 9:18-20; Job 42:7-8; Daniel 2:14-19.

One's ego does not feature at all in intercession. In our prayers, we only think of the people for whom we are praying. We experience their pain with them, we suffer their fears on their behalf, and we are consumed by the same yearnings. Jesus said, *Blessed are the merciful* (Mt 5:7). Being merciful means putting yourself in someone else's shoes, to feel as he or she feels, to think as he or she thinks, to see with his or her eyes and to experience life as he or she experiences it. This is exactly what Jesus our Saviour did for us when he was incarnated.

In our empathy and compassion, we can bring people who are troubled to the Lord and leave them with him. We need not remind him of all the facts. We need not recommend to him what he ought to do. The Holy Spirit will pray on our behalf. We cannot heal people, but we can pray for them and plead with God Almighty who can heal them through our intercession: *When Jesus saw their faith, he said, "Friend, your sins are forgiven"* (Lk 5:20).

Lord Jesus, may my prayers for my neighbours always stem from a sincere heart, filled with compassion, love and empathy.

Let us not leave one another in the lurch in terms of interest, care, and practical help; but especially let us not leave one another in the lurch in terms of prayer. – MICHAEL BAUGHEN

MUTUAL LOVE IN MARRIAGE

In the same way, husbands ought to love their wives as their own bodies (Eph 5:28).

The contents of this letter by Paul were a radical departure from the culture and customs of those days. His instructions to husbands were in direct conflict with the customary way in which husbands treated their wives at that time. Paul calls on husbands to be the loving servants to their wives in a culture where wives were seen as possessions.

Indeed, a husband must love his wife with the sacrificial love that Christ has for us. Jesus himself said, *Just as the Son of Man did not come to be served, but to serve, and to give his life as a ransom for many* (Mt 20:28). In the Scriptures, Christ is presented to us as a master as well as a servant: *And God places all things under his feet and appointed him to be head over everything for the church* (Eph 1:22). *... but made himself nothing, taking the very nature of a servant, being made in human likeness* (Phil 2:7). Jesus also gives us the command, *The greatest among you will be your servant* (Mt 23:11).

FOOD FROM THE WORD OF GOD
Ephesians 5:15-6:4; Genesis 24:34-40, 50-51, 62-66; Proverbs 5:18-20; Song of Songs 2:16-17.

We are called upon to be servants so that in so doing we may give expression to our new life in Jesus Christ. As far as marriage is concerned, men are called upon to model their attitudes on the example of Jesus. A husband expresses his love for his wife by treating her as a total equal in their life together. And he maintains his leadership by ensuring that this partnership of love works.

Holy God, you who have brought us together with your own hands, may our love for one another always resemble your love for us. Make us loving servants to each other.

The amount that two married people owe one another is incalculable. It is a debt so great that we would need all eternity to repay it. – JOHANN WOLFGANG VON GOETHE

September 26

WE ARE FIGHTING A SPIRITUAL STRUGGLE

For our struggle is not against flesh and blood, but against the rulers, against the authorities, against the powers of this dark world and against the spiritual forces of evil in the heavenly realms (Eph 6:12).

Knowing that we are involved in a struggle that is futile if we try to fight it with earthly weapons is the beginning of triumphant wisdom. Paul is very specific about our evil opponents, *For our struggle is not against flesh and blood, but against the rulers, against the authorities, against the powers of this dark world and against the spiritual forces of evil in the heavenly realms* (Eph 6:12). The immediate implication that comes to mind is that Satan is exceptionally powerful. Of course, he does not nearly possess the omnipotence of God, but in God's divine decision, he allows the evil one to temporarily rule over that part of the world that is completely removed from the mercy of God.

FOOD FROM THE WORD OF GOD
Ephesians 6:5-24; Deuteronomy 7:16; Job 1:6-12; Psalm 106:34-38; Daniel 10:4-8, 12-13.

When we are filled with Jesus (Eph 5:18) the evil powers cannot dominate us. However, we need to realise that we cannot fight against Satan with our own powers. All our efforts will be in vain. But we can buckle the belt of the Lord's strength around our waists. We can admit to our own weakness and rely on his omnipotence. We can follow Gideon's example. He reduced his 32 000 soldiers to a mere 10 000 and eventually entered into battle with only 300 men armed with trumpets and flares, and they achieved a great victory in the name of the Lord (Judg 7). We can lay down our own strength and believe steadfastly in our God who enables us to claim victory in his Name.

Not by virtue of my own power, God Almighty, but by your power I will fight the battle against the evil one until victory is achieved. Help me with this through your Holy Spirit.

God is faithful, and if we follow him faithfully, he will lead us to glorious victory.
RICHARD OF CHICHESTER

STOP COMPLAINING AND ARGUING

Do everything without complaining and arguing (Phil 2:14).

People often do not realise that their complaints and arguments are sins against God. Read again our Scripture readings of the day. God's Word puts it very clearly: *Do everything without complaining or arguing.* It is a command, not an option. God does not exclude anything. He uses the word "everything" and this undoubtedly includes everything, every situation and every task.

When we complain we are actually saying, "I do not really believe that God planned this situation. I do not believe that he could change it if he wants to." If we had in fact believed it, it would not have been necessary to complain. We would have known that our only security is to be found in God's will, regardless of what happens to us.

FOOD FROM THE WORD OF GOD
Philippians 2:5-30; Genesis 45:23-24; Psalm 34:12-15; 78:17-21; Proverbs 11:12; 17:14, 19; 20:3; 26:21.

The same God that tells us not to complain or to object, also tells us, through Paul: *Give thanks in all circumstances, for this is God's will for you in Christ Jesus* (1 Thess 5:18). How is it possible to thank God and to complain at the same time? Is it not hypocritical of us to say that we are grateful for all things, yet complain about our problems? If we persist in complaining, do we really believe that in all things God works for our good?

What is your reaction in times of trouble? Do you believe that the God who performs miracles and for whom everything is possible can change every circumstance in your life for your good?

Help me, Holy Spirit, never to contradict the will of God or to complain. For I have so often experienced that in all things, he works for my good.

Know how sublime a thing it is to suffer and be strong.
HENRY WADSWORTH LONGFELLOW

September 28

YOUR LIFE - AN EXAMPLE

Don't let anyone look down on you because you are young, but set an example for the believers in speech, in life, in love, in faith and in purity (1 Tim 5:12).

Jesus welcomes sinners and loves them. He shows genuine compassion and pity towards people, but he is also honest and condemns sin without compromise. Jesus wins sinners for God without sacrificing the purity of his life. With his arms stretched wide open, he meets people, but he expects them to lead pure lives.

FOOD FROM THE WORD OF GOD
1 Timothy 3:13-4:16; 2 Kings 22:1-2; 23:1-3, 24-25; Daniel 6:1-5.

If Jesus is our Lord and example, our compassion will be modelled on his values. Christ is merciful, but he judges severely. Some of his words are condemning and strict, but his love is everlasting. Indeed, it is actually his love that forms the basis of his judgement. The greatest enemy of our times is the fact that we prefer to be tolerant, that we do not want to condemn.

There was once a Christian woman who was cared for by a non-Christian woman who led an immoral life. One day the unbelieving woman said to the Christian woman, "You know, it's so strange: my non-Christian friends accept me. They say what I do does not matter. I am free to do whatever I like. But it is only with you that I experience genuine love and know that I am always free to come to you. But it is also only with you that I feel ashamed and sorry about my life."

This is sanctity. It rejects no one, but brings the reality of God's loving presence, his purity and holiness into a relationship.

May my life be a reflection of your holiness and love, Lord Jesus, my Saviour.

A holy life will leave the most lasting impression. Lighthouses do not blow trumpets – they simply shine.
DWIGHT L MOODY

September 29

STRIVE FOR ACHIEVEMENT FOR GOD

Brothers, I do not consider myself yet to have taken hold of it. But one thing I do: Forgetting what is behind and straining towards what is ahead, I press on towards the goal to win the prize for which God has called me heavenwards in Christ Jesus (Phil 3:13-14).

Recently we saw how a young man won a gruelling international cycling competition, breaking the world record. In an interview a commentator asked him, "What is your future goal?" Without a moment's hesitation, he answered, "My goal is to be the best cyclist in the world!"

FOOD FROM THE WORD OF GOD
Philippians 3:1-21; Psalm 63:1-8; 73:24-26.

To achieve this high goal, he was prepared to practice hard and sacrifice many things – all for a piece of gold. Why is it that so few of Jesus Christ's disciples have a similar, firm ambition to achieve for the Master? Do we go to the trouble and do we sacrifice our time to become spiritually fit? Or have we become unfit and soft? Winning a game makes high demands on an athlete's endurance – also on athletes for Christ!

Once the race has started, the athlete cannot afford to look back. He must go forward. His eyes must be fixed on the winning line, or else he has no hope of winning. In the same way, we, the disciples of God, must run our race, our eyes fixed on the Lord who encourages us. He is our trainer, referee and judge. We must not look back with yearning or discouragement, but must purposefully forget everything we have left behind – disappointments, failures, as well as past successes and victories. We must strive ahead with our eyes on the Master. He began our faith and will enable us to complete it.

Holy Lord Jesus, may I never lose sight of my goal: life with you.

If we cannot persevere during bad times, we will not be able to achieve in good times either.
ARTHUR C BENSON

September 30

WE ARE RESPONSIBLE FOR ONE ANOTHER

If anyone does not provide for his relatives, and especially for his immediate family, he has denied the faith and is worse than an unbeliever (1 Tim 5:8).

We are responsible for one another because we are Christians. All too often we see how marriages end up on the rocks, how relationships disintegrate, how people keep walking on a road that leads to destruction – without our lifting a finger. And all this because we do not love our neighbours enough to address the problem. We come up with one excuse after the other as to why we do not want to get involved, but forget God's command to help and care for our fellowmen.

FOOD FROM THE WORD OF GOD
1 Timothy 5:3-16; Leviticus 19:15-17; 2 Samuel 12:7-9, 13-14; Proverbs 10:17, 19-21; 15:31-33.

A colleague of mine told me how he became embroiled in an extramarital affair. He said he felt like an exhausted swimmer struggling all alone against the tide and waves – with no hope of swimming out of the current. He told me how he felt as if he was going under for the last time. He could see all the members of his congregation standing on the beach. Some shook their heads and wept in desperation. Others yelled out, clenching their fists in frustration and anger. Here and there were words of encouragement and gestures of goodwill. But everybody was motionless, waiting for something to happen. Nobody acted. Only one man came forward, risking everything, dived into the water and brought the poor man to safety. Not only did it save his life and his marriage, but his ministry too.

Responsibility for one another is a command not to be disobeyed.

Holy God and Father, I thank you for being allowed to belong to your immediate family. Help me through the Holy Spirit to interact lovingly with the other members of the family.

We must rediscover the full meaning of responsibility towards one another and spend less time thinking about personal rights. – PEARL BUCK

October

Prayer for October

1. To God be the glory
2. God gives us the living water
3. God sends his witnesses to all nations
4. Jesus gives us a new commandment
5. Jesus talks about the kingdom of God
6. Always be prepared
7. Christ truly rose from the dead
8. Serve one another with God's commands
9. God's reliable witnesses
10. Our lives – testimonies to God
11. God's great salvation
12. Jesus is our high priest
13. God disciplines his children whom he loves
14. Stand firm in your faith
15. Avoid the pleasures of the world
16. God listens to our prayers
17. Encourage one another in faith
18. God will punish his opponents
19. Who is king of your heart?
20. Hope in Christ's second coming
21. Christ – the light of the world
22. Christ's love for God's house
23. The power of Jesus' resurrection
24. Christ sets us free from sin
25. Jesus sought the will of God
26. Never underestimate the power of seed
27. Jesus' sympathy for lost people
28. Jesus offers nourishment for the soul
29. Jesus' suffering is followed by his judgement
30. Wait with dedication for the second coming
31. Be prepared for the second coming

Prayer for October

God of endless mercy,
we thank you that your unfathomable love covers our entire lives;
that we may rejoice at any age with the psalmist:
You hem me in – behind and before;
you have laid your hand upon me (Ps 139:5).
During this month we especially think of people
who are growing older:
people whose earthly tent dwelling is looking more battered day by day,
but people who are still internally growing in the power
of faith and prayer.
We thank you for being the Unchangeable.
Around and within us all we see is change and decay,
nevertheless, your Word assures us:
They will still bear fruit in old age,
they will stay fresh and green (Ps 92:15).
We worship you as the God who has total control over our lives:
our ideals and dreams, our strength and life expectancy.
Thank you that, with the years, you equip us and show us mercy
in wisdom and maturity, born of experience;
in quietness and peace that grow out of faith.
We thank you for having made all of life beautiful:
daybreak and the rising of the sun,
the fullness and magnificence of the noonday,
the beauty of the setting of the sun,
and the quiet of twilight and the night.
Thank you, God the Father, that you do not abandon us
in our last shift.
Thank you that you still guard over us with love and grace,
that your eternal arms are still supporting us,
just as they did in the prime of our youth and vigorous adulthood.
We thank you for this in the Name of Jesus.

Amen

October 1

TO GOD BE THE GLORY

I tell you the truth, wherever this gospel is preached throughout the world, what she has done, will also be told, in memory of her (Mt 26:13).

The incident in Matthew 26:6-13 illustrates to us in a riveting way the abundance of love. To honour Christ, this woman made an offering to him of her valuable perfume – a symbol of her hard-earned possessions. So abundant was her love that she poured every drop over Jesus. Had the oil been sold, five thousand people could have been fed from the proceeds. But because it was her most valued possession, she gladly gave it to her Master. True love never makes calculations; never tries to get away with as little as possible. Love's only desire is to always give the very best. And once love has given everything, it still thinks that the offering was too small.

FOOD FROM THE WORD OF GOD
Matthew 25:41-26:19; Genesis 8:18-21; Judges 13:15-23; 1 Kings 8:17-19.

This illustrates that there are times when common sense says, "What a waste!" – and is apparently right. But there is a world of difference between the economy of common sense and that of love. There are times when only the abundance of love can fulfil the demands of love. A gift is only a gift if it is inspired by the offering of love.

In today's passage, Jesus shows us that the scent of this sublime offering will last eternally. The dark and loveless world desperately needs such shining lights. There was so much bitterness and treason, so much tragedy around Jesus that this incident beckons to us like a lush oasis in an arid, barren desert. An offering to the Master, who made the highest sacrifice of love for our sake, is never forgotten.

Holy Spirit of God, teach me more and more how to honour my God and Father through Jesus Christ.

Praise and worship are not merely a part of the Christian life; they are the Christian life.
GERALD VANN

GOD GIVES US THE LIVING WATER

Jesus answered, "Everyone who drinks this water will be thirsty again, but whoever drinks the water I give him will never thirst" (Jn 4:13-14a).

The thirst of everyone who drinks of Christ's living water will be satisfied in all eternity. In order to get this living water, we simply have to accept Christ's invitation and come and scoop it up. The living water is free, because the cleansing blood of the Lamb has already paid for it.

FOOD FROM THE WORD OF GOD
John 4:1-26; Isaiah 12:1-6; Jeremiah 2:12-13; 17:19.

The life that pulsates and throbs through those who accept his invitation to refresh them with this living water in this sad and barren world, comes from God himself. He pours it out over them through his Holy Spirit and in so doing touches their lives and hearts so that they, in turn, can touch other thirsty souls. Anyone who is naive or arrogant enough to believe that it is his or her own charisma or ability with which he or she refreshes other people, is deceiving himself or herself.

One of the worst tragedies in people's lives is when they turn to other people in an attempt to find relief and refreshment for their spirits. They are continually deceived and disappointed. Our spirits can only find life through the living Spirit of the living God. Our eternal search and thirst for life-giving water can only be satisfied by the eternal God. We receive it when we become channels of his love and mercy through the hidden fountains of his perfect image, Jesus Christ. Then the living water flows *through* us as well as *out of* us to other thirsty souls.

Wash, relieve and cleanse me with the living water of your Holy Spirit, O God.

We can rather try to grow flowers without an atmosphere, or to produce fruit without light or heat, than to reform a man if we do not believe in the work of the Holy Spirit. – HENRY WARD BEECHER

GOD SENDS HIS WITNESSES TO ALL NATIONS

You are witnesses of these things. I am going to send you what my Father has promised; but stay in the city until you have been clothed with power from on high (Lk 24:48-49).

Every Christian has the privilege and responsibility to witness to as many people as possible about the miraculous deeds of the living Christ and the mighty deeds of the mercy of God. We must tell all people in all places of God's acts of mercy through Jesus Christ, but especially of those deeds that God has performed for us personally. We dare not evade this responsibility. Were we to do this, we would be disloyal to our God.

FOOD FROM THE WORD OF GOD
Luke 24:13-53; Psalm 9:12; Isaiah 40:9-11; 52:7-10.

There are, however, so many people who say that they are believers, but who are not impressed by this glorious truth. Their philosophy is that the task of saving people should be left in the hands of the people who were trained to do it, such as ministers. Consequently, very little of the Master's last instruction to his disciples is brought to fruition in their lives: *Therefore go and make disciples of all nations* (Mt 28:19). And because we are unfaithful to this command, the church of Christ is losing her authority in this world instead of growing. Because we are stagnating as followers of Christ instead of growing in spiritual maturity, we pay a high price.

The time has come for us to admit that spreading the gospel is our life's task, too. We have all been called to preach. The whole life of every believer should be a proclamation of the good news. Do not evade this glorious responsibility at the cost of your salvation.

Holy God, you who call your children, and equip and send them out through your Holy Spirit, show me daily to whom I should take your good gospel.

The Bible is a missionary book. Jesus Christ is the Father's first and foremost missionary to a lost world.
HAROLD LINDSELL

JESUS GIVES US A NEW COMMANDMENT

A new commandment I give you: Love one another. As I have loved you, so you must love one another. By this all men will know that you are my disciples, if you love one another (Jn 13:34-35).

With the resurrection of Jesus and at Pentecost heavenly love descended over the earth. Everyone who had received the living Christ, the true love in their lives and who chose to obey his law, started loving one another. The heathen world looked on in amazement, while some of the believers said, "See how much they love one another."

FOOD FROM THE WORD OF GOD
John 13:18-38; Exodus 19:4-6; 20:1-17.

Within a few years of Jesus having given this command of love to his disciples, the gospel had spread like a fire through the then entire known world. The miracle of God's love, the divine *agapé*, gripped crowds in the wicked Roman Empire. Is it not tragic then, that in our modern world we so seldom hear people say of Christians, "See how much they love one another"? All we see around us is suspicion, jealousy, criticism and conflict amongst Christians, churches and denominations. The unbelieving world must surely often laugh about this.

But the small group of believers who do express this divine love in their lives are warmly received by believers and unbelievers alike. The church that obeys Jesus' command for us to love one another is filled to capacity and has a tremendous impact on the world – to the glory of God. They represent the alternative to a loveless, secular society.

How does one find this *agapé* love? You find it through faith in Christ. The Word of God commands us to show love, and promises that God will grant the ability to do as he instructs (1 Jn 15:14-15).

Holy Spirit, Teacher and Guide, teach me to love as the Saviour loves me.

Take away love, and this world becomes a tomb.
ROBERT BROWNING

October 5

JESUS TALKS ABOUT THE KINGDOM OF GOD

Again, the kingdom of heaven is like a merchant looking for fine pearls. When he found one of great value, he went away and sold everything he had and bought it (Mt 13:45-46).

During the American Civil War the Union and Confederate forces were fighting just outside the city of Richmond. When night fell on the first day of battle, shouts of joy were heard from the Confederate camp. General Grant of the Union asked what was happening in the enemy camp and was told that the wife of General George Pritchett had given birth to a baby boy and that the troops were celebrating. General Grant then ordered that the bale-fires be lit and a toast be drunk. For a few precious hours, all fighting was ceased and fighting soldiers were drawn together by the birth of a baby.

FOOD FROM THE WORD OF GOD
Matthew 13:44-14:12; Psalm 96:10-13; 145:10-13; Isaiah 9:6; Malachi 4:1-2.

The good news is that another Son was born. People abandoned everything they were doing and first enjoyed the peace of the birth. There was choral singing in the skies. The shepherds were the audience. Wise Men from the east came to look for the Baby and called him the Prince of Peace. This Child started a movement that will never end. And we know that all believers will one day come to his banquet and that they will call it the wedding banquet of the Lamb. Yes, a great day is coming on which the world will change. The lion and the lamb will lie down together. People will forget about war. This is the precious pearl for which we sacrifice everything and for which we work and pray. This is the kingdom of God.

I am prepared to sacrifice everything in this world in order to attain your kingdom, O God.

If only we could look at life the way that God sees it, we would realise that nothing in this world is secular, but that everything contributes to the edification of the kingdom of God. – MICHEL QUOIST

ALWAYS BE PREPARED

So you must always be ready, because the Son of Man will come at an hour when you do not expect him (Mt 24:44).

Our Master repeatedly said that he would come again. When he went up to heaven, two angels also told his disciples on the Mount of Olives that he would come again, *Men of Galilee ... why do you stand here looking into the sky? This same Jesus, who has been taken from you into heaven, will come back in the same way you have seen him go into heaven* (Acts 1:11).

FOOD FROM THE WORD OF GOD
Matthew 24:36-25:13; Zephaniah 2:1-3; Malachi 3:1-5, 14-18.

We look forward to his coming again, because we know that our faith will then be rewarded and made complete.

This climactic event is still in the future. It will be the final fulfilment of world history. It will come suddenly and be final. It will take the unbelieving world by surprise. People will be overcome with shock and try to flee God's holy presence. At Christ's second coming, the resurrection of the believers will occur, and they will be gathered together to spend eternity with God.

We can speculate at length about the details of Christ's second coming. But the most important facts are that he is coming again and that there is still time to accept him as our Saviour. The Bible says that all people will appear before God on that day, either as their Saviour or as their Judge. *When the Son of Man comes in his glory, and all the angels with him, he will sit on the throne in heavenly glory* (Mt 25:31). Wherever you might be or whatever you might be doing, will you be ready to meet him?

Jesus, my Lord, I delight in the knowledge that you are coming again. Keep me faithful and believing until you come again in your glory.

With what would you like to be busy when Jesus comes again?
BILLY GRAHAM

CHRIST TRULY ROSE FROM THE DEAD

The angel said to the women, "Do not be afraid, for I know that you are looking for Jesus, who was crucified. He is not here; he has risen, just as he said" (Mt 28:5-6a).

According to the Scriptures, the risen Saviour appeared eleven times to individuals and groups of people before he was taken up into heaven. He appeared to:

- Mary Magdalene (Mk 16:9-11; Jn 20:10-18);
- the other women at the grave (Mt 28:8-10);
- Peter, alone in Jerusalem (Lk 24:34; 1 Cor 15:5);
- the disciples of Emmaus (Lk 24:13-32);
- ten disciples behind closed doors (Mk 16:4; Lk 24:36-43; Jn 20:19-25);
- all the disciples, including Thomas, but not Judas (Jn 20:26-31; 1 Cor 15:5);
- seven disciples while they were fishing (Jn 21:1-14);
- eleven disciples on the Mount of Olives (Mt 28:16-20);
- a group of five hundred people (1 Cor 15:6);
- James, the brother of Jesus (1 Cor 15:7) and to
- his disciples when he was taken up into heaven (Lk 24:44-49; Acts 1:3-8).

FOOD FROM THE WORD OF GOD
Matthew 28:1-20; Job 19:25-27; Psalm 47:1-9; Isaiah 53:10-13.

Yes, our Lord has risen. He has truly risen. And with these appearances to different people he wanted to give to us, too, special blessings. Pray that the Holy Spirit will give you ears to hear, eyes to see, a mouth to witness, and a heart that understands what Jesus wants to tell you through his appearances.

Risen and glorified Saviour, you did it for me, too. May my life be such that people will believe in your omnipotence.

Through his resurrection, Jesus has turned our sunsets into daybreaks.
CLEMENT OF ALEXANDRIA

SERVE ONE ANOTHER WITH GOD'S COMMANDS

So do not be ashamed to testify about our Lord (2 Tim 1:8).

Ministering God's commands to one another is not only a New Testament phenomenon. From today's *Food from the Word of God* we can deduce how Moses mapped out the principles of discipleship to the people of the Old Testament. The same principles still apply today.

Ministering discipleship may not be as exciting as the stage or the vibe of a big get-together, but we can scarcely emphasise its importance enough. The witnessing of a disciple of God, someone with vision and discipline who has totally surrendered himself or herself to God and Christ, who is prepared to pay any price so that the will of God will be executed in his or her life, is of inestimable value to the message of the kingdom of God that has to be brought to this world.

FOOD FROM THE WORD OF GOD
2 Timothy 1:1-2:13; Deuteronomy 4:9-10; 11:18-21; 31:9-13; Ezra 7:6, 10.

We received the important command in Matthew 28:19: *Therefore go and make disciples of all nations.* If you are not yet a maker of disciples, you must do what Timothy did with Paul, or Peter with James, or John with Jesus: make yourself available to a maker of disciples who can aid and educate you to become a maker of disciples yourself. Link yourself inseparably to such a teacher. Learn the art of being involved and available for service in the kingdom of God from him or her. Strive to witness with your whole life about your Lord – not just for your own sake and the sake of others whose lives are touched, but to the glory of Jesus Christ.

Lord Jesus, my perfect example, I still have so much to learn about how to make disciples for you. Grant me the guidance of your Holy Spirit in abundance.

Example is not the main way of influencing others spiritually – it is the only way.
ALBERT SCHWEITZER

GOD'S RELIABLE WITNESSES

In everything set them an example by doing what is good. In your teaching show integrity, seriousness and soundness of speech that cannot be condemned, so that those who oppose you may be ashamed because they have nothing bad to say about us (Tit 2:7).

For the sake of the credibility of our cause, it is vital that everyone who teaches others about the ways of the Lord should be blameless and upright. Luke says of Timothy, *The brothers at Lystra and Iconium spoke well of him* (Acts 16:2). Timothy had a good reputation as a Christian. He was without blame in the eyes of the Christian community in which he moved. There was nothing in his life or character that could harm the cause of Jesus.

FOOD FROM THE WORD OF GOD
Titus 1:1-2:8; Leviticus 21:6, 8; 22:9; Isaiah 50:4-7; Malachi 2:5-9.

This is why Paul invited Timothy to become his missionary companion. A deep and lasting relationship between them as well as a blessed ministry resulted from this. Titus was the same kind of person as Timothy. He was mature, his motives were pure and he showed compassion towards people (2 Cor 8:16). He demonstrated a positive attitude towards the ministry: *For Titus not only welcomed our appeal, but he is coming to you with much enthusiasm and on his own initiative* (2 Cor 8:17). There is no better way to develop a good Christian reputation amongst Christians as well as non-Christians than by following the excellent examples of Titus and Timothy.

Be irreproachable and reliable. We all ought to set these standards for ourselves, for all of us are employed in the service of God and his kingdom. Would you be prepared to make adjustments to your character if it were necessary, in order to be a reliable witness for God?

I want to be a reliable and blameless employee in your service, Master. Help me in moments of weakness through you Holy Spirit.

People seldom improve if there is no other example for them to follow than themselves.
OLIVER GOLDSMITH

OUR LIVES - TESTIMONIES TO GOD

... Jesus Christ, who gave himself for us to redeem us from all wickedness and to purify for himself a people that are his very own, eager to do what is good (Tit 2:13-14).

Whether you are a minister or a publisher, a ditcher or a pilot, a fisherman or a fruit grower, a mechanic or a carpenter, an office worker or a member of parliament, there are unique opportunities in your work because you are a reborn child of the Creator of the universe.

Whatever you do, do it well, as though you were doing it for the Lord. *If anyone serves, he should do it with the strength God provides, so that in all things God may be praised through Jesus Christ* (1 Pet 4:11b). Just as a Knysna lily that unfolds its beauty high up in the mountains, perhaps without anyone ever seeing it, does not flower in vain because God will see it – the same holds true of humans. You may live alone, walk alone and feel that no one notices you, no one realises that you bear your pain and loneliness patiently. But God knows about it. He is aware of the whispering of your heart that rises up to him, "I truly love you, O God. Accept my gratefulness while I walk lonely and alone today."

FOOD FROM THE WORD OF GOD
Titus 2:9-3:15; Daniel 6:11-16, 19-23, 25-29.

You can work for the glory of God anywhere in life. This is what makes God's love so just. No one gets a bigger opportunity than the next person. And in his kingdom, no one is without work. What pitiful people we would have been without God and the death of Jesus Christ, or without the abundant comfort of the Holy Spirit!

God the Creator, you sanctified work when you yourself created. Make me a willing and thankful worker for you in this world.

God requires your best work, not the leftovers of your fatigue. In this regard, God prefers quality to quantity. – GEORGE MCDONALD

GOD'S GREAT SALVATION

How shall we escape if we ignore such a great salvation? (Heb 2:3).

Hannah sang a song of praise to the Lord because she had found redemption (1 Sam 2:1-10). Mary's song of praise sounded at Jesus' birth when salvation came for us (Lk 1:46-55). The Wise Men from the east were overjoyed when they saw the star that guided them to Jesus' manger (Mt 2:10). The Ethiopian delighted in the discovery of salvation through Philip's ministry of the Word of God (Acts 8:39). Christians rejoice in hope and even in suffering, because they know that they have found peace in him (Rom 5:1-11).

FOOD FROM THE WORD OF GOD
Hebrews 1:1-24; Exodus 15:1-3, 6-7; Psalm 86:11-13; Isaiah 45:15-17; Habakkuk 3:2-19.

Yes, salvation and joy belong together and are inseparable. The coming of our Saviour can never be an unemotional matter. It talks directly to our hearts and makes us burst into songs of joy. We experience the same feelings as the woman who finds her lost coin, as the shepherd who finds his lost sheep, and as the longing father who sees his lost son approaching (Lk 15).

The experience of salvation is the same as that of people drilling for oil, who see the fountain of black gold shooting up into the air. It is like the joy of the soldier who returns from the trenches to his home and sees a welcoming light in the window. It is like the joy of a prisoner who walks free out of his cell and is received warm-heartedly by his friends. In our prayers, may we remember all the joy that is flowing from the mercy of God.

My soul glorifies the Lord and my spirit rejoices in God my Saviour (Lk 1:46-47).

Salvation is experiencing that God is good, and that I am a part of that goodness.
ARTHUR G CLUTTON-BROCK

JESUS IS OUR HIGH PRIEST

Therefore, since we have a great high priest who has gone through the heavens, Jesus the Son of God, let us hold firmly to the faith we profess (Heb 4:14).

There was a time when a NO ENTRY sign was put up on the gate to paradise. In the temple of the Old Testament ordinary people had no access to the presence of God. Even the high priest's access to the Holy of Holies was limited to once a year. A thick curtain separated the Holy of Holies from the rest of the temple.

FOOD FROM THE WORD OF GOD
Hebrews 4:14-6:12; Genesis 14:18-20; Exodus 28:1-3; 29:44-46; Leviticus 21:10-15.

But as soon as Jesus died on the cross, when the Righteous One died on behalf of unrighteous people, this curtain of the temple was torn in two. From that moment onwards, everyone could enter into the holy presence of God. Jesus opened the gates that were once closed to us. We may now freely step on holy ground. We have access to the mercy of God, yes, even to God himself. We are his children and he is our Father who listens to us.

Saved and justified people no longer need to say, *Go away from me, Lord; I am a sinful man!* (Lk 5:8). We may now approach our omnipotent God with all our questions. He is never too far away to hear our desperate calls. We stand before him, clothed in the righteousness of Jesus, the living Saviour. We stand before him in amazement, admiration and adoration. Yes, we may come and stand before God and say to one another, *Let us then approach the throne of grace with confidence* (Heb 4:16). And all of this only because Jesus Christ is our perfect high priest.

Jesus, perfect high priest, I praise and thank you because I may freely come to the throne of mercy through you.

If Jesus Christ is not truly God, how then can he help us?
If he is not truly human, how then can he help us? – DIETRICH BONHOEFFER

October 13

GOD DISCIPLINES HIS CHILDREN WHOM HE LOVES

Because the Lord disciplines those whom he loves, and he punishes everyone he accepts as his son (Heb 12:6).

We do not really want to be broken in the storms of life. We want to be protected from all the stresses of our day and age. We would rather be tough and self-assured than bow before God in repentance and be led to confession by the Holy Spirit. We prefer to avoid the mills of God. We ask God to grant us immunity from the oncoming tide that shakes us back and forth, and scours off our rough edges, so that we may be formed in the image of God. We beg to be saved from the discipline of problems and trials, of responsibilities, of long-lasting suffering.

FOOD FROM THE WORD OF GOD
Hebrews 11:23-12:12; Job 5:17-21; Psalm 119:65-72; Proverbs 3:11-12; Lamentations 3:31-33, 39-40.

We like using shortcuts and quick-fix solutions, believing that we can still be a rough block of rock today and tomorrow already a sculptured work of art. But God's ways are not like ours. His patience perseveres and he works accurately. His years know no end. One day is to him like a thousand years, and a thousand years like one day.

Sculpting a rock, polishing a precious stone or creating a jewel takes many long hours. Can we then expect that the honing of our hearts, polishing of our spirits, and shaping of our characters so that we may become equal to our Master will be less painful and quicker? Let us not forget that it is precisely the discipline of God that helps us to eradicate sin from our lives and strengthen our faith.

Loving God and Father, may I not only experience the pain, but also especially the love that creates jewels for your kingdom.

He who knows how to suffer, will enjoy much peace. Someone like this conquers himself and rules the world, a friend of Christ and an inheritor of heaven. – THOMAS á KEMPIS

October 14

STAND FIRM IN YOUR FAITH

First of all, you must understand that in the last days scoffers will come, scoffing and following their own evil desires (2 Pet 3:3).

Christians often say, "They laughed at me and made fun of me because I did not want to take part in what they were busy with." Or, "I was not promoted because I was not prepared to take my clients to a questionable nightclub." And, "I lost my so-called friends because I did not want to gossip along with them at their get-together." Peter offers us a perspective that will help us when people ridicule and persecute us: stand firm in the faith and let God execute his will. Wait faithfully and patiently on God – he has his own time.

FOOD FROM THE WORD OF GOD
2 Peter 3:1-18; Psalm 22:3-9; Isaiah 5:18-19; Jeremiah 17:14-18.

Even though not being accepted hurts, most of us have never really felt the pain of persecution. In certain parts of the world Christians are still physically persecuted because of their faith. They lose their homes, are thrown into jail and even killed. We, however, can also be persecuted, even if it is in a different way. Then we have to know how Jesus expects us to react: *Rejoice and be glad, because great is your reward in heaven, for in the same way they persecuted the prophets who were before you* (Mt 5:12; see also Lk 6:23). Do not resist; do not object; do not complain. Be glad.

If you are persecuted because of your faith, it means that you are truly dedicated to Christ and that others can see your dedication. You are making a difference in the world around you. You make people feel guilty so they resort to ridicule and persecution. Jesus understands this – just look at what they did to him!

*Merciful God, help me to stand firm in my faith in Jesus Christ – regardless of what the world does to me.
Help me to accept the challenges of non-believers.*

When you notice persecution, there is a strong possibility that truth is on the side of the persecuted.
HUGH LATIMER

AVOID THE PLEASURES OF THE WORLD

The world and its desires pass away, but the man who does the will of God lives for ever (1 Jn 2:17).

Today, when I look back on my life, it strikes me how things that were once important and seductive, now seem futile and even absurd. The Ecclesiastic tells of how he discovered the futility of earthly pleasure and delight. In order to do this, one needs a pure setting of priorities. Paul prays for the Philippians that their *love may abound more and more in knowledge and depth of insight, so that* they *may be able to discern what is best and may be pure and blameless until the day of Christ* (Phil 1:9-10). We must develop the spiritual ability to put first things first.

FOOD FROM THE WORD OF GOD
1 John 2:12-3:10; Psalm 65:2-4; Proverbs 28:13; Ecclesiastes 2:1; 8-11; 12:13-14; Ezekiel 18:26-28, 32.

Success in all its different guises; being well-known and highly praised; accruing money and possessions; sexual enjoyment; being cosmopolitan; traversing the universe as Satan did, examining everything and enjoying what the world has to offer – these and many other tempting things take our attention from the things that really matter: the affairs of God, for example Bible study, prayer, contemplation, fellowship, church attendance, spiritual growth and becoming mature in the faith.

When one looks back on the road that you have come, all the practices aimed at egocentric pleasure seem only to be pure fantasy. Pascal calls it "licking the world". They are all merely things that are intended to destroy the meaning of our lives on earth. For the purpose of our existence is to seek God, to find him. Once we have found him, to love him, and to enter again into a harmonious relationship with him.

Lord, my God and Father, help me to focus on the important things in life and to put all other things aside – regardless of how tempting they might appear.

Actually there is only one priority that is worth pursuing: knowledge of God.
ROBERT H BENSON

October 16

GOD LISTENS TO OUR PRAYERS

This is the confidence we have in approaching God: that if we ask anything according to his will, he hears us (1 Jn 5:14).

When you pray, do you also sometimes feel that you are disturbing God? Do you then want to hide somewhere out of shame, never to try to talk with your Father again? Do you feel like walking away from his holy presence, mumbling, "Eternal God, I am sorry for having wasted your time"? Do you sometimes feel as though there are other things and people that are more important to God than you are? Do you think that God wants you to stop talking? Does it feel as if God is looking at the world without noticing you; that he is hearing but not listening? Do you then rather leave his presence and stop praying?

FOOD FROM THE WORD OF GOD
1 John 4:13-5:21; Psalm 66:16-20; Jeremiah 42:1-11.

Do not do it! God's love calls out to you, "Do not be so quick to go away. Stay in my presence longer. Tell me how you are doing. Tell me how you really feel and why that is the way you feel. I want to know, because you are important to me and I care about you. Tell me what I can do for you. Tell me about your pain and joy, your ambitions and yearnings, about your loneliness and sorrow, of your desire for spiritual growth, faith and mercy. What can I do for you?"

Then pour your heart out to him in the knowledge that he listens to your stammering words and that he understands – even that which you have neglected to say. Then your heart will be glad that you have come to him in prayer.

O hearer of prayers, to you all flesh must come. You have been much tested during times of trouble and have always proven to be faithful.

Prayer is a conversation with God.
CLEMENT OF ALEXANDRIA

ENCOURAGE ONE ANOTHER IN FAITH

It gave me great joy to have some brothers come and tell about your faithfulness to the truth and how you continue to walk in the truth (3 Jn v 3).

In the days when I played rugby for Paarl, Boy Louw, the legendary Springbok, was our trainer. Ballie Wahl, the Springbok scrumhalf, played for the first team. All of a sudden, halfway through the season, Wahl decided to retire – and I became the first team's scrumhalf. Paarl was at the top of the log in the Western Province, and I was so nervous during every game that I could do nothing right. But old man Boy said not a single negative word, did not once lose his temper with me, nor did he once laugh at me. All he ever said was, "Just try again." And along with men like Chum Ochse, Tinus Briers, and Hugo van Zyl I appeared in the group photograph when the team from Paarl won the Great Challenge Cup against Northerns by 9-3. That year God showed me the significance of encouragement.

FOOD FROM THE WORD OF GOD
2 John verses 1-3; John verse 15; Deuteronomy 31:6-8; 1 Kings 2:1-4; Jeremiah 38:7-10; 39:15-18.

In life we are harassed by demands, bruised by anxiety and failure, broken by disillusionment, spoiled by sin. Perhaps we pretend that everything is under control, as in the match, but we are battling just to keep from drowning. We make mistakes and fall down. What we need then is encouragement – somebody who believes in us, who encourages us to get up and carry on, somebody who can give us a sense of purpose and self-confidence despite everything that is working against us. As Christians, it is our duty towards one another to encourage each other in the Name of all names – Jesus Christ.

Lord Jesus, point out someone to me today whom I can encourage, so that it really makes a difference in his or her life.

Encouragement is the oxygen of the human soul.
GEORGE M ADAMS

October 18

GOD WILL PUNISH HIS OPPONENTS

See, the Lord is coming with thousands upon thousands of his holy ones to judge everyone, and to convict all the ungodly of all their ungodly acts they have done in the ungodly way, and of all the harsh words ungodly sinners have spoken against him (Jude v 14b-15).

There will be an ocean of fire and sulphur and lost sinners will be thrown into the flames. They will writhe in pain, panic-stricken. There the fire will not be extinguished. Not even a drop of water on the tip of someone's finger to be placed on their tongues, even though they will be calling out in agony (Lk 16:19-31).

FOOD FROM THE WORD OF GOD
Jude verses 1-13; Psalm 50:16-23; Isaiah 13:6-11.

Do you think God said all of these things merely so that he could see how scared we are? No, it saddens his fatherly heart that he had to create a place like this and has to consign sinners to it, people who did not want to accept his merciful salvation. *For I take no pleasure in the death of anyone, declares the Sovereign Lord. Repent and live!* (Ezek 18:32). But, God must maintain his honour and throne and save his believing subjects. God has to punish those who sin against him otherwise he would not be a righteous God. His love gives us so many opportunities to repent and live. But his righteousness determines that his mercy will pass, and that the reward for sin is death. This is why we have to take hold of his salvation while we still have the opportunity.

God wants us to flee from sin, to realise what the punishment for sin is – and to find our salvation in Jesus Christ.

To him who is able to keep you from falling and to present you before his glorious presence without fault and with great joy – to the only God our Saviour be glory, majesty, power and authority, through Jesus Christ, before all ages, now and for evermore! Amen (Jude v 24-25).

The safest road to hell is the gradual one – the gentle slope, soft underfoot, without sudden turnings, without milestones, without signposts. – CS LEWIS

WHO IS KING OF YOUR HEART?

I have come in my Father's name, and you do not accept me; but if someone else comes in his own name, you will accept him (Jn 5:43).

Whatever God does always makes sense. It makes sense that Jesus would be a sacrifice, because a sacrifice was needed to bring man back to God. It makes sense that God used the law to instruct Israel in their need for mercy. It makes sense that Jesus Christ is our high priest. Whatever God does always makes sense. It can be studied, explained and documented in books.

FOOD FROM THE WORD OF GOD
John 5:30-6:15; Genesis 3:14; 49:8-12; Deuteronomy 18:15-22.

However, why God has done it, is entirely incomprehensible. If one looks beyond the method and studies the motive, the building blocks which were carefully stacked, come tumbling down. God's love is not logical. It cannot be neatly delineated in a thesis or explained in a sermon. Even after generations of people had treated him with contempt, he loved them. After his chosen people had nailed him naked to a cross, he still died for them. Even to this day, while millions choose to betray him for the sake of wealth and fame, he waits for them and loves them.

Yes, the love of God is incomprehensible. A bloodstained Majesty; a God with tears in his eyes; a Creator with a compassionate heart. God has become the object of the world's ridicule in order to save his children. It is unimaginable that the holy God descended in his Son to bring salvation to ungrateful people. Yet, this is indeed what he has done. Why, then, are we so stubborn and unwilling to accept it?

Jesus, living Saviour, my heart chooses you as its eternal King.

Jesus became what we are in order to make us what he is.
St ATHANASIUS

HOPE IN CHRIST'S SECOND COMING

For you know very well that the day of the Lord will come like a thief in the night (2 Thess 5:2).

What would you say of someone who has made 100 promises to you and has already fulfilled 99 of them? That he or she is honest enough to also keep that last promise to you, is it not? Jesus has already fulfilled every promise he made, bar one: that he will come again. Will he also keep this promise? Of course, he will!

Both the Old and the New Testament make mention of his second coming. Ezekiel tells of Jerusalem that will be restored, a temple that will be rebuilt, a country that will be reclaimed and of prosperity at the second coming of the Messiah. Zephaniah gives to us a new song that he will teach Israel, and he describes the overthrow of the false Christ.

FOOD FROM THE WORD OF GOD
1 Thessalonians 4:13-5:28; Job 19:25-27; Psalm 98:1-9; Isaiah 26:19; Daniel 12:1-2.

In the New Testament, Matthew compares Christ to the bridegroom who is coming to fetch his bride. Mark sees him as a master of a house who embarks on a long journey and entrusts certain tasks to the care of workers while he is away. To Luke, Christ is the nobleman who travels to a distant land to do business, leaving his possessions in the care of his workers so that they may gain something from them until his return. *In my Father's house are many rooms ... I am going there to prepare a place for you. And if I go and prepare a place for you, I will come back and take you to be with me that you may be where I am* (Jn 14:2-3). And Revelation tells of the glorious return of Christ. Along with John we can pray, *Amen. Come, Lord Jesus* (Rev 22:20b).

Lord Jesus, may I be ready and welcome you with a burning lamp when you come again.

The second coming means that all will be renewed in the kingdom of God.
JOHN AT ROBINSON

CHRIST - THE LIGHT OF THE WORLD

In him was life, and that life was the light of men. The light shines in the darkness, but the darkness has not understood it (Jn 1:4-5).

As a result of God's great mercy and of Jesus who was incarnated, the cosmic scene changed. God bowed down from heaven to enter anew into a relationship with us. Everything was changed through this sanctified drama of the incarnation of God, of his solution for fallen men.

FOOD FROM THE WORD OF GOD
John 1:1-18; Psalm 118:22-29; Isaiah 9:1; 49:5-6.

Yes, a road is laid out to God for us by the birth, ministry, death and resurrection of Jesus Christ, the road that is walked by generation upon generation of believers. They draw moral, spiritual and intellectual creativity from it. Out of it flows everything that is grand and immortal in our art, literature, music, as well as many other things. Whatever happens in this world, and whatever those who govern this world do, the truth concerning Jesus Christ and his incarnation remains undamaged and indestructible.

Jesus came to show us what *life* really is (Jn 10:10), and what our true destiny is. Instead of shadows, we have the glory of God's creation all around us. Instead of darkness, we have his light. Instead of despair, hope; instead of temporary and passing things, we have eternity. By associating with the living Christ, by delving into his teachings, by living through his life and death with him and being resurrected with him, by sharing in his love and creativity, by living *in* and *through* him, we become new people in a new world. And we walk in his light.

Thank you, Lord Jesus, for having led me out of darkness into your wonderful light, and for the difference it makes in my life.

I saw that there was an ocean of darkness and death, but also an immeasurable ocean of light and love overrunning the first, and therein I saw the unfathomable love of God. – GEORGE FOX

October 22

CHRIST'S LOVE FOR GOD'S HOUSE

His disciples remembered that it is written, "Zeal for your house will consume me" (Jn 2:17).

With this incident in the temple Jesus affirms his authority as the Messiah, the Son of God. Not only did he drive all the animals out of the temple area with a whip, but also the moneychangers. In his passionate love for the house of God, Jesus was filled with disappointment. He cleared the temple by exclaiming, *How dare you turn my Father's house into a market!* (Jn 2:16b). By calling the temple "my Father's house", Jesus asserts his unique relationship with his Father.

FOOD FROM THE WORD OF GOD
John 2:1-25; Psalm 26:1-12; 69:6-10; 84:2-8; 122:1.

When Jesus drove the moneychangers from the temple, they experienced something of God's coming wrath. In the last days people will call to the mountains and the rocks, *Fall on us and hide us from the face of him who sits on the throne and from the wrath of the Lamb! For the great day of their wrath has come, and who can stand?* (Rev 6:16-17).

We sometimes forget that God is a righteous God and that every one of us will some day stand in his presence and will have to account to him. But just as Christ cleared the temple, he also wants to clear our lives of sin. He is prepared to forgive us. How wonderful it is to know: the blood of Jesus Christ, the Son of God, purifies us of all sin (1 Jn 1:7). So what is the alternative? It is too terrible to contemplate!

Holy Spirit of God, purify the temple of my heart through the blood of the Lamb so that I may be truly pure.

The church of Christ is not an institution. It is a new life with Christ, guided by the Holy Spirit.
SERGIUS BULGAKOV

October 23

THE POWER OF JESUS' RESURRECTION

The angel said to the women, "Do not be afraid, for I know that you are looking for Jesus, who was crucified. He is not here; he has risen, just as he said" (Mt 28:5-6a).

The power of Jesus' resurrection is the power of our rebirth. Resurrection implies rebirth. Rebirth is not only our passport to heaven, but is also the power that changes us here and now. It is a gift, not merely a yearning. Paul says that he wants to know Christ in the power of his resurrection (Phil 3:10). To know Christ is to know the power that raised him from the dead.

FOOD FROM THE WORD OF GOD
Matthew 27:45-28:10; Psalm 16:8-11; 86:16-22; Isaiah 25:6-9.

All life is intended to be an Eastertide, a time of resurrection, filled with renewal. Christ wants to change our lives and make us new so that we may be as he is. And he himself is the best example there is: perfect in every sense, but more still, he comes to live within us and gives us his Spirit so that we can follow his example. When we do so, we become more and more like him. We do as he does. We love as he loves.

The power of the resurrection is the power that replaces all our disillusionment, discouragement and disappointment in life and in people with the power to change us, and to give us a fresh start. When Jesus rose from the dead he not only defeated death and Satan, but also all the little irritations which make life unbearable for us. This is why the death and resurrection of our Saviour has such an immense impact on our lives here and now.

Resurrected Saviour, thank you that your resurrection made my rebirth possible and that I could become a new person with a new life.

Christian religion is a religion of miracles and the miracle of Christ's resurrection is the epicentre and foundation of the Christian faith. – ALAN RICHARDSON

October 24

CHRIST SETS US FREE FROM SIN

For just as through the disobedience of the one man the many were made sinners, so also through the obedience of the one man the many will be made righteous (Rom 5:19).

When the angel announced the birth of Christ, he said to Joseph, *She will give birth to a son, and you are to give him the name Jesus, because he will save his people from their sins* (Mt 1:21).

Have you yet made the salvation of Jesus from sin your own? See him hanging on the cross. See him conquering sin, and the price he has to pay. He sacrifices himself so that your sins may be taken away. But Christ is not only your Saviour. Someone can save you from drowning so that you do not die an untimely death, but the one who saves you from the water cannot do more than that for you. Christ, however, is much more than just your Saviour. When the children of Israel put blood on the top and on both sides of their doorframes, that blood was their salvation. But they would still have heard the blows of the slave driver's whip had they not been released from the yoke of slavery under the Egyptians, if God had not set them free from the hand of the pharaoh.

FOOD FROM THE WORD OF GOD
Romans 5:12-6:14; Isaiah 1:18-20; Jeremiah 3:19-23; 18:7-12.

Likewise, Christ did not come to set us free just to let us remain in the prison of sin. No, he came to save us, as well as to give us victory over our quick tempers, our distorted priorities and our wicked desires. Are you a Christian who is still a slave to your secret sins? Take them to Christ. He alone gives true salvation.

Thank you, Lord Jesus, for having saved me from sin, and for having made the highest sacrifice for me, too. It fills my heart with indescribable thankfulness.

Salvation of a single soul is more important than the production and preservation of all the epic deeds and tragedies in the whole world. – CS LEWIS

JESUS SOUGHT THE WILL OF GOD

Father, if you are willing, take this cup from me; yet not my will, but yours be done (Lk 22:42).

Before we begin to pray, we must exclude our own desires from our hearts, because many of our problems actually start with our own will. And we can triumph over many problems if we are prepared to accept the will of God, whatever it might be. When we seek his will honestly and genuinely, we will find it. And in this we have the perfect example. Jesus struggled to know the will of God and it was within none other than this struggle that his victory lay. What are you doing in order to find the will of God in your life?

FOOD FROM THE WORD OF GOD
Luke 22:31-53; Psalm 86:1-13; 143:6-10.

When you are in the right state of mind to learn the will of God, do not leave the outcome to feelings or emotions. If you do this, you expose yourself to self-deception. Seek the will of God in his Word. The Spirit and the Word work together. When the Holy Spirit guides you towards the will of God, he will do it through and in accordance with the Scriptures.

Also take into consideration all the circumstances that were brought about by divine providence. It often illuminates the will of God for you in a specific situation. Struggle with God, and beg of him to reveal his will to you. Study the Scriptures, meditate on them and seek the guidance of the Holy Spirit. In this way, you will discover what the will of God is for you. And when you experience calm in your soul, you will know that God has spoken to you. Then you can act accordingly.

Lord my God, may my sincere prayer always be, "Your will be done!"

The will of God is not an itinerary, but an attitude.
ANDREW DHUSE

October 26

NEVER UNDERESTIMATE THE POWER OF SEED

Why do you look for the living among the dead? He is not here; he has risen! (Lk 24:5-6).

Never underestimate the power of seed. God did not. When his kingdom was in ruins and his people had forgotten his name, God planted his seed. When the soil of people's hearts had become hard as rock, God planted his seed. When religion had become mere ritual and the temple nothing more than a marketplace, God planted his seed. Behold the miraculous deed: see how God planted his seed in the womb of a Jewish girl. *A shoot will come up from the stump of Jesse; from his roots a Branch will bear fruit* (Is 11:1).

FOOD FROM THE WORD OF GOD
Luke 23:44-24:12; Isaiah 41:10-14; 42:1-9.

The seed of God took a lifetime to press back the stones and clods that tried to keep it underground, the stones of rigidity on arched backs, of oppression that breaks bodies and hearts, of prejudice that excludes the needy.

But the final stone was the great test of the seed – the stone at the grave and death that was rolled in front of the grave by unbelievers and sealed by Satan. For one fleeting moment, it seemed as if the Seed would remain in the earth, as if this stone was too big to be rolled away. But there, in the bowels of the earth, the Seed of God started to stir and sprout. The earth trembled and the stone moved away. And the indescribably beautiful Easter Flower bloomed. Never underestimate the power of the Seed in the hands of God.

God Almighty, with my human mind I cannot fathom this wonder, but by faith I accept it with grateful rejoicing.

Our Lord not only wrote the promise of resurrection in books, but on every leaf in spring.
MARTIN LUTHER

JESUS' SYMPATHY FOR LOST PEOPLE

When he saw the crowds, he had compassion on them, because they were harassed and helpless, like sheep without a shepherd (Mt 9:36).

Seeking and saving sinners is part of God's nature. Even shortly after man's creation, God was the one who looked for him in paradise after he had fallen: *But the Lord God called to the man, "Where are you?"* (Gen 3:9). All through the Old Testament, God is portrayed as man's Saviour: *They forgot the God who saved them, who had done great things in* Egypt (Ps 106:21; see also Is 43:11; Hos 13:4).

FOOD FROM THE WORD OF GOD
Matthew 9:18-10:10; Psalm 28:6-9; 103:1-5; Isaiah 40:9-11; Ezekiel 34:11-16.

This is why it is fitting that when Jesus came to the world as the human incarnation of God, he was first known as the Saviour. God himself chose Christ's Name to be the name of a saviour. An angel appeared to Joseph in a dream, and commanded him as follows, *She will give birth to a son, and you are to give him the name Jesus, because he will save his people from their sins* (Mt 1:21). The essence of the salvation is that Jesus came to this world to seek and save sinners. And it is precisely this truth that characterises the gospel as the good news or good tidings.

But the good news only applies to those who see themselves as sinners, who recognise and repent of their sins with regret. When we do this, he becomes our friend (Mt 11:19). Not everybody, however, wants to repent and confess his or her sins. Those who will remain outside of the mercy of God as a result of this, will one day get to know the Saviour as the Judge.

Thank you, Lord my God, for the many ways in which you show your love, compassion and mercy to me, and that you are my bestfriend.

For them who still reside in this world, it is never too late to repent. Entry into God's mercy is open and easy for those who seek and find the truth. – St CYPRIAN

JESUS OFFERS NOURISHMENT FOR THE SOUL

Then they understood that he was not telling them to guard against the yeast used in bread, but against the teaching of the Pharisees and Sadducees (Mt 16:12).

The food that Jesus offers us is the most satisfying because it is the bread and water of life. We get this food by repenting of our sins and accepting Jesus as our Saviour. Yes, he alone offers the food that gives us true life.

FOOD FROM THE WORD OF GOD
Matthew 15:32-16:20; Numbers 11:21-23, 31-33; Psalm 63:2-9; Isaiah 55:1-2.

When our Master was here on earth, crowds of people eagerly sought his help. Many sick people were brought to him so that he could touch and heal them. He gave crumbs to the Canaanite woman. He handed out bread to the Jews. Yes, they were given every opportunity to believe in Christ and accept him as their Messiah. And they did glorify the God of Israel, but this upsurge of gratitude was short-lived: *He came to that which was his own, but his own did not receive him* (Jn 1:11). They wanted to see his miracles, but they refused to conform to his requirements.

Be careful that you do not just seek God's help, forgetting to love him for his own sake. He performs miracles to this day. He is still the great healer and the source of our spiritual energy. He still has compassion for sinners and desires to set free every soul that is burdened by sin. He does not want us to get tired along the way and despair. The wilderness can place no limits on his saving mercy and the food that he provides for souls. Take it from his hands.

You broke the bread, Lord, once at the lake.
Now break the living bread for me, too!

People should pursue things that lie in the present and leave the future to the providence of God.
FRANCIS BACON

October 29

JESUS' SUFFERING IS FOLLOWED BY HIS JUDGEMENT

I tell you the truth, some who are standing here will not taste death before they see the Son of Man coming in his kingdom (Mt 16:28).

Each one of us is judged every day by the face that stares back at us from the mirror. We are judged by the people who love us, by the faces of our children, and yes, also by our dreams. We are judged in terms of the paths we do not take, but also in terms of those we have taken.

FOOD FROM THE WORD OF GOD
Matthew 16:21-17:13; Psalm 62:12; Isaiah 53:6-10; Daniel 12:1-3.

The New Testament confirms that God will draw the curtain on this earthly scene at an indeterminate point in the future. At that point, history will end and the time will come when all our days and all our judgements of ourselves and of others will themselves be judged. The Judge will be Jesus Christ. He who loves us so much and who pleads with the Father on our behalf, he who is our Advocate, will be our Judge on that day.

Romantic love is blind to everything except that which is lovely and adorable to it. The love of Christ, however, sees us with penetrating clarity and for all we are. Christ's love wants to bring about our salvation and joy so badly, that it is mercilessly opposed to everything in us that diminishes that salvation and joy. The worst judgement that love can pass is that we have held in contempt the suffering that Love endured on our behalf. This is our absolution: the mercy and righteousness of the Judge is one and the same thing. This is why Jesus suffered and died for us.

I praise you, righteous God, that he, who will one day be my Judge, is also my Saviour.

If we truly know Christ as our Saviour, our hearts are broken and cannot become hardened. Then we cannot deny others forgiveness. – MARTYN LLOYD-JONES

WAIT WITH DEDICATION FOR THE SECOND COMING

You also must be ready, because the Son of Man will come at an hour when you do not expect him (Lk 12:40).

The last message the risen Saviour gave to his followers was that he would come again (Acts 1:11). Liken this to the warning that Paul gave to the Christians at Thessalonica (1 Thess 5:1-11), and we have a good measure for life: live in expectation and patiently, and you will be doing the will of the Lord until he comes again.

FOOD FROM THE WORD OF GOD
Luke 12:35-56; Psalm 24:1-6; Isaiah 26:7-12.

Many blessings wait for the believer when the Lord comes again. The most important of these is that believers can confidently expect to be rewarded for their loyalty. Obedient Christians have the firm belief that they will be rewarded one day but along with our patient waiting for the second coming, we are admonished to live for Christ until he comes again. While we wait, we must surrender to the love of God that is constantly working in our lives.

When the love of God flows through us, we find that we can share this love with other people around us. God is love and that love is greater than we are. Therefore, it must constantly flow through us to others. People around us yearn for love, because the world in which we live is drenched with hatred. It is Satan's legacy to people. May we, as Christians who await the second coming of Christ, therefore share God's love with everybody whom he sends across our path. Then we will be ready when he comes again.

Loving Saviour, I longingly look forward to your second coming; may the Holy Spirit help me in the meantime to work and to love.

You yourself know all too well that the day of the Lord will come unexpectedly like a thief in the night.
THE APOSTLE PAUL

BE PREPARED FOR THE SECOND COMING

He told them this parable: "Look at the fig tree and all the trees. When they sprout leaves, you can see for yourselves and know that summer is near. Even so, when you see these things happening, you know that the kingdom of God is near" (Lk 21:29-31).

The second coming of the living Christ is the hope of every believer. It is the great theme of the Scriptures, and it must be our great theme in life, too. We all realise that our churches need renewal. This can only happen when hope of the second coming yet again burns in believers' hearts.

FOOD FROM THE WORD OF GOD
Luke 21:29-22:23; Psalm 119:1-8, 57-64; Proverbs 4:10-15.

Imagine a congregation of 300 members of whom 30 really wait for the second coming. What blessing, light and dedication these people can contribute to a congregation! John says, *Everyone who has this hope in him purifies himself, just as he [Jesus] is pure* (1 Jn 3:3). Those who cherish this hope need not be called upon to keep themselves pure. They do it without being told to do so. They need not be encouraged to look ahead, to deny themselves certain things, or to present themselves for service. They themselves strive to be like the Lamb.

If we do not have hope for the second coming, we are truly without hope. We must be like the parishioner who once said, "For years I knew that I was converted, but I did not know for what purpose. I only understood it when 1 Thessalonians 1:9-10 and Ephesians 4:30 became clear to me: I have been saved in order to serve the true and living God and to wait for the second coming of his Son."

With my lamp filled and brightly shining, with my eyes no longer blind, I await your future, Saviour, where I will find true joy.

Do not sadden the Holy Spirit of God, because he has put the seal on you as the property of God with an eye to the day of salvation. – THE APOSTLE PAUL

November

Prayer for November

Holy Teacher,
Origin of all true wisdom and knowledge,
we bow in worship before you.
This month, we want to dedicate all learners and students to you,
because it is the month in which their knowledge will be tested.
We profess along with the wise writer of the Proverbs:
The fear of the Lord is the beginning of knowledge,
but fools despise wisdom and discipline (Prov 1:7).
Give to everyone who is writing exams –
and also to those who struggle with the test of life –
your peace that passes all wisdom.
Strengthen them with intellectual, physical and spiritual health
and give them composure under pressure.
Strengthen their eyes, so that they can read with discernment
and distinguish the things that really matter.
Control and put their thoughts in order, so that they
can think logically.
Make their hands strong and firm so that may confidently
reproduce what they have learned.
We thank you for everyone who thinks of them
and prays for them in these times.
Be now and for every day of their lives
the way that they must walk,
the truth that they must know,
the life that they must live.
In the Name of our loving Teacher
at whose feet we sit.

Amen

November 1

LIVE LIFE TO THE FULL

Give ear and come to me; hear me, that your soul may live (Is 55:3).

Life is what you make of it. You can choose either to be happy, or to be miserable day after day. Through careful planning you may be successful, or through a reckless attitude a hopeless failure. The quality of your life depends on your mind-set and the way in which you plan and approach your future.

It may sound to you like an oversimplification of a complicated situation. Perhaps you doubt your ability to handle life. If this applies to you, it is of the utmost importance that you should thoroughly inspect your faith in Jesus Christ in the light of the Word of God. His Word gives us many examples of people whose lives were once empty and void of meaning, but who were reformed and lived dynamic lives as a result of his grace. It began the moment the Holy Spirit started controlling their lives. For Jesus said, *I have come that they may have life, and have it in to the full* (Jn 10:10b).

FOOD FROM THE WORD OF GOD
Isaiah 55:1-7; Deuteronomy 30:16-20; Jeremiah 28:20; John 11:25-26; Romans 8:12-13; Galatians 2:20.

So, if it is true that Christ came so that we may have life in abundance, do not allow his sacrifices to be rendered useless by your life. Turn to him. Walk the road of life with your hand in his loving hand. Like Paul, you will be a new creature who will discover the confidence and ability that stems from a Spirit-filled life in Jesus Christ.

Holy Spirit of God, I beg that you will reform my life in such a way that I will live every day to the full in your power and strength.

One person who has learned to control his life is better than a thousand people who have only learned to handle the contents of a book; but no one can take something out of life without God. – MASTER ECKHARDT

November 2

MAKE PEACE WITH YOURSELF

I have told you these things, so that in me you may have peace (Jn 16:33a).

So many people live with inner fear. From the moment they wake up in the morning until they go to sleep at night, exhausted, they are embroiled in a struggle with themselves. The tension exhausts them so that they are irritable and aggressive towards everyone who crosses their path.

It is definitely not God's will that people should live like this. He wants to give peace. The peace God gives his believing children overrides and permeates their whole lives. He gives us his peace so that we can use and appreciate it in every imaginable area of our lives.

FOOD FROM THE WORD OF GOD
John 16:16-33; 14:27; Psalm 122:8-9; Isaiah 55:12-13; Colossians 3:15.

If you sincerely desire this peace of God, you must first be honest with him. Be openhearted with him. Tell him about all your faults and weaknesses. Tell him about your longing to change your thoughts and life-style. Your repentance will open a new door to God for you, a door which Jesus Christ himself keeps open for you.

When God's peace flows through your life and his Holy Spirit is in control of your life, you will experience peace. The storms in your life will calm down, and you will have inner peace. God's peace does not help you escape the tough realities of life, but enables you to meet the realities and challenges of life with quiet self-confidence.

God of peace, grant me also the true, steadfast peace that you alone can guarantee me.

Where there is peace, there is God.
GEORGE HERBERT

November 3

THE GREATNESS OF GOD'S LOVE

For God so loved the world that he gave his one and only Son, that whoever believes in him shall not perish but have eternal life (Jn 3:16).

The Lord said to Daniel, *Do not be afraid, O man highly esteemed ... Peace! Be strong now; be strong* (Dan 10:19). Worry and fear can so easily become a part of our lives. Anxiety turns into fear and fear produces worries. This vicious circle eventually gets so bad that all joy disappears from our lives. Then life is without purpose or meaning.

If fear and worry rule over your life, you need to experience and realise God's love anew. The fact that God loves you is a reality that determines your attitude towards life. Believing that God's love *hems you in – behind and before* (Ps 139:5), and that his love is just waiting to find expression in your life, is the best antidote for worry and fear. These two destructive forces cannot be in your life if you are filled with God's love.

FOOD FROM THE WORD OF GOD
John 3:1-21; Deuteronomy 7:6-8; Isaiah 43:4; Daniel 10:19; John 14:15-31; Revelation 3:9.

How can we continually be aware of God's love and put an end to these destructive influences? Ask God to take away your worry and fear and to replace them with the awareness of his holy presence. In your thoughts often reaffirm God's closeness to you as well as his love for you. Always remember that he loves you, and that evil thoughts have no influence over you when his hand is over you.

You will gradually but surely become aware that the work of God's love within you is stronger than any negative thoughts.

God of love, may your love become ever stronger in my life in order that my thoughts and deeds may be formed and directed by you.

Love is God's greatest gift to us, because he himself is love; so love is also the greatest thing that God can give us. – JEREMY TAYLOR

November 4

GOD SPEAKS OUT OF THE STORM

Then the Lord spoke to Job out of the storm (Job 40:6).

Many people allege that is only possible to hear the will of God when all is quiet. It is indeed a blessed privilege to spend quiet time in God's holy presence and to experience his peace; to feel how the stress of life subsides and to have time to decide what your priorities are; to become intensely aware of God's guidance and healing and love.

But if yours is a busy and pressurised life you will find comfort in the knowledge that God spoke to Job out of a storm. In the rush of modern life that barely affords you the opportunity to stop for a while before you have to take on the next task, it sounds impossible that God could make his will known to you under such circumstances. But he is the Lord of movement and action – as well as the God of quietness.

FOOD FROM THE WORD OF GOD
Job 40:1-41:25; Matthew 26:36-46; Mark 4:35-41; Acts 27:18-26.

Through the storms of life, God can guide you when you seek him and are prepared to obey his will. Awareness of his living presence can be your share at all times and in all circumstances. Feverish activity cannot stop God when you turn to him in the midst of the storms of your life. You will find that he is already waiting to listen to you. Then your activities become positive and constructive forces, and you are enabled to do wonderful things in his name and to his glory.

Help me, Lord my God, not to allow the activities of life to separate or estrange me from you.

When you are swept off your feet, it is time to get on to your knees.
FREDERICK BECK

November 5

PEACE OF MIND

You will keep in perfect peace him whose mind is steadfast, because he trusts in you (Is 26:3).

A living faith cannot develop within a purely emotional atmosphere, because once the inspiration of the moment is over, the faith will cease to exist. Trust in a stimulating atmosphere and the quality of your spirituality will fluctuate, depending on your mood and emotions.

A disciple who is controlled by an emotional atmosphere, will not experience victorious Christianity. Paul and Silas experienced this victorious Christianity when they sang songs of praise to the Lord with their backs bloodied, shackled in chains, locked in a filthy prison cell. Their experience of the living Christ's peace rose above their circumstances and emotions. Their suffering made Christ a reality to them. Goethe said, "It is not what is *around* me, but what is *in* me; it is not what I *have*, but what I am that makes me a joyful man with peace in my heart."

FOOD FROM THE WORD OF GOD
Isaiah 26:1-5; Psalm 147:14; Luke 1:76-79; John 14:27; Romans 15:13; Galatians 5:22.

Triumphant Christianity is not determined by external factors, but by whether your heart and mind are in harmony with God, whether you know the joy of fellowship with him and are aware of his presence. When Christ is the centre of your life and you have pledged your love and devotion to him, you possess a worshipping spirit in the sanctuary of your heart that enables you always to turn to him and to experience his presence, even in the most demanding circumstances. This is peace of mind: God's peace that passes all understanding.

Thank you, Lord Jesus, that your soft footsteps of peace have also entered my life in order to give me peace of mind in all circumstances.

Peace is freedom and peace of mind.
MARCUS TULLIUS CICERO

THERE IS STRENGTH IN SILENCE

In repentance and rest is your salvation, in quietness and trust is your strength (Is 30:15b).

There are many people who are inclined to talk too much and to be unnecessarily active about inconsequential matters. They simply cannot switch off and be quiet. When they have nothing to do, they become irritable. Even though creative activities are very important in life, we must also make time to withdraw from the rush of an active life so that we may reflect on the deeper aspects of life.

FOOD FROM THE WORD OF GOD
Isaiah 30:1-18; Exodus 14:4; Psalm 65:8; Matthew 26:62-63.

Most people find it easier to let their thoughts get stuck on everyday problems instead of focusing their thoughts and their spirits on the reality of God and his unchangeable and wondrous deeds. Even a short period spent in silence with God carries feelings of balance and calmness into your life.

When we become silent in order to be alone with God, we are often inclined to want to take the stress and pressures of life with us. Consequently, this time, which is supposed to be a moment of inspiration and reflection, becomes even more disruptive. When you enter into the holy presence of God, take your Bible with you and maybe a spiritual book that inspires you, so that your thoughts may be in harmony with those of the Master. Deriving the full benefit of your quiet time with God requires dedication, perseverance and time. But the reward is immeasurable, because in silence you truly feel and experience the presence of God.

I praise you, my God, that I may enter into your holy presence in silence and in so doing may be strengthened for my life's task.

How can you expect God to speak to that quiet, inner voice that invigorates the soul, when you are constantly making such a racket with your worldly thoughts? Be still, and God will speak again. – FRANÇOIS FÈNELON

November 7

YOUR HEAVENLY GUIDE

Commit your way to the Lord; trust in him and he will do this: He will make your righteousness shine like the dawn, the justice of your cause like the noonday sun (Ps 37:5-6).

Do you get frustrated when your carefully thought out plans suddenly go wrong? Are you disappointed when all your attempts fail and your hope is dissipated? Does it disappoint you so much that you are tempted to quit and to believe that you are doomed to failure?

It may be poor consolation, but you are not the only one who feels this way. The solution to your problem is not, however, to be found in acceptance of the failure, but in investigating the true causes of your lack of success. The question you have to seriously ask yourself is: How does God fit in with my plans?

FOOD FORM THE WORD OF GOD
Psalm 37:1-20; 139:23-24; Proverbs 14:12, 25; John 14:6; Acts 2:25-28.

When you undertake something you must never forget how vitally important it is that you seek the will of God before you take the first step. He knows what is best for you. Even though his way may initially not seem to you like the right one, or even though his plans do not fit in with yours, you must realise that God's perspective on life is eternal, while yours is only momentary. This is why he can lead you to a future known to him, even though it is hidden to you.

You would not cross a busy street blindfolded if you did not have a reliable guide, would you? Why then do you not make Jesus your partner in everything you undertake? By doing this, you will undoubtedly eventually taste success.

I wanted to control my life's path myself, but now you lead me!

When you have to make a choice, but fail to do so, it is a choice in itself.
WILLIAM JONES

BEYOND OUR WILDEST DREAMS

Now to him who is able to do immeasurably more than all we ask or imagine, according to his power that is at work within us, to him be glory in the church and in Christ Jesus throughout all generations, for ever and ever! Amen (Eph 3:20-21).

We determine our abilities according to our own opinion of ourselves. If we believe that we can do something, we usually succeed. But if we say to ourselves that something is impossible, we will not even attempt it and feel even more uncertain of our own abilities and worth.

FOOD FROM THE WORD OF GOD
Ephesians 3:14-21; 1 Kings 3:5-14; Job 42:10; John 10:10.

Often we divide our lives between that which we believe we can accomplish ourselves and that which we know we can accomplish with God's help. It is only when we reach beyond our own efforts and we realise what we can achieve in the wisdom and power of God Almighty, that we enter into the exciting world of faith. Then we attempt the impossible and discover that is not really so impossible. New horizons open up to us, and our faith and spiritual lives deepen.

With faith that is growing deeper and deeper, we realise that we are totally dependent on the living Christ. When we discover that we are doing things that we thought were far beyond our abilities, we realise that we are not doing it, but Christ who works through us. We become an instrument in the hand of the Master and we live within a new relationship with him. We grow so that we may understand his ways and methods. We develop the courage required to do work for him which we never would have attempted in our own wisdom or strength.

Almighty Father, in faith I reach beyond my limited abilities and lead a life of victory that goes far beyond my wildest dreams.

Most of us do not like looking within ourselves, for the same reason that we do not like opening a letter that contains bad news. – FULTON J SHEEN

WHY DO YOU DOUBT?

Is not my house right with God? Has he not made with me an everlasting covenant, arranged and secured in every part? Will he not bring to fruition my salvation and grant me my every desire? (2 Sam 23:5).

Many people cannot believe that God loves them. They prefer to carry the heavy burden of guilty feelings as a result of their past wrongdoings. The Light of life is overshadowed by the darkness of despair, because they are so strongly convinced of their unworthiness before God. They believe that God has rejected them and left them to their own fate.

When God was incarnated in Jesus Christ, an eternal covenant of mercy was instituted by his great and eternal love for all of humanity, and for you, too (Jn 3:16). Because of this love, God gave his Son to mankind so that we could triumph over evil once and for all. In the life, death, and resurrection of Jesus Christ, we have the assurance – just as with a covenant – of the love and forgiveness of God, which has been provided for all of mankind, and for you, too.

FOOD FROM THE WORD OF GOD
2 Samuel 23:1-7; Deuteronomy 4:37-38; Psalm 145:20; Matthew 22:37; John 3:16; 1 John 4:10; 5:2.

If you have any doubt whatsoever about whether God loves you, or about your ability to receive his love, simply think about how the King of kings came to this world, how he was born and lived in humble circumstances, how the Prince of Peace suffered and died for you, how the Lord of all lords arose from the dead so that *you* may have eternal life. If you have pondered on this with dedication, you will no longer doubt God's infinite love for you.

Loving Father, help me to accept your unfathomable love at all times, so that I may overcome every doubt in my heart.

Our love for God is tested by the question of whether we seek him on account of his gifts or on account of himself. – RALPH W SOCKMAN

November 10

COME ASIDE

Come with me by yourselves to a quiet place and get some rest (Mk 6:31b).

There are many varied ways in which we can worship God Almighty. Included are financial sacrifices, service in the church of Christ and good deeds amongst the underprivileged, the sick, the elderly and the disabled. The list is endless, but one thing all people who have accepted God have in common, is that they want to show that they are disciples of Jesus Christ.

FOOD FROM THE WORD OF GOD
Mark 6:17:34; Exodus 3:1-6; Psalm 121:1-2; Matthew 14:23; Mark 4:33-34.

Even though these tokens of dedication and worship are to be recommended, it is of the utmost importance that you do not neglect the most important aspect of your Christian life in all your involvement: getting to know and love God through Jesus. So often, in their zeal for the work of the church, people forget about the Lord of the church and make very little or no time to spend in his presence. He is, after all, the head of the church which they are serving so zealously. Knowing everything about the church and doing everything for the church serves no purpose without worshipping and loving the Christ of the church.

Despite his busy and demanding programme, Jesus himself always made time to spend quality time in prayer with God, in silence. Out of these precious moments, he drew his strength for his ministry to people in need. Follow the example of the Master and your reward will be that you will be a more significant and effective witness for the God whom you love.

I love you, O Lord, my strength (Ps 18:2).

All our problems in life stem from our refusal to become quiet and reflect on God's love.
BLAISE PASCAL

THE ETERNAL SEARCH FOR GOD

If only I knew where to find him;
if only I could go to his dwelling (Job 23:3).

Man's deep yearning for God may be expressed in different ways. The first indication of spiritual hunger is a restlessness that cannot be satisfied. It is often manifested by dissatisfaction with a church that has served you faithfully all your life. When this occurs, you run the risk of becoming a spiritual wanderer, forever looking for, yet rarely finding the love and peace that passes all understanding.

One of the encouraging facts regarding spiritual hunger that is often missed or ignored, is that God is still waiting, prepared to respond to the deepest need of every person. The will of the Father is not that any soul wanders away from his love, because he or she then becomes dissatisfied with the miracle of life that God wants to give you.

FOOD FROM THE WORD OF GOD
Job 23:1-17; Deuteronomy 4:29; Psalm 69:33; 139:7-12; Hebrews 11:6.

The Word of God makes it quite clear that the heavenly Father waits to receive everyone into a full and rich relationship with himself (Jn 14:5). He desires this for all people; and therefore he sent his Son to this world. To experience this unity with God, it is vital that you must turn away from your obstinate disobedience to God's invitation, and in faith accept his offer of forgiveness. It is available to you here and now. Let his Spirit enter into your life and take control of it. Your search for God will end in joy.

By accepting you into my life, Lord Jesus, I have entered into a living association with the merciful Father. May the Holy Spirit help me to guard this relationship like a precious gem.

It is in silence that God is known and through mysteries that he reveals himself to us.
ROBERT H BENSON

November 12

HOLD ON TO YOUR PRINCIPLES

The day of the Lord is near for all nations. As you have done, it will be done to you; your deeds will return upon your own head (Obad v 15).

As a result of all the terrifying things that are taking place around us, many people are questioning the presence of God, wondering whether living a good life is worth the trouble. They refer to people who are successful because of dishonesty, to criminals who evade the law, to victims who suffer. They direct your attention to violence, oppression and injustice, asking why it seems as if injustice always triumphs.

FOOD FROM THE WORD OF GOD
Obadiah verses 1-21; Galatians 4:8-20; Colossians 2:8-9; Hebrews 3:14; 5:12; Jude verse 6.

It is very important that you do not yield to the temptation and be influenced by the events around you to such an extent that you make a compromise with this world, sacrificing your Christian principles. What is currently happening will pass. Tomorrow it will belong to history. However, the will of God shall prevail in all eternity. Consequently, we are assured that justice will always overcome. God will ultimately triumph over evil.

When life becomes too much for you, ask Jesus Christ, your living Master, to help you so that you can make a stand against the world and sin. Open your life to the influence of his Spirit so that he may give you power and strengthen your faith to remain true to your Christian principles. In the power of God, you can and will succeed. When you remain faithful to your Master, you can look forward to the day when you will enter into his glory: *Be faithful, even to the point of death, and I will give you the crown of life* (Rev 2:10b).

He who overcomes will inherit all this, and I will be his God and he will be my son (Rev 21:7).

It is always easier to fight for one's principles than to live up to them.
ALFRED ADLER

November 13

GOD'S LOVE HOLDS ON TO YOU

When evening came, the boat was in the middle of the lake, and he was alone on land. He saw the disciples were straining at the oars, because the wind was against them (Mk 6:47-48).

The disciples did what the Lord ordered them to do, and suddenly found themselves in great danger. They had to battle against the waves and the wind – and they were afraid. Even though they were where the Lord wanted them to be, it seemed as if everything was working against them. The Lord was teaching them that his children could never drift out of the realm of his love.

FOOD FROM THE WORD OF GOD
Mark 6:35-52; Genesis 32:22-32; Psalm 108:8; Matthew 26:36-46.

You also serve God to the best of your ability, and as far as you know you do his will. But things keep on going wrong. Doubt threatens to overwhelm you, and fear haunts you to such an extent that you believe your Master has deserted you. He has not. He comes walking to you just as to the disciples. In your anxiety and fear, he talks to you, too, *Take courage! It is I. Don't be afraid* (Mk 6:50b). He will join you in your storm and make it die down. And along with the storm your fear will subside. Whatever your problems might be, the Master knows about them, and you are constantly under his loving supervision. In order to experience his comfort, to know his guidance and to feel the joy of his presence, it is necessary that he should be a part of your situation and in control of your life. In every situation, he is only a prayer away from you.

My Guide and Saviour, I want to invite you to take control of my life so that, even in a storm, I will know no fear.

The wise man prays to God in the storm, not for safety from danger, but for deliverance from fear. The storm within threatens us, not the storm without. – RALPH WALDO EMERSON

INSPIRATION THROUGH DISCIPLINE

*Find rest, O my soul, in God alone;
my hope comes from him (Ps 62:5).*

Some people say, "I am going to write a book." But they never do it, not because they have nothing to write about, but because they wait for inspiration before they put pen to paper. Books like these are never written, because inspiration is not a muse who only visits writers on highly exceptional occasions. Inspiration comes to those who simply start writing. Someone once said, "Success is 99% perspiration and only 1% inspiration."

FOOD FROM THE WORD OF GOD
Psalm 62:1-12; Luke 10:1-3; Romans 7:4; 12:1-2; Hebrews 11:6; Revelation 3:8.

True inspiration is a result of discipline. The act of starting with something, whether you feel like it or not, will eventually generate inspiration. This is especially true of our spiritual lives. Every follower of Jesus sometimes feels down or even depressed, and these emotional states negatively influence our prayer lives. To us, God becomes unreal and unsympathetic. Then the big danger is that we will stop praying because we lack the desire and the inspiration to persevere in prayer. But then particularly it is of the utmost importance that we should discipline ourselves to keep praying to our God.

The Bible continually commands us: Wait for the Lord. If you are naturally impatient, you will find this a difficult command. You will be more inclined towards actions than waiting patiently. But it is when you are alone with God, seeking his will, that you receive the inspiration for the task that awaits you. The disciple who prayerfully waits for the Lord finds himself or herself at the only true source of inspiration.

Lord my God, I joyfully accept your discipline, and delight in the inspiration that you give to your children who wait for you.

Inspiration is the name of that all-encompassing operation of the Holy Spirit through which he gave the church a complete and infallible Scripture. – ABRAHAM KUYPER

November 15

LIVE YOUR FAITH

But if I say, "I will not mention him or speak any more in his name," his word is in my heart like a fire, a fire shut up in my bones. I am weary of holding it in; indeed, I cannot (Jer 20:8).

Every sincere and dedicated disciple of Jesus Christ knows what a personal relationship with the Master means to our lives. It creates such a sensation of elation that it feels as if your heart is about to explode, so full is it of the knowledge that the living Saviour lives inside you.

This feeling that begins in us as a result of our relationship with our Lord Jesus Christ creates an irrepressible urge to tell others about the wonder of our Saviour. We brim with enthusiasm in the company of our friends, acquaintances, colleagues and even strangers when we witness to them of our faith in the Lord, of his miraculous deeds and his unfathomable love for them as well as for other people.

FOOD FROM THE WORD OF GOD
Jeremiah 20:7-18; Luke 21:13-15; Acts 15:7-11; 2 Timothy 1:8; Revelation 12:11.

In the world today, there is a definite need for people who will witness enthusiastically for Christ. But perhaps it is not in your nature to be a fervent witness for the Lord. Do not allow this to discourage you. There is also another very important way of sharing the gospel with other people: the way you live and act towards other people. Jesus is the incarnation of God's Word and when he takes possession of your life, your deeds will reflect his works of love and his charity. Share your feelings of joy about your everyday relationship with the Lord with other people. With your example, you will lead them to Christ and be his powerful witness.

Holy Master, come and live in my heart so that I may reflect your love in the world where you have placed me.

Our task as laymen is to express our personal relationship with Christ so intensely that it will be contagious.
PAUL TOURNIER

November 16

THE REWARDS OF OBEDIENCE

Taste and see that the Lord is good; blessed is the man who takes refuge in him (Ps 34:8).

A well-ordered life is dependent on certain rules and standards. If this were not true, life would have broken down into a state of disorder and chaos and it would have led to complete degradation. Even in nature, animals live according to a certain set of rules. Any disobedience that disturbs the normal cycle of life may result in drastic and ruthless action being taken against the trespasser.

FOOD FROM THE WORD OF GOD
Psalm 34:1-22; 1 Samuel 14\5:22-23; Acts 5:29; Romans 6:16; Philippians 2:8; 1 Peter 1:22.

In your own life, it is very important that you should stick to the tried and tested rules governing matters such as diet, hygiene and exercise if you attach any value at all to your physical welfare. A person who considers these things, who is considerate and who bears moderation in mind, ought to enjoy all the benefits of a healthy life. On the other hand, someone who neglects his or her body will have to endure illness and disease.

Your spiritual life is also controlled by fixed rules in the form of God's commands. Disobedience to his commands will cause you to move away from God, leading to a break in your relationship. Your faith will deteriorate to such an extent that it will be virtually wiped out. However, when you remain obedient to God by keeping all his instructions, you may be assured of the fact that, through the love of God, you are certain of a life of fulfilment, joy and peace.

Master, I will trust and obey you so that I may find my joy in you.

Every truly great person first learned how to obey, whom to obey, and when to obey.
WILLIAM A WARD

November 17

OUR GOD IS THE GREAT CREATOR

In the beginning God created the heavens and the earth (Gen 1:1).

Many people expect very little of God. They believe in him and pray to him, but their prayers lack a sense of anticipation. When their prayers are answered, they ascribe it to chance. A passive attitude to the almighty Creator God, when you ask and expect nothing of him, leads to an inadequate love. When you ask and expect nothing, you can, after all, receive nothing.

God is constantly creating. He cannot be static, because he is the source of life that continually renews itself. The seasons of the year, the constant renewal of life in all its visible forms, proclaim to us a God who is constantly busy creating. God-in-action is seen in the people who accept a new life in Christ, and who live in his power and in accordance with his standards. Those who experience this new life know that only in silence can someone discover that life holds visions. They know that God provides the power to turn the visions into reality. While you wait in silence for him, creative thoughts can take shape in your mind and God the Creator will lead you in them through the Holy Spirit.

FOOD FROM THE WORD OF GOD
Genesis 1:1-31; Psalm 8:1-10; 51:12; Isaiah 65:17; Ephesians 3:9; Revelation 4:11.

When you learn to appreciate the creative power of God in this world, when you feel the same creative power operating in your mind and spirit, you know undoubtedly that God is not far from you, but an integral and creative part of your life.

Holy God, open my mind, my heart and my life to the creative power of the Holy Spirit.

Coming up with new questions, discovering new possibilities, approaching old problems from new perspectives, requires a creative imagination and is the sign of new progress in science. – ALBERT EINSTEIN

November 18

YOU CAN MEET JESUS AT THE WELL

Jesus answered, "Everyone who drinks this water will be thirsty again, but whoever drinks the water I give him will never thirst. Indeed, the water I give him will become in him a spring of water welling up to eternal life" (Jn 4:13-14).

We all feel completely powerless at times. Intellectual, emotional and physical exhaustion may be the cause of such feelings. The shock of bad news can also exhaust and weaken you. Spiritual and emotional confusion can drain your strength. If you surrender to your feelings and simply accept the situation, you run the risk of experiencing a total breakdown. The consequences can be disastrous and far-reaching. But there is a way to triumph over this.

FOOD FROM THE WORD OF GOD
John 1:1-26; Exodus 15:25; Judges 15:19; Psalm 63:2; Isaiah 55:1-3; Revelation 21:6; 22:1, 17.

In your moment of weakness, turn to the omnipotent God. Through Jesus Christ, he is the water of life, and is waiting to strengthen you with the living water that is his gift to you personally. The risen Redeemer offers himself to you. In him you can once again become strong and alive, your mind refreshed and your spirit renewed. You need no longer experience uncertainty and weakness, because in Christ you become a new creature. Filled with the Holy Spirit, you will be strengthened again, and your life will have new meaning and purpose.

Prayerfully ask the living Christ at all times to fill you with his Holy Spirit so that you may leave negative experiences and spiritual droughts behind you, and that they will not overwhelm you. Drink deep draughts from the well of faith, and conquer your weakness by his power. Boast along with Paul who was strengthened by Christ: *For when I am weak, then I am strong* (2 Cor 12:10b).

Risen and living Master, I turn to you in my moments of weakness for the strength to carry me through every crisis.

The weakness of people is often required for God's purpose with their lives.
MAURICE MAETERLINCK

LET LIFE TALK TO YOU ABOUT GOD

How many are your works, O Lord! In wisdom you made them all; the earth is full of your creatures (Ps 104:24).

One of the outstanding characteristics of Jesus' ministry on earth is the way in which he took ordinary objects and related them to spiritual matters. Bread, water, wine, coins, fishing, doors and many other everyday things and occasions were used by him in stories he told so that his listeners could understand the deeper truths about God.

In the lives of believers, ordinary things talk powerfully of God in his greatness. Family life reminds us of the paternity of God; a baby tells us about God who was incarnated in Jesus Christ and descended to our broken world to save people; friendship directs our thoughts to the friendship we can have with our Master. The overpopulation of a city that leads to sins too numerous to mention moves the hearts of all who understand charity, just like the heart of Jesus was moved when he looked out over Jerusalem and wept for her. Our whole life can tell those who are sensitive to it about a God who cares and who talks to us through his Holy Spirit.

FOOD FROM THE WORD OF GOD
Psalm 104:1-35; Exodus 9:14-17; 34:10 Psalm 8:2, 10; Isaiah 6:3; Romans 8:20-23.

In order to ensure that this is also your experience, put God at the centre of your life. Look at life through his eyes, and make his values your values. As you grow ever closer to him, you will become increasingly aware of your God who made himself known to you through his miraculous and mighty deeds.

Lord my God, make me sensitive to the lessons you want to teach me in my everyday life.

The children of Adam and Eve constantly perform the scene about the loss of paradise. We clothe our souls with messages and dogmas, losing the touch of the great life in the naked breasts of nature. – RABINDRANATH TAGORE

GOD'S WORD - OUR ANCHOR IN LIFE

The grass withers and the flowers fall, but the word of our God stands for ever (Is 40:8).

In these times of change, it seems as if the world has become a stage on which people proclaim that they have found the final answers to all life's questions. Politicians, religious leaders and self-proclaimed prophets are forever bombarding people with their cures for all the ailments of humanity, with their formulae for perfect lives, with the blueprints for their idea of Utopia.

FOOD FROM THE WORD OF GOD
Isaiah 40:1-8; Psalm 119:9, 105; Jeremiah 23:29; Matthew 4:4; John 1:1; Romans 10:8; Hebrews 4:12.

This trend, however, is not limited to the modern age. A quick look at history reveals that these voices were heard all through the ages. For a while they had enthusiastic audiences, but then they faded into obscurity, because there *was*, *is* and will always *be* only *one* true way of life – God's way. Despite all the declarations and theories people come up with, Jesus Christ, the Word of God made flesh, is still the *way*, the *truth* and the *life*. No one comes to the Father except through him (Jn 14:6). In spite of all the attacks on the Word of God from within the church as well as from outside, it has remained standing through all the ages. God and his Word remain unchanged in an ever-changing world, an anchor for his children who believe.

If you are looking for peace of mind and calmness in your spirit in the turbulent world in which we live, hold on to the living Christ and build on the foundation of the Word of God. Then you will know life in all its abundance.

Word incarnate, help me to hold firmly on to your Word so that I may find life in Christ.

People do not reject the Bible because it contradicts itself, but because it contradicts them.
E PAUL HOVEY

THE CHOICE OF LIFE

Choose for yourselves this day whom you will serve (Josh 24:15b).

The most misused gift God has given us is the freedom to choose for ourselves. Even though we are naturally inclined to sin, we only sin when we choose to do so. We can choose to live within the will of God, or to turn away from God and be disobedient to him. The choice is our responsibility – and so, too, the consequences of our choice.

People who do not believe in God walk the road that their own blind hearts have planned. They force their own interpretation on life. They measure success in terms of prestige and wealth; joy is determined by what they own; life's worth is determined from a materialistic perspective. They disobey God and commit sins without even the slightest suggestion of regret. They do not even think about the consequences of their actions.

FOOD FROM THE WORD OF GOD
Joshua 24:1-28; Deuteronomy 31:19-20; Luke 18:23-25; Hebrews 3:7-8; Revelation 3:20.

The climax of foolishness is knowing the standards Christ has laid down, yet ignoring them. Not only is it foolish, but it also keeps you from experiencing the fullness of life in Christ. When you choose to control your thoughts, focusing them on the living Saviour, you receive the strength to overcome temptations and sin. Choose to think as God wants you to think. When your thoughts, which are centred on God, are inspired by enthusiasm, it will be revealed in your life, and every body will know that you have chosen life in Jesus Christ.

Heavenly Guide, I know your road and accept it. This is why I have a breastplate against sin. I praise and thank you for it.

The strongest principle in your spiritual growth lies in the choices you make.
GEORGE ELLIOT

November 22

WHEN LIFE LOSES ITS MEANING

"I have had enough, Lord," he said. "Take my life; I am no better than my ancestors" (1 Kgs 19:4b).

It is so tragic when life loses its meaning and purpose for someone. For some people year after year passes without their achieving or doing something that is worthwhile according to them. Consequently, they start suffering from depression or boredom with life. Their thoughts and actions become negative and they seek answers to nagging questions: Is there any purpose to life? What is the use of living? Is it really worth all the drudgery and the effort?

FOOD FROM THE WORD OF GOD
1 Kings 19:1-21; Job 3:25-26; 7:16; 10:1; Matthew 25:5.

The answers to all these questions depend on your relationship with the living God. When we look away from Jesus, focusing our eyes on ourselves, we lose our sense of calling; our faith loses power and life loses its meaning and purpose. Christ must be at the centre of our lives. When someone or something else replaces him, our spiritual lives will fade and eventually die. It is impossible for Christians to live the way God intended if he is not the centre of our thoughts and lives. Then our thoughts lose inspiration, our actions lose meaning and there is no motivation for attempting anything in life.

Our lives are interwoven in God's purpose and plan for us. The spiritual worth, the reward, and the satisfaction of his will for us make life worthwhile. Christ is the power that gives our lives quality and meaning, and that fills our actions and events with purpose.

Merciful God and Father, teach me continually to walk with you so that my life will have meaning and purpose.

Man was made in the image of God with a purpose – to live in a relationship with God. If we forget this purpose, we forget who we are and what the meaning of life is. – FRANCIS A SCHAEFFER

November 23

SELECT YOUR THOUGHTS

Finally, brothers, whatever is true, whatever is noble, whatever is right, whatever is pure, whatever is lovely, whatever is admirable – if anything is excellent or praiseworthy – think about such things (Phil 4:8).

It is true that you cannot prevent destructive or contemptible thoughts from entering your mind, but it does depend on you whether you are going to reject or accept them. Sometimes you hold on to thoughts thinking that they cannot really harm you or your life. Unfortunately, before you are even aware of their influence, they have become permanent residents who eventually make their presence known in your actions and your life.

FOOD FROM THE WORD OF GOD
Philippians 3:16-4:20; Psalm 139:2; Isaiah 55:6-7; 2 Corinthians 10:4-5; Hebrews 4:12-13.

God has given you the ability to discern, so that you can select your thoughts. You and you alone can decide the nature of your thoughts and therefore the nature of you spirit. And you will surely become egocentric, bitter, unforgiving, and unchristian if you allow your mind to become polluted with immoral, negative and destructive thoughts.

In order to think dignified and noble thoughts, your spirit must be in harmony with God's Holy Spirit. He is the one who inspires you to live a good life. When you give God an honorary place at the gates to your thoughts, so that every thought meets with his approval, you will experience a surge of inspiring thoughts and you will be able to approach life with confidence.

The choice to place God in charge of your thoughts is completely your responsibility. Do not delay – invite him today to take control. Through his Spirit, he will free you of negative and destructive thoughts.

Holy Master, help me through your Holy Spirit to select the thoughts that enter my mind in accordance with your approval.

Fill your mind with good thoughts or else the enemy will fill it with bad ones: your mind can never be vacant.
SIR THOMAS MOORE

November 24

INSPIRED AMBITIONS

What you decide on will be done,
and light will shine on your ways (Job 22:28).

A don't-care attitude is the arch-enemy of ambitions. Many people have big plans to fulfil their highest aims, but somehow it never happens. They always have excuses as to why they cannot reach their goals, "The time is not yet ripe." Or, "I never had the opportunity." And, "I am still exploring all the possibilities." As the excuses become more and more, the ambitions are pushed further and further into the background, until they become shadows of dreams that will never come true.

FOOD FROM THE WORD OF GOD
Job 22:21-30; 32:8;
Ezekiel 36:26; Matthew 25:23; 1 Corinthians 9:24-27;
Ephesians 3:14-21.

Ambition is born out of creative thoughts and positive actions. You must constantly think of ways to achieve your goals. When an obstacle that threatens to divert your attention comes in your way, your aim must be big enough to let your initial enthusiasm burn clearly and brightly and to keep you on track with determination. Therefore, link yourself to ambitions that will take up all your mental, physical and spiritual abilities. Ensure that you have an aim in life that has been inspired and approved by God. Then he will provide you with the strength you need to achieve it. He will be the source to which you come back time and again in order to rekindle your spiritual energy when it starts to diminish. When your ambition is inspired in this way by God and his Holy Spirit, and is acceptable to him, you will receive the enthusiasm and inspiration to complete it to his honour and glory.

Loving Teacher and Guide, I acknowledge only you as the source of my inspiration. Protect me so that I do not stray from your will.

You might reach the top of the ladder and then discover that the ladder is leaning against the wrong wall.
A RAINE

HOW DO YOU PRAY?

So God said to him, "Since you have asked for this and not for long life or wealth for yourself, nor for your enemies ... I will do what you have asked ... Moreover, I will give you what you have not asked for" (1 Kgs 3:11-13).

In the prayer life of a Christian there is a great temptation to focus attention on the self. We are so inclined to stand before God and submit personal petitions. The serious danger of this is that our prayers soon become self-centred and that our list of personal needs are given preference over worshipping and praising God, and the welfare of others. This will lead to personal disillusionment, because we will discover that the holiness of our prayer time has made way for material demands. These can, if not answered, easily bring about a situation in which we find we have become estranged from the Hearer of prayers through our own doing. Every prayer you pray to God must echo Jesus' immortal words, *Not my will, but yours be done* (Lk 22:42). This is the ultimate exercise in faith: leaving your prayers entirely to God while you abide by God's holy will. In so doing, you admit that he is the Lord of your life and the Lord of the lives of those people about whom you are concerned.

FOOD FROM THE WORD OF GOD
1 Kings 3:2-15; Genesis 32:22-32; Psalm 13:1-2; 22:22-23; Luke 22:42; Acts 28:8.

When you leave your prayers totally and without reservation to God by trusting him unconditionally with your ultimate welfare, you will experience an unknown and bubbling feeling of peace and acceptance. You will realise that God keeps his hand on your life, and that he leads you along the perfect road.

Hearer of prayers, I lay all my needs completely at your feet, because I know that you know best what to do with them.

Our biggest problem with prayer is to "let go" and "let God".
GLEN CLARK

November 26

A MEANINGFUL LIFE

Sow your seed in the morning, and at evening let not your hands be idle, for you do not know which will succeed, whether this or that, or whether both will do equally well (Ecc 11:8).

What you get out of life is precisely that which you put into life. The rewards may perhaps not be financial prosperity, but those who dedicate themselves zealously to life and to their neighbours will eventually be rewarded. When you think about people who are lonely, embittered, judgemental and unhappy, you will often find that they have no compassion for their neighbours. Happy, satisfied people, on the other hand, are probably busy serving their neighbours in many areas.

FOOD FROM THE WORD OF GOD
Ecclesiastes 11:1-8:12; Psalm 16:1-11; 36:10; John 10:10; Romans 14:7-8; Galatians 2:20.

If you are unhappy or dissatisfied with life, think for a moment critically about what you do for others. Do you take pains to get into contact with an old friend who is experiencing problems? Do you do everything in your power to put time aside to visit someone who is ill, sad or aged? Do you offer your services and time to an organisation that renders charitable and benevolent services?

There are so many terrains open to you where you can be of service. Your active involvement will quickly transform your unhappiness into peace and acceptance. Ask Jesus to be with you and to lead you through the Holy Spirit where he can best use you to the benefit of his people who need you. He will open up the road for you and give you the ability required for the task. Perform your task and discover how life suddenly has new purpose and meaning.

Merciful Lord Jesus, I find perfect fulfilment through serving you amongst my fellow men.

One's life is filled with meaning the moment Jesus enters it.
STEPHAN NEILL

November 27

YOU ARE IMPORTANT TO GOD

So do not fear, for I am with you; do not be dismayed, for I am your God. I will strengthen you and help you; I will uphold you with my righteous right hand (Is 41:10).

Being loved by someone and loving someone yourself, feeling that you have worth in society, gives deep meaning to your life. For we need other people in our lives in order to experience contentment. This is why it is so disturbing to experience that your life is not important to anyone. Waking up in the morning and knowing that your life is not important to anyone leads to self-pity and harms your dignity and self-confidence.

FOOD FROM THE WORD OF GOD
Isaiah 41:8-20; 43:1-5; 49:1-2; Matthew 18:1-5; 1 Peter 1:19.

So what does one do to overcome this feeling that you are not important to anyone? Most importantly, it is necessary to draw your attention away from yourself and become interested in people and events around you. If you are self-centred, other people are less likely to be interested in you. However, your interest in others must not be motivated by the desire to interfere in their lives, but by a loving interest. When love becomes the dominant factor in your life, other people become more important to you than you yourself. Then your life and actions are mirroring Jesus, your perfect example.

Even though you might feel that you are not important to people, always remember that you are very precious to the Lord. He cares a great deal about you. He provides in your needs every day and has prepared a place for you in his kingdom because you are his child, whom he loves very much.

I praise and thank you, loving Master,
for thinking more of me than I think of myself.

It is always spring in the hearts of those whom God loves.
JOHN VIANNEY

GOD IS TALKING TO YOU

Gideon replied, "If now I have favour in your eyes, give me a sign that it is really you talking to me" (Judg 6:17).

How does one recognise the voice of God? Many people are confused because they pray to the Lord, yet they are never sure that he has heard their prayers and will respond to them. This inevitably leads to frustration and may have serious consequences because then one may easily misinterpret God's answers. Instead of your prayer time being a time of certainty and peace, it degenerates into a nightmare of doubt and uncertainty.

FOOD FROM THE WORD OF GOD
Judges 6:7-23; Exodus 3:5-10; Ezekiel 2:1; Daniel 5:24-27; Acts 9:3-4; Hebrews 3:7-8.

If the above scenario applies to you, it is necessary for you to seek the guidance of the Holy Spirit by opening your life to his benevolent influence. Always be sensitive to his prompting. Obtain the help of a trusted friend whom you respect. Ask him or her to be your prayer companion and example. It is a well-known fact that God often makes his will and leadership known to us through the advice someone else gives to us.

Under no circumstances should you try to negotiate with God or to force your will upon him. When you pray seriously and earnestly, leave the matter in God's hands and wait quietly and patiently for him. He will surely talk to you. When you stay in touch with Jesus through your talks with him and by spending time in reflection before him, the road will unfold before you and you will know that your prayer has been answered. God has his own perfect time, but he will definitely talk to you – just listen prayerfully.

Lord my God, I place myself in your faithful care and calmly wait for your guidance.

The degree of our faith is the degree of our prayers; the power of our hope is the power of our prayers; the warmth of our charity is the warmth of our prayers. – CARLO CARETTO

GOD CALLS YOU

***To a nation that did not call on my name,
I said, "Here I am, here I am" (Is 65:1b).***

Many people are questioning God's omnipotence and love. They look at the violence, droughts, floods, famine, plagues and wars and ask: But where is God? How can he allow all these things to happen?

We must remember that God cannot be held responsible for all the disasters in the world. They are the results of man's own sin. The free will that God out of his grace gave to man has been abused to such an extent that people now have to pay the price for it.

Furthermore, we have to remember that God is present in bad circumstances, too. He suffers along with those who suffer. He waits for people in need to hear his voice, to turn back to him, and to accept the help he is prepared to give.

FOOD FROM THE WORD OF GOD
Isaiah 65:1-2, 21-25; Genesis 3:8-9; Proverbs 1:24; Isaiah 50:2; Matthew 22:3; Romans 8:28; 1 Peter 2:9.

The solution for the destitution people experience is to be found in the abundant life that Christ offers all of us (Jn 10:10). He offers salvation and hope to everyone who comes to him, *Here I am! I stand at the door and knock. If anyone hears my voice and opens the door, I will go in and eat with him, and he with me* (Rev 3:20). What is required of us is to take a step in faith to grasp the outstretched hand of the Saviour and to experience the healing ointment of God's peace. Why not reach out to him today?

Holy God and Father, I find rest and resignation in your promises because I have heard and responded to your voice.

The road to salvation is not postponement, but to come at God's call and accept it.
DWIGHT L MOODY

November 30

REMEMBERING AND THANKING

I thank my God every time I remember you (Phil 1:3).

When your path in life becomes stony and dark clouds gather above you, suffocating all inspiration, it is time for you to become quiet and consider the past: all the experiences and blessings you have had in all the years that have passed. There were times when you wanted to break under a burden – and Someone suddenly gave you new strength, clarity and courage so that you could carry on. When disaster threatened you and it felt as though everything was lost, Someone made you get up out of the doldrums and gave you a new life of victory.

FOOD FROM THE WORD OF GOD
Philippians 1:1-11; Psalm 77:12-15;
Ephesians 5:20;
1 Thessalonians 2:12;
Revelation 11:17.

Indeed, every problem offers a new opportunity; every instance of sadness leads to consolation and joy. While you are contemplating the deeper meaning of life, you realise anew that every negative influence had its positive reverse. Then your heart is filled with joy and you rejoice, *Praise the Lord. Give thanks to the Lord, for he is good; his love is everlasting* (Ps 106:1).

The key that unlocks the door that leads to a creative life is thankfulness. There is always something in life for which you can thank God. Thank him for the good people that he has sent into your life, for the wonderful opportunities he has given you, for the friends with whom he has enriched your life, and above all for the awareness of his holy presence with you under all circumstances. Then you will approach the future with a God-given confidence and the assurance that you can triumph in the Name of Christ.

Holy God, my heavenly Father, aware of all your blessings in the past and that you are with me in Christ and the Holy Spirit, I go to meet the future with confidence.

We ought to spend just as much time thanking God for his blessings as we spend asking him for them.
VINCENT DE PAUL

December

Prayer for December

1. Divine encouragement
2. Light in the darkness
3. Trust in the Lord
4. Your haven of peace
5. The opportunity of a lifetime
6. Immanuel – God is with us
7. Are you listening, Lord?
8. Overcome your weakness
9. Forgiving love restores
10. God makes your life worthwhile
11. Your love is needed
12. Pray to God – he will answer
13. Christian love conquers evil
14. Your infallible friend
15. Start the day right
16. Christ in you
17. Stop worrying
18. Do not disappoint him
19. God is your guide
20. The weakness of indecision
21. The tragedy of being lukewarm
22. Work on your self-confidence
23. You account to God
24. Do not be afraid …
25. Was Christ born in your heart?
26. God's greatest gift
27. Never stop hoping
28. Share your pain with God
29. Our almighty Father God
30. Take my thoughts prisoner, O God!
31. Our refuge and our strength

Prayer for December

Holy and almighty God and Father,
during this time of the year you talk to us through a Child
who was born in a stable in Bethlehem and who lay
in the curve of a mother's arm and called us back
with a baby's hand to the heart of God.
We yearn at this time of the year for
the simple beauty of the Christmas tide:
for all the well-known and beloved melodies;
for everything that reminds us of the great miracle
when you who created everything came
to our lost world one night to save us for yourself.
We bow before the mystery of love,
and in the footsteps of the shepherds and wise men
we bring to you the sacrifices of our love and faithfulness.
We confess in shame that our love is not always as
warm and genuine as it ought to be.
But now, at this Christmas tide, our love wants to find your love,
and your grace to purify our love.
May we celebrate a Christmas tide of which you approve.
May the love and compassion of the festive season
be a lasting reality in our everyday lives
when we return to our daily concerns and worries.
Have mercy on all those who are suffering; who wait lonely;
who struggle with regret; who are empty and poor because of loss.
Give to them your abundant comfort.
We pray all of this in the Name of him who has come to
save people from their sin and to be for all people:
Immanuel – God with us.

Amen

DIVINE ENCOURAGEMENT

Have I not commanded you? Be strong and courageous. Do not be terrified; do not be discouraged, for the Lord your God will be with you wherever you go (Josh 1:9).

With the birth of his Son God replaced our fear with jubilant joy. When the angel appeared to Mary to bring her the wonderful news that she would be the mother of Jesus, he said to her, *Do not be afraid, Mary, you have found favour with God* (Lk 1:30b). And to the shepherds living in the fields of Ephrata the angel said, *Do not be afraid. I bring you good news of great joy that will be for all the people* (Lk 2:10).

FOOD FROM THE WORD OF GOD
Joshua 1:1-18; Psalm 27:14; Luke 2:8-15; Romans 12:8; 15:1; 2 Corinthians 1:4-5.

Our world has become a labyrinth of fear. And fear is not merely a vain fabrication: from the cradle to the grave we live in fear. We fear the world, because all around us are murders, rapes, pestilence, hatred, jealousy and vindictiveness. We fear the unknown as little children fear the dark; we fear the future, the present and the past; we are anxious about our health, our finances, the welfare of our children, our marriage; we fear growing old, and the last "feared friend" – death.

Yet, in our fear, God comes to this world at Christmas tide with his message of encouragement loud and clear, *Do not be afraid! Immanuel – God is with us.* What a tiding of great joy! The cause of our fear is removed because the Child has triumphed. Fear is replaced with joy and love. And love drives out fear (1 Jn 4:15-18). May you and your loved ones enjoy this festive season free from fear.

The Lord is my helper; I will not be afraid.
What can man do to me? (Heb 13:6).

Let me assert my firm belief that the only thing we have to fear is fear itself.
FRANKLIN D ROOSEVELT

December 2

LIGHT IN THE DARKNESS

The people walking in darkness have seen a great light; on those living in the land of the shadow of death a light has dawned (Is 9:2).

People soon become despondent during times of trouble or confusion. A spirit of downheartedness and despair threatens to overcome them. Sometimes it seems as though people allow themselves to sink into the mire of hopelessness and to willingly bow before the inevitable disaster. And once this has happened, they have great difficulty in getting up and facing life once more.

FOOD FROM THE WORD OF GOD
Isaiah 9:1-6; Psalm 27:1; Isaiah 60:1-3; John 12:46; Ephesians 5:8; 1 John 1:1-10.

Ever since the creation, there have often been times when the prospects for humankind appeared hopeless. The world has been subjected to violence, earthquakes, fires, pestilence, economic hardship and many other crises that have rocked the foundations of mankind. Yes, history proves that mankind has been confronted through the ages with circumstances that made the weak believe that everything, but everything was lost.

Yet, you should never underestimate God's omnipotence. Despite all that happens around you – including the negative events in your personal life – this fact remains firmly standing: God is in total control of his creation, and he will protect it along with his children against every form of evil and misery. No matter how desperate and futile your life's circumstances may appear, always remember that God has sent his light, his Son Jesus Christ, to this world to lead us out of all darkness into his wonderful light. This is the message of the celebration of Christ's birth: *The Lord has established his throne in heaven, and his kingdom rules over all* (Ps 103:19).

Almighty God the Creator, I praise and thank you for always being there to bring light, even in my darkest moments.

There is no choice in darkness. The light enables us to see the difference between things: and it is Christ who gives us this light. – CT WHITMELL

TRUST IN THE LORD

Even youths grow tired and weary, and young men stumble and fall; those who hope in the Lord will renew their strength. They will soar on wings like eagles; they will run and not grow weary, they will walk and not be faint (Is 40:31).

Waiting for and trusting in the presence of the Master is an ideal for which every Christian disciple strives, but it is by no means easy. Wandering thoughts, pressure and poor concentration all contribute to making the period of waiting for a God whom we cannot see difficult and uninspiring.

FOOD FROM THE WORD OF GOD
Isaiah 40:12-31; 2 Kings 1:9; Psalm 27:10-14; 130:3-7; Micah 7:7; Philippians 3:3.

Yet, viewing the time spent in the presence of God as useless and unproductive is symptomatic of a deep-seated ignorance of God's ways. Each one of Jesus' followers who has realised what God's purpose with him or her is, has spent time alone with God. When your thoughts are open to the Holy Spirit, you receive strength and inspiration.

Therefore, when you are entering a phase when you need to trust in the Lord and wait for him, keep your mind open to his guidance. Ask him, "Lord, what would you like me to do?" Maybe God will not answer you immediately. Maybe you have to wait for him for a long time. Nevertheless, one thing is certain: you cannot come to God with a positive attitude and with your heart and mind focused on him without being spiritually enriched and uplifted. Your concentration may be less than perfect; your faith may be insufficient – but when you trust in the Lord with a believing prayer on your lips, you will be aware of his presence, and you will experience that he is already waiting to meet you with his power and blessing.

Lord, give me the patience to wait for you and to trust you completely, so that I may discover your will for my life.

We must wait for God, for a long time and with humility, in wind and rain, in thunder and lightning, in darkness and cold. Wait and he will come. He does not come to those who do not wait. – FREDERICK W FABER

December 4

YOUR HAVEN OF PEACE

Peace I leave with you; my peace I give you. I do not give to you as the world gives. Do not let your hearts be troubled and be not be afraid (Jn 14:27).

All of us need something or someone to trust steadfastly. Even those who allege that they can function independently, have to admit in honesty that they sometimes trust in some or other source of strength. Even if having a reliable help in times of trouble is a great comfort, we also know that human or financial help is fallible and can sometimes leave you in the lurch.

FOOD FROM THE WORD OF GOD
John 14:15-31; Joshua 9:6; Psalm 85:9; Isaiah 52:7-10; Ephesians 2:14-17.

There is only One whose continuous care and love for you never ends, and who will never let you down: it is God himself in Christ Jesus. He calls every exhausted pilgrim to come to him with his or her burden so that he may give him or her rest (Mt 11:28). This is a peace that transcends your understanding, calms your anxious heart and allays all fear (Phil 4:7).

Accept God's merciful offer of peace by accepting Jesus Christ as your Saviour. He is the Prince of Peace (Is 9:6). Surrender to him unconditionally and his Holy Spirit will guide you and strengthen you in every circumstance. He will grant you the confidence and the ability to handle any situation that might arise. His presence will banish all fear, and his perfect love will establish the blessing of his indispensable peace in your heart.

I thank you, God of peace, that I may cherish your peace in my heart and therefore live without fear in grateful reverence to you.

Peace is not brokered around conference tables, but in the hearts of men.
HERBERT HOOVER

December 5

THE OPPORTUNITY OF A LIFETIME

See, I have placed before you an open door that no one can shut (Rev 3:8b).

A self-pitying complaint we hear all too often is, "I never got a chance in life." These people perhaps tried to get somewhere, but all their attempts failed. Inevitably, they then lose courage and feel as if life owes them something. They call their circumstances their "fate" and protest the fact that life treats them unfairly.

If this is your philosophy in life, be still for a moment and seriously think about everything that God has done for you. In Jesus Christ, he descended from heaven to be, at first, a humble carpenter. Then he became a travelling evangelist with no possessions. Despite obstacles and problems, he brought God's message of love to a cynical, deceitful and treacherous world. He was cast out, humiliated and deserted, tortured and killed in the cruellest possible manner. Despite all this, he poured out his immortal, redeeming love over all people. He triumphantly rose from the dead, and gave to you and me the comfort and strength of the Holy Spirit to be our companion on our pilgrimages.

FOOD FROM THE WORD OF GOD
Revelation 3:7-22; Psalm 78:23-25; Matthew 25:10; John 10:7-10; 20:26.

This is God's exceptional gift of mercy to you and all who will accept it. We do not deserve it, but God gives it to us freely in his unfathomable love and mercy. And no one can take it away from us. Accept his offer gratefully. Then it will be impossible for you to think that life treats you unfairly.

Eternal God, thank you for the gateway of mercy, which has been opened to me, too, through Jesus Christ. With the guidance of the Holy Spirit, I enter into your glory and love without hesitation.

The burdens of life come from us; the lightness of life comes from Christ's mercy and God's love.
MARTIN LUTHER

December 6

IMMANUEL - GOD IS WITH US

The Lord your God is with you, he is mighty to save. He will take great delight in you, he will quiet you with his love, he will rejoice over you with singing (Zeph 3:17).

When things start going wrong for you, as happens to all of us from time to time, it is easy to give in to despair, deciding to not even make an effort. Life appears to be such an unequal struggle that you find it impossible to think of victory. It feels to you as if everything is turning against you. Your problems seem totally insurmountable. Then you allow a negative spirit of helplessness and despair to wash over you and pull you down.

FOOD FROM THE WORD OF GOD
Zephaniah 3:14-20; Isaiah 7:10-14; 8:8; 41:10; Matthew 1:8-25.

If ever there were a day when all seemed lost, it must certainly have been the day that Jesus was crucified. The hopes and aspirations of so many people were shattered when the One they regarded to be the Saviour of Israel was crucified and died like a common criminal.

Then God intervened. God, who is Christ's hope and strength, transformed the apparent defeat of Good Friday into the triumphant victory of the Morning of Resurrection when Christ rose from the dead.

No matter what your circumstances might be, or how dark the future might seem, despite all the problems that affect you badly – never forget that God is always with you and that he is in total control of your life. Turn to him, put your faith and trust in him, and he will give you victory.

Omniscient God and Father, I rejoice in the knowledge that you are always with me and will never forsake or desert me. May I always remember this – especially in dark days.

The first step to victory is identifying the enemy.
CORRIE TEN BOOM

ARE YOU LISTENING, LORD?

Answer me when I call you, O my righteous God.
Give me relief from my distress;
be merciful to me and hear my prayer (Ps 4:2).

Prayer is not an automatic answering machine. Prayer is not asking God questions and instantly getting answers. Prayer is also not dictating to God what you want, and then sitting back and waiting for him to give it to you. If this is your attitude towards prayer, you will soon be disillusioned and want to call out, "God does not listen to me!"

When you come to God in prayer, know and accept that he listens to you. Lay down all your interests and concerns before him and leave them to his sound judgement. Though you may make your requests known to him, you cannot dictate to God what he ought to do. Rather ask him to show you through the prompting of the Holy Spirit what is best for you, and especially what his holy will is. And always remember: God knows what is best for you in your circumstances, because he knows your needs.

FOOD FROM THE WORD OF GOD
Psalm 4:1-8; Genesis 29:33; Psalm 6:10; 40:2-3; Jeremiah 18:18-23; 1 John 5:14-15.

When you pray like this, you will experience God's guiding hand in your life. He will guide you on the road that is best for you, even though it might differ from what you had wanted. Maybe you will have to wait a very long time for God to lead you in his ways. But whatever the situation might be, wait patiently on the Lord. He will answer your prayers in accordance with his divine will and your needs.

O Hearer of prayers, grant me the patience to quietly wait
for you when I stand before you in prayer,
so that I will understand and accept your will.

Prayer is actually standing to attention before God, the King, and being willing to obey his commands. – DONALD COGGAN

OVERCOME YOUR WEAKNESS

Finally, be strong in the Lord and in his mighty power (Eph 6:10).

There are many varied types of weaknesses that influence different aspects of our lives. For example, there are physical, emotional, mental and spiritual weaknesses. Though they appear in different guises, they all affect your welfare negatively. For some people, the consequences may be disastrous.

Physical weakness may awaken a fear in you of being attacked, whereas emotional or mental weakness may bewilder your thoughts. Spiritual weakness may have a destructive influence on your faith in God. Many a petrified soul has aimlessly wandered around in a spiritual wilderness because of this.

FOOD FROM THE WORD OF GOD
Ephesians 6:10-20; John 5:1-5; 16:25-33; Romans 8:37; 12:21; Revelation 12:11.

However, the psalmist could confirm his faith in God's omnipotence and ability, *God is our refuge and strength, an ever-present help in trouble* (Ps 46:2). This assurance was repeatedly shown to be true and certain when servants of the Lord faced great dangers and unspeakable obstacles – and overcame them.

Jesus Christ will enable you through the power of the Holy Spirit to deal with all life's challenges. He will give you the strength to triumph in his Name over all your weaknesses. Whatever your problem or difficulty might be, lay it before him and allow him to take control of your life and to lead you on the right path – the path of victory over weaknesses. In so doing, you will experience the peace that can only be achieved by following the will of Jesus.

Lord Jesus, thank you for every victory over weakness, big or small, through the work of the Holy Spirit.
Your love and mercy bring peace to my heart.

Except if there was a struggle beforehand, there cannot be victory. The helmsman is recognised in the storm; the soldier is tested on the battlefield. – St CYPRIAN

FORGIVING LOVE RESTORES

Jesus answered, "I tell you, not seven times, but seventy-seven times" (Mt 18:22).

Feelings of guilt weigh heavily on many people's consciences. Frequently they break under the weight of it and feel that they are unable or do not want to live any more. A guilty conscience also causes physical or mental indisposition and this often leads to suicide.

Jesus, who is also our Saviour from feelings of guilt, came to earth from heaven to purify and save us from our sins and guilt. Yes, God himself sent his Son to live and work amongst people like you and me, to die in a loveless manner – and to rise from the dead triumphantly and return to heaven, so that you and I can also be set free from feelings of guilt. Along with this deliverance, we have also been given eternal life (Jn 3:16).

FOOD FROM THE WORD OF GOD
Matthew 18:15-35; Psalm 32:1; 51:9-14; Matthew 6:12-15; Luke 7:36-50; Ephesians 4:31.

Is your heart's desire to have peace of mind and peace? Then accept Jesus, the living Christ, as your Saviour and surrender your life to him unconditionally. Never again do you have to be shy or ashamed to confess to him anything you have done. He invites you to confess your sins before him, as David did in Psalm 51. Go to Jesus right away. He waits for you to forgive you and comfort you with his merciful love. Experience how the weight of guilt and shame is taken from your shoulders and conscience, and how God's peace restores healing calmness to your soul.

Eternal God and Father, thank you for the assurance that you will never reject me when I turn to you and plead through the sacrifice of atonement of Jesus, my Saviour.

Confession is the first step to repentance and forgiveness.
EDMOND GAYTON

December 10

GOD MAKES YOUR LIFE WORTHWHILE

Now choose life, so that you and your children may live and that you may love the Lord your God, listen to his voice, and hold fast to him (Deut 30:19b-20a).

Many people plod along through life with neither aim nor direction. They drag themselves from day to day through a monotonous routine, without any vision of what the future may hold for them. If you are bored with your existence, if your life lacks meaning and purpose, if you feel that living is not worthwhile, take a close look at your faith in God – do it in honesty and earnestly. For it is impossible to live a life without meaning when you believe in God.

FOOD FROM THE WORD OF GOD
Deuteronomy 30:15-20; Joshua 24:13-24; John 1:4; 10:1-10; 15:1-8.

Knowing God gives a certain purpose to your life. Those who refuse to choose him, who refuse to know and love him, who refuse to live in accordance with his will, inevitably have to rely on their limited abilities to make it through life. However, when you are in a relationship with God life immediately becomes a whole new experience. Then you start to live in and through God, instead of only satisfying your own selfish aims. Your whole life goes through a total change of course. You will see your neighbours as sanctified children of God who ought to be loved and supported. Your interpersonal relationships will be better and stauncher. You will direct your mental and spiritual energy towards doing the will of God. And serving God in this way with all the love in your heart, with all the power of your mind and spirit, is the surest way to a meaningful life.

In and through you, my God and Father,
I live a full and satisfying life.

If man is reduced to nothing but a character in history, he has no choice but to subside into a completely irrational history or to endow history with human reason. – ALBERT CAMUS

December 11

YOUR LOVE IS NEEDED

You should not look down on your brother in the day of his misfortune (Obad v 12a).

When plagued by bad times, many people find that their so-called friends simply disappear. When they urgently require comfort, encouragement and support, the people with whom they had special relationships are either too busy, or for various reasons, simply not capable of helping and supporting them. Feeling rejected always hurts, but it is especially destructive if it happens to you at a time when your whole world is falling to pieces around you.

In this world which has been torn apart by sin and in which Christian compassion is so urgently needed, all of us ought to seriously and honestly look at ourselves in the light of the teachings and example of the great compassionate one, Jesus Christ. He turned no one away and turned away from no one. He showed compassion to all people and offered forgiveness to all of them, to the high and mighty as well as the meek. He did all of this out of his boundless love for people. After all, he knew the meaning of rejection all too well – yet his love, even his love for his enemies, never wavered. Even in his dying moments he in his love showed mercy to a criminal.

FOOD FROM THE WORD OF GOD
Obadiah verse 12-21; Luke 7:47; 16:19-31; 22:54; 1 John 4:7-9.

As a Christian, do you want to play a significant part in the restoration of peace, stability and reconciliation in a distorted community? Then love people with the love of Jesus Christ, regardless of who the person is or what he or she has done. Not only is it your Christian duty, it is also your privilege.

Lord Jesus, may I never forget that you love all humanity and died for all of us.

Love is the greatest of all risks … it means the giving of yourself.
JEAN VANIER

December 12

PRAY TO GOD - HE WILL ANSWER

My purpose is that they may be encouraged in heart and united in love, so that they may have the full riches of complete understanding, in order that they may know the mystery of God, namely Christ, in whom are hidden all the treasures of wisdom and knowledge (Col 2:2-3).

It is hard to believe that there are so many people who are not aware of the abundant compassion of God. Their own needs and poverty blind them to this glorious truth. Consequently, it brings about separation between them and the One who can ease their suffering, if only they would entrust it to him and obey him.

FOOD FROM THE WORD OF GOD
Colossians 2:1-15; Daniel 6:11; Matthew 6:5-15; 7:7-11; 1 Thessalonians 5:17; James 4:2.

The Scriptures assure us that God is more prepared to give to us than we are prepared to receive, and also that when we pray and believe we can receive what we ask for. Prayer is the key that unlocks the treasure houses of God. We accept that this is true, yet so few of us use the key; we enjoy so little of the abundant benevolence of God. We know that God can give what we ask for, but the obstacles that come across our path blind us. We think that they are obstacles to God, too, and that he cannot answer our prayers.

Do you do it too? Do you also think it is entirely impossible that God can answer your request while there are so many obstacles standing in the way? Such a thought pattern brings about doubt. And it is so unnecessary because how God answers your prayers is neither your concern nor your responsibility. A simple, child-like faith that prayerfully looks up to God and believes that he does in fact answer prayers – your heavenly Father gladly answers this kind of prayer.

Lord my God, I do not know how and when you are going to answer my prayers – I only know with certainty that you will do it.

God insists that we ask, not because he does not know our situation, but because we need spiritual discipline to ask. – CATHERINE MARSHALL

December 13

CHRISTIAN LOVE CONQUERS EVIL

Help, Lord, for the godly are no more; the faithful have vanished from among men. Everyone lies to his neighbour; their flattering lips speak with deception (Ps 12:1-2).

As crime increases all over the world, people are becoming increasingly aware of the presence of the evil one in daily life. We see the evidence of this in merciless acts of hate, in violation of human rights, in falling standards and in deterioration of moral conduct.

FOOD FROM THE WORD OF GOD
Psalm 12:1-8; Micah 6:8; John 4:7-9; Romans 13:8-10; 1 Corinthians 13:1-13; 16:14.

Yet, throwing one's hands in the air in desperation serves absolutely no purpose. All Christians have a duty to unite in the fight against the forces of evil, so that we can preserve the name and honour of God. We must fight the good battle persistently until the very end, because we know that the final victory belongs to God Almighty, until all eternity. The correct way of doing this is to make Jesus Christ your role model. He set the perfect example of a Christian way of life. Despite all the evil and misery of humankind, Jesus triumphed over the world and conquered death. Everything he was and did can be summed up in one word: *love.*

Therefore, express Christ's love everywhere and always. Then you will defeat the evil one in Christ's holy Name. Our love will break down every form of hatred, because the evil one has no response to the all-encompassing influence of the love of God. If we love as he loves and join in his triumphal procession through the ages, we will defeat the influences of the evil one in our tiny corner of the world.

Holy Lord Jesus, by reflecting your love in my life I contribute my little bit towards defeating the evil one in this world.

All that is needed for evil to triumph is for good men to do nothing.
EDMUND BURKE

December 14

YOUR INFALLIBLE FRIEND

I no longer call you servants, because a servant does not know his master's business. Instead, I have called you friends, for everything that I learned from my Father I have made known to you (Jn 15:15).

One of the greatest sources of joy and encouragement in life is having reliable friends, people to whom you can go for help when you find yourself in trouble. No one knows when in life such a need might arise, and knowing that you have reliable friends is always comforting.

FOOD FROM THE WORD OF GOD
John 15:1-26; Job 42:10; Proverbs 17:17; Matthew 11:19; Luke 11:5-13; James 2:23.

Yet, people can be very fickle and are susceptible to external influences. Furthermore, other responsibilities often put them under pressure. Priorities in their own lives sometimes cause them not to have time to help you. Though you may not be without help for long, you may indeed be vulnerable and without protection for a short while.

Jesus, our Lord, made it abundantly clear that he will always be with you, that he will never turn you away, leave you in a helpless situation, or forsake you (Heb 13:5). The Scriptures prove that this promise of his is true. Many Christians can also testify to the validity of this promise because they enjoyed the blessing and grace of God's friendship in times of suffering and trouble.

Do not underestimate the worth of human friends. On the other hand, never forget that your infallible heavenly Friend is always with you. He is ready to answer when you pray to him, lay your problems before him, and trust that he will deal with them in accordance with his wise judgement.

Holy heavenly Father, I thank you that I may, through Jesus Christ, be called your friend, and that you have proven this friendship innumerable times in my life.

Friendship lies more in giving love than receiving it.
ROBERT BRIDGES

December 15

START THE DAY RIGHT

Awake my soul! Awake, harp and lyre! I will awaken the dawn (Ps 57:9).

It is upsetting that so many people wake up in the morning and start complaining immediately. It determines their attitude for the rest of the day. No, rather when you wake up in the morning, think of all the wonderful things that God makes happen to you and that make life worth living. Delight in even the smallest of things: the birds singing; your family and friends; the food on your table; clothes that you can wear – yes, rejoice in the countless good things with which God fills your life.

FOOD FROM THE WORD OF GOD
Psalm 57:1-2; Genesis 19:23-28; 22:1-5; Psalm 118:24-29; Mark 16:1-8; John 20:1-2.

Be positive about everything that you are planning to undertake during the day and about all the people whom you are going to meet. Look forward with expectation and excitement to what the day might bring. Believe that these things will be good and that your Father will grant you the self confidence to meet the day with joy and dignity. Never underestimate the power of positive and creative thoughts in your day-to-day life. Tell yourself repeatedly, *This is the day the Lord has made; let us rejoice and be glad in it* (Ps 118:24). Start every new day with a prayer, and count your blessings even before you have breakfast. Your spirit will be uplifted and you will have the energy to meet the challenges of the day in Jesus' Name.

Start your day in this way, and your life will be a psalm of gratitude. You will also bless the people with whom you come into contact through the course of the day.

Holy Spirit of God, help me to start every day with a grateful heart, which purposefully meets the demands of life.

You have given me so much, Lord. Give me one more thing: a thankful heart.
GEORGE HERBERT

December 16

CHRIST IN YOU

I praise you because I am fearfully and wonderfully made; your works are wonderful, I know that full well (Ps 139:14).

We so easily forget that we are a miracle of God. We go through life aware of our surroundings and people around us, but we seldom go to the trouble of fathoming the mystery of ourselves. We love and we hate, we laugh and we cry. We are so involved in life that we seldom try to trace the causes of our actions. Sometimes our value judgements of life are shallow, and then we lose the spirit of amazement and worship that allows us to lose ourselves in love for and exaltation of God.

FOOD FROM THE WORD OF GOD
Psalm 139:1-24; John 15:1-8; Romans 15:1-6; Ephesians 3:14-21; Philippians 2:1-11; Colossians 2:6-15.

However, when God created your brain, he made a masterpiece that enables you to question and figure things out. And there are endlessly many questions begging to be answered, so many mysteries you would like to solve. With these mysteries and questions you stimulate and control your brain. If you were to neglect your brain, it would deteriorate and bring about within you a negative attitude towards life. However, if you feed it positive thoughts, especially from the Word of God, it creates a positive attitude within you to life, as well as positive thoughts.

When your spirit is filled with God and the Holy Spirit, when Christ lives in you, he controls your thoughts, and ultimately your actions, too. True Christianity is more than just intellectual acceptance of holy laws – it is when the living Christ takes possession and control of your thoughts and spirit and reveals himself to others through you.

Eternal and miracle-working God and Father, through your Spirit that lives in me, my life can be an expression of Christ's life. Help me graciously with this.

Our humanity would have been a miserable affair were it not for the miracles which God stirs within us.
FRANCIS BACON

STOP WORRYING

Cast all your anxiety on him because he cares for you (1 Pet 5:7).

Anxiety is something that we learn in life. It becomes part of our day-to-day existence and robs us of our joy, calmness and peace. We even get angry when people tell us not to worry.

A living faith in Jesus Christ is the ultimate antidote for anxiety. If you believe in him, it is impossible for anxiety to control your thoughts and deeds. However, the decision about which is going to control your life – Christ or anxiety – is up to you.

So believe that it is not true that you cannot stop worrying. If you spend just as much time on cultivating a positive faith as you waste by worrying, you will have no more problems with anxiety. However, it does take firm discipline to replace negative thoughts with positive ones of God's caring love and guidance.

FOOD FROM THE WORD OF GOD
1 Peter 5:1-14; Job 30:16-31; Psalm 38:1-23; Acts 20:24; Hebrews 2:16-18.

Do you find yourself in the awful jaws of anxiety? Be honest with God and share the deepest perceptions of your heart with him. Ask yourself in honesty whether your worry is so great that it falls outside of God's omnipotent power to do something about it. Lay your worry at his feet and confirm that he is in control. It will not always be easy, but if you set about it with the power of the Holy Spirit and if he controls your thoughts and attitude, you will in his strength overcome the habit of anxiety.

Faithful and caring Father, I place my trust in you completely, so that you may enable me to overcome my anxiety.

Anxiety does not rid tomorrow of its sadness; it only rids today of its power.
CORRIE TEN BOOM

December 18

DO NOT DISAPPOINT HIM

As a prisoner of the Lord, then, I urge you to live a life worthy of the calling you have received (Eph 4:1).

If you accept your calling as a Christian in earnest, you will know that achieving God's purpose for your life requires a lot of strength. You are called to live a holy life, a life of dedication which reflects the holiness of the Father. It means that your attitude towards your fellowmen should be balanced and that you should be prepared to forgive and to forget. It is necessary to seek and obey the will of God in every circumstance in your life.

FOOD FROM THE WORD OF GOD
Ephesians 4:1-32; Matthews 28:16-20; Acts 2:37-42; 7:54-60; Revelation 2:10; 4:20.

God has called you to live for him in this hectic world. When you preach God in an unsympathetic world, you follow our perfect example, Jesus our living Lord. He came to the world to reveal God to people. Because of the tremendous challenges that he put to people, they rejected him. It is not always easy to live for God and to reflect his way of living. The world is all too happy with its own way and unwilling to admit that God's way is the true path to life.

God does not expect you to do these things in your own strength. He has put a Godly source of strength at your disposal: the Holy Spirit. He will help you to deal with your problems with confidence, and to triumph over temptations and weaknesses. The Holy Spirit will help you to remain standing, will protect you, and his magnificence will shine through you.

Lord my God, help me to abandon my foolish struggle, and to accept your strength so that I may live to your satisfaction.

The tragedy of life is that which dies inside you while you are still alive.
ALBERT SCHWEITZER

December 19

GOD IS YOUR GUIDE

For this God is our God for ever and ever; he will be our guide even to the end (Ps 48:14).

Do not get upset when you find it difficult to understand God's guidance. Some people appear to be so certain of his guidance that you start doubting the genuineness of your own spiritual experiences. This is when you forget that God talks to different people in different ways.

God does not only use thunder and earthquakes, lightning and disaster to make his voice heard. Through a quiet, soft voice he stamps his will on those who truly desire to obey him. Some seek God's guidance without knowing God. They ask for guidance, but make no serious attempt to bring their lives into harmony with God. However, it is only when you have accepted Christ as your Saviour and Redeemer and have made him the Lord of your life, that you become sensitive to the guidance of God. In your search for a more intimate fellowship with God, prayer, contemplation and quietly waiting for God are of the utmost importance in making your spirit sensitive to the situation in which you find yourself. That of which you may have been totally unaware appears clearly before your spirit. Suddenly you realise that God is busy guiding you through simple everyday events and circumstances.

FOOD FROM THE WORD OF GOD
Psalm 48:1-14; Judges 5:7; Matthew 2:1-12; Acts 3:11-20; Hebrews 12:1-3.

Do not only seek God through the extraordinary, but also become aware of his living presence with you. Identify his guidance in the everyday events of life.

Faithful Guide, keep me sensitive and alert so that I may become aware of your guiding presence.

If we were to be prepared to learn the true meaning of discipleship ... the church and the world would be changed and the impact on society would be astonishing. – DAVID WATSON

THE WEAKNESS OF INDECISION

Elijah went before the people and said, "How long will you waver between two opinions? If the Lord is God, follow him; but if Baal is God, follow him" (2 Kgs 18:21).

Many people find it hard to make a decision. When they are confronted by this responsibility, they keep on deferring the decision, or they hesitate to do something, hoping that someone else will make the decision for them. However, life abundantly blesses those who can make positive decisions. Such people remain purposeful and are not thrown off course by every circumstance or event. Once they have made a decision, they firmly and unshakeably keep to it.

FOOD FROM THE WORD OF GOD
1 Kings 18:1-24; Job 22:21-30; 23:28; Psalm 2:7; Isaiah 19:17; Daniel 11:36.

The dominating fear that you could make a wrong decision may make you inactive, nervous and make you feel unsafe. But remember it is sometimes better to make a wrong decision and then to learn from your mistake than to remain indecisive all the time. If you lack the courage to make firm decisions and to stick to them, you will always be handicapped by your indecision.

Accept God as your Guide. In him, you have a source of wisdom that is infinitely effective and reliable. Spend enough time with him. Talk to him about every difficult decision that you have to make – and then follow the guidance he offers you. When your intuition shows you a direction which you can follow go ahead in the knowledge of God's guiding presence. Then an attitude of indecision will no longer hold back your spiritual progress.

Help me, my Saviour and Friend, to make difficult decisions with wise resolve by following the guidance of your Holy Spirit.

Not making a decision is also making a decision.
HARVEY COX

December 21

THE TRAGEDY OF BEING LUKEWARM

So, because you are lukewarm – neither hot nor cold – I am about to spit you out of my mouth (Rev 3:16).

Many people confess to the Christian faith and their faithfulness to it, but have never moved past the stage of being lukewarm in their faith. Perhaps they are afraid to dedicate themselves to Christ completely. And so, they treat him with conservative and constrained respect.

Being spiritually lukewarm reveals a lack of dedication to Christ and unwillingness to allow the Holy Spirit to work through you. This careless attitude is the direct result of neglect of your intimate fellowship with God and the powerlessness of your quiet time.

In order to get the flame of spiritual enthusiasm burning again, you need to pray every day and to do in-depth Bible study. There are no substitutes for these disciplines and no other way of reaching God and hearing his voice. When your prayer life is dynamic once more, you will experience complete oneness with God. You will discover the limitless source of power on which you rely, as well as the inspiration that you can get from living in harmony with God, Christ and the Holy Spirit. When you spend time praising and thanking God, the Holy Spirit will renew and inspire you.

Allow God's love, joy and enthusiasm to flow through you, and you will experience his uninterrupted presence. When Christ is in control, every part of your life is inspired by his glory and enthusiasm.

FOOD FROM THE WORD OF GOD
Revelation 3:7-22; Psalm 66:5-12; Isaiah 48:4-11; Malachi 3:1-5; 1 Peter 1:7; Revelation 3:18.

Fill me, O Lord, with the fire of your Holy Spirit, so that my whole life may reflect your glory with a burning heart.

Nothing great was ever achieved without enthusiasm.
RALPH WALDO EMERSON

WORK ON YOUR SELF-CONFIDENCE

The Lord is my light and my salvation – whom shall I fear? The Lord is the stronghold of my life – of whom shall I be afraid? (Ps 27:1).

Sometimes there are moments in your life when your thoughts become totally confused. You lose your sense of direction in life and your confidence melts away until it almost no longer exists. You also become uncertain of God's existence, of his love for you, your faith weakens and life loses its meaning and purpose.

FOOD FROM THE WORD OF GOD
Psalm 27:1-14; 2 Kings 18:1-8; Psalm 56:4; Isaiah 40:31; Galatians 5:10.

An effective way of rebuilding your self-confidence so that you may live a life free from the feeling of incapacity and inferiority, is being intensely aware that God is all-sufficient for you. The process of becoming aware of God's all-sufficiency for you is not something that is forced upon you from the outside by something or somebody else. No, it is a consequence of the working of the Holy Sprit of God in your life and spirit, so that his presence in your life will daily become noticeable. God lives within you, and this overwhelming truth gives you the self-confidence to respond to all of life's challenges.

When you invite the Holy Spirit to come into your heart and to take charge of your life, he drives out all debilitating fears from your life and replaces them with the knowledge that God works in your life in order to achieve his holy purpose with you. Because the presence of God becomes a daily reality for you, you meet the future with joy, peace and self-confidence.

Eternal and merciful God, I praise and thank you for driving debilitating fears from my life through the work of the Holy Spirit, and replacing them with self-confidence.

The greater and more persevering your trust in God, the greater and more persevering your self-confidence will be. – ANONYMOUS

YOU ACCOUNT TO GOD

Behold, I am coming soon! My reward is with me, and I will give to everyone according to what he has done (Rev 22:12).

Many people cling desperately to the philosophy of "eat, drink and be merry". They are sceptical about the notion that we will all one day be called to account to God for the way in which we lived our lives. Christians' attempts to keep and obey the commands of God are often the subject of people's ridicule while they are enjoying life and paying little or no attention to what awaits them.

FOOD FROM THE WORD OF GOD
Revelation 22:1-21; Proverbs 28:8; Matthew 25:14-30; 27:3-10; Hebrews 11:1-6.

Theories of the hereafter are multiple and diverse. They range from the extremes of the lake of fire, sulphur and damnation, to a heavenly utopia. No human knows what really will transpire. Therefore, it is impossible for anyone to say with certainty what will happen. The truth is, we owe God an account of the way in which we lived our lives and the manner in which we behaved during our lives on earth.

We know that Jesus Christ's death on the cross assured us of the forgiving love and mercy of God, and that he has in his compassion given the hope of salvation to us. Yet, the day will come when we have to account to God for our lives. When Peter, who betrayed Jesus, saw the sadness in Jesus' eyes, the realisation of failure made him cry. Those very eyes will one day look deeply into our souls and ask us to account for our lives.

Lord Jesus, my Saviour, help me to live as you expect of me, so that I may one day appear before God without hesitation.

We must be anchored in self-discipline if we want to successfully venture into spiritual freedom.
HEROLD E KOHN

December 24

DO NOT BE AFRAID ...

But the angel said to them, "Do not be afraid. I bring good news of great joy that will be for all the people" (Lk 2:10).

With the birth of Christ on earth, God – in his great mercy and love – came to replace our fear with rejoicing joy. The angel said to Mary, *Do not be afraid, Mary, you have found favour with God"* (Lk 1:30). Moreover, the angel who brought the message of the birth of Christ to the shepherds in the fields of Bethlehem on the first Christmas said, *Do not be afraid* (Lk 2:10).

FOOD FROM THE WORD OF GOD
Luke 2:1-20; Genesis 3:10; Isaiah 41:8-13; 2 Timothy 1:7; 1 John 4:18.

Our modern lives are so full of fear. And this fear is an overwhelming reality to us. From birth to death, we live with fear. We fear the unknown. We fear the future, we fear the present, and we even fear the past. We are afraid we might lose our health, our children, our marital partners, or our financial independence. We are afraid of growing old and of death. We are afraid of the murders, rapes and hatred that pervade our country. Always, everywhere, and in everyone there is this corroding fear of countless things.

But now, at the commemoration of Christ's birth, God sends us his good news anew: Do not be afraid! Immanuel – God is with us! It is a message of great joy. Our fear is taken away because Christ is the Victor. Our fear is replaced by love, and love drives out fear (1 Jn 4:18). Let us then rejoice in these days in the message of God, which allays all our fears.

Heavenly Father, thank you for having sent your Son to replace our fear with rejoicing gladness.

All fear is slavery.
GEORGE HERBERT

December 25

WAS CHRIST BORN IN YOUR HEART?

Today in the town of David a Saviour has been born to you; he is Christ the Lord! (Lk 2:11).

Two friends had a serious fall-out and proceeded to live in discord with one another. One of them was very unhappy about this because they had had a good friendship. He then wrote a conciliatory letter to his former friend and pleaded with him that they be friends again. But he received no response. He was deeply disappointed, but did not give up hope. He wrote again and again and again, but there was no response.

One dark, icy cold winter's night, he decided to go to his former friend's house and plead with him in person: Let us make peace and be friends again. Through biting winds and icy snow he walked to his friend's house. Nearly frozen to death he arrived there and repeated his plea with love in his eyes. His friend realised the depth of his seriousness and opened his heart to him. And they were reconciled.

FOOD FROM THE WORD OF GOD
Luke 2:8-20; Isaiah 9:1-6; Matthew 2:1-12; John 1:1-18; 1 John 5:18-20.

God is the loving friend. Between him and us a gaping chasm has appeared because of our sins. God wrote many letters to us through his prophets, but we did not want to listen. But now, in these last days, he talks to us through his own Son (Heb 1:1). God himself came to plead with us on Christmas night in the person of Jesus Christ as a child in Bethlehem, to accept him. Have you said yes to him yet?

When I try to fathom this wonder, my mind is petrified, my mouth is silenced; I see only the wonder and prayerfully remain standing before you.

Even if Christ were born in Bethlehem a thousand times, but not yet in your heart, it is a worthless event.
MARTIN LUTHER

GOD'S GREATEST GIFT

Remain in me, and I will remain in you. No branch can bear fruit by itself; it must remain in the vine. Neither can you bear fruit unless you remain in me (Jn 15:4).

If you carefully study Christ's message, you will realise that one word is written through every message: *love*. Many inspired books have been written about Christ's love for sinners. Love is also the dominating theme of the whole New Testament. And Paul tells us in 1 Corinthians 13:13 that *love* is the greatest of all of God's gifts to us.

FOOD FROM THE WORD OF GOD
John 15:1-17; John 4:1-10; 1 Corinthians 12:31; 2 Corinthians 9:15; Ephesians 2:8.

Living a life of Christian love in this broken world appears to us like an utterly unobtainable ideal. It does sound very good and noble, but impractical to us who have to struggle with all the issues of life. We find it impossible to live according to Christ's example with our own strength. We repeatedly try to achieve this, but fail time and again and are disappointed anew.

The secret to a successful Christian life that reflects the characteristics of the living Christ is to be taken into possession by Christ himself. That Jesus, the living Christ, promised to live in our hearts and minds through the presence of the Holy Spirit, is a biblical fact. When he lives within you, the path of Christianity becomes a triumphant road and a victorious way of life. God's greatest gift is the gift of himself coming into our lives and of him making us aware of his presence through love – for God is love.

Heavenly Father, your presence with me gives me certainty in my faith and you are an ever-growing reality in my life. I praise you, Lord, for you are good.

The incarnation of God would have been as great a wonder regardless of how he came into the world.
PT FORSYTH

NEVER STOP HOPING

And we rejoice in the hope of the glory of God (Rom 5:2b).

In these dying moments of the old year, it is good to rekindle the flame of our hope. Since earliest times people have had to live with problems. No nation has escaped the destruction of disasters, wars, plagues, droughts, famine, floods and countless other distressing events. All these occurrences have left a trail of destruction on people and the earth. This brings us to ask: How, then, does one handle all this destruction?

FOOD FROM THE WORD OF GOD
Romans 5:1-21; Job 13:13-28; Psalm 43:1-5; Romans 8:24-25; 1 Corinthians 15:19; 1 Timothy 4:10.

In the Scriptures we also read how one disaster after the other plagued people. They knew the pain of ridicule, death and imprisonment. They were familiar with the destructive effects of war on their lives. However, they were also intensely aware of the glorious fact that God repeatedly came to their rescue in his infinite love and saved them from their sorry plight. His love for his children and his creation is so great that he never hesitated to come to their rescue.

In our day and age, people are also desperate. They are upset, worried and disheartened. When people are annihilated, when crime and corruption increase, when senseless murders are committed, do not despair, or be disheartened. God is in control. It is his world and he faithfully guards over it. He loves his children and his creation just as much as he did in the past. Do not give up hope. Trust in God. As always in the past, he will save us, and give us his peace (Jn 14:27).

Lord my God, I come to you in doubt and despair and plead with you to strengthen my faith and love and to arouse my hope so that it will never die.

Other people see only a hopeless end, but the Christian delights in endless hope.
GILBERT BRENCKEN

SHARE YOUR PAIN WITH GOD

When I think about this, I am terrified; trembling seizes my body (Job 21:6).

We find ourselves in the last days of the old year. Ahead of us, the faint light of a new, unknown year is already flickering. What baggage are we taking with us into the new year? Many people treasure a skeleton in the closet and are afraid that it might one day be revealed for all to see. The mere thought of it robs them of the joy to which they are entitled and they lead a miserable existence because of something they did in the past in a moment of weakness.

FOOD FROM THE WORD OF GOD
Job 21:1-21; Psalm 94:11-23; 139:19-24; Isaiah 55:6-8; Matthew 12:25.

If you truly regret such a deed, ask God for forgiveness. Maybe you have already done so, but find it impossible to forgive yourself. You are clinging to something that God has forgiven long ago. Let go of it and ask the Holy Spirit to show you the direction and to place your life under his control. When he is in charge of your thoughts there will be no room for regret about sins that have already been forgiven.

Turn your back on the past. Forget what is behind you and reach for what is ahead (Phil 3:13). Let the past merely warn you of sin and foolish behaviour. Look to the future and see that when you have accepted God's forgiveness, he creates a vision for you, which eradicates all painful memories. For it is impossible to accept the freedom God grants you while are still chained to painful memories.

Holy Lord, the freedom I enjoy through your forgiveness allows me to enter the future without being oppressed by painful memories.

It is better for a man to confess his sins than to harden his heart.
POPE CLEMENT

December 29

OUR ALMIGHTY FATHER GOD

The arrogance of man will be brought low and the pride of men humbled; the Lord alone will be exalted in that day (Is 2:17).

Through all the ages, there have always been people who have wielded authority over others – in the political and economic sphere, but also within family life. In many instances, especially in our day and age, there are often cases of the abuse of authority, because people who have been placed in positions of power over subordinates grossly abuse the authority that has been entrusted to them.

FOOD FROM THE WORD OF GOD
Isaiah 2:1-22; Genesis 17:1-6; Job 5:17-18; Psalm 91:1; Isaiah 6:1-8; Revelation 4:8; 21:22.

Many people feel helpless in these circumstances. They become uncertain of themselves and tend to despair while quietly subjecting themselves to the orders of the person or people wielding the authority. In so doing they run the risk of developing a slavish attitude towards life and of thinking that there is no way out of their situation.

Regardless what the circumstance in which you find yourself might be, you must never lose your trust and faith in God's promises. He loves you and is always with you. *God has said, "Never will I leave you; never will I forsake you"* (Heb 13:5b). Also, *And surely I am with you always, to the very end of the age* (Mt 28:20). Always remember that God is omnipotent and in control. Nothing and no one can overshadow his omnipotence. Open your life to the influence of his Holy Spirit so that he can strengthen you in faith and you will be able to handle every circumstance and overcome every negative situation.

God Almighty, to you be the glory! Where you reign is splendour; heavenly is your majesty; holy your righteousness.

God is the God of promise. He keeps his word, even when it appears impossible; even when it seems as though circumstances point to the contrary. – COLIN URQUHART

December 30

TAKE MY THOUGHTS PRISONER, O GOD!

When anxiety was great within me, your consolation brought joy to my soul (Ps 94:19).

With the dying moments of the old year, a strange longing takes hold of one's heart. You have a profound longing for your home, your loved ones and friends, and the things you cannot express. Then it is good to know that these moments, too, fall under the control of our loving and almighty Father.

Your thoughts are known only to God and to you. No matter how hard you try to keep your thoughts to yourself, they are eventually revealed by your attitude and actions. Whatever you direct your thoughts to, consequently becomes the driving force in your life.

FOOD FROM THE WORD OF GOD
Psalm 94:1-23; 1 Chronicles 29:18; Job 21:27; Psalm 139:2; Daniel 2:30; Amos 4:13; Hebrews 4:13.

The popular media shape many people's thoughts. Others hungrily feed on the prescriptions of spiritual and political leaders and refuse to deviate from their prescribed ideas. Relatively few people go the trouble of thinking for themselves. However, one of the aims of disciplined discipleship is bringing your thoughts in line with the will of God. Once you have succeeded in this, your thoughts and the words you utter are no longer your own, but are inspired by the Holy Spirit.

You create your quality of life through your thoughts. Ask the Holy Spirit to help you to have Jesus Christ's attitude in your thoughts and to reflect it in your life. Time spent in silence and alone with God will give you the peace and wisdom to discipline your thoughts.

Loving God, by the power and inspiration of the Holy Spirit, I try to bring my thoughts in line with your holy will.

By space the universe embraces me and swallows me like an atom, but by my thoughts I embrace the universe. – BLAISE PASCAL

December 31

OUR REFUGE AND OUR STRENGTH

Thus far has the Lord helped us (1 Sam 7:12).

Another year has hastened to an end and we are sitting with all the memories of our successes and failures; of our joys and sorrows; of our happiness and grief; of our hope and despair. During the past year people all over the world experienced disasters: earthquakes, floods, famine and plagues. There was an unstoppable wave of crime, corruption and violence – in some areas the terrible violence of wars, too. Yet, the world has survived another year and for most people life goes on.

But in all of this, we see the hand of God that controls and keeps the destiny of his children in his omnipotent hands. The bad circumstances can mostly be attributed to humankind's greed, yearning for power, violation of human rights, disinterest and foolishness. Despite this, God stays in control and he will in his perfect time and way utilise the circumstances to man's best interest – just as he used the horror of the cross to defeat sin through the triumph of the resurrection.

FOOD FROM THE WORD OF GOD
1 Samuel 7:1-17; 2 Samuel 21:1-7; Psalm 46:1-11; 62:7-8; Jeremiah 16:19; 17:17; Joel 3:16.

Regardless of what has happened in your life during the past year, never ever forget that God is always with you. Just as he cared for you in the past, he will also care for you in the future. Put your faith and trust in the living Christ. So while you are saying good-bye to the old year, you can prepare to enter the future with God.

I know to whom I have entrusted myself, even while day changes into night; I know the Rock on whom I have built, from whom I expect my salvation.

Three things God alone knows: the beginning of things, the course of things, and the end of things. –OLD WELSH PROVERB

Register of key Scripture readings

OLD TESTAMENT

Genesis 1:1 – November 17
Genesis 39:12 – February 3

Exodus 3:14 – January 1

Deuteronomy 30:19 – December 10

Joshua 1:9 – December 1
Joshua 24:15 – November 21

Judges 6:17 – November 28

1 Samuel 7:12 – December 31

2 Samuel 22:21-22 – March 12
2 Samuel 23:5 – November 9

1 Kings 3:11-13 – November 25
1 Kings 9:3 – February 1
1 Kings 18:21 – December 20
1 Kings 19:4 – November 22

Job 21:6 – December 28
Job 22:28 – November 24
Job 23:3 – November 11
Job 40:6 – November 4

Psalm 4:2 – December 7
Psalm 12:1-2 – December 13
Psalm 19:1 – January 4, 29
Psalm 27:1 – December 22
Psalm 27:5 – May 24
Psalm 32:8 – March 14
Psalm 33:20-22 – January 13
Psalm 34:8 – November 16
Psalm 37:3-4 – March 22
Psalm 37:5-6 – November 7
Psalm 39:1-2 – January 10
Psalm 48:14 – December 19
Psalm 57:9 – December 15
Psalm 62:5 – November 14
Psalm 78:38 – March 2
Psalm 92:8-9 – January 27
Psalm 94:19 – December 30
Psalm 104:24 – November 19
Psalm 124:1-3 – January 26
Psalm 139:14 – December 16

Proverbs 29:25 – February 4

Ecclesiastes 11:8 – November 26

Isaiah 2:17 – December 29
Isaiah 9:2 – December 2
Isaiah 26:3 – November 5
Isaiah 30:15 – November 6
Isaiah 40:8 – November 20
Isaiah 40:31 – December 3
Isaiah 41:10 – November 27
Isaiah 55:3 – November 1
Isaiah 65:1 – November 29

Jeremiah 20:8 – November 15
Jeremiah 22:15 – January 28

Joel 2:12-13 – February 26

Obadiah v 12 – December 11
Obadiah v 15 – November 12

Zephaniah 3:17 – December 6

NEW TESTAMENT

Matthew 2:12 – April 19
Matthew 3:1-2 – July 22
Matthew 4:19 – September 8
Matthew 5:14 – March 30
Matthew 6:12 – April 20
Matthew 6:33 – August 6

Romans 10:9 – July 20
Romans 11:22 – March 23, September 19
Romans 13:8 – July 12
Romans 14:12 – March 16
Romans 16:17 – March 15

1 Corinthians 1:19 – January 17
1 Corinthians 2:16 – January 18
1 Corinthians 3:11 – February 5
1 Corinthians 5:8 – July 5
1 Corinthians 6:19-20 – March 17
1 Corinthians 7:3 – August 7
1 Corinthians 7:27 – August 8
1 Corinthians 8:9 – August 9
1 Corinthians 10:31 – March 18
1 Corinthians 12:11 – June 10
1 Corinthians 13:13 – July 6
1 Corinthians 14:1 – August 10
1 Corinthians 15:3 – August 11
1 Corinthians 15:22 – July 7
1 Corinthians 16:8-9 – July 13

2 Corinthians 1:3-4a – January 22
2 Corinthians 2:7-8 – September 20
2 Corinthians 3:18 – June 8
2 Corinthians 4:17 – July 3
2 Corinthians 6:4a; 6b-7 – February 21
2 Corinthians 6:17-18 – June 4
2 Corinthians 7:9 – February 15
2 Corinthians 8:2 – June 21
2 Corinthians 9:13 – August 1
2 Corinthians 10:4 – August 4
2 Corinthians 12:9 – May 16

Galatians 1:15-16 – September 22
Galatians 2:10 – August 3
Galatians 3:6, 9 – June 22
Galatians 4:4-5 – September 23
Galatians 5:1 – May 17
Galatians 6:7 – June 23

Ephesians 1:16-17 – September 24
Ephesians 2:8 – May 18
Ephesians 3:17-19 – May 1
Ephesians 3:20-21 – November 8
Ephesians 4:1 – December 18
Ephesians 5:5 – June 24
Ephesians 5:28 – September 25
Ephesians 6:10 – December 8
Ephesians 6:12 – September 26

Philippians 1:3 – November 30
Philippians 2:3 – May 2
Philippians 2:14 – September 27
Philippians 3:13-14 – September 29
Philippians 4:8 – November 23
Philippians 4:13 – July 31
Philippians 4:19 – May 3

Colossians 1:15 – February 2
Colossians 2:2-3 – December 12
Colossians 2:6-7 – February 19
Colossians 3:2-3 – January 9
Colossians 3:20 – August 14

1 Thessalonians 1:6-7 – June 11
1 Thessalonians 4:3 – January 19
1 Thessalonians 5:2 – October 20

2 Thessalonians 2:8 – July 9
2 Thessalonians 3:10 – March 20

1 Timothy 1:16 – January 20
1 Timothy 2:5-6a – June 25
1 Timothy 5:12 – September 28
1 Timothy 5:8 – September 30
1 Timothy 6:17 – May 4

2 Timothy 1:8 – October 8
2 Timothy 2:19 – 26 June
2 Timothy 3:16 – May 5
2 Timothy 12:19 – June 26

Titus 2:7 – October 9
Titus 2:13 – June 6
Titus 2:13-14 – October 10

Philemon verse 7 – May 6

Hebrews 2:3 – October 11